Constructing Counter-Culture Through Liberation Theology

Sebastian Kappen SJ (1924-93)

Constructing Counter-Culture Through Liberation Theology
Sebastian Kappen SJ (1924-93)

Mathew Thekkemuriyil Antony

2022

Constructing Counter-Culture Through Liberation Theology: Sebastian Kappen SJ (1924-93) — published by the Indian Society for Promoting Christian Knowledge (ISPCK), Post Box 1585, Kashmere Gate, Delhi-110006.

ISBN: 978-93-90569-20-5

Laser typeset by

ISPCK, Post Box 1585, 1654, Madarsa Road, Kashmere Gate, Delhi-110006 • *Tel:* 23866323

e-mail: ashish@ispck.org.in • ella@ispck.org.in
website: www.ispck.org.in

Contents

1
The Kerala Context

2
Liberation Theology: An Overview

3
A Biographical Introduction

4
Kappen on Marxism

5
Kappen on Christology

6
Kappen on Indian Religious Traditions

7
Liberation Theology and Counter-Culture

Introduction

"I am writing after much reflection, taking into consideration my responsibility both as a disciple of Jesus and a theologian."[1]

"You threaten me with the loss of my vocation if I do not conform to the norms of censorship. I do value my membership in the Society which I have served for the last 38 years and I wish to continue as a Jesuit. But not at the cost of my intellectual integrity and my loyalty to Jesus and the God who lives."[2]

These are the words of Sebastian Kappen, an Indian Jesuit, liberation theologian, social thinker, and activist in response to the Vatican's censorship of his book *Jesus and Freedom*, published in 1977. In the book, Kappen highlighted the historical human Jesus rather than the glorified Christ of the dogmas, while criticizing several other stances of the Church. Consequently, the Vatican censored the book in 1980, and Kappen became likely the first Third World progressive theologian to undergo such a disciplinary action.

Many Christian theologians around the globe started thinking innovatively and radically starting in the second half of the 1960s. This should be seen in light of the Second Vatican Council (1962-65), which was exceptionally open to liberal and progressive thinking. For instance, the Council document *Gaudium et Spes* (the Pastoral Constitution on the Church in the Modern World, promulgated by Pope Paul VI on 7 December 1965) overviewed themes, such as economics, social justice, poverty, and exploitation. The Council also promoted dialogue with other religions and cultures and acknowledged their truths through

Nostra Aetate (the Declaration on the Relation of the Church with Non-Christian Religions, promulgated by Pope Paul VI on 28 October 1965)

Immediate resonance of this openness was first reflected in the Latin American Church. Many progressive Christian theologians, including socially committed bishops, priests, nuns, and laity came forward from different Latin American countries and voiced for social causes. They started interpreting the Bible, especially the synoptic gospels (Matthew, Mark, and Luke), from the perspective of the poor. Their new way of theologizing soon received the title of liberation theology. However, I use terminologies like progressive theology, liberation theology, and theology of liberation interchangeably. Liberation theology claimed to begin from below, contrary to conventional theology that worked from the intellectual upper stratum of the Church. The proclaimed goal of liberation theology was an integral liberation of the marginalized from all forms of oppression and exploitation. For a better analysis of society, liberation theology adapted Marxist ideologies, that later provoked criticism from the Vatican. Simultaneously, it went back to the original message of Jesus and looked ahead to a total liberation of the human being, both material and spiritual. Therefore, liberation theology could be called a fundamental and "preferential option for the poor" – a maxim that was widely used in religious and political fields in Latin America during the latter half of the 20th century.

The new trend in theologizing soon spread to some Asian countries like India, Sri Lanka, the Philippines, and South Korea. In addition to the two major sources of inspiration for Latin American liberation theology (the synoptic gospels regarding the message of the historical Jesus, and Marxist ideologies), liberating elements in Buddhism inspired Asian progressive Christian thinkers, especially in India, Sri Lanka, and Korea. In the case of India, there were two generations in the development of liberation theology. The first carried the traits of liberation theology in Latin America, whereas the second had a more Indian focus, first and foremost the liberation of Dalits, i.e. outcastes who were excluded from (or found themselves entirely below within) the Hindu caste system.

The south Indian state of Kerala was a hub of the first generation of Indian liberation theologians. It had a great deal of Christians – about 20% of the population. And it was also a state where the Communist Party of India (CPI) had a strong foothold. In 1957, the CPI for the first time won the state elections and established a government that envisaged several reform policies aimed to uplift the poor. All of this appeared to be an appropriate background for progressive theologians, among whom Sebastian Kappen was one of the most important.

This book in precise an intellectual biography of Sebastian Kappen SJ as it elaborates on his intellectual formation and the development and evolution of his ideas. In view of this, I delve into the origins of his thoughts and examine his sources of inspiration. This includes his relationship with and contributions to the fields of liberation theology, his activism and aspirations to reconstruct society, and his legacy. To accomplish this task, I thoroughly explore his ideas and their development, his activism, and the context and background which transformed Kappen into a liberation theologian, social activist, and advocate of structural change.

Kappen's intellectual biography will be an expansion of certain fundamental questions and their answers. The most basic ones are: what are the particularities of the context in which Kappen lived and studied and how did they influence him? How can one interpret Kappen's activism and progressive ideas in comparison with those of other national and international progressive theologians and reformists? In what ways do his writings, publications, and correspondence stand out as channels to disseminate progressive ideologies?

I will first discuss the context in which Kappen lived and to assess its impact on his thoughts. How did religion and politics in Kerala evolve during his lifetime? To what extent did the Church in Kerala tackle social issues like poverty, illiteracy, economic exploitation, and religious discrimination? Were there reformists and progressive thinkers in India, and in Kerala in particular, who might have influenced and inspired Kappen? What did Communism in Kerala look like, and in which ways did it affect progressive thinking? Why were Communists able to score an electoral victory in 1957 for the first time through a democratic process? How did they relate to the different religious groups in the state, in particular Christians?

Along with the analysis of the Kerala context, I have also discussed the origin, inspiration, growth, and spread of liberation theology, of course, in light of the radical thoughts of Kappen. Such an analysis will help the eventual development of this dissertation. Thus, the fundamental questions in this regard are: what does liberation theology stand for? Why did it originate from Latin America? How did the Second Vatican Council contribute to its origin? Who are the leading theologians of liberation from the place of its origin? Certainly, liberation theology did not remain a local phenomenon; rather it spread to other parts of the world, including the aforementioned Asian countries. I have gone to the particularities of liberation theology in each of these countries and discuss their differences with Latin American liberation theology. Afterwards, I further narrow down my enquiry to liberation theology in India and elaborate on some of its leading progressive theologians, especially those from Kerala. At the same time, the Catholic Church's approach to liberation theology and liberation theologians comes to discussion. The Church seems to have discouraged progressive theologizing for various reasons. Thus, the book discusses those reasons, and it will look for the means that the Church used to criticize liberation theology.

The book basically consists of a critical exploration and analysis of Kappen's ideas, with the intention of dealing with questions related to his popularity and reception. Thus, it investigates the contents and evolution of his writings, especially in religious, social, and political terrains. Did Kappen stick to a particular idea throughout his life or did his thinking evolve? If so, in which direction did he move and what were his sources? In addition, it also examins how national and international events in the religious and secular world of his time differed from or converged with his ideological thinking.

Along with, I went through the ideologies that influenced Kappen, in order to understand how much they are complementary or contradictory, and how he utilized them. Being a theologian first and foremost, how did Kappen approach Marxism? Did he use Marxist concepts as means to criticize society? Did he sympathize with them and use them to target institutionalized religions, including the Christian Church? And what about the presence of other religious traditions in his progressive thinking, India being a cradle and melting pot of religions?

A critical and in-depth review of Kappen's writings and their reception will sufficiently answer the above-mentioned concerns. Very particularly, Kappen's monograph *Jesus and Freedom* is adequately discussed in consideration with the controversies and eventual censorship in 1980. Such an approach will explicate how the Society of Jesus responded to the Vatican's action and to Kappen. This will help one understand if this censorship generate discussion between Kappen, the Society of Jesus, and the Vatican, and if so, what was its content.

Figure 1. Sebastian Kappen SJ

Eventually, this book defines what kind of society Kappen proposed. Did he believe only in confronting the existing society or did he want to construct an entirely new society? If it was only some confrontation, how did Kappen stand out from other progressivists and reformers? If he wanted to construct a new society, it is important to know how he interpreted this proposal and how it would facilitate the economic, political, social, religious, and cultural liberation of man. This will ultimately facilitate the nature of such a society.

Kappen's proposal leads one to a further exploration of his influence and legacy in an extremely diversified society like India. A relevant issue that needs to be tackled is that is he remembered today – after 25 years of his death – and if, by whom. What is his impact and legacy? The key question here is to what extent can he be considered a liberation theologian rather than someone beyond that. If he was a liberation theologian, was he moderate or radical in his ideologies and criticisms? Are his thoughts only relevant to theologians or people interested in religious themes, or did he also dwell on secular subjects and can his identity transcend theology? In other words, this book reflects on Kappen's significance in contemporary society.

Figure 2. Kappen's Tomb

Endnotes

[1] Kappen's letter to Pedro Arrupe, 15 May 1981, KPA, 1.

[2] Kappen's letter to Paolo Dezza SJ, 6 September 1982, KPA, 3.

Abbreviations

AICUF	All India Catholic University Federation
AKJM	Archbishop Kavukattu Jubilee Memorial
ATC	Asian Theological Conference
BSP	*Bahujan Samaj Party* (Majority People's Party)
CBCI	Catholic Bishops' Conference of India
CCORECATO	*Comando Revolucionario Camilo Torres* (Revolutionary Command Camilo Torres)
CDF	Congregation for the Doctrine of the Faith
CDLM	Christian Dalit Liberation Movement
CEBs	*Comunidades eclesiales de base* (Basic Ecclesial Communities)
CEDI	*Centro Ecumênico de Documentação e Informação* (Ecumenical Centre for Documentation and Information)
CEHILA	*Comisión de Estudios de Historia de la Iglesia en Latinoamérica* (Commission for Studies in Latin American Church History)
CELAM	*Consejo Episcopal Latinoamericano* (Latin American Episcopal Conference)

CETRI	Centre Tricontinental
CIA	Central Investigation Agency
CMI	Carmelites of Mary Immaculate
CNBB	*Confer Âṣncia Nacional dos Bispos do Brasil* (National Conference of the Brazilian Bishops)
Comintern	Communist International
CPI	Communist Party of India
CPI[M]	Communist Party of India [Marxist]
CSI	Church of South India
CSP	Congress Socialist Party
CSRR	Centre for Socio-Religious Research
CTCH	*Confederación de Trabajadores de Chile* (Popular Front in Chile)
DP	*Document of Puebla*
DM	*Document of Medellin*
DV	*Dei Verbum* (Dogmatic Constitution on Divine Revelation)
EATWOT	Ecumenical Association of the Third World Theologians
ELN	*Ejército de Liberación Nacional* (National Liberation Army)
EPI	*Estado Português da Índia* (Portuguese State of India)
FABC	Federation of the Asian Bishops' Conference
GC	General Congregation
GS	*Gaudium et Spes* (Pastoral Constitution on the Church in the Modern World)

ICRO	Indian Christian Research Organization
IIS	Indian Institute of Spirituality
IMF	International Monetary Fund
INC	Indian National Congress
IPER	*Institut Pastoral d'Études Religieuses* (Pastoral Institute for Religious Studies)
ISAL	*Iglesia y Sociedad en America Latina* (Church and Society in Latin America)
ISPCK	Indian Society for Promoting Christian Knowledge
ITA	Indian Theological Association
Jn	John
JOC	*Juventud Obrera Católica* (Young Catholic Workers)
JSS	*Janathipathya Samrakshana Samithy* (Association for Defence of Democracy)
KADOC	Katholiek Documentatie- en Onderzoekscentrum (Documentation and Research Centre on Religion, Culture, and Society)
KARB	Kerala Agrarian Relations Bill
KCBC	Kerala Catholic Bishops' Conference
KPA	Kerala SJ Provincial Archive
KU Leuven	Katholieke Universeit Leuven (Catholic University of Leuven)
LDF	Left Democratic Front
Lk	Luke
Mk	Mark
Mt	Matthew

OA	*Octogesima Adveniens* (Apostolic Letter: The Eightieth Anniversary)
PCLM	Poor Christian Liberation Movement
PDC	*Partido Demócrata Cristiano* (Christian Democratic Party)
PRI	*Partido Revolucionario Institucional* (Institutional Revolutionary Party)
SC	Scheduled Caste
SD	*Santo Domingo Document*
SUTEP	*Sindicato Unitario de Trabajadores en la Educación del Perú* (The Peruvian National Teachers' Union)
TPI	Theological Publications in India
UCL	*Université catholique de Louvain* (French speaking Catholic University in Louvain-la Neuve)
UF	United Front
WCC	World Council of Churches
WWI	World War I
WWII	World War II

1

The Kerala Context

Kerala is an Indian state in the Malabar Coast, southwestern corner of the South Asian peninsula. It was formed on 1 November 1956. Following popular protest against the administrative division that the Indian republic had taken over from the British colonizers in 1947, the State Reorganization Act of 1956 created new states along linguistic borders. Kerala is the state where Malayalam is the dominant language. Its capital is Thiruvananthapuram (Trivandrum), in the south; two other major cities are Kochi (Cochin), in the centre, and Kozhikode (Calicut), in the north.

The word Kerala had been in use much earlier than 1956. The origin of the word is a mixture of myth and fact. Although its etymology is unclear, there are two prevalent explanations. First, Kerala is a combination of two Malayalam words, namely *kera* (coconut) and *alam* (land), i.e. *kera* + *alam* = *keralam* (land of coconuts); second, the term Kerala derived from Chera, which is the oldest known dynasty that ruled the region until the 15th century AD (Chera + *alam* = *Cheralam*, meaning the land of Cheras). *Kera* and Chera are considered the variants of the same word.

The region is historically known for its spices, especially pepper, cardamom, cinnamon, and clove, which it had been exporting since 3000 BC. In the middle ages, the Arabs enjoyed a monopoly over the maritime spice trade through the Indian Ocean, but their position was taken over by Europeans in the early modern era. The Portuguese settled in the region following the arrival of Vasco da Gama at a Kerala coastal point called Kappad, near Calicut, in 1498. In 1505, Francisco de Almeida came as Viceroy of India, settled in Kochi, and established the Portuguese State of India. In 1510, the headquarters were moved to Goa. The Portuguese traders were followed by the Dutch (1605), the British (1612), and the French (1668). European Christian missionaries accompanied all of them and carried out evangelization missions in the Malabar Coast and other parts of India.

The peculiar geographic situation has contributed to Kerala's own independent political identity. It was a narrow strip of land of almost 40,000 sq. km. wedged between a mountain range – the Western Ghats – in the east and the Arabian Sea in the west. This kept Kerala politically and culturally distinct from other parts of India. Until the closing years of the 18th century, the geographical area of Kerala consisted of two independent kingdoms – namely Travancore in the south and Cochin in the centre – and of the region of Malabar, which was part of the Kingdom of Mysore, in the north. In 1791, the Kingdom of Cochin entered into a treaty with the British East India Company and decided to be a princely state and to receive military protection from the Company. The Kingdom of Travancore accepted the British supremacy in 1795. In a new treaty concluded in 1805, Travancore agreed to pay an annual tribute of Rs. 800,000 to the Company for the protection it received. Malabar was conquered in the Third and Fourth Anglo-Mysore Wars (1792 and 1799). It was first a part of the Bombay presidency and was then added to the Madras presidency in 1800. Eventually the British dominated the region till 1947. From the 19th century onwards, they dramatically transformed Kerala. Tile factories, weaving mills, and tea and coffee plantations contributed to the economy of Travancore, Cochin, and Malabar.

This chapter is a deeper introduction to Kerala, the region where Sebastian Kappen spent a great deal of his lifetime. It will focus on three aspects that also chronologically succeed each other. First, it will discuss the history of Christianity in Kerala before and after the arrival of the European missionaries. Afterwards, it will examine the social and nationalist movements in Kerala, especially in the first half of the 20th century. Finally, it will deal with Communism in Kerala: the ideology that won an electoral victory in 1957 and has been a major player in the state ever since.

A.   The Core of Indian Christianity

Kerala has the largest Christian population of all Indian states: 5.5 million people, which is around 18.38% of the state population (census 2011). Throughout their twenty-century history, these Christians have always been a minority community. Other major religions in Kerala are Hinduism (54.73%) and Islam (26.56%). Christianity in Kerala consists of different churches, including Catholic, Protestant, Orthodox, and Pentecostal, of which the Catholic Church is the largest and dominant Christian community in Kerala. The Catholic Church in Kerala includes three *sui iuris* churches, namely the Syro-Malabar, the Syro-Malankara, and the Latin. The Latin expression *sui iuris* indicates the churches in the Catholic Church that are independent with the capacity to undertake their own administrative affairs, but in full communion with the Vatican. Currently, the global Catholic Church consists of twenty-four *sui iuris* churches under six major liturgical traditions, namely Latin, Alexandrian, Antiochian, Armenian, Chaldean, and Byzantine initiative.

Figure 3. South India and Kerala

The history of Christianity in Kerala goes back to the I[st] century AD, and the Christian community there is considered to be one of the oldest in the world. The Christians were known by different names, such as Syrian Christians, St. Thomas Christians (St. Thomas = *Mar Thoma*; the literal meaning of the Syriac word Mar is 'my Lord'; it is also used before the names of the saints and bishops), etc.[1] There are three different arguments regarding the arrival of Christianity in Kerala. The living tradition states that Christianity reached Kerala in 52 AD with the arrival of the direct apostle of Jesus, St. Thomas, in Cranganore (present-day Kodungallur).[2] Apostle Thomas established several Christian communities in India and died a martyr in 72 AD in Mylapur near Madras (Chennai), where his tomb is still preserved.[3] Many scholars, however, claim that Christianity reached Kerala through merchants from the East. There are also scholars who argue that it spread with Jewish settlers.[4] Robert E. Frykenberg, professor emeritus of History and South Asian Studies at the University of Wisconsin, USA, recently concluded that "despite contradictory and corroborative elements within various sources of the tradition, and notwithstanding whatever common features may be shared, all sources have received serious consideration."[5]

There is also a tradition according to which a migration of Syrian Christians from the Middle East to Kerala took place in the 4th century under the leadership of Thomas of Cana.[6] Syriac Christianity is an umbrella term for Eastern Christian traditions having Syriac language in their liturgy. There are also scholars who claimed that the Syrian Christians had migrated to the Malabar Coast of south India because there already existed a strong Christian community.[7] However, the date of this migration is debated. Some other scholars even argued that this migration was in the 9th century AD. The first written documents on this dated from the Portuguese period in India.[8] From the 4th century to the end of the 16th century, the Patriarch of the East Syrian Church, based in Edessa, which is also called Antioch, sent bishops to the Church in Kerala.[9] These bishops were only responsible for liturgical and spiritual matters. Archdeacons of the Church in Kerala took care of administrative affairs. Whatsoever, the Syrian Christians consider the first argument (St. Thomas tradition) to be true and valid. Until the 16th century, the Church in Kerala had a strong relationship with the East Syrian Church.

However, the discovery of the sea route to the Malabar Coast by the Portuguese Admiral Vasco da Gama in 1498 opened a new era in the history of Christianity in India.[10] Portuguese missionaries started to come to India along with the traders. The patronage right (Padroado)[11] of the kings of Portugal to rule over the local churches enabled the Portuguese missionaries to involve in the liturgical, spiritual, and administrative matters of the Syrian Christians. The Portuguese missionaries denounced the East Syrian connection of the Church in the Malabar Coast and began to introduce Latin liturgical traditions and church administrative methods. A Syriac document from c.1504 said that upon the arrival of the Portuguese, the Christians in India had to strive hard to maintain their position.[12]

Serious problems began to appear when the Portuguese bishop Don Alexis Menezes appointed and authorized a Latin bishop to rule the Syrian Christians in 1599. In a letter to the Portuguese King Philip dated 4 August 1600, Pope Clement VIII wrote that the Church of Angamaly (Cochin) lacked any endowment due to the death of Mar Abraham, the last East Syrian bishop in Kerala who ruled the Church from 1565 to 1597. Through this letter the Pope reduced the Syrian Christians to the status of a Cathedral church of one bishop who would be a suffragan to the Archbishop of Goa.[13]

Over the following decades, the Syrian Christians started agitating against the restrictions placed upon them. Their objections culminated in the Coonan Cross Oath of 3 January 1653 in which they declared that they did not want to be ruled by Latin bishops and went away under the leadership of Archdeacon Mar Thoma I.[14] The Vatican responded to the crisis by sending two groups of Carmelites under the leadership of Fr. Sebastiani and Fr. Hyacinth. Over the following decade, these envoys succeeded in reconciling 84 out of the 116 local church communities. These reconciled churches continued the East Syrian tradition and eventually evolved into the Syro-Malabar Church.[15]

Accounts about demographics of the Christians in Kerala are generally debated. The available statistics regarding the number of the Syrian Christians in Kerala during and after the arrival of the Portuguese is variant. According to the annual letters of the Jesuits in 1648 and 1654, which are in the archives in Rome, the number was only about 80,000.[16] The majority of them were settled in and around Cochin and Kottayam. Nevertheless, the number of Christians in Kerala at the beginning of the 19th century was 117,000. The number increased to 891,676 (672,124 Syrian Christians) as given in the census details of 1901. At the turn of 20th century, Christians had a growth rate of 3 percent per annum. Yet, the growth rate declined rapidly from the 1930s (it is clear from the percentage of Christian population in different censuses: 1921 - 1,376,354[17.64%]; 1931 - 1,856,024[19.52%]; 1941 - 2,263,888[20.52]).[17]

Although the Syrian Christians (St. Thomas Christians) in Kerala underwent number of divisions and subdivisions down the centuries, this section deals only with a brief history of the three *sui iuris* Catholic churches on the conviction that this will suffice for the purpose of this chapter.

The Syro-Malabar Catholic Church

The Syro-Malabar Catholic Church is an Eastern Catholic Major Archiepiscopal Church. Among the Eastern Catholic churches, the Syro-Malabar Church is the second largest with 4.5 million followers, only next to the Ukranian Catholic Church (5.3 million). The Syrian Christians claim to descend from the families who were Christianized by St. Thomas.

An important figure in the Syro-Malabar Church was Chavara Kuriakose Elias (1805-71), a Syrian Catholic priest from Kerala who was recently sanctified by the Vatican (2014). His relevance is multifold. Together with two other priests he founded India's first indigenous religious congregation on 11 May 1831 in Mannanam, of which he was the first Superior General.[18] The initial name of the congregation was the Congregation of the Servants of Mary Immaculate of Mount Carmel; and later on, it became known as Carmelites of Mary Immaculate (CMI). He also served as the Vicar General of the Syrian Christians from the 1860s. Chavara Kuriakose Elias was a pioneer in the social and educational activities of the Syro-Malabar Church. As the Vicar General, he ordered the application of the principle of 'a school along with every church' (the so-called *pallikoodam*) and this greatly contributed to the development of educational activities in the Kerala Church and society.[19] These educational institutions established by the Church were open not only for Christians but also for other people, irrespective of their religious affiliation. These schools were particularly attractive among children from the lower castes and the outcasts, who at the time were not given admission to the public schools. All these initiatives also drew other agencies and religious groups into the field and accelerated the spread of quality education in the state.

At that time, the term Syro-Malabar was not yet used to denote the Keralite St. Thomas Catholic Christians. This concept was only launched in 1923, when pope Pius XI established the Syro-Malabar hierarchy through the apostolic constitution *Romani Pontifices* and made Ernakulam the metropolitan See with three suffragan dioceses.[20] This was due to the recommendation of the Sacred Congregation for the Oriental Churches in Rome after observing the progress of the Syrian Catholics in Kerala. The term 'Syro' is used to show the relation of the Church with the Chaldean Syriac language, officially used in its liturgy, and Malabar refers to the geographical area.[21] In this decision, the title 'Syro-Malabar Church' was officially used for the first time. However, after 1923, scholars including historians and theologians used the titles 'Syro-Malabar Church,' or 'Syro-Malabar Christians,' or 'Syro-Malabar Catholics' or 'Chaldeo-Syrian' to denote the Syrian Christian community that was in communion with the Roman Church.[22]

In general, the Syrian Christian community (Syrian Christian denominations) in Kerala at the time was not a missionary community by function, especially when it came to the expansion of the Church outside Kerala. This was true mainly for two reasons. First of all, most of its converts were upper caste Hindus, particularly Brahmins (also called Namboothiris), the priestly class in Hinduism. As a result, the Christian community remained a rather closed community and thought that conversion of lower caste people would create unrest. Secondly, these upper caste converts did not want to lose their social position.[23] They indeed enjoyed various privileges under the local rulers and a high status in the society, which other newly converted Christians did not have.[24] Therefore, they remained primarily in Kerala. However, there were also counter arguments that claimed that the Syro-Malabar Christians were more interested in protecting and practicing their faith than converting the adherents of other faiths through proselytization. In addition, the jurisdictional restriction over the Syro-Malabar Church by the Latin Church also prevented the former from extending missionary activities beyond Kerala and some parts of Tamil Nadu and Karnataka.[25]

The Second Vatican Council mitigated the jurisdictional restrictions on the Syro-Malabar Church. Ever since, it has spread its mission into other parts of India, but with special permission, establishing dioceses to take care of its faithful, mainly diaspora. Some of the early established Syro-Malabar mission dioceses include Bijnor (Uttarakhand, 1972), Chanda (Chattisgarh, 1977), Jagdalpur (Chattisgarh, 1977), Rajkot (Gujarat, 1977), Sagar (Madhya Pradesh, 1977), and Ujjain (Madhya Pradesh, 1977). It also started schools, colleges, hospitals, and other charitable movements in these dioceses. As a matter of fact, both urban and rural areas had been enjoying the fruits of the Church's contributions to the education sector, social work, and curative sector of medicine.[26] Importantly, in his letter to the Bishops of India on 9 October 2017, Pope Francis declared that the Syro-Malabar Church could do its pastoral work in the whole of India by independently erecting parishes and dioceses.[27]

The Syro-Malankara Catholic Church

The Syro-Malankara Catholic Church is an East Syrian Church centered in Kerala in communion with the Roman Catholic Church and the Pope. The history of the Malankara Church goes back to the 16th century. When the 84 local church communities, reclaimed by the Carmelite missionaries who were sent to the Malabar Coast by Rome, formed the Syro-Malabar tradition, there were still 32 left. The apostolic commissaries could not regain those 32 church communities. Archdeacon Mar Thoma I, the leader of the Coonan Cross Oath, demanded he be consecrated bishop. Rome rejected this demand, and Mar Thoma I and his followers were excommunicated in 1663. Soon he declared allegiance to the Syriac Orthodox Church of Antioch in order to form a separate church. The newly separated group acknowledged the Antiochean Patriarch and the Antiochean liturgy. In 1836, it even strengthened its connection by officially approving the Antiochean liturgy and canon law. From then on, it became known as the Malankara Church. With the Synod of Mulanthuruthy in Kerala in 1876, the Malankara Church came under complete supremacy of the Antiochean Patriarch.[28] In the following years, it underwent many splits.

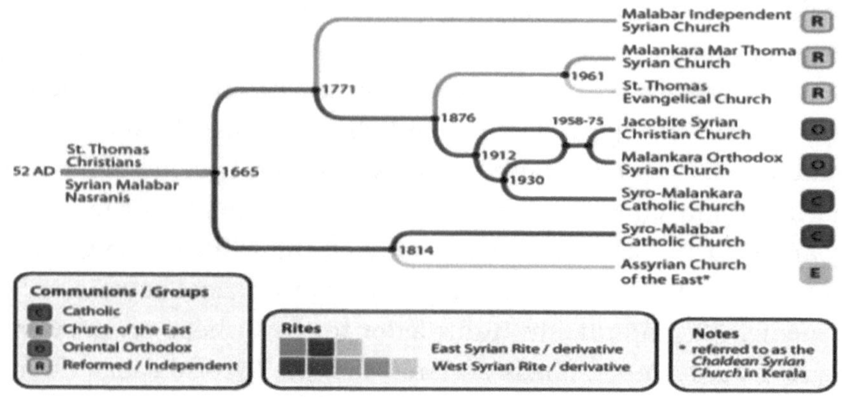

Figure 4. Division within the St. Thomas Christians in Kerala[29]

In fact, there were always attempts in the Malankara Church for a reunion with the Catholic Church from the time of the division. Major attempts and initiatives were taken by Mar Thoma IV (1686-1728), Mar Thoma V (1728-64), and Mar Thoma VI (1761-1808). However, the Roman Catholic Church did not want the reunion to take place. The Vatican was afraid that this would lead to a reunification of all Syrian Christians and to its loss of control.[30] By the beginning of the second quarter of the 20th century, the Syro-Malankara Bishop Geevarghese Mar Ivanios (1882-1953), along with four others, strived to reunite and enter in communion with the Roman Catholic Church. Eventually, the reunion took place on 20 September 1930.[31] Soon after, on 11 June 1932, Pope Pius XI established Syro-Malankara hierarchy for the reunited community, through the Apostolic Constitution *Christo Pastorum Principi*.[32] Along with this declaration, the Pope also erected an Archeparchy in Trivandrum and an eparchy in Tiruvalla, suffragan to Trivandrum. In 1933 Trivandrum Archeparchy became the Metropolitan eparchy and Mar Ivanios became the first Metropolitan bishop. The

Syro-Malankara Catholic Church experienced a speedy growth after its reunion and the establishment of Syro-Malankara hierarchy.

The Roman Catholic Church (Latin Church)

The term Latin Church here stands for the Roman Catholic Church. The history of the Latin Church in India began in the last decade of the 13th century with the visit of John of Monte Corvino, a Franciscan missionary, who came to the southeast coast of India (Madras/Chennai) and preached the gospel in 1291, en route to China.[33] The first Latin diocese in India was erected in Quilon (Kollam), Kerala on 9 August 1329 by the then Pope John XXII. It died a silent death and we do not know anything about the first bishop's last years except that he was martyred.[34]

The Portuguese Jesuit missionaries undertook revitalized missionary activities later in the 16th century as they reached the Malabar Coast. Franciscan, Dominican, and Augustinian religious orders also sent missionaries to different parts of India. In our discussion about the Latin Church in the Malabar Coast we concentrate more on the Jesuit missionaries and their contributions. This is specifically for three reasons. First of all, the history of the Latin Church in the Malabar Coast, especially in Travancore, Cochin, and Malabar district, was mingled with that of the Syrian churches. In our discussion of the history of these Syrian churches, we already acquired basic knowledge about the Latin Church. Secondly, Jesuit missionaries quickly grew into the most important Roman Catholic missionary society in India, expressly in the Malabar Coast. And finally, we will focus on the progressive theological and secular thinking and contributions of the Indian Jesuit, Fr. Sebastian Kappen, at the later stages of this study.

The Society of Jesus is a religious order in the Catholic Church, founded by the Spanish priest St. Ignatius Loyola (1491-1556) in 1540. Traditionally, European monastic men and women were expected to live in communities that allowed them to participate as a group in daily routines. However, Ignatius Loyola made some innovations and granted freedom to the members of the Society to actively engage in apostolic work.[35] This provided opportunity to the zealous members of the Society to find their own charisma and open up their own areas of mission.[36] The Society immediately started sending out missionaries to different parts of the world to carry out the evangelical mission. The Jesuit mission in India began with the arrival of St. Francis Xavier (1505-52), known as the second apostle of India, in Goa on 6 May 1542.[37] Though he began his missionary activities in Goa, he later came to Kerala and the fishery coast of Tamil Nadu.[38] Xavier adapted a method of cultural dialogue in order to reach the people easily. For instance, he applied the means of singing the creed and the Christian doctrines knowing that singing was an integral part of the Indian culture.[39] In his letter of 1545, Xavier narrated his experience in Travancore. He used to collect people in one place and teach catechism. He translated the basic prayers in the Catholic Church into vernaculars and learned them by heart to teach.[40] Cultural adaptation was very much part of the Jesuit method and Xavier might have learned it from Ignatius Loyola, the founder of the Society of Jesus and a proponent of acculturation. Xavier stayed in India for three years and left for Portuguese Malacca (in today's Malaysia) in 1545. In 1548, he came back to Goa, but again left for Malacca in the following year.[41]

The first Jesuit province in India was Goa (1549). It was the third province of the Society, after Spain and Portugal. The second province in India, Malabar, with its headquarters in Cochin, was created as a vice province in 1602 and as a province in 1605. By the mid-18th century, the Jesuit establishments in the Goa Province were the richest in India with 132 members and 12 houses. The case was almost similar regarding the Malabar Mission.[42] It had 51 members and 8 establishments. At the death of the Archbishop of Cranganore/Kodungallur in 1754 the Viceroy and the Archbishop of Goa wanted to have the post for a Jesuit, for the Jesuits used to hold the office of the *Father of Christians (Pai dos Cristãos)* in India.[43]

In the Malabar district, Jesuit missionaries were the pioneers from within the Church in the field of education; but in Travancore, the Jesuit educational institutions are of relatively late origin. Jesuits deployed a wide range of activities, but were especially important for their education, which they considered the means for the socio-economic development of the marginalized sections in the society. In other words, education itself stood as a synonym for social uplift. Along with their social activities, the missionaries decided to provide them training in carpentry, smith works, paper manufacturing, etc.[44] They founded a great number of educational institutions in Kerala. St. Joseph's School (Calicut, 1793),[45] St. Michael's (Kannur, 1865), Kristuraja Lower Primary School (Calicut, 1943),[46] Sarvodaya School (Echome, Wayanad, 1950), AKJM High School (Archbishop Kavukattu Jubilee Memorial, Kanjirappally, 1961),[47] Loyola School (Trivandrum, 1961), Loyola College of Social Sciences (Trivandrum, 1963), and St. Xavier's college (Trivandrum, 1964) are the most renowned Jesuit educational institutions in Kerala. The latter, St. Xavier's, helped educate the students of the fishermen of the coastal area. Nirmala ITC Pariyaram, Edatva ITC, and Training programs in Attappady, etc. provided job oriented training to the youth. Jesuits focused on two essential responsibilities of education: acculturation and socialization. Their central point of concern was the conversion of students into agents of social change. Similarly, they have also been running a couple of retreat centers aiming for an integral development of the human person. Institutions like Sameeksha (Kaladi), Lumen Jyothis (Kochi), etc. invested great energy in penetrating into the intellectual world with Christian thinking and visions.[48]

Educational institutions in Malabar were established not only by the Jesuits and the Syrian Christians, but also by the Protestant missions that settled in great numbers in the 19th century, especially under the auspice of the Basel Evangelical Missions, a German based Protestant Christian missionary organization founded in 1815. It was initially known as German Missionary Society and later as Basel Evangelical Missionary Society. It started missionary activities in India in 1834.[49]

These missionary initiatives accelerated the process of social transformation. At the Fifth International Seminar on Indo-Portuguese History held at Cochin in 1989, the Indian historian M.G.S. Narayanan categorically explained how the Portuguese (Jesuit) presence in Malabar challenged the Hindu society. Jesuits' initiatives for the material and spiritual uplift of the people of the Malabar Coast, irrespective of their caste and creed, motivated the Hindu community. The Hindu community felt the need to fight social evils, including the elements of injustice in the Hindu caste system.[50] This called the Hindu orthodoxy to search for retrospective and corrective measures to block the flow of the low castes from Hinduism. Although the fundamental reason for all discrimination, the caste system, continued to be strong in south India until the 20th century, the reformative attempts from certain corners within Hinduism should also be seen from this point of view.

B.   Reformist and Nationalist Agitation in British India

Even after the arrival of the Dutch, French, and the British, the Portuguese presence continued, but was confined mainly to Goa. In 1954, India demanded the Portuguese leave India. The negotiation continued for seven years and in 1961 the Portuguese State of India was merged with the Indian Union through a military operation. The Dutch and French presence ended in 1825 and 1954 respectively. At the same time, the second half of the 18th and the first quarter of the 19th centuries roughly represent the period of the rise and consolidation of British India. The British East India Company conquered entire territories and turned other states and provinces into indirectly ruled vassals. Protests against the British appeared in several parts of India, especially in the closing years of the 19th century under the banner of the Indian National Congress (INC), which was founded in 1885.[51] In the mid-1910s Mahatma Gandhi (1869-1948) took over the leadership of the nationalist and anti-British movements at the national level.[52] Simultaneously, huge cries for social transformation were also heard elsewhere in India, in many cases even long before the nationalist feeling was centre-staged.

The case was no different in the southwestern part of the South Asian peninsula, where the social reform movements also preceded the nationalist movements. Yet, there were also some differences and particularities. In this section, we limit our discussion to the historical context of Kerala in the first half of the 20th century, focusing only on the very essential areas that are necessary in further developing this research.

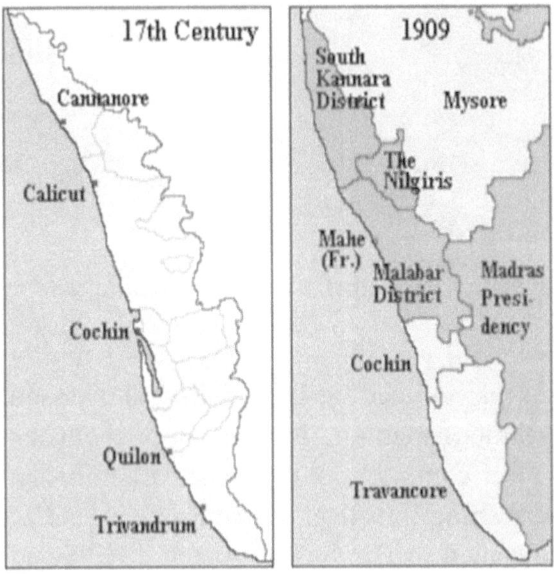

Figure 5. Kerala: 17th and early 20th centuries[53]

The British colonization inspired Indians to reflect on their own society. One of the first and most famous modernization or reformist movements appeared in Bengal in the 1820s. Over the 19th century, this Bengal Renaissance gained national importance, and other regions followed suit. Reformist movements in Kerala were mostly based on religious matters, particularly on the injustice and discrimination in Hinduism towards low castes and Dalits.[54] Even though such discrimination existed all over India, Kerala practiced caste discrimination and untouchability in their most complex forms. For that reason, besides the national level social reform movements, there were many local initiatives that took the severity of the caste problem into consideration. Three Keralite reformists proved to be the most prominent by the beginning of the 20th century: Chattampi Swamikal (1853-1924), Sri Narayana Guru (1856-1928), and Mahatma Ayyan Kali (1863-1941).

Figure 6. Chattampi Swamikal, Sri Narayana Guru, and Ayyan Kali[55]

Chattampi Swamikal was born to a high caste family in southern Travancore.[56] In his younger age he travelled all over south India, met many Hindu religious men and learned more about the religion and its scriptures. After coming back to Travancore in his late twenties he indulged in abolishing injustice, discrimination, and untouchability, all of which prevailed in Hinduism.[57] Being a Hindu sage, Swamikal went against the caste-ridden Hindu society and stood with and voiced for the marginalized. He aspired to construct a casteless society. His perspectives on religion had an inclusive nature, for he taught that all religions were different pathways to God. Second, in addition to the books on Hinduism, he also wrote a book on Christianity in Malayalam: *Chrsitumatha Chedanam* (*Hindu Critique of Christianity*). The book provided his understanding of Christianity, and also argued that Christian missionaries misinterpreted the scriptures and the teachings of Jesus.[58]

Sri Narayana Guru, a disciple of Chattampi Swamikal, continued to carry on his guru's teachings. Unlike his guru, he was born into a low caste Hindu family (Ezhava), which gave him the bitter experience of social discrimination. Narayana believed in the equality of all humans and fought to mitigate caste discrimination.[59] He caught society's attention in Kerala by condemning the Brahminic hegemony and its monopoly over matters related to temples and prayer ceremonies (*pooja*). In his protest against the ban on the low castes from entering the temples, he established more than sixty temples for them, which in fact was a right belonging to the Brahmins. His strong and revolutionary teaching was that caste degenerated men and therefore should be abolished. He considered the caste system to be a meaningless and foolish institution that enabled the strong and the rich to subjugate the weak and the poor. His idea of humanity was reiterated in his famous dictum: "one caste, one religion, one God for mankind."[60] In addition to building temples, Narayana Guru initiated also the establishment of schools and temples for the lower castes and untouchables.[61] A major step in this regard was the founding of the SNDP (Sri Narayana Dharma Paripalana Yogam or Sree Narayana Trust) in 1903 as a charitable organization for the educational and spiritual empowerment of the Ezhavas and other low castes. Narayana Guru strongly advocated that education would liberate people and urged the low caste section of the society to educate its children.[62] Due to his endeavors, the Ezhava community obtained a strong presence in the political, social, and economic fields in Kerala.

Mahatma Ayyan Kali, a third major social reformer from Kerala, also was born into a low caste Hindu family (Pulaya). Just as his contemporaries, he also struggled to eradicate untouchability. He strongly argued for the rights of the Pulayas, specifically for their right to use public roads, which were off limits to them. Because of the continued efforts, the Pulaya community gained a representative in the Travancore State Assembly in 1910. Ayyan Kali became the nominated representative in 1912 and remained in the Assembly for 28 years. His major objectives were to secure education, employment, and land for the lower castes. Having realized the relevance of education in social advancement, he constructed a school in Vengaloor, in the Travancore princely state, for low caste children, especially from the Pulaya community.[63] Soon after that, through several strikes and protests, he forced the Nairs (one of the high castes) to admit Pulaya children in the schools granted by the government. To achieve this, he mobilized the Pulayas and instructed them to refrain from working in the fields and farms of the Nair landlords. Moreover, due to his consistent demand, he in 1924 achieved full-fee concession education for Pulaya children and half-fee concession for other backward classes. All of this was a great success. However, Ayyan Kali excluded Pulaya Christians (newly converted Christians from the Pulaya community) from these benefits.[64]

Indeed, in their fight against caste discrimination, Chattampi Swamikal, Sri Narayana Guru, and Ayyan Kali not only targeted the exploitation of the high castes but also the conversion attempts from other religious groups, especially Christians. Despite their inclusive approach to other beliefs, all these reformers reacted against what they called the exploitation of the economic and political poverty of the low castes by other religious groups. Chattampi Swamikal wrote against Christian missionaries and the many conversions taking place during his time. In the introduction to his book on Christianity he noted that Christian missionaries lured the poor and uneducated low caste Hindus to convert by giving clothes and food products.[65] He respected Christianity but opposed these practices, in particular, mass conversion.[66] According to Sri Narayana Guru, moving from one faith to another out of conviction was not a serious offense, but conversion for material benefits was unjustifiable. Guru initiated the reconversion to Hinduism of families who had converted to Christianity due to poverty and discrimination.[67]

There were still other political and socio-religious movements throughout Kerala, focused on injustice and social discrimination. Although in Malabar, being under direct British rule, there existed less caste discrimination in the administrative machinery, the low castes and untouchables were still out of the mainstream of the society. This was due to the fact that their social and economic status was dependent on and determined by their rank in the caste hierarchy. In Cochin and Travancore, the situation was even worse since they did not have representation in the administrative structure.[68]

Gandhi and Kerala

The reformist movements were given new impetus by the national events that took place at the beginning of the 20th century. At the national level, a stronger collective form of anti-British sentiment appeared. One of the most revolutionary means of agitation was the Swadeshi (self-sufficiency) movement, which instructed the people to give up all foreign products and promote Indian goods. The movement mainly targeted the exploitation in the textile sector. The British cheaply exported cotton as raw material to the home country and imported the costly finished textile products back to the Indian markets, which depleted the Indian economy. At the national level, the Swadeshi movement received revitalized momentum in the years following Lord Curzon's communal based Bengal partition in 1905. It even led to a split within the Indian National Congress (INC), which initially was a very moderate party that only argued for more Indian representation in the British Indian institutions.[69] Peace returned when the partition was revoked in 1911 (the moment when New Delhi was created as the new capital of British India), but tensions again rose with the return of Mahatma Gandhi (1869-1948) to India in 1915 and the frustration following unfulfilled expectations after the First World War. Indian independence as a reward for their support to the British in the War was the expectation of many Indian nationalists.[70] Gandhi, who had studied law in England and had stayed in South Africa since 1893, quickly began organizing protests against the British in various forms, such as agrarian and labor reform demonstrations, non-violent and non-cooperation protest, and civil disobedience.

Like in other parts of India, in Kerala the prevailing anti-imperialist and pro-nationalist movements in secular as well as religious sectors became more active after WWI. The Travancore Civil Rights League (1918) stood up for the abolition of untouchability and the uplift of the marginalized, looking forward to a stronger mobilization against the British. During its conference held in 1919, it even cooperated with Christians and Muslims.[71] Likewise, in Malabar, the fifth Malabar District Political Conference of 28 April 1920, under the patronage of the INC, was one of the significant events towards a nationalist movement.[72] In the presence of Annie Besant (1847-1933), a prominent British socialist and supporter of Indian self-rule, the Conference rejected the Montague-Chelmsford Reforms (gradual introduction of self-governance) and demanded constitutional reforms and freedom from the British.[73] Furthermore, unrest that had been growing among the landless peasants all over Kerala led to uprisings. An example of the culmination of such minor agitations was the Mappila Revolt in Malabar in 1921. It was mainly organized by landless Muslims against the British authority and the Hindu landlords. Other peasant protest followed in many other parts of Travancore, Cochin, and Malabar.[74]

Eventually, the Keralite socio-religious reformist movements joined the mainstream of political movements for independence. A collective and organized outburst of this nationalist feeling started with the first visit of Gandhi to Kerala on 18 August 1920.[75] His presence in Calicut gained particular attention for the fact that this city was the place where the European colonization in India started in 1498. The visit was part of a mobilization campaign for his non-cooperation movement against the Rowlatt Acts and the British policy of levying excessive land-tax.[76] However, Gandhi's visits to Kerala also had a different and more socio-religious agenda.

Gandhi's second visit to Kerala in March 1925, during the Vaikom Satyagraha, is a good example of this. The Vaikom Satyagraha of 1924-25 was a movement that developed around the Vaikom temple in the district of Kottayam, primarily against untouchability and, more specifically, the ban on the low castes from entering the temple. Gandhi subscribed to the movement, visited the temple, and accordingly fueled his popularity in Kerala. He continued to engage in the socio-religious reform movements over the following years. During his third visit, from 9 to 15 October 1927, he called on the Maharaja and Maharani of Trivandrum to discuss untouchability.

Gandhi's taking over of the leadership of Congress in 1921 and his visits to Kerala made the INC even more popular. This encouraged the Kerala faction of the party to engage in and lead social reform movements. Following the Vaikom line, the Kerala unit of the INC – the KPCC (Kerala Provincial/Pradesh Congress Committee) – launched a *satyagraha* in the Guruvayur temple in Trichur (in the Malabar district) in November 1931, with the blessing of Gandhi, for securing the right for untouchables to enter the temple. The non-violent protest was initially unsuccessful. The *satyagraha* leaders went on hunger-strike several times, but their action was called off in 1932 due to the intervention of Gandhi.[77] INC activists and leaders continued their struggle, and finally the low castes attained the right to enter the temple when the Maharaja of Travancore issued the historic Temple Entry Proclamation of 1936.[78]

The Nivarthana or Abstention movement of 1932 followed the Guruvayur Satyagraha of 1931. This protest was initiated by representatives of the lower castes and Muslim and Christian minorities, again under the auspice of the INC, for adequate representation in public services. Eventually, due to many protests, the lower castes and other minorities received representation.

Gandhi visited Kerala once again, from 10 to 22 January 1934, between the Nivarthana agitation and the Proclamation of 1936. He addressed the public in various meetings and engaged in discussions with communities from the lower stratum of society.[79] Gandhi also visited many Hindu religious places, including Sivgiri Math where Sri Narayana Guru died and was buried. Also, during his fifth and final visit in January 1937, he contributed to the socio-religious reformations in Kerala. On 21 January, Gandhi opened a private temple at Kottarakkara for all the caste communities.

Still, all of these actions should not eclipse that Gandhi, in fact, supported the caste system and actually contributed to strengthening this peculiar Indian social system. According to Gandhi, each person was born into a caste that had been assigned with a duty or profession in society. If somebody did not respect this accordingly, he or she committed a crime.[80] Therefore, in effect, Gandhi ideologically differed with the above-mentioned social reformists, who all wanted to abolish the caste system. This became clear during his visit to Sri Narayana Guru in 1925, who confronted Gandhi on his view on the difference among human beings based on caste.[81]

However, like these Kerala reformists, Gandhi was also very much concerned about conversion to Christianity. As explained above, the 19th and early 20th century witnessed mass conversions of low castes to Christianity in Kerala. Although he was born into a Hindu family, Gandhi was very open to Christianity. In an interview in 1920, he even admitted that he once had wished to convert due to his devotion to the teachings of Jesus, especially the non-violent approach.[82] On 22 September 1922, he wrote in his weekly journal *Young India* that the Sermon on the Mount contained the essence of Christianity and that someone who rightly understood it would acknowledge the fact that no religion was false.[83] Later, however, he came to the conclusion that Christianity did not have anything Hinduism lacked. He believed that he could be a good Christian too if he lived as a good Hindu.

Even while Gandhi had a positive understanding of Christianity, he totally rejected conversion. For him, Christianity was a religion of the West and conversion to Christianity was therefore a kind of aping of Europeans. He went so far as to say that Indian Christian converts committed violence against the mother country and that every conversion to Christianity contained an element of denationalization.[84] On 21 March 1929 Gandhi wrote in his weekly journal *Young India* that the contribution of Christianity to national life had a negative character. He might have considered materialistic civilization and the imperialistic exploitation of the British in India as part of Christianity.[85]

Gandhi's criticism of Christianity is the major explanation of his socio-religious commitment in Kerala. He did not actually advocate the cause of the low castes and the untouchables, but instead first and foremost wanted to prevent them from turning to Christianity. This was made clear by his indifference towards similar actions against untouchability in north India. There, Dr. Ambedkar (1891-1956), a social reformer, politician, and the principal architect of the Constitution of India, largely campaigned against discrimination towards untouchables and advocated their political rights and social freedom, and most importantly abolition of caste system. Gandhi's ideological difference with Ambedkar on caste and untouchability throws light on his genuineness. The sole purpose of Gandhi's Temple Entry struggle (especially his visit to Vaikom Temple in 1925) was to put an end to the conversion of low castes to Christianity. He promoted *satyagrahas* to open the temples for the low castes only in Kerala, but not in north India.[86] The reason was that the conversion movement in north India had not become a menace. On the contrary, mass conversion had mainly been taking place in Kerala.[87]

The conflict between Gandhi and Ambedkar popped up at the First Round Table Conference in 1930.[88] Ambedkar argued for a communal electorate, believing that it would unify the Dalits to stand for their rights and equal status with the upper castes in the society. Gandhi, on the other hand, took an anti-Dalit stand in this matter and claimed that no separate electorate should be permitted. He went on an indefinite fast (Yeravada Fast, 20-26 September 1932) to protest when the British Prime Minister Ramsay McDonald decided in favor of Ambedkar and the Dalits. Gandhi's point of argument was that it would disintegrate Hindu religion and society.[89] Eventually, the British government had to yield to the demands of Gandhi, and certain clauses in the decision were withdrawn.

C.   Communism and Church in Kerala

Communism has been very important in Kerala, especially from the formation of the first Communist government in 1957. Since then, Communists in Kerala have scored several electoral wins and formed governments, the latest in May 2016. This section discusses the particularities of Kerala Communism: the history of the Communist movement in Kerala before and after the formation of the state in 1956, the first Communist government's policies, (with a special preference to the Kerala Agrarian Relations Bill (KARB) and the Education Bill), and the impact on and attitude of the Catholic Church. This background will help us understand Sebastian Kappen's relation with Communism, as will be discussed in Chapter IV and VII.

The Communist Party of India (CPI) originated in the early 1920s. It took birth in Tashkent, Uzbekistan, where M.N. Roy (1887-1954), an Indian radical activist and political theorist, created an Indian Communist Centre and a training school for Indian revolutionaries in 1920. From 1922 onwards, these institutions started contacting embryonic Communist groups in British Indian cities like Mumbai, Chennai, Kolkata, and Lahore. Initially, they worked as a radical wing within the INC, but in 1929, the Comintern forced the CPI to dissociate itself.[90] However, in 1933, the socialist wing within the INC formed the Congress Socialist Party (CSP), and the CPI started collaborating with it. In this way, the CPI succeeded in gaining control over local INC units, especially in Kerala, Orissa, Maharashtra, and Bihar. It was not a strong supporter of INC, since it strived for a people's democracy rather than an independent republic, but it did not try to interfere in the events that led to Indian independence on 15 August 1947.

The CPI decided to adapt the democratic process by participating in the general election in 1951, which it considered a platform to popularize Communist policies and mobilize people for the revolution. This tactical move led to international criticism, especially from China.[91] Still, the party performed well in some regions of south India and in 1951-52 won 16 seats in the Indian parliament (on a total of 489 seats). It decided to cooperate with the progressive policies of the Congress government. This collaboration even intensified when Nehru grew closer to the Soviet Union (despite his policy of Non-Alignment: not aligned with or against one or more sovereign states).[92] An extreme left wing in the CPI was unsatisfied with this pleasing of the INC, but they lost importance when Khrushchev during the 20th Communist Party of Soviet Union (CPSU) Congress argued for a peaceful and slow transition to socialism.

Kerala was one of the regions where Communism was especially popular. A first instance could be the Communist League, formed in Trivandrum in 1931.[93] During the 1930s, Communism found increasing interest, especially among the educated middle class. On 26 January 1940, the CPI officially came into existence in Kerala. In 1948 the CPI contested in the Travancore state election and secured 10 percent of the votes. By the early 1950s, Communism succeeded in attracting the poor and landless lower caste in large scale. Subsequently, in the first election in the integrated Travancore-Cochin state from 10 December 1951 to 5 January 1952, it won 13.3 percent of the poll. In the 1954 Travancore-Cochin election, the Party improved its performance (16.2 percent votes) along with its allies.

Malabar also was supportive of the CPI. It had a significant Ezhava population, which predominantly were economically backward working class and therefore a successful target group of the CPI. Besides, in Malabar the presence of Christians, who were mainly INC oriented, was less until the late 1940s. As the 1950s rolled in, Syrian Christians in Travancore-Cochin migrated in large scale to Malabar in search of agricultural land. This, however, did not affect Malabar's Communist affiliation.[94] For instance, in the 1954 election, the CPI secured 38.3 percent of the poll in the region.[95] When this region was annexed to Travancore-Cochin in 1956 to form the state of Kerala, the percentage of the Ezhava population in the state increased from 22 to 26, which further helped Communists in the state politics.

All of this indicated the pro-Communist mind of Kerala society even before the formation of the state in 1956. This extraordinary popularity was the result of various factors. Most importantly, the INC was the working platform of the leftists. When these leftists founded the CSP in 1934, the party continued to collaborate with the INC, and the latter's popularity helped the former's reception in Travancore, Cochin, and Malabar. This further encouraged the Communists. When the Kerala wing of the CPI was officially established in 1940, it attracted many due its fight against caste divisions, class divisions, landlessness, and the communal based party politics among the non-Communist parties in Kerala.[96]

Immediately after the formation of the state in 1956, the CPI started preparing for the forthcoming election to the state Legislative Assembly by drafting an election manifesto. It severely criticized the INC and put forward fourteen reform actions.[97] The Communists even compared Kerala to Chinese Yenan, expecting it to radiate the power and influence of the party to the whole nation. Yenan, as the headquarters of the Chinese Communist Party, was the center of the Chinese Communist revolution from 1936 to 1948. The manifesto proved convincing, and in the election, which was held in February-March 1957, the CPI captured 65 out of 126 seats (the number includes five CPI-backed independent candidates). The CPI continued to state that it would adhere to the framework of the federal constitution.[98] M.N. Govindan Nair, then general secretary of the Kerala wing, declared in New Delhi on 20 March 1957, immediately after the election result was made public, that the party would not go for a Red Revolution.[99] Also, the post-election response from various corners acknowledging the new move gave the Communists more dynamism. The Prime Minister Jawaharlal Nehru's invitation to the CPI in Kerala to form the government boosted the party. In fact, Nehru expected the Communists to fully embrace the democratic path and he believed that by taking over the responsibility of a government, the party would discipline itself.[100]

The Communists came to power on 5 April 1957, appending a memorable moment in history. While the INC seemed undefeatable because of the charismatic leadership of Nehru, a Communist party had seized power in a democratic way, through the electoral process. The victory led to the formation of the first Communist government in Kerala under E.M.S. Namboothiripad as the Chief Minister.[101] The government had two major challenges in actualizing Communist agenda in the state: it had to simultaneously work within the limits of the federal constitution and execute the slow transition to Communism.[102] The two fields in which it mostly profiled, were land reform and education.

The Kerala Agrarian Relations Bill (KARB), presented in the Legislative Assembly on 21 December 1957, was considered one of the revolutionary steps of the new Communist government.[103] Its major goals were ceiling on land holdings, fair rents, debt relief, fixity of tenure, and redistribution of the surplus land.[104] The bill aimed to collect the surplus land to form a land bank from which the government could appropriately distribute to the landless.[105] However, before its disbanding, the Communist government was unable to get the KARB approved in the Assembly. This was mainly due to the protest of opposition groups under the leadership of the INC. Next to these groups, the two leading agitators against the bill were Syrian Christians and the Nair Service Society (NSS), a semi-political and semi-religious group of Nairs, one of the upper castes.[106] This may be strange, since temples, churches, and other religious institutions were exempted from the provisions of the land reform policy. Yet, many plantation grounds and *kayal* (back waters) were in the hands of Christians and Nairs, and these areas were subject to the bill.

The other most noted reformation of the government was the Kerala Education Bill of 1957. The draft bill, which was published on 7 July 1957 and discussed in the Kerala Legislative Assembly, proposed a substantial reform in the education sector. On 2 September 1957, the government passed the bill in the Assembly.[107]

First and foremost, the bill called for compulsory and free elementary education in the state. To realize this, it intervened in finances, for instance stipulating that fees collected from private school managements could go to the state exchequer, and that the government would pay the salary of the teachers either directly or through the school. It also interfered with the nomination of new teachers, stating that the manager of the school had the freedom to appoint the teachers, but only from a list prepared by the State Public Service Commission, and that the management could not dismiss a teacher without the prior written approval of the concerned government officer. In other words, it increased the state's influence in education. The government, under clause 14 and 15 of the bill, even had the freedom to take over schools for a period of not more than five years either on account of public interest or by paying compensation. Local, district and state level committees were established to advise the government on educational matters.[108] In addition to this, the inspection, control and supervision of schools remained the responsibility of the government even though the administration of the school was under the management.[109]

With this new bill, the government especially aspired to control private schools run primarily by religious communities. Underlining all the above-mentioned proposals, then education minister Joseph Mundassery noted that the government also wanted to stop the custom of using schools as prayer houses, limit corporal punishment, stop teacher and student participation in strikes, and reserve seats for the backward people in society.[110]

The making of the Education Bill was a difficult task for the government. Already during the formation of the bill, the government had to face protest from various sectors of society, especially religious minorities. The Catholic and Protestant churches were the leading agents. Through their criticism of the bill, they also intended to denounce Communism. This is not a surprise: in particular, the Catholic Church had always reacted against Communism ever since the latter's inception, through the means of papal encyclicals, such as *Quadregesimo Anno* (1931), *Divini Redemptoris* (1937), and *Ad Apostolorum Principis* (1958).[111] They also referred to the experiences of the Church under different Communist regimes in East Central Europe and Latin America.[112]

In Kerala, the Church first targeted the anti-religious ideology of the Communists, arguing that the latter's control of education would result in the brainwashing of the young students. The Catholic Bishops, the Malabar Catholic Association, and the Protestant Christian Association protested the injection of atheism and materialism into the mind of the future generation.[113] It also fiercely opposed a later governmental decision to change the syllabuses and textbooks. The committee deputed by the government to deal with this did not have Christian representation, even though the majority of the private educational institutions in Kerala was established and run by Christian managements.[114] The Church argued that the government wanted to discredit or negate faith in God, religious consciousness, and moral values. But it also played a nationalist card: it reproached the Communists who highlighted the achievements of Communist China and Russia instead of those of India. This would reduce the patriotic feeling of the new generation and turn them into admirers of the Communist countries.[115]

Secondly, the Catholic Church pointed out that the rights of the minority religious groups were violated. The Constitution of India guaranteed minorities the right to freely profess, practice and propagate one's religion (§25) and to "establish and maintain institutions for religious and charitable purposes" (§26). Above all, Article 30 conferred the right to all minority groups – based on religion or language – to establish and administer educational institutions of their choice. Moreover, in granting aid the State should not discriminate against any minority institution.

On 22 May 1958, the Supreme Court of India observed that certain clauses in the bill, for instance those on taking over the school and forbidding the collection of fees from the students, indeed violated the minority's rights. This, along with pressure from the side of the Church and other organizations, forced the government to review the bill. Finally, after much deliberation, the Education Bill became law on 19 February 1959.

Since the minority institutions were not satisfied with various regulations in the bill, the Christian, Muslim, and Hindu managements decided to keep their educational institutions closed at the beginning of the 1959-60 academic year.[116] The Kerala Catholic Bishops' Conference's meeting at Ernakulam in March 1959 evaluated the circumstances and declared: "we call upon our people to take all necessary action uniting with other communities to change the harmful clauses of the Kerala Education Bill."[117] At a convention held at Kottayam on 3 May 1959, these three managements even went further and took the decision to strive for ending the Communist rule in the state. On 7 May, sixteen Catholic Bishops in Kerala issued a pastoral letter criticizing the bill and called for a *hartal* on 12 June.[118] *Hartal* is a form of civil disobedience and protest, which involves the voluntary shutdown of shops, offices, workplaces, etc. The Malayalam daily *Deepika* instructed the people to wear black badges and to use black flags during the silent processions.[119]

On 12 June 1959, the in/famous *Vimochana Samaram* (Liberation Struggle) against the government broke out. The Church played a key role. The protestors effectively made use of the press belonging to the Church. Additionally, special groups of volunteers called the 'Christopher community' (*Shanti sena*) assisted the agitation. Many mass protests took place, some of them ending in violence. As a result, the government resorted to *lathi* charges, police shootings, and the arresting of protestors. Major police shootings were at Angamaly on 13 June, killing seven protestors, at Pulluvila and Vettukad on 15 June, killing two and three respectively, and at Cheriathurai, Trivandrum on 3 July taking two lives. Hundreds of people were hurt in the police actions. Chief Minister E.M.S. declared that no enquiry into the shootings was possible.[120]

The events in Kerala gained national and international attention. Consequently, it turned into a serious matter between the state and the central government. On 31 July 1959, the President of India dismissed the state government and declared Presidential rule. The state legislature was brought under the authority of the Indian Parliament until the next Assembly election in February 1960. The Education Bill of the Communist government, in effect, was revoked.

Communist leaders like Thomas Issac later accused the CIA of conspiracy.[121] Recent research has confirmed that the United States indeed assisted the INC in toppling the government and financially backed a coalition of the INC, the Praja Socialist Party (PSP), and the Indian Union Muslim League (IUML) to defeat the Communists in the 1960 election.[122] This triple alliance won the 1960 Assembly election and formed a new government. The CIA continued its anti-Communist operations by propagating in and outside India that the first Communist government in Kerala was a failure.

A reversal from the policies of the Communist government was explicit under the INC led coalition government. In 1962, the High Court made the KARB insignificant. The government brought new Land Reformation Laws in 1963, which were a diluted version of the 1957 KARB.[123] In the education sector, also, the government did not take any revolutionary steps against the interest of the religious groups and private managements.

Meanwhile, years-long left-right ideological conflict within the CPI at the national level culminated in a split in 1964. Thirty-two left-wing members of the National Council left the CPI and created a new party, the Communist Party of India [Marxist]. This CPI[M] took a more independent stance than the CPI regarding the relationship with the Soviet Union and China, and emerged to be the leading party among the two. In Kerala, different left-wing parties, including the CPI, joined forces in 1965-66 and formed a United Front (UF) under the aegis of the CPI[M]. The UF registered a massive victory in the 1967 Assembly election, with CPI[M] winning 52 seats and the CPI 19 (of a total of 133). In 1967, the Communists for a second time assumed power in Kerala. The new government decided to continue with the reformative steps of the 1957 government and introduced changes to the Land Reform Laws.

In the 1970 Assembly election, the CPI left the CPI[M] alliance and made a coalition with the IUML and Kerala Congress, a regional political party. This was a successful move: the new coalition won the election and was in power from 1970 to 1977. Gradually, the Communists tried to mitigate the conflict with the religious groups, especially with the Christian Church. In 1979, E.M.S. – who still was the foreman of the CPI[M] – observed that the Church reduced its blind criticism of Communism in Kerala. It could also be understood as a policy of non-interference in each other's matters.[124]Meanwhile, the left-wing parties expanded their coalition in 1976 as the Left Democratic Front (LDF) under the patronage of the CPI[M] against the INC led United Democratic Front (UDF). The LDF formed government again during 1980-81, 1987-91, 1996-2001, 2006-11, and from 2016 to date.

At national level also, the CPI[M] grew fast and its vote share of 4.2% in 1967 increased to 6.7% by 1991. On the contrary, CPI deteriorated, and the vote share went down from 5.2% to 2.5% during the same period. This was partly due to new splits. In 1967, far-left radicals in the Bengal village of Naxalbari created a new party called the Communist Party of India [Marxist-Leninist] (CPI[ML]). These Naxalites – as they are commonly called – convened in Kolkata in 1969 and called for armed revolution, denouncing the electoral process. Later, there were many more minor splits among the Communists. Newly created parties were, among others, the Marxist Coordination Committee (MCC, 1971), the Marxist Communist Party of India (MCPI, 1983), the Communist Marxist Party (CMP, 1987), the Janathipathya Samrakshana Samithy (JSS, 1994; Democracy Protection Committee), and the Party of Democratic Socialism (PDS, 2001).

Although the first Communist government was in Kerala, Communism was also strong in a few other Indian states. The CPI in West Bengal entered into national electoral politics with the first general election of 1951 and won 3 out of 26 parliamentary seats in the state. In the state Assembly election of 1952, the CPI had 10.76% of the total votes polled and bagged 28 out of the 238 seats. In 1977, the Left parties formed a Left Front and in the State Assembly election of that year, the CPI[M]-led Left Front gained a massive victory by winning 231 out of 294 seats.[125] The Left Front also won the next six Assembly elections (1982, 1987, 1991, 1996, 2001, and 2006) in the state and formed the government between 1977 and 2011.[126] Besides Bengal, the tiny northeastern state of Tripura had a strong Communist presence.

After receiving the status of a state in 1972, Tripura was ruled by a Left Front led by CPI[M] between 1977 and 1988 and then again since 1993.

One obviously may wonder to what extent these Communists were true Communists: they acted in a democratic environment and formed coalitions. Authors like Nossiter argue that their program was far from Marxism and Leninism and that these parties should be seen as variations of state parties, such as AIADMK in Tamil Nadu and TDP in Andhra Pradesh and Telangana. Still, the CPI and CPI[M] had a Communist identity and profile. It made use of many symbols from the Soviet Union and had a progressive program, mainly focusing on three areas. The first was agrarian and land reforms.[127] They encouraged agricultural and forest based small-scale industry, protected the sharecroppers from land eviction, distributed land to the landless, reduced land tax, enhanced laborer's wage rates, and introduced the food-for-work program funded by the central government. Secondly, they gave preference to improving the quality of education. Finally, they attempted to alleviate poverty and ensure proper health care for all.[128]

In sum, the last decades of colonial rule – and the first decades of Sebastian Kappen's life – witnessed different social and political movements in Kerala. Local reformists argued for the suppression of caste and the emancipation of Dalits. Importantly, these foremen objected conversion to Christianity, which was a widespread phenomenon in Kerala. They were joined by the INC and Gandhi, albeit for different reasons. Freedom fighters subscribed to an agenda of nationalism. Communists grew from the 1930s onwards and have regularly ruled Kerala since 1957. Though in conflict with Communism, the entire Church did not completely reject Communist ideologies. Pointedly, Communism gained the interest of several clergymen in the state. Sebastian Kappen was one of them.

Endnotes

[1] Brock, *An Introduction to Syriac Studies*, 1.

[2] D'Souza, *In the Steps of St. Thomas*, 23. *Acts of Thomas*, an apocryphal book (not in the canon of the Bible), was written between 180 and 230 AD. Its original is in Syriac. *Acts of Thomas* was popular in the ancient times, for there existed Greek, Latin, and Armenian versions of it. It consists of thirteen acts including the description of the journey of Apostle Thomas from Jerusalem to India. Cf. Neill, *A History of Christianity in India: The Beginning to AD 1707*, 26; Neill, *The Story of the Christian Church in India and Pakistan*, 17; and Kuriakose, *History of Christianity in India: Source Materials*, 2. For an English version of the *Acts of Thomas*, cf. Hennecke, *New Testament Apocrypha* (1965-1973).

[3] Neill, *A History of Christianity in India*, 33.

[4] Neill, *A History of Christianity in India*, 30. For a more detailed history of the St. Thomas Christians in India, cf. Menacherry, *The St. Thomas Christian Encyclopedia of India*, Vol. 2 (1973) and Perumalil and Hambye, eds., *Christianity in India: A History in Ecumenical Perspective* (1972).

[5] Frykenberg, *Christianity in India: From Beginning to the Present*, 90-3.

[6] Baum and Winkler, *The Church of East: A Concise History*, 53.

[7] Neill, *A History of Christianity in India*, 42-3.

[8] For instance, scholar Richard M. Swiderski has written about the uncertainty of the dates of the arrival of and identity of such a group of Christians in Kerala. Cf. Swiderski, *The Blood Weddings: The Knanaya Christians of Kerala* (1988), and Kuriakose, *History of Christianity in India*, 3-5.

[9] Fortescue, *The Lesser Eastern Churches*, 358-9.

[10] Gama, *The First Voyage of Vasco da Gama 1497-1499*, 5.

[11] The Portuguese term *Padroado* means patronage. It was an agreement between the Catholic Church and the Catholic government of Portugal. According to this agreement, the Holy See could transfer the administrative power over the local churches to the Portuguese King.

[12] Kuriakose, *History of Christianity in India*, 21.

[13] Pope Clement VIII, "*In supremo militantis*: The Imposition of Portuguese Patronage over the Church of Angamaly," 68-73.

[14] Coonan Cross Oath was a public avowal of the St. Thomas Christians in Kerala against the Portuguese dominance. The Christian community declared that they would not submit themselves to Portuguese administration either in ecclesial or in secular matters.

[15] Frykenberg, *Christianity in India*, 135-7.

[16] I quote these figures from the citations of Joseph Thekkedath. Cf. Thekkedath, *History of Christianity in India, Vol. 2: From the Middle of the Sixteenth Century to the End of the Seventeenth Century (1542-1700)*, 24-5.

[17] These details are taken from a working paper by K.C. Zachariah under the title "The Syrian Christians of Kerala: Demographic and Economic Transition in the Twentieth Century," 13-4. Cf. https: opendocs.ids.ac.uk/opendocs/bitstream/handle/20.500.12413/3027/wp322.pdf? sequence=1%2520%5baccess-ed%25205%2520November%25202015%5d.%2520%25E2%2580%259CReligious%2520Demography%2520of%2520India,%25E2%2580%259D%252038,%2520http://www.cpsindia.org/dl/religious/summary3c.pdf%2520%5baccessed%252028%2520June%25202017%5d.

[18] The co-founders are Fr. Palackal Thoma Malpan (1780-1841) and Fr. Porukara Thoma Kathanar (1799-1846).

[19] Kariyil, *Church and Society in Kerala: A Sociological Study*, 46.

[20] The suffragan dioceses were Trichur, Changanacherry, and Kottayam. Pallath, *Important Roman Documents Concerning the Catholic Church in India*, 202.

[21] Mathothu and Nadackal, eds. *The Church of St. Thomas Christians Down the Centuries*, 120.

[22] Kuriedath, *Authority in the Catholic Community in Kerala*, 10, footnote, 38. For more details about the history of the Kerala Syrian Christians of the last two centuries, cf. Koodapuzha, *Indian Church History* (1980); Koodapuzha, *Faith and Communion of the Indian Church of the St. Thomas Christians* (1982); Podipara, *Thomas Christians* (1970); and Podipara, *The Rise and Decline of the Indian Church of the Thomas Christians* (1979).

[23] Soares, *Catholic Church in India: A Historical Sketch*, 11.

[24] Robinson, *Christians of India*, 40-1. Also cf. Bayly, *Saints, Goddesses and Kings: Muslims and Christians in South Indian Society, 1700-1900*, 273-6.

[25] For more details, cf. Kochuparampil, "The St. Thomas Christians of India: Ecumenical and Missiological Challenges," 243-60.

[26] Houtart and Mercinier, *Church and Development in Kerala*, 321.

[27] "Letter of His Holiness Pope Francis to the Bishops of India," http://w2.vatican.va/content/francesco/en/letters/2017/documents/papa-francesco_20171009_vescovi-india.html [accessed 23 October 2017].

[28] Pallath, "The Syro-Malankara Catholic Church," 261-2.

[29] http://sharbtho.blogspot.be/2013/04/ [accessed 6 August 2017].

[30] Pallath, "The Syro-Malankara Catholic Church," 262.

[31] Tisserant, *Eastern Christianity in India: A History of the Syro-Malabar Church from the Earliest Time to the Present Day*, 79. For more details, Brown, *The Indian Christians of St. Thomas* (1982) and Richards, *The Indian Christians of St. Thomas, Otherwise Called the Syrian Christians of Malabar: A Sketch of their History, and an Account of their Present Condition, as well as a Discussion of the Legend of St. Thomas*. Cf. https://archive.org/stream/indianchristian00richgoog#page/n12/mode/2up [accessed 23 April 2015]. The author was a missionary from the Church Mission Society (CMS) to the Hindus in Travancore and Cochin for thirty-five years.

[32] Pope Pius XI, "*Christo Pastorum Principi*, Apostolic Constitution concerning the Erection of a new Ecclesiastical Province of Antiochean Rite for the Syro-Malankara Faithful in the Malabar region of the East Indies," 264-73.

[33] Neill, *A History of Christianity in India*, 71. Also cf. "Medieval Source Book: John of Monte Corvino: Report from China 1305," http://legacy.fordham.edu/halsall/source/corvino1.asp [accessed 10 July 2015].

[34] Frykenberg, *Christianity in India*, 117-8.

[35] Ferrao, "Keynote Address of Archbishop Filipe Neri Ferraro at the Inaugural Session of the International Conference 'In Honour of St. Francis Xavier: Jesuit History, Culture and Identity," 12.

[36] Some of the great Jesuit missionaries to India after Francis Xavier were Robert De Nobili (1577-1656), who was the pioneer of inculturation in Madurai (Tamil Nadu), John de Britto (1647-93), who continued the act of inculturation after De Nobili, Peter Caironi, founder of Chirakkal Mission in Kerala, Joseph Taffarel, James Montenari, Michael Vendramin, Aloysius Delzotto, Linus Maria Zucol, and Constant Lievens.

[37] Pinto, "The achievements of the Jesuit educational mission in India and the contemporary challenges it faces," 17.

[38] Jagatheesan, "St. Francis Xavier," in The St. Thomas Christian Encyclopedia of India, 16.

[39] Ferrao, "Keynote Address of Archbishop Filipe Neri Ferraro," 15-6.

[40] "The Hand of Xavier in the Pearl Fishery Coast," *Pro Deo et Partia*, Series No. XXV, 104-6. Cited from Kuriakose, *History of Christianity in India*, 32.

[41] For more details, cf. *Christianity in India*, 128-30.

[42] Institutions in the Malabar mission included the Mother of God School, Cochin, Quilon School, Syrian Seminary of Santa Cruz in Cranganore, Jesuit Scholasticate at Cochin, etc.

[43] Shastry, "Marques de Pombal and the Jesuits of Goa," 51-2. For a detailed history of the Jesuits from their arrival in Malabar to the 19th century, cf. Ferroli, *The Jesuits in Malabar*, vol. 2 (1951).

[44] Few historical writings that will hugely support our queries about the missionary contributions in Malabar are Ferroli, *The Jesuits in Malabar*, vol. 1 (1939) and Kurup and John, *Legacy of Basel Mission and Herman Gundert in Malabar* (1993).

[45] "St. Joseph's Boys' Higher Secondary School, Kozhikode," http://www.stjosephsboysschool.org/index.php [accessed 13 July 2015).

[46] Pinto, "The achievements of the Jesuit educational mission in India and the contemporary challenges it faces," 15. For more details, cf. Verstraeten, "Jesuit Colleges in India in the Restored Society," 52-64.

[47] "AKJM School, Kanjirappally," http://akjmschool.net/history.aspx [accessed 13 July 2015].

[48] Kunnukal, "Jesuit Education in India Today and Tomorrow," 109.

[49] Kurup, *Peasantry Nationalism and Social Change in India*, 114.

[50] Cited in de Souza, "Why Cuncolim Martyrs? An Historical Re-Assessment," in *Jesuits in India: In Historical Perspective*, 39. Selvaraj, *Christianity and Social Transformation: The Kerala Story* (2002). The author is a known missiologist in India. He studied in Delhi University and in Union Biblical Seminary, Pune and obtained doctoral degree from SAIACS (South Asia Institute of Advanced Christian Studies), Bangalore.

[51] INC is one of the oldest political parties in the world. The party was founded in 1885 by Allan Octavian Hume (1829-1912), Dadabhai Naoroji (1825-1917), and Dinshaw Wacha (1844-1936). It had been a pivotal agent in the Indian National Movement. INC formed the government after the first general election in 1952 and held power for the next 25 years, forming government for five consecutive terms (1952-1957; 1957-1962; 1962-1967; 1967-1971; 1971-1977).

[52] Cf. Reddy and Gandhi, "Introduction," in *Gandhi and South Africa: 1914-1948*, 5; Gandhi, *Satyagraha in South Africa: The Selected Works of Mahatma Gandhi*, vol. 2 (1968); and du Toit, "The Mahatma Gandhi and South Africa" (1996).

[53] http://www.zum.de/whkmla/region/india/xmalabar.html [accessed 6 August 2017].

[54] Caste system is an age old uniquely Indian institution which categorizes people into four major classes with thousands of sub-classes called castes and sub-castes respectively. The four major castes are Brahmins (priestly caste), Kshatriyas (warrior caste), Vaisyas (traders, artisans, farmers, etc.) Sudras (entitled to serve other castes). The people of the lower castes historically remained economically, socially, politically, culturally, and religiously poor, oppressed, marginalized, and exploited. Dalits were the people who were not included in the caste frame.

55 Swamikal, http://www.veethi.com/india-people/chattampi_swamikal-photos-2025-14524.htm; Haindava Keralam, http://www.haindavakeralam.com/sree-narayana-gurus-greatest-messages-hk4825; and Ayyan Kali, https://twitter.com/hashtag/ayyankali [accessed 3 November 2017].

[56] Menon, *Social and Cultural History of Kerala*, 201.

[57] Pillai, *Chattampi Swamikal*, 141. The full name of Swamikal was Sree Vidyadhiraja Parama Bhattaraka Cattampi Swamikal. As a reformist, he was against the conventional interpretation of the Hindu Scriptures.

[58] Swamikal, *Hindu Critique of Christianity* (Malayalam), https://archive.org/details/KristumataChedanam-ChattampiSwamikal-EnglishTranslation [accessed 10 July 2017].

[59] Rajayyan, "Sri Narayana Guru and Social Reform," 43-4.

[60] Menon, *Kerala History and its Makers*, 226-7.

[61] Guru, *The Word of the Guru: Life and Teachings of Narayana Guru*, 24 and Jones, *The New Cambridge History of India: Socio-religious Reform Movements in British India*, 180.

[62] Vaidyar, *Thoughts of Sri Narayana* (Malayalam), 73.

[63] Chentharassery, *Ayyan Kali*, 52.

[64] T. Chentharassery, *Ayyan Kali*, 69-70.

[65] Swamikal, *Hindu Critique of Christianity* (Malayalam), 10-1.

[66] Nair, "The Dynamics of Kerala Politics," 259.

[67] Panickar, "Narayana Guru on Conversion," http://www.hinduismtoday.com/modules/smartsection/item.php?itemid=4292 [accessed 5 November 2015].

[68] Nossiter, *Communism in Kerala: A Study in Political Adaptation*, 66.

[69] Biswas, "Paradox of Anti-Partition Agitation and Swadeshi Movement in Bengal (1905)," 38-9.

[70] Cf. Biswas, "Paradox of Anti-Partition Agitation and Swadeshi Movement in Bengal (1905)," 53-4. Also cf. C.N. Trueman, "India and World War One," http://www.historylearningsite.co.uk/world-war-one/india-and-world-war-one/ [accessed 24 October 2017].

[71] Cf. Sadasivan, *A Social History of India*, 507.

[72] Cf. Pillai, *A History of Congress in Kerala*, 13.

[73] Hardgrave, Jr., "The Mappilla Rebellion, 1921: Peasant Revolt in Malabar," 65. Also cf. "The Montague-Chelmsford Reforms (1919)," http://historypak.com/montagu-chelmsford-reforms/ [accessed 16 October 2015.

[74] Houtart and Lemercinier, *Church and Development in Kerala*, 19.

[75] For the details given about the five visits of Gandhi to Kerala, I depended greatly on Nair, "Gandhiji's Visits to Kerala-Gandhiji Remembered on 30 January," http://www.spiderkerala.net/resources/4928-GANDHIJI-S-VISITS-TO-KERALA-GANDHIJI-REMEMBERED.aspx [accessed 9 September 2015].

[76] Hardgrave, Jr., "The Mappilla Rebellion, 1921," 66-7. Through this Act the British could arrest and imprison anyone without trail and judicial procedures on charge of anti-British activities. Due to the nationwide protest, the Act could not be implemented.

[77] For more details, cf. Krishna, "Synthesising the Gandhi-Ambedkar-Narayanaguru-Marx Visions for *Dalit* Liberation"; Singh, "Wellness and Welfare: A Longitudinal Analysis of Social Development in Kerala, India"; and Jeffrey, "Temple-Entry Movement in Travancore, 1860-1940," 4.

[78] P. Krishna Pillai, A.K. Gopalan (later Communist leaders), K. Kelappan, Mannath Padmanabhan, and N.P. Damodaran were at the fore front of the *satyagraha*.

[79] *Harijan* is a Samskrit word meaning 'child of Hari or Siva,' a Hindu God. Gandhi popularized this term by attributing it to the Untouchables.

[80] Sunder, *They Burn: The 160000000 Untouchables of India*, 32. Selvaraj, *Christianity and Social Transformation*, 28. For more details, cf. Prashad, *Untouchable Freedom: A Social History of a Dalit Community* (2000).

[81] Mason, *Christianity and Race: The Burroughs Memorial Lectures, 1956*, 21.

[82] Polak, *Mr. Gandhi: The Man*, 40.

[83] Cited from Kuriakose, *History of Christianity in India*, 323.

[84] Gandhi, *Young India*, 20 August 1925.

[85] Gandhi, *Young India*, 21 March 1929.

[86] Keer, ed. *Dr. Ambedkar: A Memorial Album* (1982); Omvedt, *Dalits and the Democratic Evolution: Dr. Ambedkar and the Dalit Movement in Colonial India* (1994); and Bhatia, *Dr. B.R. Ambedkar: Social Justice and the Indian Constitution* (1994).

[87] Bakshi, *Gandhi and Status of Harijans*, 121.

[88] Round Table Conference between India and England was the initiative of the British Government to discuss the constitutional reforms in India. It was a series of three Conferences between 1930 and 1932.

[89] A brief description about the Yeravada Fast is available from the articles "The Previous Fasts," *The Indian Express*, 4 March 1948 and "Gandhi's Fast to Fight Caste Injustices," *The New Indian Express*, 16 September 2011. For additional details, cf. Gandhi, "Ambedkar and Separate Electorates Issue," 1328-30.

[90] Nossiter, *Marxist State Governments in India: Politics, Economics and Society*, 14; Kaye, Communism in India, 6; and Nossiter, *Marxist State Governments in India*, 15.

[91] Basu, *Towards Naxalbari (1953-1967): An Account of Inner-Party Ideological Struggle*, 32.

[92] Nossiter, *Marxist State Governments in India*, 17, and Nossiter, *Communism in Kerala*, 105.

[93] Nossiter, *Communism in Kerala*, 65.

[94] A. Jayasankar, *Communist Rule and Liberation Struggle* (Malayalam), 58, and E.M.S, *Communist Party in Kerala* (Malayalam), 507-8.

[95] Cf. Election Commission of India, "Statistical Report on General Election, 1954 to the Legislative Assembly of Travancore-Cochin" (New Delhi: Election Commission of India). The pdf version is available on http://eci.nic.in/eci_main/StatisticalReports/SE_1954/StatRep_TravCochin_1954.pdf [accessed 22 July 2015] and Fic, *Kerala, Yenan of India: Rise of Communist Power, 1937-1969*, 43.

[96] These details are from the works of Selig Harrison, Kathleen Gough, Donald S. Zagoria, and Jeffrey, as cited in Nossiter, *Communism in Kerala*, 96, footnote, 2. I went to the original sources for more details. Cf. Harrison, *India; The Most Dangerous Decades*, 193-9; Gough, "Kerala Politics and the 1965 Elections," 64-5; Zogaria, "The Social Bases of Communism in Kerala and West Bengal"; Jeffrey, "Matriliny, Marxism, and the Birth of Communist Party in Kerala, 1930-1940," 77-98; and Vadassery, "The Kerala Experiment," 92.

[97] Nossiter, *Communism in Kerala*, 122; Fic, *Kerala, Yenan of India*, 34, 64-6, and 68-9; and Lieten, "Education, Ideology and Politics in Kerala 1957-59," 4.

[98] Maitra, *Marxism in India: From Decline to Debacle*, 238.

[99] M.N. Govindan Nair asserted that the line of the party is not violent upsetting of everything, but it wanted to serve the people, working within the limits of the constitution. Cf. Fic, *Kerala, Yenan of India*, 84.

[100] Fic, *Kerala, Yenan of India*, 78. Fic argued that the CPI in Kerala went contrary to the expectations of Rajendra Prasad and Jawharlal Nehru by rectifying the phrase 'Tactical Line.' Communist rule, according to Fic, was nothing but a systematic exploitation of the institutions of parliamentary democracy for its own interests i.e. the dictatorship of the proletariat, which, indeed, appeared to be a peaceful process.

[101] Nossiter, *Communism in Kerala*, 147-8.

[102] Pillai, *Left Movement and Agrarian Relations 1920-1995*, 62. To know more about the slow transition, refer to the PhD dissertation of Victor M. Fic titled "Peaceful Transition to Communism in India, 1954-1957: A Comparative Case Study of Kerala" (1962).

[103] E.M.S. *Communist Party in Kerala* (Malayalam), 528.

[104] Nossiter, *Communism in Kerala*, 149; Lieten, "Education, Ideology and Politics in Kerala 1957-59," 4; and Gough, *Village Politics in Kerala*, 416.

[105] Singh, *Communist Rule in Kerala*, 36.

[106] Nossiter, *Communism in Kerala*, 152-3.

[107] Raj, "Politics of Educational Management," 265.

[108] Cf. Dhanuraj, "Story of 1957 Education Bill in Kerala," 9; E.M.S., E.M.S. on Education (Malayalam), 138; Gopalan, *Kerala, Yesterday and Today* (Malayalam), 121; Bhaskaran, *Communist Movement in Kerala* (Malayalam), 38; Jayasankar, *Communist Rule and Liberation Struggle* (Malayalam), 119; Windmiller, "Constitutional Communism in India," 27; and Raj, "Politics of Educational Management," 263-4.

[109] Lieten, "Education, Ideology and Politics in Kerala 1957-59," 8.

[110] Schoenfeld, "Kerala in Crisis," 243, and Sato, "Social Security and Well-being in a Low-income Economy," 291.

[111] *QA* 36, 112, 113, 116, 128; *DR* 3-5, 8-16, 18-20; *AAP* 7-9.

[112] Cf. Fic, *Kerala, Yenan of India*, 80-2, and Thundiyil, *The Hidden Agenda*, 21.

[113] Lieten, "Education, Ideology and Politics in Kerala 1957-59," 10.

[114] Mathew, *Communal Road to Secular Kerala*, 146. Among the private educational institutions in Kerala, majority of them were established and administered by Christian managements. Having no one invited from the side to the Syllabus Committee was a clear indication of the impending regulations over the private education sector.

[115] Kumbalakuzhy, *Liberation Struggle* (Malayalam), 128.

[116] *Deepika*, 28 May 1959.

[117] *Deepika*, 20 March 1959.

[118] Jayasankar, *Communist Rule and Liberation Struggle* (Malayalam), 230-1.

[119] *Deepika*, 11 June 1959.

[120] For more details, cf. Kumbalakuzhy, ed., *Image* (Malayalam), 153-4.

[121] For more details, cf. Issac, *The Unseen Sides of the Liberation Struggle* (Malayalam), 248-60, and Ajayan, "Midterm Election in Kerala in 1960 and the American Government," 217.

[122] Ajayan, "Midterm Election in Kerala in 1960 and the American Government," 213.

[123] Jayasankar, *The Communist Reign and the Liberation Struggle* (Malayalam), 343.

[124] E.M.S., *Religious Faith and the Communists* (Malayalam), 23.

[125] Maitra, *Marxism in India*, 243-5.

[126] Nandi, "Communism through the Ballot Box: Over a Quarter Century of Uninterrupted Rule in West Bengal," 171-94.

[127] Nossiter, *Marxist State Governments in India*, 139-42.

[128] Öktem, "A Comparative Analysis of the Performance of the Parliamentary Left in the Indian States of Kerala, West Bengal and Tripura," 324, and Nossiter, *Marxist State Governments in India*, 163-7.

2

Liberation Theology: An Overview

The second half of the 20th century, especially the 1960s and following decades, witnessed an unconventional development in the Catholic Church in the form of liberation theology. Liberation theology evolved as a praxis oriented movement within the Latin American Church in order to resist the dehumanizing character of the established economic and political systems, which first challenged economists and then Christian theologians.[1] In order to liberate the poor and the marginalized, some Latin American theologians, bishops, and priests championed a new mode of theologizing in their Church by analyzing the historical praxis of liberation. Their ideas soon spread to other parts of the world. This chapter is a study of the birth and development of liberation theology. In the first four sections we deal with the definition and preliminary notions of liberation theology, liberation theology in Latin America, liberation theology in Asia (Sri Lanka, the Philippines, South Korea), and liberation theology in India in particular. We will critically assess the commonalities and particularities, as well as the convergence and divergence among different liberation theologies. The fifth and final section inspects Catholic Church's approach to and teaching on liberation theology, inter alia by means of the two CDF[2] documents on liberation theology, namely *Instruction on Certain Aspects of the Theology of Liberation* (1984) and *Instruction on Christian Freedom and Liberation* (1986). Rather than giving a comprehensive overview, this chapter wants to facilitate a framework for further reference.

A.   Liberation Theology: Definition and Preliminary Notions

Although there were various liberation activities in the Church already in the 1950s or even before, especially from Europe in the form of Left Catholicism and Christian trade unions,[3] the term *liberation* gained greater significance after it began to appear alongside the term *theology* in the late 1960s. Most of the initial literature on liberation theology was either in Portuguese or in Spanish. The Portuguese word for liberation is *libertação,* a combination of *liber* (free) and *ação* (action) which does not have a proper English translation coupling *free* and *action*, if not libera[c]tion.[4]

Liberation theology was not, as many feared, a new theology created to totally demolish the conventional methods of theologizing, but only a new way of *doing* theology in the Church.[5] However, this new way gave the impression that liberation theology was against the conventional aptitude of theologizing. This impression was further fueled by at least three elements. First, liberation theologies were designed for specific contexts taking into account the political, economic, social, and cultural milieus in the concerned societies. This contextual focus made it different from the traditional mode of theology and theologizing for the Church, which was universal and paid little regard to the different religious and cultural backgrounds of the local churches.

Second, liberation theology was different because of its praxis oriented and radical way of theologizing that sought to explore and eradicate the root cause of poverty and suffering. Traditional theology had more of an intellectual background and a spiritual interpretation of the world. Progressive theologians, on the contrary, attempted to encounter material problems as they were, instead of being locked up in the spiritual interpretation of material deprivations. No liberation theologian defined charity as almsgiving; for them, charity rather was true and committed struggle for social justice. Liberation theologians advocated a conversion of theories and doctrines into praxis, which essentially formulated a theology from below.[6]

Third, the liberation theologians kept themselves distinct from conventional and orthodox theologians and the dogmatic and doctrinal hegemony of the West that prevailed in the Church. They called to re-write this Western dominant Christian theology according to different contexts, whether in Latin America, Asia or elsewhere.[7] The renowned English priest and theologian Christopher Rowland argued in agreement with the ideas of the Latin American liberation theologian Jon Sobrino (1938), that European theology was interested in "thinking about and explaining the truth of faith." At the same time, liberation theologians claimed that faith ran "parallel to real life and is in dialectical relationship with it."[8]

Gustavo Gutiérrez (°1928) defined liberation theology as a "theological reflection based on the gospel and the experiences of men and women committed to the process of liberation in the oppressed and exploited land of Latin America. It is a theological reflection [...] born of shared efforts to abolish the current unjust situation and to build a different society, freer and more human."[9] Highlighting its practical dimension, Christopher Rowland called liberation theology "[...] a way, a discipline, an exercise which has to be lived rather than acquired as a body of information."[10] *The Brill Dictionary of Religion* recognized the comprehensive nature of liberation theology in dealing with Third World realities via Christian faith. Liberation theology, as discussed in the dictionary, was a theological movement to alter the elements in the Third World that denied a fuller human life.[11]

Liberation theology emerged from the oppression and discrimination that prospered in the so-called neo-colonial era, which reached its climax in the 1960s and in the first half of the 1970s in Latin America with the neo-fascist regimes.[12] Economic monopolization concentrated wealth into a few hands, that is to say: the multinational companies that functioned as a continuation of the post-colonial economic imbalances. Although the economy had been growing, this led to protests among industrial workers, poor and landless peasants, students, and many other left-wing groups. Progressive theologians joined them.[13]

Liberation theologians also had Christian sources of inspiration. Importantly, they have depended very much on the Bible in formulating a theology from below. The story of the deliverance of the Israelites from the slavery in Egypt as described in the book of Exodus (chapters 1-15) stands as a model of liberation, as it is very much related, according to the liberation theologians, to the dehumanizing realities of the Third World. In the New Testament, the synoptic gospels (Matthew, Mark, and Luke) are considered to be the major source of inspiration. Many liberation theologians indeed aimed at going back to the original meaning of the message of Jesus.[14]

In addition, liberation theology also followed the wave of the modernization of the Church. Particularly after the Second Vatican Council (1962-65), a large number of theologians explored the meaning of the term liberation, inspired by the reformative measures of the Council, despite the accusation that the Third World bishops had no voice in the Council.[15] The Council documents like *Gaudium et Spes* (Pastoral Constitutions on the Church in the Modern World, 1965) and *Dignitatis Humanae* (Declaration on Religious Freedom, 1965), had a crucial role in this search for the unexplored meaning of the term. Instead of depending on theological and philosophical intellectualism in the formulation of theological reflections, these documents concentrated on concrete life experiences and social sciences.[16] Likewise, the social teachings of the Church immediately after the Council, like *Populorum Progressio* (On the Development of Peoples, 1967) and *Octogesima Adveniens* (The Eightieth Anniversary, 1971 – the pastoral letter of Pope Paul VI), accentuated vigorous actions and thoughts of radical priests. The Pope condemned the world-wide phenomenon of imbalance between the rich and the poor and asked rich nations to spend their superfluous wealth at the service of poor nations.[17]

Liberation theology, therefore, worked as an umbrella term to bring together different liberationist ideologies to actualize a "dialectical interweaving of theory and practice."[18] In this entwining process, progressive theologians reiterated the significance of both religious and non-religious factors. The spiritual and secular character made liberation theology a unique movement that posed a challenge to every form of established presuppositions in religion, economy, and society.[19] As the term liberation stood for an integral development of the human person, liberation theology exhorted the conventional orthodox theology and its proponents to engage with the social and political world. Understanding the relevance of an integral approach to human life, liberation theology worked on liberation from situations of injustice and exploitation; liberation from anything that hindered the fuller development of a human person; and liberation from sin. This view of integral liberation thus consisted of both secular and religious dimensions of human life.[20] While elaborating the essential elements of liberation theology, *The Encyclopedia of Christianity* acknowledged the integral, analytical, and reflective approach of liberation theology to the fundamental problems of human life.[21]

Although liberationist movements started in Latin American countries, it did not take a long time to reach African and Asian churches and other parts of the world. Similarities in the existing contexts of the Latin American, African, and Asian countries made liberation theology transnational.[22] As a result, it developed into African liberation theology, Black theology in America, *minjug* theology in South Korea, theology of struggle in the Philippines, Dalit theology in India, etc. Of course, they all had their own accents. African liberation theology strived for regaining African identity that was lost due to cultural imperialism, obviously next to tackling the problems of poverty and the manifold ways of marginalization. Proponents of Black theology dealt with racism, and social and political marginalization.[23] Asian liberation theology had to tackle the reality of religious and cultural pluralism alongside socio-economic issues.

B.   Liberation Theology in Latin America

The beginning of the second half of the 20th century witnessed new ways of proclaiming the gospel in the Latin American Catholic Church based on progressive theologizing. This innovation was simultaneously an ecclesial and social process.[24] It became a significant movement in Christian theology since the 1970s, when it started to be addressed as liberation theology. There were many champions of liberation theology, and we will not discuss all of them. Interestingly, many of the liberation theologians in Latin America, native or foreign, were Jesuits.

Latin America appeared to be the perfect breeding ground for liberation theology. Key characteristics made the continent very fertile for the growth of a progressive theology: severe political and economic exploitation, strong Christian presence, and growing popularity for Marxist ideologies. First, the political developments of the era infringed human rights and further made the 1950s to early 1980s a period of dehumanization.[25] Power was concentrated in the hands of government officials, Catholic clergy, and land and mine owners. As a result, the traditional economic and political exploitation that had been prevailing in the continent culminated and led to the economic crisis in the 1960s.[26] The economic problems were mainly due to the opening of the Latin American markets to the global economy, which allowed external capital transactions to take place, further leading to domination by multinational companies.[27] Additionally, the debt of these countries alarmingly increased due to uncontrolled borrowing from the agencies like the IMF and World Bank. Eventually, capital flight and foreign debt depleted the Latin American economy.[28] Politically, the Latin American countries suffered from the maldistribution and misuse of power, which in turn infringed human dignity, freedom, and rights. Therefore, there had to be both an economic and political change in these countries.[29]

Secondly, Latin America had a strong Christian presence, certainly compared to other parts of the Third World: 90% of the Latin American population was Christian. However, the Church had been indifferent and unresponsive to the economic and politically exploitative systems.

Moreover, the Church hierarchy was accused of being a land-holding oligarchy.[30] Yet by the 1960s, interestingly, many bishops, priests, nuns, and lay leaders committed themselves to ending the status quo. In Brazil, for instance, they created Basic Ecclesial Communities (CEBs) in the 1960s. These CEBs, which were also known as Basic Christian Communities or Small Christian Communities, later spread to other Latin American countries.[31] Consisting of small groups, they took up social, economic, political, and spiritual issues into discussion and analysis, making use of the Bible and the experience of the people. These CEBs became one of the springboards of Latin American liberation theologians.[32] Pope Paul VI's condemnation of the oppressive structures in Latin America in 1968, further accelerated the Church's liberating mission.[33]

Thirdly, the presence of Marxism also greatly influenced liberation theology, which at a certain stage was even called Christianized Marxism. For instance, the establishment of a socialist administration in Cuba by Fidel Castro in 1959 gave confidence to other regions that had been undergoing severe economic and political exploitation.[34] The Cuban revolution indeed proved that changes were possible. Latin American economists and political thinkers began to reflect, making use of Marxist categories in order to understand and evaluate the societal problems.[35] They had an impact on theologians, who included thoughts on the meaning of Christian values and their relevance in Latin America in the debates on poverty and underdevelopment. Although Pope John XXIII excommunicated Castro in 1962 for suppressing the institutions of the Catholic Church in Cuba, the Christian progressive thinkers did not turn back from assimilating Marxist views on the poor, capitalists, and imperialism.[36]

Some Key Figures

All such actions and thoughts were first attached to the label of liberation theology by Gustavo Gutiérrez in 1968. Gutiérrez is a Peruvian progressive theologian and a Catholic priest from the Dominican Order. Since he played a vital role in developing and popularizing progressive theologizing, he is called the father of liberation theology. Gutiérrez studied medicine at the National University of San Carlos in Lima, Peru. In the beginning of the 1940s, especially during his studies, he was an active member of the Catholic Action, an originally French movement that had been initiated in the 1920s by the Catholic lay philosopher Jacques Maritain, like the Young Catholic Workers (JOC) in Belgium founded by Josef Cardijn in 1925. The Catholic Action aimed at tackling the decline of the Church's influence among French, Spanish, Italian, and Belgian people, and at fighting the popularity that socialism had been gaining among factory workers. Through the efforts of Rome and the Latin American churchmen, the movement was imported to Latin America in the 1930s to deal with similar developments.[37] In the 1950s, Gutiérrez studied in Europe: first psychology and philosophy at the Catholic University of Louvain, Belgium, then doctoral studies at the IPER (Pastoral Institute for Religious Studies) of the Université Catholique in Lyon, France, and eventually in Rome to further deepen his knowledge in theology.[38] In Europe, Gutiérrez became fascinated with the *nouvelle théologie* (new theology) and its objective to fundamentally reform Catholic theology by finding alternatives to neo-scholasticism and the challenges of modernity.[39]

Back in Peru, Gutiérrez founded the San Bartolomé de Las Casas Institute in Rimac, Lima, to study the cultural background and the plight of the poor.[40] In doing so, he was also greatly influenced by the Brazilian educator and philosopher Paulo Freire (1921-77).[41] Freire became one of the first liberators in Latin America and his works – including *Education as the Practice of Freedom* (1967) and *Pedagogy of the Oppressed* (1970) – became the voice of and for the poor. Freire strived to release the peasants from socio-cultural enslavement and to conscientize them about the causes of their oppression by means of education. Gutiérrez claimed that Freire's first book had great influence on the second general meeting of the Latin American bishops in 1968.

Gutiérrez used the phrase liberation theology for the first time when he addressed pastoral workers and theologians at Chimbote, Peru, in

1968.[42] Two of his most significant early works discussed the theme of liberation: the book titled *Lineas Pastorales de la iglesia en America Latina* (1968) and the article "Toward a Theology of Liberation" (1970), which is a mimeographed copy of his address in Chimbote in 1968 – *Hacia una Teologia de la liberacion*.[43] In the early 1970s, Gutiérrez wrote a ground-breaking book on liberation theology, initially in Spanish (*Teología de la liberación: Perspectivas*, 1971), and then in English (*A Theology of Liberation: History, Politics and Salvation*, 1973). This book became the official textbook of liberation theology as it dealt with theological, political, and sociological issues. In it Gutiérrez defines liberation theology as a "critical reflection on Christian praxis in the light of the Word."[44] The concept of liberation theology was further spread by the American black theologian James H. Cone's *A Black Theology of Liberation* (1970). Both Gutiérrez and Cone used the term liberation independently, but there existed a common link between them: they both advocated secular/material liberation on the one hand and religious/spiritual on the other.[45]

Of course, there were many more progressive theologians and activists. We will briefly discuss only three of them, namely Camilo Torres Restropo, Hélder Pessoa Câmara, and Óscar Arnulfo Romero: the three progressive theologians and activists who are mentioned in the very few references that Sebastian Kappen made on Latin American liberation theology.[46]

Camilo Torres Restropo (1929-66) was a Roman Catholic priest from Colombia who studied sociology at the Catholic University of Louvain, Belgium, and graduated in 1958 with a dissertation on *The Proletarianisation of Bogotá*. Back in Colombia, his concern for the poor prompted him to co-found the Faculty of Sociology at the National University of Colombia in 1960. However, the conservative Catholic hierarchy was anxious about his revolutionary activities and Torres had to give up all his positions at the National University.[47] In 1964 he started organizing the United Front of the People, an organization to support the political left. In the following year, Torres joined the

National Liberation Army (ELN), a guerrilla movement, to combat the established exploitative systems in Colombia. He believed that "if Jesus were alive today, he would be a guerrillero," a quote that has influenced many progressive and radical thinkers and activists.[48] Torres was killed in 1966 during an operation against the Colombian military.[49] His name, however, lived on. For instance, a group of socially committed Catholic priests and university students in the Dominican Republic in 1970 founded the Revolutionary Command Camilo Torres (CCORECATO).[50] In this way, Torres was a clear predecessor of liberation theology in Latin America.

Another renowned social activist who strived for the liberation of the poor was the Brazilian archbishop Hélder Pessoa Câmara (1909-99), who is reputed for his quote: "When I give food to the poor, they call me a saint. When I ask why they are poor, they call me a communist."[51] Câmara in 1952 became the auxiliary bishop of Rio de Janeiro (1952-64) and in 1959 the archbishop of Olinda and Recife (1964-85). He was known as the bishop of the slums for his action for the poor, such as the establishment of the Banco da Providência to facilitate financial assistance. However, he was also critical of the military dictatorship in his country and of the Church in the West, specifically its transition to ultra-comfort and luxury, white dominance, and unilateral anti-Communism.[52] His radical thinking and actions brought much criticism from the conservative Catholics, who accused him of promoting armed struggle.[53] However, unlike Camilo Torres, Câmara was an advocate of non-violent protest. He was a Nobel Prize nominee in 1973 for his social reform efforts, and the American diocese of Davenport, Iowa awarded him with the *Pacem in Terris Award* in 1975 on account of his fight for peace and justice.[54]

A third important activist was Óscar Arnulfo Romero (1917-80). Romero was born to a middle-class family in El Salvador, studied theology at the Gregorian University in Rome, became the auxiliary bishop of the Archdiocese of San Salvador in 1970, the bishop of Santiago de Maria in 1974, and ultimately the archbishop of San Salvador in

1977. Although Romero liked to keep his distance from socio-political controversies, the political and economic repression taking place in El Salvador disturbed him very much.[55] The torturing and killing of priests and nuns, workers' union leaders, and teachers and students by the ruling aristocracy, prompted Romero to raise his voice. He accused the Salvadoran military dictatorship for violating human rights. In protest, he wrote a letter to Colonel Arturo Armando Molina, the then president, to stop violence against the poor. However, the president's military, which had the support by the U.S. military, continued the violence and labeled those priests and social activists, as well as Romero himself, as Communists.[56] In February 1980, the Catholic University of Leuven awarded him with an honorary doctorate. In the same year, on 24 March 1980, Romero was assassinated during a Holy Mass in the Divine Providence Hospital chapel.[57]

As progressive thinkers, there were many similarities in their thoughts and activism. All the three were Church leaders, as Camilo Torres was a priest, and Hélder Câmara and Óscar Romero were bishops. They represented Colombia, Brazil, and El Salvador respectively, which were predominantly Christian like other parts of Latin America. They all, like many other progressive theologians, raised their voices against the violation of human rights and every form of political and economic exploitation in Latin America, especially in their own respective countries.[58] Pastoral commitment to the poor was the major impetus for the revival initiated by the progressive theologians.[59] They also assimilated a Marxist way of social analysis into their progressive Christian theologizing. Marxism categorized the class society on economic terms, taking into account the exploitation – the haves and have-nots, the capitalists and the proletariats, the oppressors and the oppressed – and strived for a classless society.[60]

Pedro Arrupe and the Society of Jesus

Another important observation is that liberation theology was very much related to the Society of Jesus – e.g. Ignacio Ellacuría, Jon Sobrino (both of them were Spanish but worked in El Salvador), Juan Luis

Segundo (Uruguay) were each Jesuits. This is not surprising given that the emergence of liberation theology as a new branch of theologizing and the assumption of Pedro Arrupe to power as the Superior General of the Society of Jesus took place in the same era. The liberal and progressive thinking of Arrupe, therefore, might have inspired many Jesuits to commit themselves to social justice. The following analysis of the life of Arrupe will give a basic understanding of the Society of Jesus' approach to liberation theology.

Pedro Arrupe was born on 14 November 1907 in Bilbao, Spain. In 1927, after his studies at the Medical School of the Universidad Complutense, Madrid, he joined the Society of Jesus. Unfortunately, he could not continue his priestly studies in Spain because the Republican government dissolved the Jesuit order and expelled its members from the country in 1932. Arrupe continued his studies in Netherlands and Belgium, and was finally ordained a priest in Marneffe, Belgium, in 1936. He then moved to the USA in order to complete his theological studies at St. Mary's Seminary in Kansas, and to do his Tertianship in Ohio, where he served Hispanic immigrants. In the United States he also obtained a doctorate in medical ethics.[61] Arrupe's personal experiences played a great role in formulating his thoughts: not only the political turmoil in Spain – including the dictatorship of Primo de Rivera from 1923, the anti-Catholic Republican regime from 1930, and the Civil War between 1933 and 1936 – but also the First and Second World Wars.[62]

In 1938, Arrupe went to Japan as a missionary, where he first engaged in social services under the patronage of the Jesuit University in Tokyo, and eventually, after WW II, became Jesuit vice-provincial (1954-58) and Jesuit provincial for Japan (1958-65). During his Japan period, Arrupe also visited Latin American countries, where he was struck by the poverty and exploitation. Arupe also participated in the final session of the Second Vatican Council and engaged himself in the discussion on *Gaudium et Spes*. In May 1965, just before the close of the Council, the 31st General Congregation of the Society of Jesus elected Arrupe as the 28th Superior General of the Society of Jesus.[63]

Arrupe aimed to continue the spirit of the Second Vatican Council by reorienting the Society accordingly and countering the conservative stance of the Catholic Church. This led to his later title of 're-founder of the Society of Jesus.'[64] He attended the Medellin Conference of 1968 and was inspired by the new ideas he had. Over the following years, he motivated the members of the Society to be active in social issues and to contribute to the growth of the theology of liberation. In an address to the 10th International Jesuit Alumni of Europe, in Valencia, Spain, in July 1973, Arrupe emphasized the need of an inevitable change in the world. This address had been called radical, because Arrupe exhorted his priests to strive for social justice and inculturation.[65] He proposed that Jesuit education should impart effective means of attaining justice, strong interference for change in the society, and active involvement in reforming unjust structures.[66]

Nearly ten years after the 31st General Congregation in which he was elected Superior General, Arrupe convened a new one. The General Congregation was the highest authority in the Society of Jesus and was convened only for very significant matters related to the whole Society, such as the death of the Superior General and the election of a new Superior General.[67] However, the 32nd General Congregation, which lasted from 2 December 1974 to 7 March 1975, was an exceptional meeting, since it came together for a different reason. Arrupe aspired for the liberation of the poor from all kinds of exploitation and oppression and convened the General Congregation to proclaim the Society's strong commitment to reading and addressing the signs of the time.[68] The meeting reflected his call and concluded, inter alia, that the Society of Jesus would support its members in their initiatives towards establishing justice and would sustain and defend them when they were unjustly discouraged or persecuted.[69] The 32nd General Congregation also mentioned the need for inculturation, especially in the context of the Third World.[70] In the following years, Arrupe put these ideas into practice. When in 1977 a Salvadoran death squad, the White Warriors Union, threatened the 47 Jesuits who were working for the poor in the country, Arrupe replied that it was the mission of the Society to fight for justice and that his priests would not back down. Likewise, for example, in June 1978, while responding to the 'Conclusions of the Jesuit Conference of India on the Report of the Commission on Inculturation,' he instructed the Jesuits in India and Sri Lanka "to go forward with confidence."[71]

The Church's observation about Arrupe's use of Marxist ideologies was valid to an extent. Still, Arrupe's point was that social analysis could adopt certain methodological viewpoints that were close to Marxism. Arrupe stated that there were occasions when Christians had to share a number of Marxist views in order to deal with social issues. Yet, he emphasized, this was only an adoption of a method – making use of the substance of the Marxist explanations to the social reality and applying them to the present society – and not a promotion of Marxist philosophy.[72] Arrupe therefore encouraged the use of Marxist elements in social analysis and tried to engage in dialogue with Marxists.[73] He found the scope of applying their means of social analysis while dealing with issues related to economic interests, property structures, exploitation of an entire class, class struggle, and even ideologies camouflaging injustice.[74]

Arrupe's commitment to the social causes and the theology of liberation did not mean that he supported Marxism in its totality. In a letter written in 1980 to the Jesuit Provincial Superiors in Latin America, the Superior General explained that one could employ Marxist means in social analysis as long as one was able to distinguish it from Marxist philosophy, which contradicted Christian beliefs.[75] In other words, he insisted that Jesuit theologians and pastors should use Marxist analysis judiciously and discriminatingly.[76] Importantly, Arrupe discouraged a total reliance upon Marx's views for two reasons: first, the risk of identifying Marxist means with its philosophy, and second, the reductionist nature of Marxism that would trim down politics, culture, and religion as realities totally dependent on economic relations.[77] Even when he supported Marxist analysis, he did not exclude the element of risk in it and referred to *Octogesima Advenience* in which Pope Paul VI warned that it was illusory and dangerous to accept Marxist elements.[78] Moreover, Arrupe relied upon the document of the Latin American Bishops' Conference at Puebla in 1979 to state that Marxist analysis leads to a "total politicization of Christian existence" or to a conversion of the language of faith to that of social sciences.[79]

However, Pope John Paul II was discontented with Arrupe's radical stance and assimilation of Marxist ideologies. By the close of the 1970s, the Society's liberal and innovative activities brought the Jesuits into ideological conflict with John Paul II, who regarded Arrupe as being overly permissive and found elements of Marxism in his thoughts and in the liberation theology he was supporting. Moreover, Arrupe's encouragement and support to the liberal and progressive Jesuits drew the Pope's suspicion. In June 1981, the Pope summoned the Pontifical Commission for Latin America. The conclusion of the Commission condemned Arrupe's position that a division between the doctrine and the analysis of Marxism was possible.[80] Subsequently, on 5 October 1981, John Paul II appointed a personal delegate to the Society of Jesus. This seemed to be the culmination of the Pope's discontent with Arrupe's liberal ideologies ever since the former became the Pope in 1978. As we will see in Chapters V and VII, this conflict on account of the radical stance and Marxist orientation would also affect Kappen's relation with the Congregation of the Doctrine of Faith.

The Conferences

Next to the commitment of the individuals and the connection with the Jesuits, liberation theology was also subject to a kind of institutionalization. While initially many young priests joined revolutionary groups, or formed their own associations, liberation theologians gradually convened in official meetings, especially in the Conference of the Latin American Bishops (CELAM) at Medellin, Colombia (1968), Puebla, Mexico (1979), and Santo Domingo, Dominican Republic (1992).[81]

The CELAM was established in 1955, after the model of the National Conference of Brazilian Bishops (CNBB) and under the initiative of bishops Hélder Câmara (Brazil) and Manuel Larrain (Chile). It aspired to regain ecclesial unity that had been lost with the end of colonial period in the early 19th century. The first Conference (CELAM I) took place from 25 July to 4 August 1955 in Rio de Janeiro, Brazil. It elected Jaime de Barros Câmara (1894-1971), the Archbishop of Rio de Janeiro, as its president and Bishop Manuel Larrain (1900-66) as its vice-president. [82] The second Latin American Episcopal Conference (CELAM) was held in Medellin from 26 August to 6 September 1968, after the two major preparatory meetings in Mar de Plata, Argentina (1966)[83] and Itapoan Bahia, Brazil (May 1968).[84] It coincided with Pope Paul VI's visit to attend the International Eucharistic Congress.[85] CELAM II was a remarkable moment in the history of the Church, for it sharpened the question of social justice and replaced the status quo model with a catalyst model. It was during this Conference that the bishops explicitly articulated their decision to opt for the poor and to distance themselves from the rich class, though it was not a completely *ex novo* idea.[86]

Medellin's 'option for the poor' was the need of the time for various economic and political reasons.[87] The Latin American countries, except the socialist state of Cuba (1959),[88] were controlled by the Pentagon. Oligarchy and dictatorship had become the norm. Nevertheless, there were also signs of the emergence of a social and political consciousness, inter alia, with the rise of organizations like the Institutional Revolutionary Party (PRI) in Mexico, the Christian Democratic Party in Chile (PDC) and the radical Popular Front in Chile (CTCH). Besides, the Peruvian military revolution (1968) under the leadership of Juan Francisco Velasco Alvarado and the subsequent left-leaning and pro-poor Revolutionary Government of the Armed Force, and the progressive reforms in the agrarian sectors in these countries fueled the popular revolutions in different parts of Latin America.[89] Medellin in fact accentuated such popular revolutionary movements by declaring its empathy with the poor and the oppressed of society.

The conclusions of the Medellin Conference are divided into three sections: human promotion, evangelization, and structure of the Church. Most importantly, the council prioritized the problems of the multitudes of people in Latin America and the need to liberate them. With this term, it meant the integral development of the human person. This further showed the political dimension of pastoral work. However, the effectiveness of the Medellin contribution has to be challenged. The phraseology of the council's conclusions provided only certain theoretical observations condemning injustice as an institutionalized violence.[90] Of the sixteen statements it produced, only three – on justice, peace, and poverty – could make an impact. For the rest, it identified problems rather than planning their eradication.[91]

Yet, Medellin opened the door for further action. It motivated activists to commit themselves to the cause of the poor.[92] Hélder Câmara, who played a significant role in organizing the CELAM at Medellin, for instance, convinced the government in 1970 to form a committee to study the social and economic problems in Mexico. In Nicaragua, hundreds of CEBs started functioning and promoting social activism among young activists. In 1972, a Commission for Studies in Latin American Church History (CEHILA) was founded in Quito, Ecuador, as an independent research organization under the guidance of CELAM. Its most important contribution was the publication of a huge amount of literature in support of the theology of liberation in Latin America.[93] For instance, it undertook a rereading of Latin American history that took into account the social and political factors along with both popular and institutional religious history.[94] CEHILA also succeeded in acting as an ecumenical agent among different churches and formed a Protestant group to answer the needs of Protestants. In fact, by encouraging progressive thinking both from the Catholic and Protestant sides, liberation theology became not merely a Catholic movement. Instead, it stood for the eradication of the miseries of the people of Latin America irrespective of creed; with the sole purpose of attaining integral liberation.

Another example of an organization that encouraged and contributed to the liberation movement in Latin America was the Ecumenical Centre for Documentation and Information (CEDI), which the Brazilian environment pioneer Carlos Alberto Ricardo founded in 1974 in Sao Paulo and Rio de Janeiro.[95] The CEDI developed a network of organizations and individuals who worked on matters related to indigenous tribal people.[96] It organized the peasants and the poor against the military regime and reacted against multinational agencies like the International Monetary Fund (IMF) and the World Bank.[97] In 1981, the organization also added environmental issues to its agenda. Nevertheless, the primary concern remained the indigenous people.[98]

The third CELAM conference was inaugurated by Pope John Paul II at the Basilica of Our Lady of Guadalupe in Puebla, Mexico, on 27 January 1979, and lasted until 13 February. The central theme of discussion was the 'Evangelization in Latin America's Present and Future.' Unlike Medellin, the opponents of liberation theology, including the Colombian Bishop Alfonso Lopez Trujillo, controlled CELAM III.[99] Trujillo, who had been an expert at the Medellin conference of 1968, was consecrated bishop in 1971 and appointed as the general secretary of CELAM in 1972. Although he studied Marxism and was familiar with its revolutionary ideologies, he was conservative and opposed theology of liberation. In his phrasing, he wanted to avoid conflicts with Latin American governments, who increasingly arrested, tortured, exiled, and assassinated progressive Christian thinkers. In preparation for the Puebla conference, Trujillo systematically attempted to prevent progressive theologians from being selected to attend the conference as he "excluded opposition at Puebla, and pushed ahead with orthodoxy".[100]

However, the progressive theologians eventually were content with the Puebla conference. On the one hand, there were three non-condemnations – Marxism as a methodology of analysis (although CELAM III condemned classical Marxism), liberation theology, and socialism as an alternative; on the other there were three condemnations – namely capitalist liberalism, state sponsored violence, and claims for national security.[101] Still, Puebla went against the spirit of Medellin in many ways. For instance, it put forward the gospel as the fundamental reason for cultural unity within Latin America, unlike Medellin, which had not only counted on the Christian presence but also the ethnic elements. In addition, Puebla stepped back from Medellin's accommodation of cultural changes and negative approach to the arrival of universal urban-industrial culture and condemned the secularization process.[102] It therefore took steps back in the process of the liberation of the poor.

1992 was the 500th anniversary of the evangelization of Latin America and it was, by all means, an occasion to convene a fourth CELAM. Pope John Paul II approved the central theme of discussion for this CELAM meeting on 12 December 1990: 'New Evangelization, Human Promotion, Christian Culture.'[103] The conference was held in Santo Domingo, in Dominican Republic from 12 to 28 October 1992. After the term of Trujillo as the General Secretary of CELAM ended in 1984, the conservative wing's control over CELAM had diminished. Unlike in Puebla, the progressive bishops unanimously raised voice for an inculturated evangelization.[104] The *Santo Domingo Document (SD)* considered culture a cultivation of what is humane and highlighted its pro-nature and pro-community traits.[105] In this way, it acknowledged and appreciated all existing cultures, whether they were pre- or post-Colombian. As a matter of fact, a re-reading of SD provides the notion of the need of a baptism of the Church by different cultures and not vice versa. This constituted a shift in the Church's approach with regard to its understanding of evangelization which until then had been a process of exclusive giving without assimilation. SD used 'evangelization of culture' and 'inculturation' as equivalent terms.[106] Inculturation could be understood in general terms as the acquisition of the norms and normativity of a culture or ideology by another culture or ideology. Through this process, an ideology gets access to foreign cultures.

The CELAM conferences had been instrumental in the development of liberation theology in Latin America. They generated an enormous impact in Latin America toward acknowledging individual cultures, criticizing all forms of exploitations and oppressions of the oligarchies, and uniting the Church as a corrective force that could even threaten the established oppressive systems.[107] The primary concern of Medellin was human development, i.e. the empowerment of the marginalized class. Puebla concentrated on the evangelization and the integral development of the ethnic groups recognizing and respecting their dignity. Likewise, Santo Domingo appreciated the relevance of cultures and promoted inculturation.[108]

Puebla and Santo Domingo, however, did not surpass the spirit of Medellin. They were both criticized for their theoretical approach. The Church, opting for the poor and empowering them to denounce every form of oppression as encouraged in Medellin, eventually turned into theoretical expressions like evangelization and inculturation.[109] Unlike that of the previous conferences, Santo Domingo's Christology was a familiar one. While Medellin and Puebla put forward the historical, i.e. human Jesus, Santo Domingo foregrounded Jesus as Christ.[110]

C. Asian Liberation Theology

Latin America may have been its cradle, but liberation theology was also important in other continents, for instance, Asia. Christianity is a minority religion in Asia, accounting for only 4.5% of the total population. Still, the continent produced a number of important Christian thinkers, including some liberation theologians. This section attempts to know what liberation theology meant in an Asian context and to what extent it can be considered a continuation of Latin American liberation theology. It will do so by focusing on four key countries: Sri Lanka, the Philippines, South Korea, and India. At the outset, all of these countries have their own distinct features that gave particular characteristics to liberation theology in each of them. We will discuss the most important of them.

By differentiating Asian liberation theology from other liberation theologies, we do not intend to isolate the Asian reality from the global reality. Liberation theologies everywhere stood for the integral liberation of the poor, marginalized, and oppressed, and so, it was not the fundamental charisma but the context in which they applied it that made them different. Asian liberation theology's desire to go in terms with the global reality was rightly acknowledged by James H. Cone in 1979, in a conference held in Wennappuwa, Sri Lanka, on 'Asia's struggle for a full humanity: Toward a relevant theology.' The task of the conference was to make sure that Asian reality was not divorced from the global reality.

Sri Lanka

One of the key countries for Asian liberation theology is Sri Lanka. This is not surprising: it has a century-long history of colonization – first by the Portuguese, then by the Dutch, and finally by the British. According to the 2016 census, it has an important Christian population of 7.4% of the ca. 20 million; versus 70.2% Buddhists, 12.6% Hindus, and 9.7% Muslims.[111] The Catholic Church is the biggest church among many other Christian churches, such as the Anglican, Methodist, Baptist, Salvation Army etc. Liberation theology was first promoted in Sri Lanka by the Anglican bishop Lakshman Wickremesingha (1927-83) and the Catholic bishop Leo Nanayakkara OSB (1917-82), the latter who was deeply influenced by the Second Vatican Council. They were followed by two liberation theologians of renown, namely Tissa Balasuriya (1924-2014) and Aloysius Pieris (1934).

Balasuriya did his higher studies in Ceylon, Rome, Oxford, and Paris. Along with Bishop Leo, in 1971 he established the Centre for Society and Religion (CSR) to encourage inter-ethnic and inter-religious dialogue in the context of Buddhist nationalism and tension between religious communities. He also wanted the Centre to be a common platform where Hindus, Buddhists, Muslims, and Christians could come together and exchange their views. In the following years, he was also a founding member of the Ecumenical Association of the Third World Theologians (EATWOT, 1976), the Civil Rights Movement (CRM), People's Action for Free and Fair Election (PAFFREL, 1987), and the

Asian Meeting of Religious (AMOR). Balasuriya fought for ethnic peace, justice, human rights, and the urban and rural poor, and in this struggle utilized Marxist ideologies. He wrote extensively on progressive theology, but his 1994 *Mary and Human Liberation* became controversial. The Congregation for the Doctrine of Faith (CDF) found certain dogmatic errors in his teachings, especially in this book, and excommunicated him on 2 January 1997.[112]

Balasuriya considered human freedom to be a human right. He observed that rights to political freedom, freedom from any kind of torture, and freedom from imprisonment, along with other basic needs, were fundamental and must be guaranteed. He said this considering the plight of the South Asian villages that were suffering from preventable causes. It also was a call for the Church in Asia to struggle for human rights and freedom, and to motivate the movements striving for these values by promoting compassion, sharing, etc.[113]

Aloysius Pieris is a renowned proponent of the theology of liberation in Sri Lanka and a contemporary of Balasuriya. Scholars consider him one of Asia's most innovative theologians.[114] Pieris was the first non-Buddhist to secure a doctoral degree from the Buddhist University of Sri Lanka. He is an inclusivist who fostered Buddhist-Christian dialogue in the country. This could be assumed to be the fundamental difference between Pieris and Balasuriya. Pieris' liberation activities were not limited to understanding Buddhism and Asian Christianity. He actively engaged himself in the undertakings of various organizations. One of them was the Devasarana Collective Farm initiated by Yohan Devanand, an Anglican monk, in 1971. Devasarana was an innovative project that brought together unemployed youth and poor peasants to cultivate collaboratively in order to liberate themselves from poverty. It was indeed a sign of solidarity with the poor farmers in the country. Likewise, the Tulana Research Center for Encounter and Dialogue, which he founded in 1974, still functions as the centre for retreat and reflection, social animation, and inter-religious dialogue.[115] His works are predominantly compilations of the essays he wrote in the 1970s and

1980s.[116] The most widely read volume is *Fire and Water: Basic Issues in Asian Buddhism and Christianity* (1996).

Pieris and Balasuriya criticized the Asian Church for their failure to understand the cultural and religious diversity in Asia. First of all, the Asian Church depended on theology imported from the West. This pulled them back from formulating an indigenous theology according to the needs of the Asian contexts, taking into consideration the religious, cultural, political, and economic situations of Asian countries. As a result, the faithful in the Third World had become "theologically inarticulate oppressed people."[117] They had been provided with a prefabricated theology made in a Western colonial mold. Pieris phrased this as follows: the Asian Church failed to become the "Church *of* Asia," rather, it remained a "Church *in* Asia."[118] According to him, the Church *in* Asia should become an inculturated Church in order to be the Church *of* Asia. When Pieris addressed the Asian Theological Conference (ATC) in Sri Lanka in 1979, he critically pointed out that the primary attention of the Church deviated from the 'Third Worldness' and 'Asianness' of Asian theology because it focused too much on the religious character.[119] Many scholars continued to hold this view after Pieris. For instance, Peter C. Phan, the American theologian of Vietnamese origin, reiterated what Pieris argued. The Asian Church had to be "baptized in the Jordan of Asian religion and on the Calvary of Asian poverty."[120] However, the Vatican had a discouraging approach towards promoting the 'Asianness' of the Church. Referring to the Filipino bishop Francisco Claver, Phan said that one of the curia bishops in Vatican, during the Asian Synod in Rome in 1998, instructed the Asian bishops not to use the expression 'Church of Asia.' As a result, the Asian Church was caught up between classical western theology and the newly emerged Latin American theology of liberation. Or, in secular terms, the Asian Church was struggling between capitalist developmental ideologies and Marxist socialism.[121]

A second reason for the failure of the Asian Church was its rigid organization and leadership. Balasuriya commented that this was widening the gap between the ordinary faithful and the hierarchy.[122] Asian Churches' dependence on Western theology caused the Bishops' Conferences in Asia to disregard the socio-economic problems of the Asian countries. Only in a few countries did the bishops denounce capitalism and become spokesmen for the poor and the oppressed.[123] In the very first chapter of his *Planetary Theology* of 1984 Balasuriya criticized the indifference of the Church and Christians towards the immense human suffering around the world. He found this theology "culture-bound," "Church-centered," "male-dominated," "aged-dominated," "pro-capitalist," "anti-Communist," "overly theoretical," and "non-revolutionary."[124] In addition, the Asian Churches failed to cultivate a horizontal relationship among themselves, and only developed a vertical relation with Rome. Criticizing the structural and institutional nature of these churches, Balasuriya pointed out that they created only westernized bourgeois through their educational institutions.[125] Pieris also criticized the Church for not going beyond the limits of dogmas and doctrines to the realm of praxis. In his view, religion had not only a liberating aspect but also an enslaving nature, justifying poverty. In his *Asian Theology of Liberation*, Pieris claimed that the Asian churches had been teaching how to be poor by pointing out the spiritual and soteriological relevance of poverty in human life, but they disregarded the need of the struggle for the poor.[126] Jon Sobrino's understanding of liberation from dogmatic faith (originally Kantian) and from every form of alienation (originally Marxian) seemed to have influenced Pieris in this regard.[127]

The third reason for the failure of the Asian Church was its disrespect towards other Asian religions and cultures. For Balasuriya, the theology of the Christian West was only Church-centered as it was predominantly mono-religious. Importing this Church-centered theology to a multi-religious and multi-cultural context weakened the latter's religious and cultural balance.[128] He questioned some of the fundamentals of Catholic faith like original sin, the godhood of Jesus, and the motherhood of Mary. This, not surprisingly, put him in conflict with the Vatican.[129] According to Balasuriya, talking about the privileged place of Mary, Jesus, and the Church would always be offensive to the dialogue partners. For him, religion was only significant when and as long as it contributes to the liberation of man on this earth.[130]

Balasuriya and Pieris not only criticized the Asian Church and explained its failure, but also developed ideas of freedom and liberation, especially focusing on their area of interest, i.e. human freedom and inter-religious dialogue respectively. As an advocate of human freedom, Balasuriya considered capitalism (along with the West and the institutional Church) to be curtailing this freedom. He resorted to the liberating elements in socialism for the retrieval of the lost freedom and for instance, in the 1970s, supported the Third World demand for a New International Economic Order (NIEO).[131] While Balasuriya emphasized material liberation, Pieris argued for an integral liberation of the human person, both spiritual and material.[132] In Pieris' view, concentrating more on the transcendental dimension of liberation reduced liberation to something that could only be understood in mystical terms. If the first meaning of liberation is religious, the second should be secular or vice versa – liberating the people from every form of oppression.[133]

The pro-socialist mind of Balasuriya was evident also in his support of socialist China. Especially in the 1980s, he applauded China's achievements in overcoming its manifold problems like poverty, unemployment, and foreign dependency, and considered them an example for other Asian countries.[134] Balasuriya's support of Chinese socialism should also be seen as a criticism of the Church which traditionally opted for the right wing of the political spectrum.[135] But he also genuinely championed an Asian revolution. His ideas were not different in content from the conventional understanding of revolution that intended a rapid and radical transformation of the prevailed political, social, and economic structures.[136] His appreciation for the Latin American theological evolution[137] and the Chinese model development should be considered in connection with this rapid and radical revolution.

As a Buddhist scholar, Pieris worked more in the field of the Buddhist-Christian relationship. Through his works he attempted to provide a systematic and nuanced understanding of Buddhism and Asian Christianity. His stay with a Buddhist monk in order to understand the depth of the Buddhist way of life helped him develop a more indigenous form of Christian prayers including the Holy Mass, the highest liturgical celebration for Catholics. He incorporated the Buddhist mindfulness (*sati-patthana*) and awareness into the Christian prayers. This method was later called 'the Contemplative Mass,' 'the Silent Eucharist,' and 'the Buddhist Liturgy.'[138] By reiterating the relevance of mindfulness, he actually criticized the ritualistic nature of the historically and traditionally evolved Christian celebrations.

This dialogue was not easy, since many Buddhist revivalists, such as Anagarika Dharmapala, were critical of Christianity. According to them, Jesus was a mere spiritual dwarf in front of the Buddha. Initially, Pieris tried to tackle this criticism by means of the Christology of St. Paul, the apostle, who tried to present "Jesus Christ as the one cosmic mediator and as the metacosmic Lord over all visible and invisible forces of the universe."[139] However, this was not something new to Asia since the Buddhist missionaries did the same with Buddha long before Jesus. They had enthroned the Buddha over all elements of nature and all gods, spirits, and personified cosmic forces.[140] In contrast to his previous attempt to project Jesus as the once cosmic mediator, Pieris later in his *Love Meets Wisdom* (1988), blamed the Church's attempt to implant the cosmic Christ in Asia where there already was a cosmic Buddha who was placed above all elements of nature and all gods, spirits and personified cosmic forces.[141] Pieris stated that Christology had to avoid competition with Buddhology.[142]

The Philippines

Liberation theology also penetrated the Philippines. This is not surprising. With 87% of the population belonging to Christianity (and 11% to Islam and 2% to traditional indigenous religions) according to the 2015 statistics, it is one of the two Christian countries in Asia, next to East

Timor (96%). Moreover, the country was a Spanish colony from 1521 to 1898 and it accordingly had a common history with Latin America. For instance, the agricultural feudal system and the government's assistance to the landlords increased the gulf between the rich and the poor.[143]

In the second half of the 20th century, socially committed Christians came together to work for the liberation of the oppressed. Just as elsewhere, they were inspired by factors like Marxism, the Second Vatican Council, Latin American liberation theology, and experience in the West. Carlos H. Abesamis SJ (1934-2008), Vitaliano R. Gorospe SJ (1924-2002), José de Mesa (°1946), and Edicio De la Torre (°1943) were among the most pronounced progressive theologians. Their common agenda was the struggle for the marginalized.

The KU Leuven alumni Carlos H. Abesamis and José de Mesa – a lay theologian born in Manila – rather found inspiration in Western liberal ideologies to work for the poor and the oppressed. Abesamis began a seminary system in which the candidates to priesthood had to maintain regular contacts with marginalized communities. To his surprise, he received enormous support from the Archbishop Jaime Sin. José de Mesa focused on creating an indigenous theology by tapping the wealth of the Filipino culture.[144] Vitaliano R. Gorospe, professor and former chairman of the Department of Theology at the Ateneo de Manila University, was inspired by Gutiérrez's *A Theology of Liberation*. Besides his academic initiatives, he, like Edicio, also was very much involved in the problems of the poor farmers of Laguna.

Edicio dealt not only with theology, but also with agriculture, education, and politics. Also, he stood out among the other three progressive thinkers on account of his affinity to Marxist ideologies. Being greatly influenced by the ideologies of Marx and Mao Tse Tung, he committed himself to the poor and the oppressed and especially in the 1970s strove for farmers' rights and land reforms. He was the founder of Education for Life Foundation (ELF), a non-governmental organization that engaged in leadership development. He contributed much to the fields of democratization and development through education and leadership programs. Like Camilo Torres, he in 1972 joined the underground left against the reign of President Marcos.[145] He endured various regulatory measures from the state including imprisonment.

The Filipino liberation theology also enjoyed support from the Filipino Communist parties like the Communist Party of the Philippines (CCP) and the Socialist Party of the Philippines (SPP). Since the 1930s, both parties had been working among the poor peasants, organizing peasant movements. Interestingly, the emergence of liberation theology in the Philippines prompted the Communist parties to collaborate with progressive theologians, having found similarities in their mutual goals. Subsequently, the Communist parties offered their support to the revolutionary activities of the progressive theologians, though the latter were not all that equally fascinated by Communist ideologies. The same goes for the National Peoples' Army (NPA), the armed wing of the Communist Party of the Philippines, founded in 1969. As a matter of fact, the Communist parties succeeded in attracting the socially committed Christians to Communist/Marxist ideologies. At the same time, the Christians who opted for the poor had to face challenges both from the state and the Church that labeled them Communists. Indeed, the mainstream Church in the Philippines was more inclined to see Communism as a bigger problem than the injustices in the society.[146]

Filipino liberation theology eventually developed a broader perspective. The Maoist orientation, and the armed struggles of the Communist parties in the 1980s against the Marcos regime and United States interventionism increased the number of Christians who were attracted to those parties. This gave momentum to the development of a Filipino version of liberation theology, similar to Latin American liberation theology. This enthusiasm led to the non-violent overthrow of Ferdinand Marcos' dictatorial regime in 1986 through the People Power Revolution. The role of the progressive thinkers in mobilizing the middle class played a crucial role in this victory, and as a result, the priest Louie Hechanova coined the phrase 'theology of struggle,' which is the Filipino theology of liberation.[147]

Unfortunately, unlike Latin American theology, the Filipino contribution to liberation theology has received little attention from international scholars, mainly due to the lack of sufficient literature.[148] Still, the Filipino progressive theologians collaborated with other liberation theologians. François Houtart's (whom we will discuss in Chapter III) participation in a seminar held in Baguio City in 1976 was one such inspirational example. Likewise, their contact with the EATWOT and other such international organizations and theologians inspired them to continue their struggle. By the mid-1980s, a number of literary works appeared in the profile of Filipino liberation theology.[149]

South Korea

According to the census of 2015, South Korea also has a substantial Christian population of 27.6% (versus 15.5% Buddhists, 1.7% followers of other religions, and the rest without a formal religion). It now is the most developed country in Asia, with the highest per capita income, and a fully functioning modern liberal democracy, but from the 1960s to the 1980s, it underwent periods of military dictatorship. Christian progressive theology considerably contributed the transformation of Korea.[150] The economic growth of South Korea in the 1970s also had a dark side since laborers were often exploited in factories. This provoked nationwide protest and conscientization, often under a Christian banner. At the same time, intellectuals also suffered from the dictatorship of Park Chong-hee, who ruled the country from 1961 to 1979. He ousted and imprisoned many progressive Christian professors.[151]

Korean liberation theology has been called *minjung* theology. The term is a combination of two Korean characters, namely *min* (people) and *jung* (mass). *Minjung* means the ordinary people; more particularly in this context the economically, socially, and politically oppressed people.[152] Two scholars, Ahn Byung-mu and Suh Nam-dong, launched the term in 1975. *Minjung* theology, though influenced by Latin American liberation theology, is therefore a contextual theology or a theology of the ordinary people.[153] Undergoing the many-sided problems of the dictatorial regime, they felt the need for a change. They were encouraged by a variety of organizations, such as the student movements of the 1960s, the Seoul Metropolitan Community Organization (SMCO) – an organization created to tackle the needs of the urban poor –, the House of Dawn – a charitable organization for the education of girls –, etc.[154] Christian groups like the Christian Ecumenical Youth Council, Priests Corps for the Realization of Justice, Catholic Young Workers Organization, Church Women United, Human Rights Commission of the National Council of Churches, etc. had also been inspirational in the struggles for human rights.[155]

Minjung theology revolved around the principles of *han* and *dan*. *Han* has different meanings but is related to a feeling of resentment, depression, repressed anger, and helplessness.[156] *Dan* on the other hand functioned as a means to resolve the tensions of *han* by bringing about a personal and social transformation of the resented person or society.[157] This two-level transformation constituted the non-violent struggle of the *minjung* for liberation.

Minjung theology over time refined itself in order to withstand the suppressive steps of Park Chong-hee. Although it initially focused only on economic and cultural conditions, it eventually addressed political and social issues as well. This led the *minjung* to further the struggle for democracy during the dictatorial reign of Jeon Du Whan from 1980 to 1988, even though he suppressed the *minjung* demonstration in 1980.[158]

The sources of *minjung* were not limited to the Bible and the Church, but also included Buddha Siddharta (Amita Buddhism), Shamanism, Marxism, Latin American liberation theology, and the experience of the *minjung*. Amita Buddhism was a form of Buddhism that focused more on the present world, unlike Buddha Maitreya, which concentrated on the Buddha of the coming world. Distinguishing itself both from traditional Christian and Maitreya Buddha preoccupations (other worldly) and rigid Marxist class analysis (materialistic), *minjung* theology took a more inclusive middle stand. The very life of the *minjung*, including their suffering, pain, aspirations, and struggle, was the core of its theology. Historians like Takashi Hatada remarked that the history of Korea from its beginning had been a history of suffering.[159] *Minjung* theologians used the Bible not as a norm but only as a source of reference that further enabled a socio-political reading.

A good example is the deep study of the gospel of Mark by Ahn Byung-mu (1922-96), the father of *minjung* theology. Ahn Byung-mu identified a particular group of people in the gospels who were close to Jesus. They were neither disciples nor members of the ruling class and Byung-mu called them *ochlos* (crowd/mass),[160] and decided to use the term *ochlos* instead of *laos* (God's people) to denote the ordinary faithful.[161] He thought that liberation theology should focus on contemporary *ochlos*, which he identified as the poor and the marginalized who, just as in the Bible, were nowhere in the religious or political scenario. Still, this does not mean that *minjung* theology neglected Jesus. On the contrary, Jesus remained the strength and inspiration of the *minjung* as he became one with them. The *minjung* theology is identified with the strength of the powerlessness of Jesus and is called a "politics of powerlessness."[162]

The proponents of *minjung* theology awaited a *minjung* millennium with peace and justice as its landmark.[163] Conversely, the *minjung* theologians found an unholy relationship in the country between religious and political messianism. Therefore, the challenge of the *minjung* theology in Korea was to engage in a permanent and unfinished revolution to bring an end to religious and political messianic promises by actualizing a society of peace and justice. This would be possible, according to Kim Sung-Hae, a leader of the South Korean sectarian church called Yoido Full Gospel Church, through an effective blending of the native values with the gospel values. Admittedly, only the initial few decades in the two-century history of the Korean Catholic Church assimilated native values. Writings of Chŏng Yak-Chŏng (*The Essence of Catholic Teaching*, 1795) and Chŏng Ha-Sang (a lengthy apologetic letter, 1839) stood out as the examples for using native resources. Later, with the arrival of French missionaries, native values gave way to the Western value system and theologizing. The Korean *minjung* theologians therefore advocated a search for disregarded indigenous elements.[164] A good example was *Pastoral theology*, a bimonthly published by the Catholic Conference of Korea since 1967 that, along with issues like social justice, Church involvement in politics, social participation of the Church, and farmers' problems, also elaborated on inculturation (and also closely followed the development in Latin American liberation theology). Another example is the Catholic Farmers' Movement, which started in 1966.[165] Needless to say, the South Korean liberation theology was an utmost contextual theology, reading the signs of the time.

A Brief Comparison

The analysis of Sri Lankan, Filipino, and Korean liberation theology demonstrates that practices in Asia cannot be lumped together. Its inherent diversity in the social, religious, and cultural spheres made focal points of theological discourses slightly or largely different based on context. While Sri Lankan theologians stressed the dehumanizing aspects of poverty and injustice, and on multi-religiosity, Filipino and Korean theologians mainly worked on the social, political, and economic aspects of human life. Nevertheless, themes like Third World poverty, interreligious dialogue, inculturation, and integral liberation remained at the center of Asian liberation theology. The integral liberation they brought about consisted not only of the spiritual and the material but also of the cultural and the religious liberation. Their initiative for inculturation and interreligious dialogue helped cultural and religious groups come out of exclusive thinking and promote peaceful coexistence.

Asian liberation theologies showed a number of similarities and dissimilarities with Latin American liberation theology. All of them had a preferential option for the poor. Both Latin American and Asian liberation theologies also looked into the original meaning of the message of Jesus in the synoptic gospels. Additionally, they had common sources of inspiration, such as Marxist social analysis and the Second Vatican Council.

Nevertheless, the differences outnumbered the similarities. Most importantly, the religious context of Latin America and Asia was different, as the former was primarily Christian, and the latter was predominantly multi-religious. For this reason, it was impossible for Asian liberation theology to present Jesus as the sole liberator since there were many liberators, mythical and historical, and of different religions. Therefore, unlike in Latin America, Asian liberation theology could not be defined as a reinterpretation of the gospels. Rather, it had to take into account the scriptures and traditions of other religions. Asian liberation theologians emphasized cooperation and peaceful coexistence among religions. They therefore promoted inculturation by adapting the liberating elements in the Asian religions and cultures. Another important difference is the fact that the Church in Latin America, including some prominent bishops, was more supportive of progressive thinking and theology of liberation than the Asian Church and its hierarchy.

D. Liberation Theology in India

Indian liberation theology is primarily a critical approach to imported theology, especially because the latter is alien in the pluralist context of India.[166] This critical approach complemented the hallmark of liberation theology in general, which is contextualized interpretation of the gospels with a preferential option for the poor. Since the 1970s, a number of progressive theologians were also active in India. Many of them identified with Latin American liberation theology by explicit or implicit references in their writings. Nevertheless, some scholars, such as the Kerala theologians Paul Puthanangady and Mathew Paikada, claimed that liberation theology in India was still in its formative stage. By the time they made this observation – from the late 1980s onwards –, liberation theology had started to fade away. Since liberation theology in India became less influential during the time it was expected to emerge into a strong discipline, it should be understood as a theology that died before blossoming. According to Puthanangady, liberation theology in India did not fully succeed in becoming contextualized, because Indian liberation theologians were busy analyzing liberation theology elsewhere from a theoretical perspective.[167] Paikada also followed this line of thought by commenting: "[...] theology has to be deeply rooted in the socio-political and religious situations of the people."[168] We assume, therefore, that Indian liberation theology underwent more a conceptualization than contextualization. Still, this does not mean that there has not been a praxis-oriented liberation theology in any form in India.

First Generation Liberation Theology

One can clearly distinguish two generations of progressive Christian thinkers in India. The first generation was mostly in line with Latin American liberation theology, and its major proponents were Christian theologians from south Indian states, especially Kerala and Tamil Nadu. The most important ones from Kerala included Sebastian Kappen SJ (1924-93), Samuel Rayan SJ (1920), M.M. Thomas (1916-96), and Paulose Mar Paulose (1941-98). The relatively strong Christian presence in these states produced more theologians and the Marxist background, particularly in Kerala, challenged those from the state to get out of the traditional Christian ghettos. They were all very well convinced of the need of constructing a new theology of liberation for India and went a long way in this regard. Each also produced a considerable amount of literature, especially during and after the 1970s. The Second-generation theology emerged in the early 1980s.

Samuel Rayan is a widely read Jesuit theologian and a staunch proponent of liberation theology. He graduated from the Gregorian University in Rome in 1960. He was then appointed as the chaplain to the Kerala division of the All India Catholic University Federation (AICUF), which provided him with the opportunity to motivate students. Rayan also cooperated with the World Council of Churches (WCC) as a consultant to its commission of Faith and Order, from 1968 to 1983, and with the EATWOT. He has also worked as the sectional editor of the journal *Jeevadhara*, which published the articles of progressive theologians including his articles, from its start in 1971. As an Indian liberation theologian, he promoted adapting elements from religious and cultural realities in creating a theology of liberation.[169]

Figure 7. Samuel Rayan, M.M. Thomas, and Paulose Mar Paulose[170]

M.M. Thomas belonged to the *Mar Thoma* Church – a Syrian Christian Church based in Kerala – and became first and foremost known as a renowned ecumenist and was considered a great bridge-builder between Christian churches, and organizations. His connection with the World Student Christian Federation (WSCF) and the WCC gave him a good deal of international exposure. As he made it clear in his *Salvation and Humanization* (1971), his theology revolved around the spiritual dimension of the Christ-event (birth, death on the cross, and resurrection)[171] and for this reason he focused less on the secular understanding of liberation.[172] However, he is one of the Asian theologians and Christian activists who strived for the cause of the marginalized and the poor even before Latin American liberation theology considered the poor to be the central point of its theological discourse.[173]

Paulose Mar Paulose was a prominent figure in the religious and political circles of Kerala from the late 1970s to his death in 1998. He became bishop of the Chaldean Syrian Church in Kerala in 1968. The Chaldean Syrian Church is an Indian Christian Church that traces its origin to St. Thomas. As a priest and bishop, he distinguished himself from others with his affinity for certain political and secular ideologies, believing that religion and politics are not fundamentally different. In his progressive thinking, he criticized priestly hegemony and questioned many of the basics of Christian faith. For instance, his criticism of the idea of life after death, his denial of the teaching on retribution according to one's deeds on earth, his emphasis on the possibility of error in the Bible due to its human authorship, etc. made him a controversial figure in his Church. Paulose sought the liberation of people during their life on earth, and especially exhorted young people to strive for a new social order. He said: "what shall be the role of Christian youth? I would say that they should be a dissenting minority; they should be non-conformists [...] to stand as the community of Jesus, as a dynamic force within the society, acting as a dissenting minority."[174] Two of his major works, both in Malayalam, namely *Freedom is God* (1996) and *What Right have You to be Silent?* (1998) disseminated his ideas of dissent.

Samuel Rayan, M.M. Thomas, and Paulose Mar Paulose all wrote on theology of liberation. Additionally, they expressed their understanding of inculturation, pluralist culture, Indian religious tradition, Marxism, etc. in formulating their progressive thinking. Their thoughts and ideologies will return in the following chapters.

Despite the fact that Latin American liberation theology influenced and motivated Christian progressive thinkers in India, the contextual differences between Latin America and India also made the latter's liberation theologies different, as was the case with other Asian progressive theologies. Due to the heterogeneous religious and cultural context of India, Indian theology of liberation had to strive for religious and cultural liberation along with economic liberation. Therefore, the challenge for Indian Christian theology of liberation was to integrate the reformative elements of various religious traditions with biblical and Marxist elements of social analysis which would finally bring about an integral development of the human person, both material and spiritual. In the words of Michael Amaladoss, the task of Indian liberation theologians was to effectively blend the economic, political, social, cultural, and religious dimensions of life.[175]

In a 2005 book called *On the Banks of the Ganges: Doing Contextual Theology*, Felix Wilfred, an Indian theologian, recalled that the process of liberation in India was an interreligious project.[176] In fact, this interreligious project has facilitated ongoing direct and indirect interreligious dialogue. This must be seen in line with the statement of the Indian Theological Association (ITA, a theological forum of Catholic theologians of India founded in 1976), which at its eighth annual meeting at Pariyaram, Kerala in 1984 proposed an indigenous theology. Although 1984 was the year the CDF and the Vatican produced a document criticizing liberation theology, ITA decided to take 'Towards an Indian Theology of Liberation' as the central theme of the ninth annual meeting.[177] Accordingly, the ninth annual meeting at the Sacred Heart Seminary at Poonamallee, Chennai, from 28 to 31 December 1985 also reiterated that the Church and its theologians should strive to design an Indian theology of liberation in order to evolve a new hermeneutics to understand and interpret the Indian religious scriptures and symbols that would provide an integral vision on liberation.[178]

Veritably, Indian liberation theologians have integrated not only the scriptures and symbols of religions but also other methodologies like Marxism, which had already been in use in Latin America.[179] Marxist ideologies were very dominant in some parts in India, especially in Kerala and West Bengal (both often ruled by Communist parties). These ideologies were used in secular social analyzing, which we will elaborate in Chapter IV.

Another important difference was the fact that the Church in India was already in its transformative path prior to the Second Vatican Council and the rise of Latin American liberation theology.[180] Especially from the 1950s, it was very clear from the institution and later functioning of the Catholic Bishops' Conference of India (CBCI) and other individual Catholic Bishops Conferences in Asia. The Federation of the Asian Bishops' Conference (FABC), formed in 1972, also carried out the liberating mission of these individual Bishops Conferences.[181] Both organizations had been making revolutionary decisions in line with the liberation of the people. The Second Vatican Council did not have a groundbreaking influence on these organizations.

Initial attempts of Indian liberation theologians in the 1970s had taken mostly a theoretical form. This should be due to the influence of conventional theology, which is a mere god-talk, on them during the early period of their transition to a new way of theologizing. As a result, they did not initially manage to explore the challenging aspect of theology, namely the day-to-day experience of real human life. Or in other words, in an era in which god-talk had primacy over praxis, they had been struggling to bring balance between these aspects. Even among the leading progressive Christian thinkers, there were differences in how they made use of the different means of social analysis like Bible, reformative elements in the Asian religions, etc.

Second Generation

Dalits are those who are not included in the caste frame, and are better known under their outdated names, such as parialis, outcastes, or untouchables. Traditionally, Dalits were considered an impure and polluting people and therefore were physically and socially excluded from mainstream society.[182] Dalit is a self-chosen word and means 'oppressed.' According to the 2011 census, there are about 200 million Dalits in India, which made up 16.6% of the country's total population. The number of Christian Dalits is estimated to be approximately 20 million. As a matter of fact, nearly 75% of the Indian Christian population consists of Christian Dalits.[183] As per article 341 of the Constitution of India, the government of India instructed not to use the term Dalit officially. The official term used in the Constitution is Scheduled Castes (SCs). Yet, Dalits are synonymously known as 'outcastes' (people outside the caste structure), '*Harijan*' (a Gandhian term which means people of God [Hari = God; jan = people]), 'Avarrias' (casteless), 'Panchamas' (fifth caste), 'Chandalas' (the worst of the earth), and 'depressed classes' (a term used from British Colonial days).[184]

According to Aloysius Pieris, the lower castes and the Dalits were living under a religiously enforced socio-economic slavery established by the Brahminic orthodoxy.[185] The Jesuit Dalit activist Prakash Louis observed that the caste system regarded the Dalits as people unworthy to live with the caste people. They had been undergoing poverty, degradation, humiliation, and even gender discrimination for centuries.[186] Maria Arul Raja SJ, another Dalit activist, pointed out that Dalits were neglected in the job sector, and there existed an institutional hatred in the secular and democratic state of India against them. This institutional hatred had been perpetuating two negative tendencies throughout history: first, the superiority and domination of the caste Hindus were established and maintained, and second, the sense of backwardness and inferiority complex of Dalits was reinstated. These phenomena have led to relentless conflicts between caste Hindus and Dalits.[187]

The second-generation liberation theology, also called the Dalit liberation theology, became a prominent branch of theology from the early 1980s onwards and has become the prominent branch of liberation theology in India, even today. One of its main features was that its leading figures came from the Dalit Christian communities.[188] Dalits converted to Christianity were initially called Christians of Scheduled Caste Origin or Harijan Christian. Later, the Christian Dalit Liberation Movement (CDLM) in its meeting in Hyderabad in 1984 opted the term Christian Dalits. The National Convention of Catholic Christians in Mumbai in June 1989 approved another new name, Dalit Christians, believing that this would acknowledge the human dignity of the Dalits.[189]

The Dalits as a whole were increasingly threatened by the national corporate companies, especially in the 1970s and 1980s. Additionally, the liberalization of the Indian economy from the early 1990s and the subsequent inflow of multi-national corporate companies increased this threat. These national and international agents together infringed upon the freedom and rights of the poor by taking up their ancestral properties in order to establish huge factories. In several parts of India, Dalits were being displaced from their land by the government in order to launch new gold and coal mine projects. They had no more access to the forests and its resources upon which they had been relying for their livelihood.[190] The ruthless urban exploitation of rural resources that actually belonged to the Dalits of the region further pushed them to utter poverty and unrecoverable situations.

As it was impossible to change one's caste, the only means of liberation for the Dalit people was to revolt. The major means towards this end included Buddhism, the Bhakti movement, Dalit *sahitya* (Dalit literature), and tribal revolts. First of all, the absence of caste-based discrimination in Buddhism made it attractive to Dalits. As a result, a large number of Dalits, including B.R. Ambedkar, embraced Buddhism in October 1956. In a mass conversion event held in Lucknow, the capital city of the Indian state of Uttar Pradesh in 1957, 15,000 Dalits converted to Buddhism. After this, similar conversions took place in different parts of India.[191] Secondly, the Bhakti movement was a form of revolt among Hindus fighting discriminations based on caste and gender. Thirdly, a revitalized Dalit literature began appearing from the 1960s from low caste and outcaste poets and writers. It was mainly based on themes, such as untouchability, poverty, oppression, exploitation, revolution, criticism of the Hindu religious and social system, etc.[192] It often gave the floor to famous revolutionaries, such as Marx, Lenin, Mao, Ho Chi Minh, and Martin Luther King Jr. It was also heavily influenced by revolutionary literature from, inter alia, Pablo Neruda and Vladimir Mayakovsky.[193] The literature helped Dalits in their struggles liberate themselves from the religious and ideological captivity of the Brahminic religiosity and to develop a more secular world view.[194] Fourthly, the economic, social, and educational backwardness of the Dalits became rich soil for radical and revolutionary Marxist movements. The Maoist Naxalite movement, which was birthed in 1967 as a result of the split in the Communist Party of India [Marxist] (CPI[M]), recruited many Dalits into their militant struggle against the landlords.[195]

Yet another significant means of protest was conversion to Christianity.[196] In this process, Dalits would assimilate some of the Christian religious and cultural values, which they did not practically comprehend since their motive was not religious but to escape discrimination.[197] Dalit conversion started with their contact with the

Christian missionaries from the 16th century. Although there were conversions among the Dalits, "mass conversions," as indicated by Robert E. Frykenberg, a scholar of the history of Indian Christianity, took place much later, especially in the 20th century. By the beginning of the 20th century, approximately one million Dalits embraced Christianity.[198]

Within the Christian Church, however, Dalits were subject to another type of discrimination, namely internal inequity. They indeed experienced discrimination from high caste and class Christians. The statement of the National Seminar on Dalit Ideology organized by the Department of Dalit Theology of the Gurukul Lutheran Theological College and Research Institute in Chennai in 1989 clearly articulated this oppression. In fact, without any regional difference, the converted Dalit Christians were considered second class Christians by the high-class Christians.[199] For example, Dalit Christians had separate seats in the churches, separate areas in cemeteries, separate communion cups, and in some places even separate church buildings.[200] However, the Department of Dalit Theology did react against it.

In addition to the discrimination within the Church, Dalit Christians were also marginalized by Hindu fundamentalists. Using local influence, they denied the Dalit Christians the benefits of governmental laws for the emancipation of the Dalit community including compensatory reservations. For instance, the Dalits converted to Christianity are denied of the quota of seats in education and employment, which the non-converts enjoyed, since Article 341(3) of the Constitution of India prescribes that Dalits lose their status as Scheduled Caste once they start following foreign religions like Christianity and Islam. As a result, there is also a tendency among some Dalits Christians to reconvert to Hinduism in order to regain their status as SC.

All of this discrimination fueled the Dalit liberation theologians that held aspirations for Dalit empowerment. They realized that Dalit conversion to Christianity in itself could not be taken as a means of liberation in its fuller sense. Conventional theology and biblical interpretations could not liberate unless and until they were understood from the perspective of the economically and socially unprivileged Dalits. Therefore, such an interpretation of theology and the gospels could be a connecting link between the first and the second generation liberation theologies. Dalit liberation theologians, therefore, should exploit the first-generation liberation theologians' radical interpretation of the gospels.

Despite its slow but progressive transitions, the Church in India still very much mirrored the remnants of the superiority of the traditional Christianity. In its attempt of inculturation, the traditional Church appropriated only the high caste concepts like Vedanta, Yoga, Ashrams, etc. to develop the terms like 'Christian Vedanta,' 'Christian Yoga,' and 'Christian Ashrams.' The reason behind this is that the first Christians of India, especially from the I[st] century to the arrival of the Western missionaries in the 16th century, were said to be high caste Hindus: the priestly class Brahmins. Therefore, this appropriation of the high caste concepts was to highlight the traditional Christians' conformity to their former Brahminic tradition. We assume that such a Brahminic self-distinction of the traditional Christians imposed a secondary status upon the Dalit Christians in the Church.

This being the situation, Dalit Christian leaders came forward to protect the identity and faith of their community, and hence the second-generation liberation theology.[201] Dalit Christian theology, therefore, was a product of the Dalit's self-consciousness of their alienations both inside and outside the Church. The primary goal of Dalit theology was to liberate the Dalits from their historically conditioned inferiority.[202] There had been serious initiatives towards the cause of Dalit liberation starting in the early 1980s. Besides, few non-Dalit Christian theologians, especially from the south Indian states of Kerala and Tamil Nadu, also felt the need of theologizing for and being sensitive to the life problems of the Dalits.[203]

As a matter of fact, Dalit and non-Dalit Christian authors and theologians published extensively on Dalit liberation, giving way to a solid Dalit liberation theology. They interpreted the gospels from a Dalit point of view, even calling Jesus a Dalit. The central figure in Dalit theology is Jesus who experienced the Dalit brokenness in his suffering and death. A clear articulation of this Dalit brokenness is explicit in the Dalit creed developed by M.E. Prabhakar: "Our cries for liberation from harsh caste-bondage were heard by God, who came to us in Jesus Christ to live with us and save all people from their sins."[204] Moreover, in developing a Dalit liberation theology, the Dalit theologians saw an interconnection between the struggle of the Dalits and that of the marginalized and the poor in the Bible. They particularly identified with chapter four of the gospel of Luke, which is about Jesus' prophetic mission for the poor, the oppressed, and the sick. Today the Dalit theologians consider Luke's chapter four as the manifesto of Dalit liberation theology, called the 'Nazareth Manifesto.'

Along with these individual scholars and theologians, a number of Dalit organizations emerged. The CDLM was established in 1984 and actively intervened in matters pertained to Dalit rights. It organized three major rallies – first in Chennai (one in November 1978 and one in September 1988) and then in New Delhi (August 1990) – in order to publicize the problems of the Dalit Christians. The Poor Christian Liberation Movement (PCLM) launched a series of activities, such as awareness programs, vocational training programs, and income-generating programs.[205] The Dalit Liberation Education Trust (DLET), based in Chennai, concentrated on Dalit education.[206] In sum, it aspired toward the implementation of the policies formulated by Mohandas Gandhi and Dr. B.R. Ambedkar for uplifting the poor and the oppressed and the formulation of a Dalit-consciousness among the Dalits.

Unlike the Latin American and first-generation liberation theologies, the Dalit theology did not focus on Marxist social analysis. One of the major reasons of this rejection could be inferred from Kerala's political history. The popular force that in 1957 had led to the victory of the CPI in Kerala was predominantly made up of Dalits and other oppressed people. However, the Dalits observed in the course of time that the Communists did not fully commit itself to constructing a more egalitarian and casteless society. Caste played a significant role in formulating trade unions, electing their leaders, selecting candidates for local elections, etc. The eventual failure of the different Communist governments in Kerala in establishing a classless and casteless society forced the Dalit movements in other parts of the country not to completely rely on Marxist ideologies.[207] Admittedly, the different Communist parties feared that their commitment to the causes of the Dalits and the poor would drive away the middle class and the rich.[208]

E.   The Vatican and Liberation Theology

Having discussed liberation theology in various contexts, it is fitting to examine the Vatican's attitude towards it. Pope John Paul II and CDF Prefect Cardinal Ratzinger – later Pope Benedict XVI – did not continue Paul VI's neutral approach. The latter's simultaneous appreciation and criticism was said to have the specific intention of keeping liberation movements affiliated to the hierarchy. John Paul II and Ratzinger, in contrast, followed the strategy of attacking liberation theology.[209] They thought it had been mushrooming as a radical sect within Christianity, especially in Latin America since the 1960s. They also had the impression that liberation theology received undue emphasis and publicity.[210] John Paul II was uncomfortable with the liberation theology that assimilated Marxist ideologies, violated individual rights, and led the priests and nuns to politics.[211] As he had lived in Communist Poland, he was afraid that Communism would infiltrate into the Church via liberation theology, both in ideological and practical ways.

As a culmination of the Vatican's cautious approach, the CDF, under the prefectship of Cardinal Ratzinger, promulgated two consecutive documents on liberation theology: *Instruction on Certain Aspects of the Theology of Liberation* (1984) and *Instruction on Christian Freedom and Liberation* (1986). Both documents contained criticism against liberation theology, albeit with a different intensity. Although Ratzinger did not clearly spell out the names of any progressive theologians in the two documents, his intent was clear.

The introductory positions of both documents took a mild approach to liberation theology. Instead of a total dismissal right at the beginning, the documents seemed to be appreciative of its positive sides. The first letter recognized the observations of the two milestones in the history of progressive theology, namely the Medellin (1968) and the Puebla (1979) Conferences of the Latin American Bishops (CELAM), and the second one even affirmed the need of a theology of liberation. Additionally, the CDF conveyed that the warning against the dangers of liberation theology "should in no way be interpreted as a disavowal of all those who want to respond generously with an authentic evangelic spirit to the 'preferential option for the poor.'"[212] Some scholars concluded that the documents were not against liberation theology, but only targeted its most exaggerated views.[213]

The CDF, however, also expressed significant criticism of liberation theology, which completely overshadowed its introductory positive affirmation. The major censure of both documents was the idea that the liberation movement initiated a deviation from the mainline Church. The CDF accused liberation theologians of using liberation theology as an instrument to attack the authority of the Church. This argument seems to have emerged due to the general understanding among the liberation theologians that the hierarchical Church belonged to the oppressive class. The CDF's charge went even further and claimed that these theologians promoted the idea of a Church of the poor, in order to oppose the hierarchical Church.[214] As a matter of fact, the CDF tried to detect the elements in liberation theology that in its eyes could negatively affect the orthodoxy of the Church.

First, the CDF claimed that so-called liberation theology was aimed only at the economic, political, and social liberation of the human person, but not at his spiritual liberation. The CDF, in contrast, did not tolerate any attempt to confine the concept of liberation purely to worldly programs. It reminded that the integral liberation of the human being had three indispensable pillars, namely "the truth about Jesus the Savior," "the truth about the Church," and "the truth about man and his dignity."[215] Understandably, the CDF observed that liberation in its real meaning had both spiritual and material realms. It therefore refuted liberation theologians for proclaiming an earthly gospel, which focused only on the material realms and politicized the message of Jesus.[216]

The second criticism dealt with dogmatically relevant themes. The CDF disagreed with liberation theology regarding the concepts of salvation, sin, and freedom. It reproached liberation theologians that their struggle for "human justice and freedom in the economic and political sense constitutes the whole essence of salvation."[217] According to Ratzinger, the primary duty of the Church was to preach the death and resurrection of Jesus that facilitated the liberation from the bondage of sin. It was sin that caused evil and unjust social structures.[218] But liberation theology reduced sin to oppressive and exploitative social structures, which, in effect, negated the concepts of evil and personal sin.[219] The concept of freedom also met with different interpretations. According to the CDF, freedom was more spiritual than social and economic liberation on earth, which only created a better condition for real freedom, but not liberation as such.[220]

Finally and most importantly, liberation theology adopted a Marxist method of social analysis and, according to the CDF, affirmed and promoted class struggle and violent revolutions in society.[221] The CDF rejected the ideological and functional significance of Marxism, but was in principle close to certain Marxist interpretations of revolution and work. Rather surprisingly, it acknowledged the right of the poor to revolt as a last resort — even to recourse to armed struggle in order to establish justice.[222] In this way, it opened the door for dialogue with liberation theologians, emphasizing that their views were not completely different, and just had different accents. While the CDF stressed spiritual liberation, liberation theology put material liberation higher on the agenda.

The CDF documents met with various reactions. Some found the documents positive since they did not fully ignore the demand for structural change in the established systems.[223] Others doubted the genuineness of the CDF's openness and referred to the experience of progressive theologians who were either censured or silenced by the CDF, such as Hugo Assmann (1984) Leonardo Boff and (1984, 1992), to which we will come back in Chapter V. Leonardo Boff was quite clear about the primacy of the anthropological element over the ecclesiastical elements. Calling for a new incarnation of the Church, he made a plea for criticism to promote theological reflection and to eventually disturb dogmatism.[224] Likewise, the Latin American Church considered the documents a blow to human rights.[225] The seemingly positive attitude towards liberation theology, especially in the first chapter of the first document, came under the question of authenticity. Allegedly, this chapter was not originally meant by Ratzinger, but insisted upon by Pope John Paul II as a strategic move to bring liberation theology under the control of the official Church.[226]

In the five sections of this chapter, we have tried to understand liberation theology both from a wider perspective and from particular contexts. The underlining features of liberation theology are its praxis orientation and contextualization, which essentially distinguish it from conventional Christian theology. From our analysis, it is clear that liberation theology is neither against the Church nor its teachings. Rather, it introduced a new mode of theologizing, i.e. a radical rereading of the liberating messages of the gospels. In doing so, liberation theology challenged armchair and Western dominant Christian theology. Both in Latin America and Asia, economic and political oppression as well as other dehumanizing elements in secular and religious domains inspired progressive Christian thinkers to act. Along with the gospels, Marxist ideologies and other local elements – institutions like CELAM, CSR, and religious ideologies like Buddhism – contributed towards constructing a theology of liberation. However, the last section of this chapter blamed the Vatican for its rather discouraging attitude towards liberation theology. The Vatican's criticism of liberation theology was mainly for its preference for political, economic, and social liberation to spiritual liberation, unorthodox perspectives on Church teachings, and

Marxist assimilation. As a matter of fact, this attitude of the mainstream Church weakened progressive theologizing.

Endnotes

[1] Illickamury, "Roman Document on the Theology of Liberation: A Theological Appraisal," 432.

[2] Congregation for the Doctrine of the Faith (CDF) is the body in the Roman Curia responsible for defending Catholic faith and doctrine. The Congregation was founded in 1542 by Pope Paul III (1468-1549) in order to fight the heretical teachings. Today the head of the Congregation is called the Prefect of the Congregation for the Doctrine of the Faith. Until 1968, the Pope was the head of it, and after that, one of the Cardinals was appointed Prefect. Cardinal Franjo Seper became the Prefect in 1968 and he served his office until 1981. Cardinal Joseph Ratzinger (Pope Benedict XVI) took over the office in 1981 and remained as the Prefect till his election as the Pope in 2005. The present Prefect is the Spanish Jesuit Archbishop Luis Francisco Ladaria Ferrer (from July 2017).

[3] For more details, cf. Gerard and Horn, "Left Catholicism in Western Europe in the 1940s," 13-44, and Pasture, "Multi-faceted Relations between Christian Trade Unions and Left Catholicism in Europe," 228-46.

[4] Boffs, *Introducing Liberation Theology*, 11.

[5] Tamez, "Liberation Theology," 5438.

[6] Cousineau, "Preferential Option for the Poor," 374, and Rowland, ed., *The Cambridge Companion to Liberation Theology*, 2.

[7] Turner, *An Introduction to Liberation Theology*, 2.

[8] Rowland, ed., *The Cambridge Companion to Liberation Theology*, 3.

[9] Gutiérrez, *A Theology of Liberation: History, Politics, and Salvation*, 12 and 209.

[10] Rowland, ed., *The Cambridge Companion to Liberation Theology*, 2.

[11] Mattes, "Liberation Theology," 1095.

[12] Castelo Branco, Brazil (1964), Hugo Banzer, Bolivia (1971), and Augusto Pinochet, Chile (1973). Cf. Mattes, "Liberation Theology," 1095.

[13] Mattes, "Liberation Theology," 1097, and Lazar, *Latin American Politics: A Primer* (1971).

[14] Gutiérrez, *A Theology of Liberation*, 61.

[15] Cf. Balasuriya, *Jesus Christ and Human Liberation*, 133.

[16] Sawyer, *The Poor are Many: Political Ethics in the Social Encyclicals, Christian Democracy, and Liberation Theology in Latin America*, 34.

[17] Cf. *OA* 4; Boffs, *Introducing Liberation Theology*, 86-7.

[18] Sweetland, "Liberation Theologies," 484.

[19] Turner, *An Introduction to Liberation Theology*, 1.

[20] Gutiérrez, *A Theology of Liberation*, 175-7.

[21] Schubeck, "Liberation Theology," 260-1.

[22] The Boff brothers clearly elaborated the national and transnational character of liberation theology in *Introducing Liberation Theology* (1987) from Orbis Books, Maryknoll. This work provided a thorough and comprehensive account of liberation theology.

[23] Johnson, "Black Theology," 963-7, and Cone, *Liberation: A Black Theology of Liberation*, 483.

[24] Irvine, "Liberation Theology in Late Modernity: An Argument for a Symbolic Approach," 930-1.

[25] Illickamury, "Roman Document on the Theology of Liberation," 432.

[26] The role of the liberationists in Peru is elaborately discussed in the works like *The Emergence of Liberation Theology: Radical Religion and Social Movement Theory* (Christian Smith, 1991) and *Political Process and the Development of Black Insurgency* (Doug McAdam, 1982). Catholic Action movements in the beginning of the 20th century had also been the precedent forms of liberation theology. For instance, youth and student organizations like *Juventud Obrera Catolica* (JOC), *Juventud Estudiantil Catolica* (JEC), and *Juventud Universitaria Catolica* (JUC). Cf. Peña, "Theology in Peru: An Analysis of the Role of Intellectuals in Social Movements," 35, and McGovern, *Liberation Theology and Its Critics: Toward an Assessment and Planas, Liberation Theology: The Political Expression of Religion*, 24-7 and 106-11.

[27] Morley, Machado, and Pettinato, "Indexes of Structural Reform in Latin America," 14, http://www.rrojasdatabank.info/eclacsa/lcl1166.pdf [accessed 24 June 2015].

[28] Pastor, "Capital Flight from Latin America," 1. For more details about capital flight economic problems in Latin America, cf. Fatehi, "Capital Flight from Latin America as a Barometer of Political Instability," 187-95 and Vos, et al., eds., *Who Gains from Free Trade? Export Led-led Growth, Inequality, and Poverty in Latin America* (2006).

[29] Lazar, "Introduction," 3.

[30] Rush, "CELAM III: Policy is Science, Growth," 55.

[31] Williams, "Liberation Theology and Its Role in Latin America," http://web.wm.edu/so/monitor/issues/07-1/6-williams.htm [accessed 24 June 2015].

[32] Bruneau, "The Catholic Church and Development in Latin America: The Role of the Basic Christian Communities," 538.

[33] Colonnese, ed., *The Church in the Present-Day Transformation of Latin America in the Light of the Council: Second General Conference of Latin American Bishops, Bogotá, 24 August, Medellin, 26 August - 6 September, Colombia, 1968*, 20.

[34] For more details on the relationship between the government and the Church in Cuba, cf. Treto, *The Church and Socialism in Cuba* (1988).

[35] Illickamury, "Roman Document on the Theology of Liberation," 433.

[36] *Chronicle Telegram*, "Pope Excommunicates Castro," 3 January 1962.

³⁷ Cf. Smith, *The Emergence of Liberation Theology*, 80. For more details, also cf. Adriance, *Opting for the Poor*, 20.

³⁸ Brown, *Gustavo Gutiérrez*, 22.

³⁹ Martinez, *Confronting the Mystery of God*, 111.

⁴⁰ Gutiérrez named the institute after bishop Bartolomé de Las Casas (c.1484-1566), the bishop of Santiago, Chile, who vigorously resisted along with many other bishops, the humiliating subjugation of the native Americans by the Spanish military with the blessing of the Church. Pablo, *Death of Christendoms, Birth of the Church*, 28.

⁴¹ Gutiérrez, "The Meaning and Scope of Medellin," 75.

⁴² Sweetland, "Liberation Theologies," 484.

⁴³ Gutiérrez, *Lineas Pastorales de la iglesia en America Latina: Analisis teologico* (1970); Hennelly, ed., *Liberation Theology: A Documentary History* (1990); and Schubeck SJ, "Liberation Theology," 259.

⁴⁴ Gutiérrez, *A Theology of Liberation*, 13. For an elaborate discussion on the theology of liberation for th e poor in Latin America, cf. Gutiérrez, *We Drink from Our Own Wells: The Spiritual Journey of a People* (1984).

⁴⁵ Fabella, "Liberation," 122-3.

⁴⁶ Kappen, *From Faith to Revolution* (Malayalam), 65.

⁴⁷ Larsen, "Camilo Torres: 40 Years after the Death of a Fighter for Latin American Freedom," http://www.marxist.com/camilo-torres-catholic-marxism170206.htm [accessed 2 May 2015].

⁴⁸ Cf. "Chesucristo: The Christification of Che," 78-87.

⁴⁹ Sawyer, *The Poor are Many*, 44.

⁵⁰ Rosario-Cruz, "Remembering Padre Camilo Torres," http://eliacin.com/2009/03/remembering-padre-camilo-torres/ [accessed 8 March 2017].

⁵¹ Cited in Rocha, *Helder, the Gift: A Life that Marked the Course of the Church in Brazil*, 53 (It was the English edition of the Portuguese book *Helder O Dom: uma vida que marcou os rumos da Igreja no Brasil* in 1999).

⁵² Câmara, *Church and Colonialism*, 18-35.

⁵³ Lernoux, *People of God: The Struggle for World Catholicism*, 341. The author has also written another book to elaborate the changes in the Latin American Church especially after the emergence of progressive theological thinking, namely *Cry of the Poor: The Struggle for Human Rights in Latin America, the Catholic Church in Conflict with the U.S. Policy* (1980).

⁵⁴ *Pacem in Terris* (Peace in the World) was an encyclical letter by Pope John XXIII in 1963, exhorting the people to secure and maintain peace in the world.

⁵⁵ Pelton, *Monsignor Romero: A Bishop for the Third Millennium*, 5.

⁵⁶ Brockman, *Romero: A Life*, 62-79.

⁵⁷ Pelton, *Monsignor Romero*, 11. For more details about the last days of Romero, also cf. Brockman, *The Word Remains: A Life of Óscar Romero*, 205-23.

58 Berryman, "Church and Revolution," 2.

59 Rowland, ed., *The Cambridge Companion to Liberation Theology*, 5; Illickamury, "Roman Document on the Theology of Liberation," 434.

60 For details on the Marxist analysis of society, cf. Wright, *Class Structure and Income Determination* (1979).

61 Bruke, ed., *Pedro Arrupe: Essential Writings*, 19, and Zeyen, *Jesuit Generals: A Glimpse into a Forgotten Corner*, 80.

62 Zeyen, *Jesuit Generals: A Glimpse into a Forgotten Corner*, 79; Bruke, ed., *Pedro Arrupe: Essential Writings*, 15-21; and Smith, *The Emergence of Liberation Theology*, 133.

63 For more details about the 31st General Congregation, cf. *Documents of the Thirty-First General Congregation* (s.d.).

64 Hitchcock, *The Pope and the Jesuits: John Paul II and the New Order in the Society of Jesus*, 68.

65 Arrupe's address to the Tenth International Congress of Jesuit Alumni of Europe, Valencia, Spain, 31 July 1973. Arrupe, "Men for Others: Education for social justice and social action today," 173.

66 Pedro Arrupe, "Men for Others," 8.

67 Constitution of the Society of Jesus, 680.

68 Hitchcock, *The Pope and the Jesuits*, 76.

69 GC 32, Decree, 4, no. 28; Centrum Ignatianum Spiritualitatis, *Follow-up on General Congregation XXXII*, 7; and Amaladoss, "Introduction," ix-xii.

70 GC 32, Decree 4, nos. 53-6. Cf. *Documents of the Thirty-Second General Congregation of the Society of Jesus*, 44.

71 Cf. Arrupe, "Letter of Approval and Presentation to the Indian Assistancy," 7-10.

72 Arrupe, "Marxist analysis by Christians," 690.

73 This was clear from Arrupe's visit to Cuba and the meeting with Fidel Castro in 1973. Cf. Bishop, *Pedro Arrupe, S.J: Twenty-Eighth General of the Society of Jesus*, 252.

74 Arrupe, "Marxist analysis by Christians," 690. It was first published in *Civilta Catolica* (4 April 1981), the Jesuit review. Also published by Orbis Books in 1990. Arrupe, "Marxist analysis by Christians," 307-13.

75 Arrupe, "Marxist analysis by Christians," 689.

76 Forrester, *Forrester on Christian Ethics and Practical Theology: Collected writings on Christianity, India, and the Social order*, 407.

77 Hebblethwaite, "The use of Marxism," 5. Cf. http://archive.thetablet.co.uk/article/12th-march-1983/5/the-uses-of-marxism [accessed 14 December 2015].

78 *OA* 34.

79 Puebla Document, no. 545; Arrupe, "Marxist analysis by Christians," 692; and Goff, "Puebla: Bishop's De-liberation?" 43, https://nacla.org/sites/default/files/articles/A01304043_1.pdf [accessed 9 May 2015].

[80] Hebblethwaite, "The use of Marxism," 5, and The Spanish edition of the *L'Osservatore Romano*, 29 November 1981.

[81] Gutiérrez, *A Theology of Liberation*, 61 and Illickamury, "Roman Document on the Theology of Liberation," 435.

[82] Enrique, *A History of the Church in Latin America: Colonialism to Liberation, 1492-1979*, 113.

[83] Barba, "Moral Agency in the Context of Social Sin: The Perspectives of the Latin American Bishops (CELAM) and John Paul II," 49.

[84] Cf. "A New Church: From Medellin to Puebla," http://opcentral.org/resources/wp-content/uploads/sites/11/2014/09/crisis02.pdf [accessed 8 May 2015].

[85] Pfeil, "Toward an Understanding of the Language of Social Sin in Magisterial Teaching," 70. It was the 39th Eucharist Congress that held in Bogotá, Colombia in 1968. The theme of the Conference was 'The Eucharist and the Bond of Love.' Cf. Monte, "Pope Paul's Visit to Bogotá Focuses on Poverty Problems," 1.

[86] Gutiérrez, *A Theology of Liberation*, 118.

[87] Torres and Eagleson, eds., *The Challenge of Basic Christian Communities: Papers from the International Ecumenical Congress of Theology, February 20-2 March 1980, Sao Paulo, Brazil*, 78-80.

[88] The Cuban experiment was a positive and pragmatic alternative by the youth and the progressive section of the clergy to fight poverty and inequality.

[89] Enrique, *A History of the Church in Latin America*, 130.

[90] The Second General Conference, no. 4.

[91] Cleary, *Crisis and Change: The Church in Latin America Today*, 44-6.

[92] Rending, ed., *Christianity and Revolution: Thomas Borge's Theology of Life*, 2, and Girardi, *Faith and Revolution in Nicaragua: Convergence and Contradictions*, 26-32.

[93] Bethel, *Ideas and Ideologies in Twentieth-Century Latin America*, 282. Examples of CEHILA literature are *Para Una Historia de la Evangelizacion en America Latina* [*Toward a History of the Evangelization of Latin America*, 1975] and *Materiales Para una Historia de la Telogia en America Latina* [*Materials for a History of Theology in Latin America*, 1980]. Cf. Foster, "The Historiography of Christianity in Ecumenical Perspective," 122, and Anderson, "The State of Missiological Research," 27.

[94] Braton, "History and Theology," 238.

[95] Angela Alonso, "Hybrid Activism: Paths of Globalization in the Brazilian Environmental Movement," 22, http://onlinelibrary.wiley.com/doi/10.1111/j.2040-0209.2009.00332_2.x/epdf [accessed 7 June 2015].

[96] Schmink and Wood, *Contested Frontiers in Amazonia*, 116.

[97] The funding was mainly from Germany (Brot für die Welt – a communion of evangelical churches), Norway (Norwegian Church Aid, NCA), and the Netherlands (Interchurch Organization for Development Cooperation, ICCO).

[98] Alonso, "Hybrid Activism: Paths of Globalization in the Brazilian Environmental Movement," 24.

[99] Three famous opponents who controlled CELAM III were Roger Vekemans, a Belgian Jesuit and a member of the staff of CELAM, Cardinal Sebastiano Baggio, the president of the Pontifical Commission for Latin America, and Alfonso Lopez Trujillo, the General Secretary of CELAM. Cf. Smith, *The Emergence of Liberation Theology*, 210.

[100] Smith, *The Emergence of Liberation Theology*, 211. Among those excluded, were the bishop and activist Sergio Méndez Arceo (1907-1992), bishop Samuel Ruiz (1924-2011) – both from Mexico –, Miguel Obando y Bravo (°1926) from Nicaragua, and bishop Pedro Casaldáliga (°1928) from Brazil.

[101] Goff, "Puebla: Bishop's De-liberation?" 43, https://nacla.org/sites/default/files/articles/A01304043_1.pdf [accessed 9 May 2015].

[102] *DM* 6.1 and 8.2; *DP*, 461and 421. For more details, cf. Sarmiento, "The Awareness of the Latin American Church to the Reality of the Indigenous Cultures," 3, http://www.sedosmission.org/web/en/mission-articles/doc_view/841-the-awareness-of-the-latin-american-church-to-the-reality-of-the-indigenous-cultures-i-part [accessed 8 May 2015].

[103] Cf. CELAM, *New Evangelization, Human Development, Christian Culture*, 57-148.

[104] *Inculturation* is a term used mainly in the circle of Christian academicians and churchmen to indicate the cultural adaptation by the Church in non-Christian cultures.

[105] *SD* 228b.

[106] To know the terms evangelization and inculturation in detail, cf. CELAM, *New Evangelization, Human Development, Christian Culture*, 57-60.

[107] Sobrino, "The Winds in Santo Domingo and the Evangelization of Culture," 168-70.

[108] Sarmiento, "The Awareness of the Latin American Church to the Reality of the Indigenous Cultures," 6.

[109] CELAM, *New Evangelization, Human Development, Christian Culture*, 168.

[110] Sobrino, "The Winds in Santo Domingo and the Evangelization of Culture," 177.

[111] Department of Census and Statistics, Sri Lanka, http://www.statistics.gov.lk/PopHouSat/CPH2011/index.php?fileName=pop43&gp=Activities&tpl=3 [accessed 19 June 2017].

[112] Some of his widely read books are *Jesus Christ and Human Liberation* (1976), *Sri Lankan Economy in Crisis* (1981), *The Eucharist and Human Liberation* (1979), *Planetary Theology* (1985), and *Mary and Human Liberation* (1994).

[113] Balasuriya, "Organization for Human Rights and Development," 25-30.

[114] Phan, "Reception of and Trajectories for Vatican II in Asia," 315.

[115] The library at Tulana has an extensive collection of books that deal with major Asian religions, Sri Lankan history, and cultural studies.

[116] *Love Meets Wisdom: A Christian Experience of Buddhism* (1988) and *Asian Theology of Liberation* (1988).

[117] Balasuriya, *Jesus Christ and Human Liberation*, 103 and 112

[118] Pieris, *An Asian Theology of Liberation*, 45, and Phan, "Reception of and Trajectories for Vatican II in Asia," 305.

[119] Pieris, "Towards an Asian Theology of Liberation: Some Religio-Cultural Guidelines," 75.

[120] Pieris, *An Asian Theology of Liberation*, 45-50.

[121] Pieris, "Towards an Asian Theology of Liberation," 89.

[122] Balasuriya, *Jesus Christ and Human Liberation*, 103-4.

[123] Balasuriya, *Jesus Christ and Human Liberation*, 112-3.

[124] Balasuriya, *Planetary Theology*, 1-8.

[125] Balasuriya, *Jesus Christ and Human Liberation*, 102.

[126] Pieris, *Asian Theology of Liberation*, 57-8. Jesus' reference to the poor in the gospels (Mk 14, 5-7 = Mt 26, 9-11; Mk 10, 21= Mt 19, 21 = Lk 18, 22; Lk 14, 21; Lk 16, 19-22; Lk 19, 8; Lk 21, 1-4 = Mk 12, 42; Jn 12, 5-8; Jn 13, 29) cannot be limited to the 'poor in spirit' or the 'spiritually poor.' The conventional understanding and teaching of the Church must be re-read taking into consideration the really, materially poor. Cf. Abesamis, "Some Paradigms in Re-reading the Bible in a Third-World Setting," 24-5. Referring to Moltmann, Pieris complained that the Church has disregarded the social dimension of theology. Cf. Pieris, "Christ Beyond Dogma: Doing Christology in the Context of the Religions of the Poor," 228, and Moltmann, *The Trinity and the Kingdom of God*, 199-201.

[127] Sobrino, *The Principle of Mercy: Taking the Crucified People from the Cross*, 1. Besides Buddhism, Marxism also was an area of interest for Pieris, for he depended considerably on Marxist ideologies in analyzing society. Moreover, the interest of bishops Lakshman Wickremesingha and Leo in indigenous Marxist Socialism encouraged Pieris' research.

[128] Balasuriya, *Jesus Christ and Human Liberation*, 103-4.

[129] Schaeffer, *National Catholic Reporter*, 13 (14 June 1996).

[130] Toolan, "Heresy or Hokum in Sri Lanka?" 5.

[131] Balasuriya, *Jesus Christ and Human Liberation*, 119.

[132] Fabella, "Liberation," 123.

[133] Ariarajah, "Liberation in World Religions," 124-5.

[134] Rowland, ed., *The Cambridge Companion to Liberation Theology*, 58; Balasuriya, *Jesus Christ and Human Liberation*, 99.

[135] Balasuriya, *Jesus Christ and Human Liberation*, 118.

[136] Balasuriya, *Jesus Christ and Human Liberation*, 92.

[137] Balasuriya, *Planetary Theology*, 12-3.

[138] Pieris, "What kind of Church do we wish to be?" 428, and Pieris, "Spirituality as Mindfulness: Biblical and Buddhist Approaches," 38-51.

[139] Pieris, "Buddhism as a Challenge for Christians," 181.

[140] Pieris, *Love Meets Wisdom: A Christian Experience of Buddhism*, 87.

[141] Pieris, *Love Meets Wisdom: A Christian Experience of Buddhism*, 83-8.

[142] For a better evaluation of the Christology of Pieris, also cf. Phan, "Jesus Christ with an Asian Face," 406-11.

[143] Amaladoss, *Life in Freedom*, 12, and Miras, "Doing Theology in the Philippines: A Study on the Theological Methods of Selected Filippino Contemporary Theologians," 82.

[144] De Mesa, "Dr. José de Mesa's Online Publications," http://www.dlsu.edu.ph/library/webliography/fpub/jose_demesa.asp [accessed 23 March 2015]. His thesis is entitled "Providence as God's Concern for his People in the Lowland Filipino Context: An Attempt at Theological Re-rooting of a Gospel Theme," (1978).

[145] "Edicio dela Torre," https://www.youtube.com/watch?v=43HMyW0n_X0 [accessed 23 March 2015].

[146] Miras, "Doing Theology in the Philippines," 83.

[147] The term evolved during a discussion meeting of a small group of Christians at St. Scholastica's College in Manila in 1982. Cf. Harris, "The Theology of Struggle: Recognizing Its Place in Recent Philippine History," 96.

[148] Miras, "Doing Theology in the Philippines," 6.

[149] Following are some of the works of the above mentioned Filipino theologians: *The Four Faces of Asia: A Summary Report on the Asian Bishops' Meeting , Manila, November 23-29, 1971* (1971); *The New Christian Morality and the Filipino* (1973); *Filipino Values Revisited* (1988); and *Forming the Filipino Social Conscience: Social Theory from a Filipino Christian Perspective* (1997) by Gorospe; *The Mission of Jesus and the Good News to the Poor* (1987); *A Third Look at Jesus* (1991); and *Backpack of a Jesus-Seeker* (2006) by Abesamis; *In Solidarity with the Culture: Studies in Theological Re-rooting* (1987) by Mesa; and *The Philippines: Christians and the Politics of Liberation* (1986) by De la Torre. Major contributions from other authors to the field of progressive theology included *Points of Departure: Essays on Christianity, Power and Social Change* (edited by Mario Bolasco with De la Torre, 1994); *Red Revolution: Inside the Philippine Guerrilla Movement* (Gregg Jones,1989); and *Marcos Against the Church: Economic Development and Political Repression in the Philippines* (Robert Youngblood, 1990).

[150] For instance, *The Korean Minjung in Christ* (David Kwang-sun Suh, 1991); *Minjung Theology: The People as the Subjects of History* (Commission on Theological Concerns of the Christian Conference of Asia, 1983); and *An Emerging Theology in World Perspective: Commentary on Korean Minjung Theology* (edited by Jung Young Lee, 1988) are some of the major works.

[151] Ahn Byung-Mu was a persistent critique of the dictatorship in Korea. He was also under house arrest for some time. Many were imprisoned, and many others escaped from the country in the 1970s. Cf. Küster, "Jesus and the Minjung Revisited: The Legacy of Ahn Byung-Mu," 1 and Amaladoss, *Life in Freedom*, 4.

[152] Lee, "Minjung Theology: A Critical Introduction," 3.

[153] Liberation theologies in Latin America and other Third World countries had considerable impact on Korean progressive theologizing. At the same time Korean *minjung* theology distinguished itself from other forms of liberation theologies in many ways. While economic oppression and poverty were the central themes of Latin American liberation theology, for Korea it was the political, social, and cultural oppression. It was also the case with other Asian countries.

[154] Rowland, ed., *The Cambridge Companion to Liberation Theology*, 48.

[155] Lee, "Minjung Theology: A Critical Introduction," 7.

[156] The minjung's feelings are due to the oppressive systems existed in Korea. For instance, the massacre of 2,000 Kwangju citizens by the Chun's regime in 1980 left deep feelings of resentment in the minds of the minjung. For more details about the minjung feeling, see the minjung poet Tong Hwan Moon's understanding to the term han. Cf. A. Sung Park, "Minjung Theology: A Korean Contextual Theology," http://www.biblicalstudies.org.uk/pdf/ijt/33-4_001.pdf [accessed 31 March 2015].

[157] Amaladoss, *Life in Freedom*, 4-5.

[158] Küster, "Jesus and the Minjung Revisited," 12.

[159] Hatada, *A History of Korea*, 142. It is cited from Jung Young Lee, "Minjung Theology: A Critical Introduction," endnote, 5, page 25. Lee did not fully agree with Hatada by arguing that there were times Korea was autonomous and powerful enough to fight the invaders. To substantiate his argument Lee also has referred to Sohn Pow-Key, et al., *The History of Korea* (1970).

[160] For more details about *ochlos*, cf. Balz, "ochlos," 553-4; Arndt, Danker, and Bauer, *A Greek-English Lexicon of the New Testament and other Early Christian Literature*, 746. Dχλος is a Greek term that generally means "people," "crowd," or "masses." In the New Testament the term Dχλος occurs 175 times mainly in the gospels, Acts, and Revelation. In general sense of the term, it implies "a relatively large number of people gathered together." The term Dχλος can on the one hand refer to a casual gathering of a great number of people without any particular reference to crowd or throng (cf. Mt 9, 23.25; 15, 35; Mk 2, 4) and on the other hand it can also point to "a gathering of people that bears some distinguishing characteristic or status" mainly in contrast to the rulers (Mt 14, 5; 15, 10; 21, 26; Mk 11, 18, 32). For a detailed understanding of the term from a Korean sociological point of view, cf. Küster, "Jesus and the Minjung Revisited," 5-6.

[161] Still, the manifesto of the *minjung* speaks of the people of God. It is articulated as "The People of God and the Mission of the Church" and which is in fact the documentation of the Christian Conference of Asia (CCA) in 1979. Cf. Volker, "Jesus and the Minjung Revisited: The Legacy of Ahn Byung-Mu," 12.

[162] Cf. Kwang-Sun, "A Biographical Sketch of an Asian Theological Consultation," 15-37.

[163] Lee, "Minjung Theology: A Critical Introduction," 14.

[164] Sung-Hae, "Liberation and Inculturation: Two Streams of Doing Theology with Asian Resources," 67.

[165] Sung-Hae, "Liberation and Inculturation," 74.

[166] Paikada, *Indian Theology of Liberation as an Authentic Christian Theology*, xvii-xviii.

[167] Puthanangady, ed., *Towards and Indian Theology of Liberation*, ix, and Paikada, *Indian Liberation Theology as an Authentic Christian Theology*, xviii.

[168] Paikada, *Indian Liberation Theology as an Authentic Christian Theology*, xviii.

[169] Rayan, "Commonalities, Divergence, and Cross-Fertilizations among Third World Theologies," 198-9.

[170] Jesuit theologian Fr. Samuel Rayan, http://ajournotalks.blogspot.be/2013/05/by-shalet-jimmy-published-in-new-indian.html; Dr. M.M. Thomas, images and memories, http://drmmthomas.blogspot.be/; and Paulose Mar Paulose, http://csipass.blogspot.be/2012/03/blog-post_20.html [accessed 3 November 2017].

[171] Thomas, *Salvation and Humanization*, 2.

[172] For more details, cf. Philip, *The Encounter between Theology and Ideology*, 89-108.

[173] Sugirtharajah, "Liberation Theologies," 129. For more details on Thomas' contribution to Dalit theology, cf. Bird, *M.M. Thomas and Dalit Theology* (2008).

[174] Paulose, "Be a Dissenting Minority," viii.

[175] Amaladoss, "Liberation Theologies and Indian Experiences," 726.

[176] Wilfred, *On the Banks of the Ganges: Doing Contextual Theology*, 95.

[177] Pathil, "What happened at Poonamallee? A Brief Report," 1.

[178] Statement of the Indian Theological Association, "Towards an Indian Theology of Liberation," 20 (no. 48).

[179] Puthanangady, ed., *Towards an Indian Theology of Liberation*, viii.

[180] Paikada, *Indian Theology of Liberation as an Authentic Christian Theology*, 129.

[181] For further details, cf. Sin, "The Future of Catholicism in Asia," 15.

[182] Cf. Kunnath, "Anthropology's Ethical Dilemmas: Reflections from the Maoist Fields of India," 740-52; Arul Raja, "A Dialogue between Dalits and Bible: Certain Indicators for Interpretation," 41; and Kananaikal, *Christians of Scheduled Caste Origin*, 1.

[183] Massey, "Dalit Movements," 220.

[184] Oommen, "The Emerging Dalit Theology: A Historical Appraisal," 19.

[185] Pieris, *An Asian Theology of Liberation*, 103.

[186] Louis, "Discriminated Masses of India: Dalits and Minorities," 10.

[187] Arul Raja, "Negotiating with Contemporary Social Change: Emerging Dalit Theological Sensibilities," 87. For more details, cf. Arulraja, *Jesus the Dalit: Liberation Theology by Victims of Untouchability an Indian Version of Apartheid* (1996).

188 Prabhakar, "Developing a Common Ideology for Dalits of Christian and Other Faiths," 66-8.

189 Prabhakar, "Developing a Common Ideology for Dalits of Christian and Other Faiths," 66-7.

190 Wilfred, *On the Banks of Ganges*, 88; Sobrino and Wilfred, eds., "Globalization and its Victims," (2000). For more details about the landless Dalits, cf. Kunnath, "Smouldering Dalit fires in Bihar, India," 309-25.

191 Cf. Bellwinkel-Schempp, "Roots of Ambedkar Buddhism in Kanpur," 221-44.

192 Gokhale-Turner, "Bhakti or Vidroha: Continuity and Change in Dalit Sahitya," 29. Untouchability is abolished in India by law. Article 17 of the Constitution of India states that its practice in any form is forbidden.

193 Gokhale-Turner, "Bhakti or Vidroha," 37.

194 Pieris, *An Asian Theology of Liberation*, 104. For more details, cf. Nemade, "The Revolt of the Underprivileged," 113-23 (taken from the endnote of Aloysius Pieris, *An Asian Theology of Liberation*, 135).

195 For recent examples, cf. Kunnath, "Smouldering Dalit fires in Bihar, India," 314-5.

196 Arul Raja, "Negotiating with Contemporary Social Change," 85.

197 Jayakumar, *Dalit Consciousness and Christian Conversion: Historical Resources for a Contemporary Debate*, 306-7.

198 Frykenberg, *Christianity in India: From the Beginnings to the Present*, 33-4.

199 For more details, cf. Nirmal, ed., *Towards a Common Dalit Ideology*, 130, and Prabhakar, "Developing a Common Ideology for Dalits of Christian and Other Faiths," 67.

200 Manickam, *Studies in Missionary History: Reflections on a Culture-contact*, 173.

201 Prabhakar, "Developing a Common Ideology for Dalits of Christian and Other Faiths," 66-8.

202 Pui-lan, *Discovering Bible in Non-Biblical World*, 12; Arul Raja, "Reading the Bible from the Dalit Location," 87-91; and Webster, *The Dalit Christians: A History*, 35-6.

203 Some of the prominent figures in this field are George Koilparambil, Masilamani Azariah (a Bishop in the Church of South India [CSI]), Xavier Irudayaraj, Jose Kananaikil, Arvind P. Nirmal, James Massey, and M.R. Arulraja. Koilparampil, *Caste in the Catholic Community in Kerala* (1982); Azariah, *The Unchristian Side of the Indian Church: The Plight of the Untouchable Converts* (1985); Irudayaraj, *Emerging Dalit Theology* (1990); Kananaikil, *Christians of Scheduled Caste Origin* (1990); Nirmal, *Towards a Common Dalit Ideology* (1991); Webster, *The Dalit Christians: A History* (1994); Pui-lan, *Discovering Bible in Non-Biblical World* (1995); Das and Massey, *Dalit Solidarity* (1995); Arulraja, *Jesus the Dalit: Liberation Theology by the Victims of Untouchability, an Indian Version Apartheid* (1996); Jayakumar, *Dalit Consciousness and Christian Conversion* (1996); Robinson, *Christians of India* (1996); and Massey and John, *Rethinking Theology in India: Christianity in the Twenty-first Century* (2013).

204 Cited from Robinson, *Christians of India*, 199-200.

[205] "PCLM: Poor Christian Liberation Movement," http://www.dalitchristian.com/index.php/about-pclm [accessed 6 April 2015].

[206] Raj, *Dalit Theology and Dalit Liberation: Problems, Paradigms and Possibilities*, 39.

[207] Ayrookuzhiel, "The Ideological Nature of the Emerging Dalit Consciousness," 87-8.

[208] A.K. Gopalan, a Communist leader from Kerala commented in 1968 that the Communist parties should give up the fear of losing the support of the middle class and the rich. Cf. Sugirtharaj, "Developing a Common Dalit Ideology: Is it a Myth of Reality?" 34.

[209] Pasture, "Religious Globalization in Post-war Europe: Spiritual Connections and Interactions," 96.

[210] For more details in this regard, cf. Budde, *The Two Churches: Catholicism and Capitalism in the World-System* (1992); Burdick, *Looking for God in Brazil: The Progressive Catholic Church in Urban Brazil's Religious Arena* (1993); Keogh, *Church and Politics in Latin America, Levine, Popular voices in Latin American Catholicism* (1990); and Drogus, "The Rise and Decline of Liberation Theology: Church, Faith, and Political Change in Latin America," 465-8.

[211] Cf. McGovern, *Liberation Theology and Its Critics*, 15-9.

[212] CDF, *Instruction on Certain Aspects of the Theology of Liberation*, introduction.

[213] Illickamury, "Roman Document on the Theology of Liberation," 440.

[214] CDF, *Instruction on Certain Aspects of the Theology of Liberation*, X. 13; XI. 15; XI. 10.

[215] CDF, *Instruction on Certain Aspects of the Theology of Liberation*, XI. 5. Originally this idea belonged to John Paul II, who conveyed it during his opening address at Puebla Conference in 1979 (Section I. Para.1). See also, cf. Illickamury, "Roman Document on the Theology of Liberation," 439-40.

[216] *Christian Century*, "Backing for the Poor," 408-9.

[217] CDF, *Instruction on Certain Aspects of the Theology of Liberation*, VI. 4; X. 6.

[218] CDF, *Instruction on Christian Freedom and Liberation*, no. 75.

[219] CDF, *Instruction on Certain Aspects of the Theology of Liberation*, introduction; IV. 2, 12, and 15.

[220] CDF, *Instruction on Christian Freedom and Liberation*, no. 31.

[221] Rayan, "Instruction on Christian Freedom and Liberation," 228.

[222] CDF, *Instruction on Christian Freedom and Liberation*, nos. 78-83.

[223] Cf. Rayan, "Instruction on Christian Freedom and Liberation," 236-9.

[224] Boff, *Jesus Christ Liberator: A Critical Christology for Our Time*, 44-6.

[225] Illickamury, "Roman Document on the Theology of Liberation," 431; Cox, *The Silencing of Leonardo Boff: The Vatican and the Future of World Christianity*, 178-88; and Bahmann, *A Preference for the Poor: Latin American Liberation Theology from a Protestant Perspective*, 50.

[226] Brown, "The Roman Curia and Liberation Theology," 552-4.

3

A Biographical Introduction

Sebastian Kappen was born in Kodikulam, a remote village in Idukki in the British princely state of Travancore, on 4 January 1924.[1] Travancore, being located at the southernmost tip of the Indian subcontinent, consisted of the present central and southern Kerala, and the district of Kanyakumari, which is in present day Tamil Nadu. It was an independent kingdom and between 1798 and 1805 became a princely state in British India. Travancore was neither conquered by nor annexed to British India, but established a subsidiary alliance with British India and was part of the system of indirect rule. The British East India Company provided protection to the state, which in return had to pay a fixed annual tribute to the Company. Until the beginning of the second half of the 20th century Kodikulam was part of the Karimannur village union. The social system was oppressive. Landless tenants worked under the landlords and were paid in the form of paddy or other agricultural produce. Agriculture was the major source of income for the landlords and livelihood for the tenants. In 1951, a new panchayat (local body of governance system in the Indian subcontinent) was created with an area of 45 square kilometers and a population of 10,000, making Kodikulam its headquarters: twelve kilometers away from the nearest town Thodupuzha.[2]

This chapter begins with an investigation into Kappen's childhood and education, including his Jesuit formation in different parts of India.

Later, we analyze his two influential stays abroad – as a doctoral student in Rome (1959-62), and as a visiting professor in Louvain-la-Neuve, Belgium (1970). This will provide an overview of the ideologies and personalities that influenced and motivated Kappen. Then we examine his activism back in India from 1962 to his death in 1993. Finally, we will briefly analyze his major works, which will expectantly facilitate an overview of Kappen's thoughts and activism.

A.   Childhood and Education

Kappen was born into a traditional and land-owning Syro-Malabar Christian family. Since it was believed that the Syrian Christians' ancestors had been converted from high castes, they enjoyed high social status and respect in society.[3] Many of them possessed land and were economically stable like other high caste Hindus. Although the Syrian Christians were a minority within the region, numerous landless *kudiÿans* (tenants) worked under them all throughout the year for their livelihood.[4] Kappen later wrote in his unfinished autobiographical notes that as a young boy he knew every plant and tree in the family property; his mind and body, and above all his very being were intimately bound up with the Mother Earth.[5] He always enjoyed assisting his father Kuriakose (derived from the Syriac Aramaic name Quriaqos) in agricultural works, which helped him realize the dignity of manual labor.[6] The biotic-spiritual bond with his father helped him nourish and sustain. He also had great intimacy with his mother Annamma (a culturally loaded name with the meaning 'the one who provides food'), whom he compared to a fathomless ocean. He remembered her as a nurturing, emotionally mature woman who cared for the family the best she could. In fact, in the family, Kappen learned the dignity of hard work and the nobility of personal character from his father and mother respectively.

Figure 8. From left: Fr. Kuriakose Kappen Sr. (1856-1937), Monsignor J.C. Kappen (1898-1970), Fr. Kuriakose Kappen Jr. (1890-1956), and Fr. G.C. Kappen SJ (1925-83).[7]

The Kappen family had many important religious members who influenced the young Sebastian. Fr. Kuriakose Sr. (1856-1937) was the senior-most among them. He founded the St. Ann's Church in Kodikulam in 1902 as a parish church in the Archeparchy of Ernakulamm-Angamaly.[8] Kappen's father's uncle and namesake was a well-known local priest (Fr. Kuriakose Kappen Jr., 1890-1956) who pioneered recording the history of the Kappen family. Monsignor J.C. Kappen (1898-1970; Monsignor is an honorary title the Catholic Church gives to the clergy for their valuable service to the Church) worked as the vice-postulator of the canonization of St. Alphonsa (1910-46), the first saint from Kerala. Fr. G.C. Kappen (1925-83) belonged to the Society of Jesus and worked as a pastor in the diocese of Calicut. However, this does not mean that all of the Kappens were entirely pious. Fr. Kuriakose Jr. was known for his rebellious nature. His criticism of the Church hierarchy led to his ecclesiastical suspension.[9] Kappen's father was also critical in religious matters. Along with the basic lessons on the humanizing character of work and the need for intimacy with nature, he gave the young Sebastian food for his intellect and stimulated him to think widely and secularly. Kappen learned from his father that religion and religious matters had a hypocritical side. The father instilled in his son a passion and love for personal development. No wonder, Kappen's most cherished memory of his father was the words of advice he received: "wherever you go, try to excel."[10]

Even years before Kappen received this *mantra,* he was deeply motivated by his father to excel in whatever he did. Kappen's middle school was St. Joseph's English school (established in 1934) at Karimannoor, 8.5 kilometers away from his home in Kodikulam. The young boy was very good in studies and other extracurricular activities like arts and sports. He was particularly interested in Malayalam and English languages and literature. As Travancore was a princely state in British India, English was treated as a prominent language. Speaking English was considered a status symbol that provided job opportunities. The young Kappen was delighted to participate in debates and to argue with those who were skilled in English.[11]

After successfully completing middle school, Sebastian joined a high school established in 1859 by Carmelite Fathers (CMI) in Vazhakulam, twenty kilometers away from Kodikulam. According to him, the most enriching thing he received in the school was his acquaintance with the intellectual arguments of Thomas Aquinas to prove the existence of God. As he was a boarding student, Kappen did not go home daily. This provided him with ample opportunity to dialogue with his teachers and the priests who were in charge of the boarding. It was one of the Carmelite priests who introduced Aquinas to Kappen. Even though Kappen could not fully grasp the argumentations of Aquinas, his acquaintance with the great 13th-century theologian and philosopher sparked off his intellectual quest at a young age.[12]

The philosophical arguments for the existence of God presumably influenced Kappen very much. He tried to integrate both intellectual and spiritual matters during his school days at Vazhakulam. As a boarding student he attended daily Mass, spent hours in prayer and meditation, and strictly adhered to other spiritual activities like weekend confession. He also developed a special devotion to the Sacred Heart of Jesus, with the help of *Jesus, King of Love* (1929, published by the Convent of the Sacred Hearts and Public Adoration) authored by Mateo Crowley

(1875-1960), a Peruvian Catholic priest and the founder and apostle of the enthronement of the Sacred Heart.[13] Crowley encouraged the enthronement of the Sacred Heart in families and promoted adoration during night. He was an ardent devotee of the Sacred Hearts of Jesus and Mary and once said that he could not think of anything other than becoming a religious. Kappen's own words that he was often "transported to an ecstasy of devotion with tears rolling down" his eyes indicate that he was deeply challenged by Crowley.[14]

In fact, Crowley had an Indian connection. On a visit to India he reached Cochin, Kerala on 18 August 1939. Fr. Aurelio OCD received him at St. Joseph's Pontifical Seminary, Aluva. From 21 August to 23 September 1939, Crowley preached retreats to the priests at Kottayam, Changanacherry, and Trivandrum. Afterwards, he went to Tuticorin in Tamil Nadu to visit the families who had already enthroned the Sacred Heart. He then traveled further to the north, inter alia, to Goa, Bangalore and Mylapore, where he continued to conduct retreats for priests, nuns, seminarians, and lay people. After spending five months in India, Crowley left for Ceylon on 24 January 1940.[15]

Although Kappen and Crowley did not meet in person, the former must have developed special devotion to the Sacred Hearts of Jesus and Mary during or shortly after the latter's visit. Eventually, however, this new pietism and Kappen's intellectual quest formed an internal conflict between reason and faith. It provided a sense of sinfulness that made a teenager's normal thoughts, words, deeds, and desires seem impure and wrong. It also developed a sense of scrupulosity. Kappen confessed later that the sense of sin paralyzed his creativity and "killed once and for all the poet and artist" in him.[16] Arguably, he developed his piety at the cost of his reasoning power and creative thinking.

Kappen's personal conflict seems to have made him neutral regarding the socio-political developments in British India in the 1930s and 1940s. He did not indeed engage himself in the nationalist or reformist movements, including the fight for independence under the leadership of Mohandas Gandhi. Kappen only took part in some of the anti-imperialist campaigns, but later pointed out that it was not his "political conviction" but "youthful excitement" that had prompted him to do so.[17] In other words, Gandhi was not an inspiration in the life of the young Sebastian Kappen. Although Gandhi's ideas on Indian and Western Christianity, conversion and indigenous identity of Christians in India, contribution of Christianity to national life,[18] etc. had been circulating all over India, Kappen did not seem to be influenced by those ideas. Of course, the lack of political conviction could be due to many reasons. Kappen himself acknowledged later that he was confined to his family, school, and parish.[19]

On 27 June 1944, at the age of twenty, Kappen joined the Society of Jesus to mark the initial formation of novitiate for two years. Interestingly, it was one of the Syro-Malabar Carmelite priests (CMI), Fr. Florence, who was aware of the intellectual capacity of Kappen during his school days (he was in charge of the boarding house at Vazhakulam when Kappen stayed there), instructed him to join the Society of Jesus, believing that Jesuit formation would foster his intellectual pursuit.

Although there existed Rite differences, it was common in Kerala for candidates from the Syro-Malabar Catholic Rite to join religious congregations and orders in the Roman Catholic tradition. This inter-ritual flow (mainly from Syro-Malabar to Latin Rite) was due to several factors. First, there were only a few indigenous Syro-Malabar religious congregations in Kerala; second, there was a strong presence of Latin religious congregations; and third, the Syro-Malabar Church had only a limited jurisdiction. Indeed, while the Roman Catholic Church enjoyed jurisdiction all over India, the Syro-Malabar Church's area of jurisdiction was limited. As the religious congregations in this church could not accommodate the large number of young people who aspired to religious life, these candidates joined the Latin congregations, which provided them with the opportunity to work outside the jurisdiction of the Syro-Malabar Church. More than half of the Catholic missionaries working in India (including both foreign and local) were from the Syro-Malabar Church.

Kappen's priestly formation took place in four places, namely Calicut (Kerala), Kodaikanal (Tamil Nadu), Mangalore (Karnataka), and Pune (Maharashtra). The first two phases of his formation, i.e. his novitiate and juniorate, were at Calicut. During the two years of novitiate (1944-46) at Christ Hall in Calicut, Kappen learned more about Western Christian spirituality from his Novice-Master Fr. Aldo Maria Patroni SJ (1904-88). Fr. Patroni was originally from Sernio, in the Province of Sondrio in Italy. Shortly after his priestly ordination on 21 November 1934, he came to Kerala, where he later, in 1948, would become the last foreign bishop of Calicut. His noble character attracted young Kappen and this soon grew into a deeper master-student relationship. While the master introduced Western, and especially Jesuit spirituality to Kappen during their evening walks, the student showed him the world of Malayalam. During his subsequent juniorate, from 1946 to 1949, Kappen learned Latin, Greek, and English while also studying Biblical history and spirituality. Later, he would acknowledge that he went through the process of de-indigenization during those years, but also admitted that this formation gifted him with an open mind to Western culture.[20]

Eventually, by 1949, Kappen equipped himself to more seriously pursue his search for truth. The Society sent the 25-year old Kappen to the Sacred Heart College of Shembaganur in Kodaikanal, a beautiful hill city in the territory of the present-day state of Tamil Nadu, to study classical scholastic philosophy, Thomistic in particular, for three years.[21] Candidates aspiring for Catholic priesthood traditionally underwent philosophical formation for a period that slightly varied according to the different modes of formation in different religious orders or dioceses. Normally, the candidates did philosophical studies before they started theological formation, since philosophy is considered the handmaid of theology (*ancilla theologiae*). One of the most important philosophers he further explored during the philosophical formation was the philosopher cum theologian Thomas Aquinas (1225-74) of whom Kappen had acquired preliminary knowledge during his schooling. Aquinas was known for integrating reason and faith, arguing that both originated in God and were inevitable in finding the truth. He was famously known in the academia of both philosophy and theology for his five arguments for the existence of God. Learning Thomistic philosophy helped young Kappen, as he later recalled, to concentrate on the themes he engaged himself with.[22]

At the Sacred Heart College, Kappen was also inspired by the advice of the Spanish Jesuit priest-professor Emilio Ugarte (1903-?) who suggested he read more classical works. Fr. Ugarte was very much connected with the formation programs of the Jesuits in India. He was born in Murguia-Amezaga, Spain. After joining the Jesuits in 1919 he travelled to Shembaganur in Tamil Nadu (India) in 1921. In 1929, he went to Enghien, Belgium, for his theological studies and returned to India in 1937 as a professor in the Sacred Heart College of Shembaganur. He remained there till his retirement in 1985.[23] Ugarte taught philosophical psychology and related subjects and wrote many books.[24] Simultaneously, he was very much concerned with social justice. In Shembaganur he started a home for the handicapped and constructed homes for the farm-workers of Sacred Heart College. Last but not least, Ugarte did a great and long service to intellectual dialogues. In Ugarte "East and West, tradition and modernity, science and humanities, and the human and the transcendent seem to blend so effortlessly."[25] It was no wonder that the young Kappen, who always sought truth was inspired by such a great psychologist-philosopher. Several of Ugarte's thoughts, such as the sense of social justice and the combination of Eastern and Western traditions, will return in Kappen's later life in a more sharpened version.

Kappen secured a Licentiate in philosophy from Sacred Heart College in 1952 and went to St. Joseph's Interdiocesan Seminary, Mangalore, Karnataka, to teach for a period of two years. St. Joseph's was first established in 1763 and reestablished in 1878 when the Jesuits took it over from the Carmelites. The seminary initially was of the diocese of Mangalore. When the diocese was bifurcated into two dioceses – Mangalore and Calicut – in 1923, it became an interdiocesan seminary.[26]

From 1952 to 1954 Kappen taught at St. Joseph's. His appointment was a part of the *practicum* of the candidates under formation, especially after the philosophical studies. During this period of regency, candidates would be appointed either for teaching in seminaries or doing administrative works in various institutions. Usually, the superiors selected candidates with good academic interest and teaching skills. Kappen's appointment was an acknowledgement of his intellectual caliber and his progress over the past years. His engagement at St. Joseph's helped him acquire practical and general knowledge and consolidate and conceptualize the philosophical convictions that he had earned during his studies at Sacred Heart College.

Another significant period in his formation was from 1954 to1957, which he spent doing his theological studies in De Nobili College, the Jesuit formation house at Pune where Fr. Ugarte was Rector between 1967 and 1972. De Nobili College is one of the biggest and oldest Jesuit institutions in India. In Pune, Kappen could learn more about the ecclesiastical system, the hierarchical phenomena, and the intellectual and academic character of traditional theology.[27] This theological formation was the last phase of priestly formation. Kappen was ordained priest on 24 March 1957, at the age of thirty-three.[28]

As his superiors wanted him to be a seminary professor, he was asked to study Indian philosophy and religion. Kappen started exploring Indology. His prior basic knowledge in Sanskrit helped his further reading about Indian history. At Pune, he acquainted himself with Indian sources, such as the Hindu sacred literature of Vedas and Upanishads. His study on Indian philosophy and Hindu scriptures enabled him to acquire proper knowledge about Indian schools of thought and religions. An in-depth knowledge about the Indian philosophical and religious tradition allowed him at a later stage to criticize the religious institutionalization through his books and articles.

Kappen combined this with another two years of formation called Tertianship at Pune. It is the final period of formation in the Society of Jesus. During this period, he underwent, like any other tertian, a silent thirty-day retreat to focus on the spirituality of St. Ignatius of Loyola. He finished his Tertianship in 1959.

B.   Inspiration through Foreign Contacts

In 1959, the Society of Jesus sent him to Rome to pursue doctoral studies at the Pontifical Gregorian University, which initially was called Roman College and established by the Jesuits in 1551. Samuel Rayan had been doing his studies at Gregorian as Kappen's predecessor until 1960. Kappen was in total conformity with the traditional religious interpretations of the scriptures both of Christianity and Hinduism when he left for Rome. The one and a half decade-long formation in India had turned him into an academically disciplined person enabling himself to cope up with the intellectual West. Rome would now transform him into a liberal and progressive thinker.

There are still different accounts of Kappen's higher studies in Rome. While authors like Ajit Muricken wrote that Kappen's superiors wanted him to study theology, other scholars like Sebastian Painadath SJ argued that Kappen went to Rome for doctoral studies in Marxism. Muricken claimed that at a certain point Kappen decided to write a thesis on St. Augustine, despite his expertise in Indology, but at the end landed on Marxian thought on religion. In Muricken's view, an immediate inspiration for Kappen to study Marxism was the newly elected Communist government in Kerala in 1957 and the conflict between the Kerala Catholic Bishops Conference and the government.[29] Kappen, being a priest fully conformed to traditional theological interpretations, took it for granted that Marxism was top to bottom anti-Christian. According to Muricken, Kappen, after dropping his plan to study theology, dreamed of studying Marxism to equip himself with intellectual arguments to fight Communism after his return to Kerala.[30]

Interestingly, as Kappen delved into the writings of Karl Marx in Rome, he found them inspirational. In particular Marx's "Ökonomisch-philosophische Manuskripte" (1844) prompted Kappen to learn more about religious alienation and praxis. The "Economic and Philosophical

Manuscripts" were a collection of Marx's writings in Paris between April and August 1844. It was an unfinished work and rough draft. According to Muricken, Kappen learned German to study the manuscripts in their original language, but in 1959 the Foreign Languages Publishing House in Moscow published the English translation. However, we may assume that Kappen worked with the German version, to which he systematically referred. The writings mainly dealt with economics and philosophy in order to discuss the worker's alienation from the product. Marx severely criticized religion for alienating the human being from what he is.[31] This critic of religion challenged the traditional Christian in Kappen.

Eventually, Kappen's further reflections led him to writing a doctoral thesis on the Marxian critic of religion under the guidance of Joseph de Finance (1904-2000), a French Jesuit and professor at the Pontifical Gregorian University. He defended his doctoral dissertation on 14 April 1961, two years after his arrival in Rome. His thesis is titled "Praxis and the Emancipation of Man from Religious Alienation according to the Economic and Philosophical Manuscripts of Karl Marx." This title is slightly different from what is given in later publications, namely "Religious Alienation and Praxis according to Marx's Economic and Philosophical Manuscripts of 1844."[32] Contrary to the presupposed idea that Kappen wrote in German or in French, the dissertation is in English.[33] However, his expertise in French and German helped him make use of the literature in those languages for his work.

The dissertation does not have any acknowledgements and does not give the names of the jury members. Including the introduction, it consists of six chapters: "Introduction: Biography of Marx," "Religious consciousness in general," "Economic praxis and genesis of religion," "Praxis and the emergence of the new man," "The consciousness of the new man," and "An evaluation." It spreads out in 240 pages including a bibliography of 6 pages. Kappen referred to 52 sources in total, of which 12 are the original writings of Marx, and the remaining 40 are secondary literature. Among the 52 sources, only two are in English, the rest being either in German or in French.

Pages 61 to 87 deal with the central theme of the dissertation, namely alienation. Kappen examines alienation from products, productivity, and from the essence of man. In the concluding part (pages 222-34), he comments on why Marx criticized religion and wrote on religious alienation. He identifies two major reasons: first, the intellectual prejudices of Marx and second, the inefficacy and exaggerated other-worldliness of Christianity. Kappen thus simultaneously criticized both Marx and (institutionally established) Christianity. Although he would further develop these thoughts over the following decades, it is important to note that he had already then phrased them.

Having completed his studies in Rome, Kappen returned to India in 1962 and started working in the Lumen Institute in Ernakulam, Kerala, together with Samuel Rayan, who by then was back from Rome. During this time, Kappen worked also as the chaplain of the Newman Association, a movement of learned laity who often met (and meet) in local circles to discuss political, social, religious, and other topics.[34] Back in Kerala, Kappen did not intervene in political developments. After the collapse of their first government in 1959, the Communists came back to power in 1967. The political society in Kerala was once again witness to various tensions between the Church and the government over the new educational policy. Kappen's anti-institutional mind remained silent when the Communist government of Kerala issued the Kerala University Bill in 1967 to subject the community-run private colleges. When the Keralite bishops reacted against this bill, Kappen responded simply by saying that he was not interested in dealing with such issues. He sustained this attitude even in the following years, continuing to tell his friends that he was not an activist and he did not want to be known under any particular label or title.[35]

In spite of his stay abroad, Kappen did not seem to maintain intensive contacts with foreign theologians or clergymen. Only in the early 1970s, did he go abroad again. He visited the Maryknoll Seminary in New York as a guest professor in 1970.[36] Unfortunately, we do not have more details of this visit. Fr. Aurel Brys SJ later commented that

Kappen opened doors for himself, and it was reasonable for the pro-progressive Maryknoll Seminary to invite him as a guest lecturer.[37] His second stay, in 1970, was in Leuven, and this is better documented since this was an element in a long friendship with François Houtart, who became a major source of inspiration in Kappen's academic life.

François Houtart (1925-2017) was a Belgian Catholic priest and Marxist sociologist who in 2009 won the UNESCO-Madanjeet Singh Prize for the promotion of tolerance and non-violence, and was a Nobel Peace Prize nominee in 2011. He was ordained a Catholic priest in 1949, obtained a licentiate in Socio-Political Sciences from the Catholic University of Leuven in 1952, and completed his post-graduation from Chicago University in 1954. Houtart became professor of sociology at the University of Louvain – initially in Leuven and from the early 1970s onwards in Louvain-la-Neuve – and in 1956 founded the Centre for Socio-Religious Research (CSRR).[38]

Houtart was close to the working-class community, especially via the Young Christian Workers movement (YCW– founded in Belgium by Joseph Cardijn in 1924; better known under its French name Jeunesse Ouvrière Chrétienne [JOC]). He increasingly became convinced that the working class was against the Church because of the latter's alliance with the bourgeoisie. In an interview from 2005, Houtart recalled situations from the 1950s in Brussels and other European cities, confirming how far the Church stood from the poor and how few priests sided with the working class.[39]

In the 1950s, Houtart regularly traveled to Latin America, especially to Cuba, Haiti, Nicaragua, and Brazil. There, he was acquainted with the working class, but also got to know bishops and conducted social and religious research. Some of his noted books in English are based on these experiences, such as *The Challenge to Change* (1964), *The Church and the Latin American Revolution* (1965), and *Church and Revolution* (1970). Houtart also had an influence on the Second Vatican Council. The Brazilian Archbishop Hélder Câmara, who was the vice-president of the Latin American Bishops Conference (CELAM), asked Houtart just before the start of the Council to prepare a synopsis of his research and to distribute it among all the Council fathers in order to give them an in-depth understanding of the situation in Latin America.[40]

Houtart actively participated in the Second Vatican Council and served as the secretary of the sub-committee which drafted the Pastoral Constitution called *Gaudium et Spes*. This document became a powerful instrument in the social teaching of the Catholic Church in the post-conciliar years. Houtart revealed that the Council was a unique opportunity to introduce certain radical transformations in the Church.[41]

Appreciating his great service in the Second Vatican Council, the Latin American bishops invited Houtart to assist in preparing the Medellin conference of 1968. However, he did not attend the conference since he was banned by the Vatican. The Holy Sea indeed issued a veto on him because immediately after the Council he was very much involved in the political and social problems in Vietnam by cooperating with the Communists. However, the Vatican disciplinary action did not prevent Houtart from further establishing contacts with other Asian countries. In 1968, Tissa Balasuriya invited him to Sri Lanka. On his way, Houtart first visited Kerala and then some other Asian countries like Japan, Korea, Hong Kong, Indonesia, and the Philippines. It was during this travel that Houtart and Kappen met for the first time.

The meeting between Houtart and Kappen was the beginning of a new collaboration, especially in the area of sociology of religion. Kappen's proficiency in French facilitated their exchange of ideas and their influence on each other. After their meeting in 1968, Houtart read Marx and literature on Marx more closely in the library of the University of Peradeniya (Kandy, Sri Lanka) and Kappen gained a new interest in using Marxist means in social analysis.[42] Prior to the meeting, Kappen had indeed written very few articles with a secular nature. From the late 1960s onwards, he started publishing on revolution, liberation, development, etc. Just as Houtart was active within youth organizations in Belgium, Kappen started working for and among the youth in Chennai in the 1970s. Along with this active life with people, both of them were also were very much interested in exploring Buddhism for its progressive ideologies.

Houtart's visit to Asia, especially India and Sri Lanka, was indeed a turning point in his life. He learned more about Hindu and Buddhist cultures and decided to do his doctoral studies on Buddhism in the context of Sri Lanka. He eventually attained his PhD on *Religions and Ideology in Sri Lanka* from the Catholic University of Leuven in 1974 and published it as a book in Bangalore in the same year with the help of the Theological Publications in India (TPI).[43] Houtart also worked in the editorial boards and advisory bodies of many journals including the Catholic journal of *Concilium* (1960-99), which published one of Kappen's articles.[44] Houtart continued publishing on Sri Lanka and even India in the following years with Geneviève Lemercinier.

Geneviève Lemercinier was a collaborator and assistant of Houtartat at the Université catholique de Louvain in Louvain-la-Neuve, and a co-founder of the Centre Tricontinental (CETRI), a non-governmental organization founded in Louvain-la-Neuve in 1976 with the goal of promoting justice and social security in Asia, Latin America, and Africa. Interestingly, her doctoral dissertation was on Kerala: *Religion et Ideologie au Kerala: Modes de Production et Fonctions Sociales de la Religion*, from the Université catholique de Louvain in 1977. CSRR published it in 1983 under the title *Religion and Ideology in Kerala*. According to Houtart, Lemercinier was helpful in his academic life, especially with her theoretical and methodological approach, which complemented his philosophical approach. In his words, "her methodological competence in the elaboration of the cultural models and her vast knowledge of the literature [...] were of immense assistance."[45] He appreciated her for the scientific contribution to sociology of religion at the University and of CETRI for over 20 years. Moreover, she accompanied Houtart in his travels to and work in Asia and Latin America for more than thirty years.

After their meeting in 1968, Houtart and Kappen kept in contact. The former invited the latter for a return visit and in February and March 1970, Kappen was a guest professor of ecclesiology at the CSRR at the Université catholique de Louvain.[46] During this time Kappen stayed at Mrs. Brys (born Diane Schelstraete, in Drongen), the mother of the Jesuit missionary Aurel Brys who worked in Ranchi, India. Fr. Brys was not in Belgium at the time, but still recalls his mother's words about Kappen. For her, Kappen was a quiet and gentle man who was constantly reflective. After his return to India, Kappen contacted Mrs. Brys twice, once to thank her, before she died in 1996.[47]

Over the following years, the contact between Houtart and Kappen continued. The former wrote a long introduction to the latter's book *Jesus and Freedom* in 1977. In the preface of the book, Kappen acknowledged that Houtart was a continuous source of inspiration, especially for his "deep humanity and profound concern for the underprivileged."[48] Also, the choice of the publishing house may have been determined by their collaboration. The book appeared with the American publisher Orbis Books, with which Houtart had a connection and had published, inter alia, *The Church and Revolution* in 1971.[49] Orbis Books belonged to the Maryknoll Mission (MM). Kappen had stayed at the Maryknoll Seminary as a visiting professor in the beginning of the 1970s and developed a personal relationship with the Maryknoll Mission.[50] This publisher was mainly known for books on the theology of liberation and progressive Christian thinking. A Nicaraguan priest called Miguel D'Escoto (1933), who belonged to the Maryknoll Mission, had founded it in 1970. The publisher became well known soon after publishing Gustavo Gutiérrez's *A Theology of Liberation* (1971).

In 1979, Houtart published two new books on Kerala, for which he had returned to the state. Kappen was working in Chennai during this time, but he must have helped Houtart, who made use of the archives and libraries of local Jesuit institutions, especially at the Lumen Institute at Ernakulam and the Socio-religious Centre in Calicut, two places where Kappen had lived.[51] Both of Houtart's works – *Church and Development in Kerala* and *Catholic Hospital System in India* – positively acknowledged the role and contribution of the Church in Kerala in various fields like education, culture, sociology, politics, and health care.

The books remained purely secular, and surprisingly, Houtart made no reference to Kappen. This may suggest that Kappen was a less significant intellectual friend to Houtart than Houtart was to Kappen.

C.   Increasing Activism

In 1970, Kappen moved from Ernakulam to Calicut, the same place where he spent the initial years of his formation and started working in the St. Joseph's Boys' high school. Later he left the Jesuit house and shifted his stay to a small house called *Archana* and then to *Sevanikethan* in the village of Thenjipalam. His life in the countryside further inspired him to deepen his reflections on the ordinary people and the realities of their living conditions. From then, he always chose to live outside Jesuit institutions in order to avoid their comfort and security, and to imitate Jesus who had always been with the people. At the same time, as a member of the Society, he was in contact with the nearest Jesuit house and, importantly and as he recalled, never thought of leaving his priesthood.[52]

In Ernakulam and Calicut, Kappen had a wide circle of friends including students, intellectuals, Communist leaders, and the professors at the University of Calicut with whom he found the scope of exchanging progressive ideologies. He also used to visit scholars like M.G.S. Narayanan, a renowned historian in India.[53] Such kind of meetings and conversations helped Kappen strengthen the ideas he had been developing since his stay in Rome. Moreover, during this period, he also taught at the Vidyajyoti college of theology in New Delhi (a Jesuit institution) and the Papal seminary in Pune (the national seminary for India).

For Kappen, these encounters were indeed a learning process to challenge his own understandings and convictions in the field of both philosophy and theology. In 1972, he published his first book with National Book Stall at Kottayam under the title *From Faith to Revolution*. Rather than further elaborating on the philosophical and theological presuppositions, he wanted to go back to the original meaning of the message of Jesus and to shake off all the centuries-old layers of interpretations of Jesus and the gospels. Kappen stated that philosophy and theology, as means, should contribute to constructing a new society from below. He did not want to confine his freedom to the means, i.e. to the joy of mere philosophizing and theologizing. It is this radical Kappen that will further return in successive writings.

Kappen moved from Calicut to Chennai in 1975. In the capital of Tamil Nadu, he engaged himself in gathering and teaching youth, and publishing books and articles. He settled in a slum area, where the poor and the marginalized people were concentrated, and in 1976 founded the Centre for Social Reconstruction. Two of his close relatives, his niece Mercy Kappen and his nephew Sebastian Vattamattam, assisted him in running the organization. Mercy had earlier worked as his secretary and had joined him to Chennai. Kappen worked hard to form a new generation committed to the messages of the historical Jesus and Marx without depending on interpretations and intermediaries. He occasionally collaborated with student movements, namely AICUF, a Jesuit initiative, and the Student Christian Movement of India (SCMI).[54] Besides, he used to invite people to his residence to give classes.[55] As a result of Kappen's contact and friendship, many young people who were engaged in social issues and activities used to come and stay with him in order to learn more about Jesus and Marx. The human suffering that he encountered in Chennai moved him deeply, because he considered it a means not only for intellectual thought, but also for being one with them.[56]

Many of Kappen's guests in Chennai were passionate social activists. For instance, Sadanand Menon, a nationally reputed arts editor, teacher of cultural journalism, and expert on politics, ecology, and art, later recalled the energy and inspiration he received from Kappen. When such activists had to temper their radical activism due the state of Emergency between 1975 and 1977, they found Kappen as the apt teacher to take them to the roots of radical theories. In a series of lectures over the following four years, Kappen introduced Kant, Hegel, Feuerbach, Marx,

Heidegger, Husserl, Wittgenstein, and other philosophers to those who approached him. Menon later called Kappen as one of his greatest gurus.[57]

The Centre for Social Reconstruction did not have the structure of an institution, because that was not Kappen's intent. From the slum he moved to a small house where he started publishing journals and leaflets with the assistance of Ajit Muricken, who, together with Philip Mathew, in 1987 wrote a study on Kappen: *Religion, Ideology, and Counter-Culture.* In 1976 Kappen set up the English journal *Anawim* (Hebrew for poor or oppressed), a tract introducing Jesus to the contemporary man. Kappen decided to initiate it due to the demand of progressive Christian thinkers and young socially committed activists who had often been engaging in discussions about how Christians should respond to the problems of poverty and injustice in India. Kappen continued *Anawim* for eight years and stopped it in 1984.

Likewise, he published two other periodicals. Thirteen issues of *Socialist Perspectives* occasionally appeared between 1978 and 1982, promoting independent socialist thinking in Asia, but were stopped in 1982 due to financial shortage. In that year, however, he established *Negations*, a journal of culture and creative praxis. Kappen was the editor of this quarterly; Sadanand Menon and Aloysius Pieris were the associate editors. The first issues appeared in Chennai; later, the enterprise moved to Trivandrum. Kappen discontinued it with the January-March issue in 1985 since he had received little feedback from Church circles and from Marxists. He felt as if he was conducting a monologue.[58]

In Chennai, Kappen experienced a complete return to Marx. He published an article entitled "The Marxist and Christian Dialectics of Liberation" in 1977.[59] After his thesis in 1961, Kappen had not written much on Marx or Marxism, apart from a couple of small articles referring to Marxist ideologies and a chapter in *From Faith to Revolution.* Now, sixteen years after his PhD, he looked back to Marxism in order to compare it with religion in general and Christianity in particular.

In 1977, Kappen published one of his most important books: *Jesus and Freedom*. It was the outcome of decade-long reflections and discussions on Christian life and faith. His target group was the educated youth who wanted to radically commit themselves to the gospel values. The book was a clear indication of his convictions about the historical human Jesus, and, beginning with his 1975 article "Jesus Today," Kappen no longer made use of the terms Christ and Jesus Christ. Although the distinction between these terms is passingly referred in few other places in this dissertation, we make a detailed analysis in Chapter V. *Jesus and Freedom* clearly fitted in the climate of the era and closely connected with the thoughts of liberation theology. Indeed, also elsewhere, radical and progressive thinkers criticized the hierarchy and the institutionalized Church through their writings. This prompted the Vatican to scrutinize their books, to censor many of them and to ban their authors. *Jesus and Freedom* was no exception. This will also be discussed in greater detail in chapter V.

The Vatican censored *Jesus and Freedom* in 1980. The Congregation for the Doctrine of the Faith found certain dogmatic errors, especially regarding the godhood of Jesus. The book and the author underwent thorough scrutiny between 1980 and 1982, which led to the prohibition of Kappen from publishing books without the prior permission of the superiors of the Society of Jesus.[60] However, this did not prevent him from writing. Along with several articles, Kappen also worked on two new books, again with unconventional theological positions. Yet, it seems that he waited for the controversies and the conflict with the Congregation for the Doctrine of the Faith to come to end before he published them. In 1983, *Jesus and Cultural Revolution: An Asian Perspective* appeared. The book shed light on another area of Kappen's interest, namely counter-culture. It was a compilation of lectures he delivered at the seminar on 'Third-world Theologians in Dialogue' in New York back in 1979. The second work also came out in 1983 under the title *Marxian Atheism*. These books are discussed in detail in the following section of this chapter, which is on the works of Kappen.

Kappen's classes on Marxism were not limited to the Centre for Social Reconstruction in Chennai. He often travelled to teach about Marxism, art, culture, tradition and modernity, etc. We have retrieved details of some of these classes. The first among them, for a social action team in February 1982, focused on Marxism. Kappen's niece Mercy recorded the class, and today it is available online.[61] Kappen presented Marxism as a philosophical thought and described its evolution and development by focusing on the influence of Hegel and Feuerbach. He also elaborated on Marx's vision of religion, which he explained with the help of the concepts of capitalism, alienation, and revolution. Another example is his after-dinner talk on "the prophetic role of the Christians in contemporary India in the world of art" at the Papal seminary, Pune, in 1983. The talk was mainly about the artistic forms of the prophecy of Jesus through poetic languages, parables, and stories. He explained the need for prophecy to take such artistic forms in India to make it appealing to a wider section of the people.[62]

Shortly before the publication of *Marxian Atheism*, i.e. by the end of 1983, Kappen had moved to Bangalore. It was merely a change of location, not of a shift of the activities he had been carrying out in Chennai after the Vatican ban. In Bangalore, Kappen continued the journal of *Anawim*. After two years, Kappen went back to Trivandrum.[63] Surprisingly, his stay in Trivandrum was challenging. As a controversial figure and liberal thinker Kappen had to face objections even from the local Church. For instance, the Archbishop of Trivandrum, Jacob Acharuparambil OFM Capuchin (1919-95), wrote a letter to Mathew Pullattu SJ, the then Provincial Superior of the Kerala Province of the Society of Jesus, on 1 March 1985, expressing his anxiety over Kappen's stay in Trivandrum. The Bishop conveyed his fear that the priests of his diocese "who oppose the teachings of the Church and authority in the Church, will find encouragement and support from Rev Fr Kappen." In order to prevent this, the Archbishop asked the Provincial Superior to transfer Kappen from his eparchy. The Provincial Superior did not seem to have responded to this call.[64]

Kappen did not retire from his mission of writing, as he found his pen the strongest weapon he could ever have wielded. In the following years he wrote extensively on counter-culture and Indian Communism and Marxism. He also compiled many of his articles into books. In 1985, when Kappen was still in Trivandrum, he published *Jesus Today*, a collection of articles that he himself, Samuel Rayan, and George M. Soares Prabhu (1929-95) had written for *Anawim*.

In 1990, after having lived in Kerala for five years, Kappen moved back to Bangalore.[65] Beetween 1989 and 1992, he published six books: five in Malayalam and one in English.[66] Besides Marxism and liberation theology, he dealt with subjects like environment, art, culture, counter-culture, Marxian ideologies, socialism, etc. In Bangalore, just as in Trivandrum and Chennai, he was in contact with intellectuals, environmentalists, artists, and college students. As a part of it, he gave a series of talks on the themes of tradition, modernity, and counter-culture at the United Theological College, an inter-church seminary in Bangalore.

C.F. John, a Bangalore based artist who knew Kappen from 1987 and had frequent contact with him, revealed that Kappen was interested in painting during the last three years of his life.[67] Kappen started painting in 1990, according to John, to overcome the loneliness he felt towards the end of his life. His paintings were the reflection of his meditations. In the beginning he worked on small pieces of paper, but later John gave him canvases of two and a half feet. Some of his paintings conveyed messages. The two examples below illustrate that injustice is the first outcome of the use of power, and power can create a vicious world. This is clearly depicted in his painting with the pond and crane. When John suggested to Kappen that the crane was a romantic figure in the picture, the latter denied it and said that it was a symbol of power. According to Kappen, there are fish in the pond and the crane thought that they gain salvation when it eats them. He sarcastically criticized the legitimization of the exploitation of the weak by the strong, by giving the very act of exploitation the color of liberation. Likewise, the second painting represents an old woman going in the direction of a water source. Towards the end of his ascetic life, Kappen had also been thinking that he should go back to the source of his life. C.F. John recalled that the woman in the painting had only few personal belongings with her, just as Kappen himself.

Figure 9. Painting by Kappen: The crane and the pond

**Figure 10. Painting by Kappen:
The old woman going towards the water source**

In Bangalore, like in every other place where he stayed, Kappen lived a very minimal life identifying himself with the poor and marginalized. His health gradually deteriorated. In 1991, while he was giving a talk on the First Gulf War, he had a first heart attack. He was afflicted with asthma, spondylosis, and high blood pressure as well. In May 1991, he suffered a second heart attack. The doctors prescribed a heart surgery, but Kappen refused to undergo this since such treatments were unaffordable to the majority of the people.[68] Presumably, his superiors insisted he receive treatments. Kappen died on 30 November 1993 at the age of 69 while he was undergoing the treatment at Lake Side Medical Centre, Bangalore. He is buried in the cemetery of the Provincial House in Calicut. He could not publish some of his final writings, but they posthumously appeared with different publication houses like Visthar, Manusham, and Indian Society for Promoting Christian Knowledge (ISPCK).

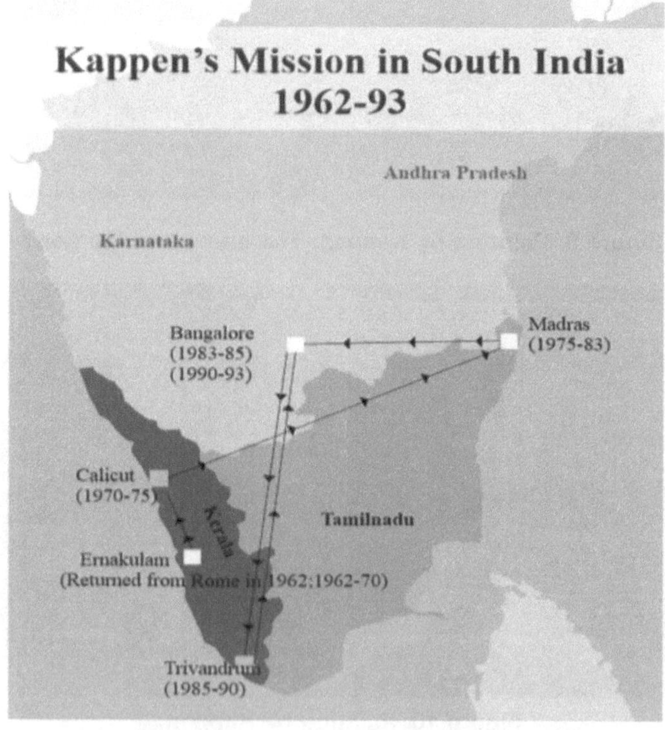

Figure 11. Kappen's Mission in South India, 1962-93

D.   A Bibliographical Note: Brief Sketch of the Works of Kappen

This section gives a brief introduction to Kappen's works in view of facilitating a proper and closer understanding of his thoughts as the research progresses. Kappen wrote extensively both in English and in his mother tongue Malayalam. He authored 17 books and about 80 articles including his tracts and editor's notes published in his journals *Anawim, Negations,* and *Socialist Perspectives.* Six of these books (and two of his articles) were published posthumously. His major books are: *From Faith to Revolution* (Malayalam, 1972), *Jesus and Freedom* (1977), *Marxian Atheism* (1983), *Jesus and Cultural Revolution: An Asian Perspective* (1983), *Jesus Today* (1985), and *Liberation Theology and Marxism* (1986). After his death, inter alia, *Tradition, Modernity, and Counter-culture: An Asian Perspective* (1994), *In Search of the non-Christian Jesus* (Malayalam, 1999), *Hindutva and Indian Religious Traditions* (2000), *Jesus and Culture: Selected Writings of Sebastian Kappen S.J.* vol. 1 (2002), and *Jesus and Society: Selected Writings of Sebastian Kappen S.J.* vol. 2 (2002) appeared.

Kappen's articles were published in different national and international journals, such as *Review for Religious* (St. Louis, Missouri), *Vidya Jyoti* (Delhi; before 1975 named *The Clergy Monthly*), *Vaidikamithram* (Kerala), and *Jeevadhara* (Kerala). Among these journals, *Jeevadhara* stood out with the highest number of Kappen's articles. It is an international theological review that was set up in 1971, and investigated the most relevant issues in theology, including human problems and ethical, political, and social concerns.

By the time Kappen's first book came out in 1972, he had already published about ten articles. His first published article in English, as available today, came out in 1964 under the title "The Eucharist and the Quest of India for a New Vision of History," two years after his return from Rome. The article conveyed the what-and-how of his initial thoughts and ideologies. It was an analytical study of the cyclic nature of time in Indian tradition and of the future orientation of Christianity.[69] Kappen, relatively new to the Indian intelligentsia, believed that the West had certain vital elements to contribute to Indian tradition. This observation stemmed from the overemphasis of Indian tradition on the cultic past, which ignored the present and its values towards constructing the future. This reference to Western culture would come back in his later writings. For instance, in his article "Christian Participation in Social Work," published in 1968, he depended greatly on Western Scholars, such as Edward Schillebeeckx, Henri de Lubac, Marie-Dominique Chenu and so forth.[70]

In the late 1960s, Kappen made a big step forward from his conformity to traditional theology with a claim for an integral view of the two interlocked aspects of the Church – the secular and the sacral. He also began using Marxist terms, for he reiterated the communitarian dimension of humanity and the importance of human labor. Both community/society and labor are two inevitable factors that constitute Marxism. By bringing them in the discussion on Church and social work, Kappen tried to contribute to an integral perspective – growth and development of both the Kingdom of God and the earthly city.[71] The Second Vatican Council and its documents, especially the *Decree on the Apostolate of the Laity* (*Apostolicam Actuocitatem*)[72] and *Church in the Modern World* (*Gaudium et Spes*; as mentioned earlier in this chapter, Houtart also contributed to its constitution),[73] significantly influenced Kappen in this regard. Moreover, placing himself on the line between the Church and the secular world, he could develop a language that helped him secularize theology.[74]

Kappen's life and intellectual horizon further opened to accommodate the evolution that had been taking place. In 1969, Kappen published "The Role of the Church in National Development." At that time, he was a guest professor at De Nobili College, Pune, where he had studied theology from 1954 to 1958 and had done his Tertianship in 1958-59. As we find in the article, his teaching career opened up new vistas. Firstly, he started thinking very seriously about the human being's earthly welfare and the means to acquire this. He did not mention the salvation of the soul (i.e. the spiritual responsibilities of the Church), but claimed that the Church should concentrate more on the earthly welfare of the people of India. Secondly, following his encounters as a teacher in the seminaries, he thought of challenging the social commitment of the younger generation. Becoming a serious social thinker, Kappen was very much concerned about caste distinctions and voiced for equality and dignity of all human persons.[75]

Kappen further refined his ideologies in the following years. The most significant among his articles during this period were "Christianity as Liberation" (1970), "The Christian and the Call to Liberation" (1971), and "Christianity and India's Development" (1972).[76] The main thrust of all these articles was the Church's role in a revolution, which according to Kappen was a radical transformation of the prevalent social system and a process of humanization – humanization that overcame every form of inequality, injustice, alienation, and class antagonism.[77] Kappen began appearing in the gown of a social thinker rather than that of a theologian. His conviction that the Kingdom of God had to be inserted into the material world, just like the Word had become flesh in Jesus, revealed his interest for the material or secular well-being of humanity.

His travels to Belgium and the U.S. in the beginning of the 1970s provided him with an open intellectual and liberal space to articulate himself, ever after his return from Rome in 1962. This gave him a great opportunity to formulate and express his visions on the Church. Kappen now was ready to write his first book *From Faith to Revolution* (1972). It was a compilation of the ideas inherent in his speeches and articles from the previous years. Kappen considered this book as a partial solution to the absence of scientific research in the field of religious sociology in Kerala.[78] In fact, this book worked as a catalyst for the transformative efforts of radical clergy and socially committed common man. The 1970s were the golden period of liberation theology in Latin America and Kappen himself found the inspiration and courage to flag off certain serious thinking about the social commitment of different faiths.[79]

From Faith to Revolution was a vivid articulation of the transition in Kappen's thoughts that had been taking place in the previous years. As he overcame the hurdle of his own so-called orthodoxy with a kind of semi-orthodoxy having 'met' Marx in Rome in 1959, he now, thirteen years later, wanted to put aside his semi-orthodoxy, giving way to liberal and secular perspectives. Admittedly, Kappen made a shift from Christ to Jesus Christ that paved the way to his portrayal of a more human Jesus Christ. For Kappen, the term Christ, which he often used in his initial articles, stood for the glorified/deified Jesus and the term Jesus for the historical human Jesus. Kappen's intellectual evolution prompted him to strive for a consensus between Christ and Jesus that apparently resulted in Jesus Christ, an integration of God and human or transcendence and immanence. According to Civic Chandran, a famous Keralite writer, this book had inspired not only progressive Christian thinkers in Kerala but also left-wing readers.[80]

Kappen continued publishing articles in different journals after his first book. In 1973 he wrote "The Future of Christian Education and Christian Education of the Future" for *Jeevadhara*. His major concern during this period was the interference of religious groups, especially the Church, in the field of education. According to him, the secular society was getting matured and the Church had to acknowledge it and eventually relinquish its domination of society. An assessment of the service of the Church in the education sector encouraged him to propose an attitudinal revolution in the Church, enabling itself to step back from its "be-all and the end-all of everything" attitude.[81]

In the same year Kappen wrote another article, namely "The Goals of Revolution," in which he gave a clear and explicit definition of revolution. He wrote that revolution was a "radical and rapid transformation of a social system" that transformed society into a new entity in which human dignity is held high.[82] Kappen used numerous Marxian terms in this article, such as socialization, labor, state property, private property, capitalism, production, etc. Speaking in terms of human dignity, which is not central to Marxism, and economics, which in religion is less prioritized, Kappen foresaw a revolution unlike the conventional one. The socialist and theologian in him envisioned a revolution both by religious and economic means, for a better society. Therefore, one could find Kappen in the beginning of 1970s as a revolutionary socialist who is neither an anti-Communist Catholic priest nor an anti-religious Marxist.

However, Kappen's criticism of the Church had become clear in the changing theological atmosphere. The Second Vatican Council and the emergence of various liberal and progressive movements in different parts of the world had given a new vigor to theologizing. In India, most importantly, the All India Seminar on the Church in India Today in 1969 emphasized the need for focusing on a contextualized theology, indigenization, socio-economic development, inter-religious dialogue, etc.[83] By the early 1970s theological literature largely accommodated the term liberation in place of development.[84] Issues of social justice were widely discussed. The CBCI declared in 1974 that it would focus on preaching the good news that implied an integral liberation of the whole man.[85] It also acknowledged that the poor had an unfavorable impression of the Church in India, and that the latter had reduced itself to a corporate institution running schools and hospitals. Such a contextual background gave tremendous impetus for Kappen to be more critical about the Church.

The changing theological atmosphere in Kerala in the 1970s was also clear from the writings of Christian thinkers and theologians, which included both criticisms and suggestions. The journal *Jeevadhara* provided a rather comprehensive understanding of the political, economic, social, and religious context in Kerala in the 1970s by publishing articles of progressive thinkers from Kerala including Kappen. Its continued insistence for a change in the Church's approach towards various societal issues also indicated the need for a revised theology. First of all, many progressive thinkers thought that conventional theology had matured and needed a shift from its mere focus on one's soul and its liberation. Secondly, this shift should take place by considering the temporal aspects of human life. In fact, theologians, such as Samuel Rayan, M.M. Thomas, Paulose Mar Paulose, etc. called for a theology of liberation in Kerala.[86] They also advocated for the integration of secular and religious dimensions of life in order to avoid the problem of identifying the Church in Kerala with a collection of ritualistic practices.[87] Thirdly, for its praxis orientation, the Church was reminded of the need to awake from the academic and spiritual slumber. It had to put aside the undue supernaturalism that ignored the temporal side of human life, and the triumphalist self-image that it borrowed from abroad. The Church had to create its own image by being the voice of the voiceless.[88] Fourthly, as Samuel Rayan pointed out, the Church had to take into account the Marxist criticism that it neglected the concrete realities of human life.[89] It had been subject to a renewal after the Second Vatican Council, but it still had to grow in order to strip its corporate identity.[90] In India, the Church's identity was based on its institutions and leadership, which created a negative impression.[91] Fifthly, progressive writers laid a huge stress on the prophetic dimension of the life and mission of Jesus, rather than on the cultic Jesus, expecting that the prophetic Jesus would inspire the Church towards a permanent renewal and revolution.[92] All five of these points will be further discussed and elaborated in the following chapters. This revolutionary spirit also had to give importance to eradicating "injustices, alienations, and institutional violence of socio-economic systems."[93] Finally, they were critical of the capitalist trend of the time and challenged the Church to escape capitalism since it was essentially dehumanizing. As an alternative, they invited the individual believer to collaborate with genuinely committed revolutionary movements.[94]

Kappen adopted these thoughts and continued publishing large numbers of articles in different journals and magazines. He wrote "The Jesus Fellowship" (1974) when he was living in Calicut. Frequent contact with the secular world enabled him to view the Church from the vantage point of an outsider. As a result, he criticized Christian triumphalism since it hindered opportunities for fruitful dialogue with other religious groups. Instead, he wanted to provide a new definition to the Church that would turn it into an institution that considered itself a means of integral liberation.[95] In addition, Kappen developed a closer affinity to the human Jesus, leaving behind the Christ whom he had been frequently dealing with in his earlier writings.

In 1975, Kappen published two articles in *Jeevadhara*: "Values in Crisis: A Socio-Philosophical Analysis of the Indian Situation" and "Jesus Today." The first one was about his understanding of values and their role in the society, dealing with issues like the secularization of values, the values of capitalism, and the religious monopoly of values. Kappen tried to diagnose the fundamental problems in society. He engaged himself with social problems like unemployment, price hikes, failure in law and order, vested interests of the political parties, and corrupt governments and bureaucracy. Even though they could be seen as the general problems of any society, Kappen considered them to be fundamental in India. In fact, he served as an inspirational figure among social activists; right at the time they needed one most.[96] For this he had to essentially come to a conclusion regarding the Jesus of history and the Christ of faith. This is evident in the article "Jesus Today," and we will further elaborate it in Chapter V.[97]

"Jesus Today" was a condensed form of a book that appeared two years later, in 1977: *Jesus and Freedom*, which became one of Kappen's most popular works and was eventually censored. Kappen wrote *Jesus and Freedom* after moving from Kerala to Chennai in 1976. However, he emphasized in his preface that the book was the outcome of decade-long reflections and discussions on Christian life and faith. The major intellectual sources of his critical approach towards established religions in this book, though he did not say explicitly, appeared to be the theology of liberation, the synoptic gospels with a preference to the gospel of Mark, and his knowledge of Marxist ideologies. Besides, he acknowledged that the immediate sources of inspiration were the groups of students he interacted with in classrooms and the intellectuals he encountered at seminars and academic discussions. These conversations led them to analyze society in a radical way, especially with the help of the socially oriented questions evolved in them.[98]

The censorship did not stop Kappen from writing. On the contrary, the 1980s saw the apogee of his publications. In 1983, Kappen published *Marxian Atheism*, which was essentially an edited version of his doctoral dissertation. Much more than a mere reproduction, it was the result of his over two-decades-long study of Marxism and experience with Marxists. It delved not only into the "Economic and Philosophical Manuscripts of Marx" but also into Marxism as a whole. The goal of the work was to educate a broader readership about Marxian philosophy, critic of religion, and atheistic humanism.[99] Kappen provided the common man with a deeper understanding of Marx's critical approach towards religion. However, he was not in total conformity with Marxian criticism of religion and ended his book with a critical evaluation.

Another major publication from 1983 was *Jesus and Cultural Revolution*. In the book, Kappen argued that every vicious and exploitative structure had to be demolished and a new culture, counter to the previous, had to be established.[100] And this, in India's case, could only happen after going back to the original meaning of the message of Jesus. According to Kappen, history had always been witnessing to established groups of people who wanted to maintain the heritage and infallibility of the culture in which they belonged. He called this phenomenon cultural hegemony. As long as the powerful defined the norms and customs of society, oppression of the weak by the strong and exploitation of the poor by the rich would be the culture.[101] The silence of the weak and the poor legitimized the laws of the strong and the rich. This being the established culture, Kappen strived to construct a counter-culture by denouncing the existing vicious exploitative structures. It was for this reason that Kappen, unlike many other contemporary progressive thinkers, depended on assimilating the liberating elements of religious and philosophical movements in order to construct a counter-culture. Most importantly, besides presenting Jesus as the prophet of counter-culture, he also considered the teachings of Buddha, Marx, and the Bhakti movements. As the title of the book indicated, Kappen expected a cultural revolution and the dawn of a counter-cultural era in India through the agents of Jesus, Marx, and Buddha. Notably, his interest in Buddha also appeared in other texts, for instance, the paper he presented at the seminar on 'The Significance of Jesus for Asia,' in Vidya Jyoti, New Delhi, in April 1982.[102] His concentration on Buddha could also be viewed as a follow-up to his quest for dialogue with other religions.

In his life and writings, Kappen remained different from other progressive thinkers. Many other liberation theologians accommodated indigenous elements in the process of liberation, but they only incorporated those elements that were in conformity with those of the Church. Kappen had a wider vision that enabled him to take more radical steps. In fact, he built *Jesus and Cultural Revolution* on his *Jesus and Freedom* and went beyond that to see the relation between the teachings and life of Jesus. In the chapter on Kappen's understanding of Jesus, we will further investigate how he inserted Jesus into the "repressed culture of the downtrodden and the marginalized" by denouncing the powerful Brahminic Sanskrit tradition in Hinduism.[103]

Kappen's first book to deal explicitly and exclusively with liberation theology and Marxism was published in 1986 under the apt title *Liberation Theology and Marxism*. It was essentially a search for platforms for dialogues between Marxism and Christianity. Kappen believed that a proper understanding of the convergence and divergence between the two sides would facilitate certain areas of collaboration. Most importantly, he declared a parting of ways with theological terms like God, sin, grace, salvation, and heaven, claiming that the concepts were burdened with layers of meanings and interpretations. He substituted the term God with Divine,[104] and defined liberation as the integral development of the human person, liberating him/her from every form of alienation. His initial inspirations for liberation theology were the Bible, the Second Vatican Council, and the social teachings of the Church.[105] Gradually, however, radical progressive thinkers, including Kappen himself, looked to certain Marxist ideologies to analyze the social problems. Kappen asserted that Marxism and Indian theology of liberation had a long way to go in dialogue and co-operation in order to liberate Indian society from every form of oppression, irrespective of whether the problem was political, economic, cultural, social, religious, etc.

Kappen's heritage continued through his posthumous works, *Tradition, Modernity, and Counter-culture* (1994), *In search of the non-Christian Jesus* (1999), and *Hindutva and Indian Religious Traditions* (2000).[106] In *Tradition, Modernity, and Counter-culture*, Kappen dealt with the unquestionable hegemony of religion and the exploitative capitalist system. According to him, religion had tamed God. The God of authentic religion was partial to the poor; but the God of the theocratic society had become partial to the rich. Furthermore, God had been effectively muted in contemporary society to make him neutral in principle, and this legitimized the hegemony of the ruling class.[107] Kappen proposed a counter-culture to break down the hegemony of the past over the present. In fact, one can see a genuine attempt in his *In Search of the non-Christian Jesus* to overcome the hegemony of the past by rediscovering the historical Jesus and the original meaning of his message. On the one hand Kappen advocated a theology of liberation and on the other he strived for liberation from theology.[108] In *Hindutva and Indian Religious Traditions*, Kappen addressed the issue of growing Hindu religious and nationalist fundamentalism in India, which he believed had never been part of its culture before.[109] It was one of the issues Kappen dealt with during the last years of his life, undoubtedly inspired by the rise of the BJP and the tensions around Ayodhya. Unfortunately, he died before he could further elaborate on the subject.

This chapter introduced us to different facets of Kappen's life. Importantly, we analyzed his childhood and education, priestly formation, studies in Indology, foreign stays, activism, and major works. All these seem to have helped him become a liberation theologian and social thinker. In the following chapters, these analyses will contribute to an understanding of the major transitions in Kappen's life, of which we have discussed the fundamental shift – decision to become a Jesuit – in this chapter.

Endnotes

[1] Kappen, "Ingathering," 10; Muricken, "S. Kappen: The Man and his Contribution to the Study of Counter-Culture," 9-31; and Painadath, "Preface," vii-xiv.

[2] "Kodikulam Grama Panchayat," http://lsgkerala.in/kodikulampanchayat/history/ [accessed 17 November 2015].

[3] Joseph, *George Joseph, the Life and Times of a Kerala Christian Nationalist*, 28.

[4] Cf. Menon, *The History of Freedom Movement in Kerala: 1600-1885*, 56, and Varier, Village Communities in Pre-colonial Kerala, 13.

[5] Kappen died shortly after he started writing an autobiography. The few pages he wrote are published in *Ingathering: Autobiographical Writings and Selected Essays*, edited by Sebastian Vattamattam (2013).

[6] Kappen, "Ingathering," 10-1.

7 "Kappen Kudumba Yogam, Pala," http://www.kappenkudumbayogam.org/wp-content/uploads/2015/04/Web.pdf [accessed 17 November 2015].

[8] Today it is a parish church in the diocese of Kothamangalam, which was erected on 26 July 1956 by the then Pope Pius XII, bifurcating the Ernakulam-Angamaly Archeparchy.

[9] Kappen, "Ingathering," 12.

[10] Kappen, "Ingathering," 13.

[11] Of course, these facts should be approached critically, since they are based on Kappen's own memories at the last phase of his life.

[12] Muricken, "S. Kappen: The Man and his Contribution to the Study of Counter-Culture," 10.

[13] "Fr. Mateo Crawley-Boevey, ss.cc.: Founder and Apostle of the Enthronement of the Sacred Heart," http://www.menofthesacredheartsohio.com/x_pdf/fr-mateo-final%20 2007.pdf [accessed 12 October 2017].

[14] In his unfinished autobiographical notes, Kappen called Crowley's book *Christ the King*, but this seems to be a mistake. Cf. Kappen, "Ingathering," 13.

[15] "Fr. Mateo in India," http://www.ssccpicpus.com/userfiles/file/LIBRARY/13.%20 SS.CC.%20Personages/SSCC%20Brothers/20.%20Mateo%20Crawley%20(1875-960)/ Fr.Mateo%C2%B4s%20trip%20in%20India.docx [accessed 22 October 2015].

[16] Kappen, "Ingathering," 13-4.

[17] Muricken, "S. Kappen: The Man and his Contribution to the Study of Counter-Culture," 10.

[18] Kuriakose, *History of Christianity in India*, 321-3, 343-4, and 368.

[19] Painadath, "Preface," vii.

[20] Kappen, "Ingathering," 17.

[21] Sebastian Kappen's name is given in the Catalogue of the Madurai Vice-Province of Jesuits because the Sacred Heart College, Shembaganur where he did his philosophical studies was under Madurai Vice-province. Cf. *Catalogus Viceprovinciae Madurensis* (Madurai: Typis De Nobili, 1949, 1950, and 1951), 35, 35, and 34.

[22] Muricken, "S. Kappen: The Man and his Contribution to the Study of Counter-Culture," 11. For a better understanding of Thomistic philosophy, cf. Aquinas, *Summa Theologica: Literally translated by Fathers of the English Dominican Providence* (1947-1948); Martin, ed., *The Philosophy of Thomas Aquinas: Introductory Readings* (1989); and Gilson, *Thomism: The Philosophy of Thomas Aquinas* (2002).

[23] Between 1937 and 1985, he also worked as the Rector of St. Paul's Seminary, Trichy (1942-48) and of De Nobili College, Pune (1967-72).

[24] Some of his publications are: *Notes of Youth Psychology* (1953); *Ideal Personality* (1961); *Lay Sanctity the Need of the Hour* (1962); *Vacation and Psychology* (1963); *Philosophical Psychology* (1964); and *Experimental Psychology* (1972).

[25] Gispert-Sauch, "The Concept of Person and Indian Thought - An Attempt at a Cross-cultural Dialogue," 27. In order to honor Ugarte for his contributions, the Sacred Heart College published a collection of essays in 1986 from Chennai. Cf. Amaladass, Raj, and Elampassery, eds., *Philosohpy and Human Development: Essays in Honour of Father Emilio Ugarte, S.J.* (1986). Some of the leading Jesuits who collaborated with this publication were Anand Amaladass (professor of Indian Philosophy at Sacred Heart College), Salvino Azzopardi (professor of philosophy at Jnana Deepa Vidyapeeth (JDV), Pune), Joseph de Finance (Gregorian University, Rome), Joseph Marneffe (professor of philosophy at JDV), Mariasusai Dhavamony (professor, Gregorian University, Rome), and George Gispert-Sauch (professor in theology and Indian religions, Vidya Jyoti, New Delhi).

[26] "St. Joseph's Interdiocesan Seminary," http://stjosephseminarymangalore.org/HISTORY.html [accessed 15 July 2015]. Again, in 1980, during his visit to Mangalore to take part in the centenary celebration of the reorganization of the seminary, Fr. Pedro Aruppe, the then Superior General of the Jesuits, expressed his will to hand the administration of the seminary over to the Interdiocesan Board of Administration. The Sacred Congregation for the Evangelization of Peoples approved it by its decree dated 15 July 1992 with effect from 1995.

[27] Varghese, "New Insights of Ecclesiology in Sebastian Kappen's Understanding," 60.

[28] Kappen, *Jesus and Culture: Selected Writings of Sebastian Kappen S.J.*, vii-viii.

[29] KCBC, "Pastoral Letter," 139.

[30] Muricken "S. Kappen: The Man and his Contribution to the Study of Counter-Culture," 12.

[31] Cf. Marx, "Economic and Philosophical Manuscripts," 61-219.

[32] Painadath, "Preface," viii. The title of the dissertation is given slightly different in Jayaseelan, *Towards a Counter-culture: Sebastian Kappen's Contribution*, 6 ("Praxis and Religious Alienation According to the Economic and Philosophical Manuscripts of Karl Marx"). I consulted the original copy of the thesis at the archives of the Ufficio Dottorati of the Gregorian University in May 2016, after months of mails and in very strict circumstances (I may be the first one to use the original copy, but only for two hours and without copying or taking notes).

[33] Vattamattam, who compiled and edited many of the works of Kappen, and D.C. Kizhakkemury, an Indian freedom fighter, activist, and writer, have said in their talks on Kappen that he wrote his dissertation in German and French, respectively. The talks are available on https://www.youtube.com/watch?v=aOEuNeDOcEA ("Sebastian Vattamattam introducing Fr. Sebastian Kappen") and https://www.youtube.com/watch?v=KdMK0WdZeVU (D C Kizhakkemury on Fr. Sebastian Kappen"), [accessed 8 August 2016].

[34] The current chaplain of the Association is Dr. Abraham Adappur SJ, who also was at the Lumen Institute when Kappen came back from Rome to Ernakulam.

[35] Interview with Sebastian Vattamattam, Kottayam, 22 September 2014. For more details, Nossiter, *Communism in Kerala*, 371.

[36] Vattamattam, "Sebastian Kappen (1924-1993)," 3-4.

[37] Interview with Aurel Brys SJ, Heverlee, 12 November 2016. Fr. Brys is a Belgian missionary working in Ranchi, north India.

[38] Sahabandhu, "Portraying the person and works of François Houtart." From the interview of the Sri Lankan Methodist minister Jerome Sahabandhu with Houtart at Louvain-la-Neuve in July 2005. http://www.iese.ac.mz/lib/noticias/2009/houtard.pdf [accessed 11 February 2016].

[39] Interview of Jerome Sahabandhu with Houtart.

[40] For these details, I depended on the interview of Jerome Sahabandhu with Houtart. I also made use of the books Houtart co-authored with Geneviève Lemercinier, with the purpose of learning more about Houtart's life. For instance, they include: *Genesis and Institutionalization of the Indian Catholicism* (1981); *The Great Asiatic Religions and their Social Functions* (1982); *Size and Structures of the Catholic Church in India: The Indigenization of an Exogenous Religious Institution in a Society of Transition* (1982); *Church and Development in Kerala* (1979); and "Social Functions of Religion in Pre-Capitalist Societies: The Case of Kerala," 91-108.

[41] Interview of Jerome Sahabandhu with Houtart.

[42] A better example for this is Houtart's *Religion and Ideology in Sri Lanka* (1974). Interview of Jerome Sahabandhu with Houtart.

[43] Houtart, *Religion and Ideology in Sri Lanka* (1974).

[44] Kappen, "Spirituality in the new Age of Recolonization," 27-35.

[45] Houtart, *Religion and Ideology in Sri Lanka*, vii.

[46] Email contact with the archivist of Louvain-la-Neuve, 28 February 2016. Nicolas Delpierre, Archives de l'UCL, Université catholique de Louvain. For the moment, the archives are not inventoried and cannot reveal further details about these contacts.

[47] Although Fr. Aurel Brys could not meet Kappen in Belgium, they met twice at Pune, in India. Interview with Aurel Brys SJ.

[48] Kappen, *Jesus and Freedom*, viii.

[49] Houtart and Rousseau, *The Church and Revolution: from the French Revolution of 1789 to the Paris Riots of 1968; from Cuba to Southern Africa; from Vietnam to Latin America* (1971).

[50] Vattamattam, "Sebastian Kappen (1924-1993)," 3-4.

[51] Houtart and Lemercinier, *Church and Development in Kerala*, v.

[52] Interview with C.F. John, Bangalore, 19 September 2014; Vattamattam, *Towards a Counter-culture* (Malayalam), 17.

[53] Interview with Sebastian Painadath SJ, Ernakulam, 15 September 2014.

[54] A movement of the university students founded by Fr. Carty SJ in 1924, envisioning a just society.

[55] Interview with Sebastian Vattamattam.

[56] Interview with Mercy Kappen, Bangalore, 19 September 2014.

[57] Menon, "Kappen: The Advocate of Radical Consciousness," 169-70.

[58] Chandran, "Forward" to *Towards a Counter-culture* (Malayalam), 12.

[59] Kappen, "The Marxist and the Christian Dialectics of Liberation," 53-67.

[60] Arrupe's letter to Kappen, 27 May 1981, KPA, 1.

[61] Details from the index of Vattamattam, *Towards a Counter-culture* (Malayalam), 167-84. Online source is "Fr. Sebastian Kappen: Marxist Study Class, Part I," https://www.youtube.com/watch?v=Ng76tVHVv94 [accessed on 3 November 2016].

[62] Online source is "Fr. Sebastian Kappen's Talk on Art," https://www.youtube.com/watch?v=cuuRgQzd2Lk [accessed on 10 January 2016].

[63] Stayed at Anawim, T.C. 11/307 TVM-695 003.

[64] Archbishop Jacob Acharuparambil's letter to Fr. Mathew Pullattu SJ, the then Provincial Superior of the Kerala province, 1 March 1985, KPA, 1.

[65] 930, 1 Block, HAL 111 stage, Bangalore 560 008.

[66] Kappen, *Envrionment, Culture* (Malayalam) (1988); *An Introduction to Marxian Perspectives* (Malayalam) (1989); *The Source of Art* (1991); *Prophesy and Counter-culture* (Malayalam) (1992); *The Future of Socialism* (Malayalam) (1993); and *The Future of Socialism and Socialism of the Future* (1992).

[67] Interview with C.F. John.

[68] Vattamattam, *Towards a Counter-culture* (Malayalam), 17-8.

[69] Kappen, "The Eucharist and the Quest of India for a New Vision of History," 51-60.

[70] Kappen, "Christian Participation in Social Work," 586-94.

71 Kappen, "Christian Participation in Social Work," 590.

72 Pope Paul VI, *Decree on the Apostolate of the Laity*, promulgated on 18 November 1965.

73 Pope Paul VI, *Church in the Modern World*, promulgated on 7 December 1965.

74 Joseph, "Sebastian Kappen, 1924-1993," 117.

75 Kappen, "The Role of the Church in National Development," 59-75.

76 Kappen, "Christianity as Liberation," 12-3; "The Christian and the Call to Revolution," 29-45; and "Christianity and India's Development," 47-62.

77 Kappen, "The Christian and the Call to Revolution," 30-2, and Kappen, "Christianity and India's Development," 49.

78 Kappen, *From Faith to Revolution* (Malayalam), 9-10.

79 Interview of Prof. Idesbald Goddeeris with François Houtart, 22 April 2014.

80 Chandran, "Forward" to *Towards a Counter-culture* (Malayalam), 8-9.

81 Kappen, "The Future of Christian Education and Christian Education of the Future," 58 and 64.

82 Kappen, "The Goals of Revolution," 51.

83 Orientation Paper F, "Responsibility of the Church in India Today" at the All India Seminar on the Church in India Today, Bangalore, 15-25 May 1969, 231-60.

84 For more details about the theology of development, cf. Bauer, *In Search of a Theology of Development* (1969) and *Towards a Theology of Development* (1970).

85 CBCI, "Declaration of CBCI on Evangelization," 6.

86 Kallumkalpurayidom, "The involvement of the Kerala Church in Politics," 71.

87 Puthumana, "A Christian Evaluation of Kerala Politics," 85.

88 Chethimattam, "Towards a Theology of Liberation," 25-34.

89 Rayan, "Human Well-being on Earth and the Gospel of Jesus," 36-7.

90 Manalel, "Should the Church be Poor?" 336.

91 Rayan, "Wealth and Power and the Catholic Church in India," 351.

92 Prabhu, "Jesus the Prophet," 217.

93 Thannikot, "The Liberating Church," 327.

94 Kappen, "Values in Crisis: A Socio-Philosophical Analysis of the Indian Situation," 22-3.

95 Kappen, "The Jesus Fellowship," 196.

96 This is clear from the memoirs of Kappen that are presented by social activists in the Kappen memorial lectures since the death of Kappen.

97 Kappen, "Jesus Today," 171.

98 Kappen, *Jesus and Freedom*, preface, vii.

99 Kappen has explained the purpose of the book in its preface. Kappen, *Marxian Atheism*, 1-3.

[100] Kappen, *Jesus and Cultural Revolution: An Asian Perspective*, 15-28.

[101] Kappen, *Jesus and Cultural Revolution*, 19-26.

[102] Kappen, "Jesus in the India Context," 217-21.

[103] Kappen, *Jesus and Cultural Revolution*, Forward, 7.

[104] Kappen, *Liberation Theology and Marxism*, 8.

[105] Kappen, *Liberation Theology and Marxism*, 9.

[106] Visthar published his *Tradition, Modernity, and Counter-culture: An Asian Perspective* from Bangalore. *In search of the non-Christian Jesus* (Malayalam) came out in 1999 from the Manusham publications and in the following year the same publisher released his *Hindutva and Indian Religious Traditions*.

[107] Kappen, *Tradition, Modernity, and Counter-culture*, 9. Also cf. "Sebastian Kappen talks on Tradition and Modernity: Part I," https://www.youtube.com/watch?v=kP7pVKn5qoU and [accessed 30 June 2017].

[108] Kappen, *In Search of the non-Christian Jesus* (Malayalam), 45-58.

[109] Kappen, *Hindutva and Indian Religious Traditions* (2000).

Kappen on Marxism

Sebastian Kappen began writing on Marxism in 1959 during his doctoral studies in Rome. After defending his PhD dissertation, "Praxis and the Emancipation of Man from Religious Alienation according to the Economic and Philosophical Manuscripts of Karl Marx" in 1961, he no longer focused much on Marxism until the close of the 1960s; rather, during this period, he wrote articles related to theological and Rite issues within the Church in Kerala. However, as we have discussed in Chapter II, the Second Vatican Council's openness towards progressive theologizing and his encounters with Houtart (Chapter III) inspired Kappen, who resumed writing on Marxism. This chapter aspires to explore Kappen's understanding of Marxism. In view of this, we examine to what extent his study of Marxism was limited to certain Marxist ideologies and terms and/or related to the Church in India or the cultural, religious, political, and economic contexts existing in the country. The chapter consists of three sections, where we will analyze Kappen's thoughts on three major topics, namely capitalism, alienation, and revolution. Each section will analyze when he started using the idea in question, what he wrote about it, and possibly how his thoughts developed further.

A.   Capitalism

The concept of capitalism was infrequently debated in Kerala, at least until the arrival of Communism in the state in the 1930s. Among theologians, it did not evolve into a relevant subject of discussion, even though the Vatican already produced two encyclical letters by then, namely Pope Leo XIII's *Rerum Novarum* (1891) and Pope Pius XI's *Quadragesimo Anno* (1931), dealing with social issues. Kappen also dealt with the notion less systematically, certainly compared to other topics, such as alienation and revolution. Still, he provided an academic approach to capitalism. We find his first reference to the concept in his doctoral dissertation, where he basically attempted to analyze Marxian criticism of capitalism. After this, his analysis of capitalism re-appeared towards the end of the 1960s. In this section, based on his fragmentary writings on the concept, we will see how Kappen analyzed capitalism against the various aspects of man's life in society. In view of this, we will first briefly discuss the general notions of the Marxian teaching on capitalism and then the way Kappen understood it, along with interrogating how the context in which Kappen lived inspired him in his critique of the capitalist system.

How did Marx view capitalism? Capitalism is a system primarily based on the private ownership of the means of production and their effective operation for creating profit. A capitalist economy inevitably included factors like private property, wage labor, price systems, competitive markets, etc. For Marx, labor was the most essential characteristic of human life. It allowed self-realization, which eventually generated real freedom. But in the capitalist system, the laborer loses this freedom to individuality because an invisible division splits his day into two parts. In the first part he produces the value equal to his wage, but the value he generates in the second part – what Marx referred to as surplus value – goes to the capitalist whose only intention is to extract as much as possible from the worker. Thus, the laborer sells one part of his labor for survival and the capitalist takes the rest away. In order to avoid this inherent exploitation, Marx proposed a socialist society, basically inspired by the ideologies of equality and solidarity. He advocated the abolition of private ownership of the means of production and the concept of profit.[1]

As discussed in Chapter I, in the late 1950s Kappen experienced Communism in Kerala. When the CPI took power in Kerala in 1957 it was expected to do something concrete to deal with the semi-feudal, pro-capitalist system in the state. To what extent the Communists in Kerala succeeded in this mission is matter for debate. Admittedly, they played a vital role until and after the formation of the state in partially abolishing Kerala's feudal and semi-feudal agrarian system. However, on their march toward a socialist society, they did not succeed in passing the capitalist phase – to phrase it in their own discourse. They did not eliminate the capitalist system, but even encouraged state capitalism, in which the state owned and operated the means of production for the purpose of profit, like other private institutions and capitalists. This shift has several causes. First of all, as one of the states in the Indian federal system, the Kerala state and government have to abide by the constitution of India, which essentially does not promote the fundamental Marxist ideologies of "the proletarian revolution" and the subsequent dictatorship, "the collapse of capitalism," and "the withering away of the state."[2] Secondly, the Communists themselves acknowledged the importance of parts of the capitalist system in Kerala, namely industrialization and large-scale production, and the foreign-invested plantation sector.[3] Thirdly, the capitalist interests of many of the Communists held them back from adopting true Marxist ideology. Therefore, coping with the economic environment of the state was an issue of survival for the Communists. As a part of this, the Communist governments also promoted public sector undertakings by investing heavily in profit-oriented sectors, such as industry, agro-based companies, (and more recently, information technology).

This is the general context in which Kappen wrote on capitalism. He criticized the capitalist policies of the Communists in Kerala. The Communists, being part of a federal system alien to Communism, did not have any alternative but to conform with the public-private sector and the pro-capitalist economic system. Therefore, Kappen's criticism of capitalism had manifold aspects: it laid bare capitalism in its real form, then targeted the capitalist interests of the religious institutions in India and elsewhere, and eventually also criticized the capitalist lenience of the Communists.

The growing criticism of Latin American capitalism could also be mentioned here. Behind Kappen's criticism of the capitalist character of the religious institutions in Kerala and India, we find his reference to the Latin American situation. Being a Jesuit progressive thinker, Kappen learned about the reaction against capitalist exploitations in Latin American countries and the way in which the local Church tackled it by emphasizing a preferential option for the poor. He was mainly informed by three sources: the works of Christian progressive thinkers, the works of Communist authors who wrote about Latin American capitalism and the liberationist movements, and the Indian priests of the Society of Jesus and the sisters of the Medical Mission Congregation who worked in Latin American countries.[4] Eventually, Kappen also painted a clear picture of the economic and political exploitation that existed there in the 1960s. He was quite optimistic about certain events, such as the Medellin Conference of the Latin American Bishops (CELAM, 1968), which condemned liberal capitalism. In light of this progressive transition of the Church in Latin America, Kappen expected that his criticism would change the institutionalized and capitalist nature of the Church and its institutions in Kerala.[5]

Kappen's Understanding of Capitalism

Although Kappen did not dedicate volumes specifically to the theme of capitalism, it appeared directly and indirectly in his writings concerning Marxism. He dealt with the subject over a wide spread of time, from the late 1960s to his death.[6] Kappen occasionally wrote about capitalism, but without really expanding on the concept. For instance, he said in 1969: "after twenty years of planning [Five Year Planning in India], the gulf between the rich and the poor is widening."[7] Still, there was an eventual evolution in his understanding of capitalism. This is clear from his early writings, especially those from before *Jesus and Freedom* (1977). In his *From Faith to Revolution* (1972), Kappen makes a short criticism of capitalism also by making some random references to Church documents like *Rerum Novarum* (1891), *Gaudium et Spes* (1965), and *Populorum Progressio* (1967). The reason for the lack of overemphasis on the topic in his writings could only be an assumption that the relatively well-educated society with a strong Marxist presence was already aware of it either through the works of left-leaning authors or through the struggles of Marxists in the state. In *Jesus and Freedom,* he provided a rather clear picture of capitalism as he understood it. This is because Kappen wrote the book in a non-Communist context (Chennai) and therefore felt the need to conceptualize capitalism, before criticizing it.

Kappen adequately reflected on the definition and the legacy of capitalism through theoretical explanations. For him, it was a "negation of the social dimension of man" and a "license for few to exploit many." Competition was its hallmark, "law of the survival of the fittest reigns economic life," and its result was profiteering and consumerism.[8] It goes without saying that Kappen's thoughts on capitalism developed in line with those of Marx. In order to analyze capitalism in his books and talks, Kappen used Marxian terms, such as bourgeoisie, means of production, surplus value, wage, slavery, working class, exploitation, praxis, etc. At the same time, his understanding of capitalism was not only as an economist but also as a sociologist and Christian progressive thinker. He interpreted capitalism from different perspectives by relating it with society, culture, imperialism, Church, and Marxism, and therefore we assume that it was also evolving.

First of all, from a sociological point of view, Kappen examined how the capitalist system affected the creation of a classless society. For this, he resorted to the ideas of Marx, who said man must create a world for himself. Marxism is different from other philosophies in the way it looks at the world. Whereas other philosophical thoughts gave various interpretations to the world, Marxism concentrated on the need to transform it.[9] Kappen reiterated the Marxian argument and found transformation more important than mere interpretation. This transformation was in fact an act of humanization attained through praxis. In the process of constructing a new world, man, his labor, the fruit of his labor, etc. were co-related and complementary. However, the capitalist and bourgeois system prevented the construction of a classless society. For Kappen, capitalism therefore was to be demolished for the sake of a new world order.[10]

Secondly, we see how Kappen treated capitalism from a cultural viewpoint. Kappen's posthumous work called *Tradition, Modernity, and Counter-culture* in 1994 presented a different understanding of the capitalist system, wherein he said that capitalism prevented the proper articulation of the inhibited creative spontaneity of the worker. He explicated this from a cultural perspective. Only when certain conditions are met, does a piece of art or a poem become perfect. But in bourgeois modernity, capitalism rules; maximizing production and profit are the maxims.[11] Therefore, when labor is being tapped from the laborer, nothing other than the required quality is produced. In a way, the capitalist system stagnates the creativity and spontaneity of a worker and can therefore be considered dehumanizing.

Thirdly, Kappen went back to imperialism to explain capitalism. By the beginning of the 1990s India witnessed an accelerated transition to globalization and liberalization. Prior to that, its economy was only partially open to foreign markets. The main objective of the new policy was strengthening the fledging economy in order to achieve self-reliance. Lifting up the Indian restrictions to the world market in 1991 strengthened capitalism. Kappen commented on these political changes, but did not change his approach to capitalism. Along with his argument that capitalism is exploitative and dehumanizing, he also started writing on imperialism. In light of Marx's criticism of capitalism, Kappen claimed that capitalism is a form of imperialism that exists even now, in the contemporary world.[12] For instance, he spoke of an invisible imperialism through agents like the United Nations, the World Bank, and the International Monetary Fund.[13] Kappen criticized the capitalist countries' invasion into the interests of developing countries. In the case of India, this created a dual economy: one for the rich and one for the poor. The goal of production turned to be the satisfaction of the rich, while the poor were deprived of basic needs. He said that if India managed to meet the needs of its own people, capitalist countries like America would lose millions of consumers.[14] Thus, in reality, capitalism did not make India self-reliant but instead, turned it into a more dependent country.

Finally, Kappen found capitalism to be a solid instrument for criticizing both the Catholic Church and Marxism. He strongly criticized them for their ever-increasing capitalist orientation. The Church and Marxism were far away from their original forms in which they were detached from pro-rich orientation. He also put forward certain antidotes against their own capitalist character. He referred to the Council documents, especially *Gaudium et Spes*, in condemning the excessive concentration of private property and the means of production in few hands.[15] The Church and Marxism had to first liberate themselves from the clutches of capitalism and pro-rich attitude and then try to construct a classless society as Marx envisioned.

Kappen's Criticism of Capitalism: The Why and How

Kappen's liberal borrowing from Marxist interpretation of capitalism helped him make his criticism broader. For this reason, his criticism cannot be limited to something that is exclusively from an Indian point of view. His censure of capitalism could be categorized into two: general and particular or contextual. The general criticism mainly targeted the issue of the concentration of the means of production and the dehumanizing character of capitalism. The particular one predominantly consisted of criticism from the perspective of certain specific contexts – Latin America, India, (and Kerala). Kappen saw capitalism as a foreign invention, as one of the serious problems that India was facing, as a catalyst in the alliance between religion and politics, and as an exploitation of the submissive religious mind of the ordinary people.

Regarding the general criticism, the fundamental point was the concentration of the means of production – both agricultural and industrial – into a few hands. This accumulation further led to the flow of wealth into the hands of the rich, creating a wide disparity in income and opportunity, which eventually sidelined a great deal of the common people. As a result, the working class remained stagnant or became poorer.[16]

For this reason, Kappen considered the capitalist mode of production as a "great threat to the *true* development of man" and therefore as a dehumanizing factor.[17] The growing grip of the capitalist mode of production in its real sense ignored and questioned human dignity, because in the process of the maximization of production, the worker and his labor were commoditized and considered objects rather than human beings.[18]

Moving from general criticisms to more particular ones, Kappen understood capitalism as a product of the West that was exported to or imported by other parts of the world. He especially elaborated on this aspect in several articles and extracts in the journal *Socialist Perspectives* that he published during his activist period in Chennai. For instance, his article called "The Present Cultural Crisis" (1980) stated that capitalism was not of Indian origin; rather, it had been introduced by the capitalist colonial powers. Subsequently, capitalism led to the creation of a consumer class, the concentration of the means of production, the marketing of products, the maximizing of profits, etc. By arguing so, Kappen shed light on the eventual circulation of private interest, consumerism, inequality, and bourgeois culture.[19] In 1985, he said the same with regard to Latin American countries. In his view, the capitalist system in Latin America was not a creation inside the continent alone; it was also the consequence of certain outside elements, introduced mainly by the CIA and American transnational companies.[20] Kappen's reference to the CIA indicated his strong anti-capitalism and sympathy to the left-wing. It is also interesting to note the leftist argument that the CIA secretly supported and funded the Church in Kerala in the Liberation Struggle against the Communist government between 1957 and 1959. The left-wing leaders considered it as the support of a capitalist power to a capitalist institution in order to wipe out Communism from Kerala.[21] Kappen does not refer to this and only frames the CIA in a Latin American context.

Kappen's critical approach presented capitalism as one of India's serious problems.[22] The capitalist and corporate systems became powerful enough to steer economic, social, and political life. In a capitalist society, the economic development did not reach every section in the society. His argument was essentially on behalf of the Dalits in India. The Dalits were a prime example in this regard as they were under great threat from the national and multi-national companies who, with the help of the government, infringed their freedom and rights by taking away their ancestral properties in order to establish huge factories. The Dalits were being displaced from their land by the government in order to launch new gold and coal mine projects and other industries. They practically no longer had access to the forest and its products upon which they had been relying for their livelihood.[23] In Kappen's words, the aftermaths of capitalism were "the proliferation of slums, the marginalization of the tribals and the outcastes [the Dalits], the destruction of traditional handicrafts and the ecological ravages wrought by profit-oriented production." This inspired him to challenge the Indian capitalists to replace "production for profit" with "production for social needs."[24]

Furthermore, Kappen criticized the capitalist system for providing a platform for the alliance between politics and religion that would eventually generate a bourgeois ethics in society. This observation was particularly in light of the pro-Congress party approach of the Church in Kerala. For Kappen, the Indian National Congress (INC) did not have support from the poor and the working class because of its pro-rich and pro-capitalist slant. The Church's Congress-orientation and anti-Marxist attitude showed the capitalist nature it projected in the state. In 1969, he wrote: "the history of the Church in Kerala since independence is a record of alliance with conservative socio-political forces."[25] Moreover, according to Kappen, both the Church and the INC had been trying to protect the vested interest of the rich and the powerful.[26] For this reason, Kappen developed the thought from an ethical perception that capitalism in any society created division. Private property and the consequent private interests, backed by religion and politics, forced man to erect barriers with his fellow beings. According to Kappen, what Marx repudiated was the bourgeois ethic that promoted "private property, private interest, competition, and consumerism."[27] In doing so, Marx's primary intention was to highlight the exploitative and dehumanizing aspect of capitalism, but not the elimination of the capitalists as a whole. Subsequently, he strived to develop a humanism that was intrinsically based on the interests of the working class.[28] Kappen even suggested the abolition of private property, a Marxian proposal, to eradicate the economic categorization in society.[29]

Finally, the submissive mind of the working class in Kerala and India due to the country's religious, social, and cultural traditions also contributed to the establishment of bourgeois ethics. The working class accepted the concentration of wealth into a few hands as a part of the system, which was mainly due to the religious and social values that taught that wealth is associated to birth. The acutely caste-ridden Kerala society considered the higher castes, especially the Brahmins (the priestly class), as repositories of knowledge and bearers of economic privileges. This fostered the capitalist assumption that intellectual labor was superior to manual labor, a clear instance for the traditional religious backing of capitalist structure.[30] In the case of Kerala, this had eventually smothered the urge of the marginalized landless tenants to revolt against the capitalist structure under the aegis of Marxism.

In sum, Kappen's critical analysis indicated two important institutions that should challenge capitalism: Marxism and religion, with particular emphasis on the Catholic Church. Kappen was both a pro-Marxist and a Christian theologian; at the same time, he was a strong critic of the capitalist lenience of the Marxist parties and the Church in Kerala. Both required a retrospective analysis, and in turn are to engage in constructive collaboration in creating a better social order in which the human person was the subject. His initiative for such a society was obvious in his preferential option for the poor and the marginalized – especially the Dalits – that strengthened the Dalit liberation movements in India.

B.   Alienation

In Marxian terms, alienation can be understood as any form of estrangement of human existence from its essence in the natural and material sense into an objectified alien being.[31] The concept of alienation, however, has a rather complex history and a number of different disciplines have been using it. It dates back to the Judeo-Christian tradition and continued to appear in Roman law and German idealism, especially in the writings of Hegel (1770-1831), such as *Phenomenology of Spirit* (1807). Bruno Bauer, a disciple of Hegel, applied the concept of alienation in his dealing with religion. He focused more on the estranged self-consciousness of man, which for him was an aftermath of the intrusion of religion. Ludwig Feuerbach further developed these thoughts, especially in his *The Essence of Christianity* (1841). It was from these predecessors that Marx adopted this idea for his critique of capitalism and religion. He explained the concept further in his "Economic and Philosophical Manuscripts"[32] and "Thesis on Feuerbach" (1845).[33]

With regard to the concept of alienation, Marx depended on Hegel. According to Hegel, man journeys to become himself because of the process of alienation. This journey is through the act of labor, which helps him become what he ought to be. However, Marx's view on alienation was also fundamentally different. While Hegel considered man as a spiritual being and highlighted the alienation of consciousness, Marx thought that man is related to nature and therefore focused on material alienation. And whereas Hegel saw alienation as something positive, Marx deemed it negative. He considered it something that makes man what he is not supposed to be through various means that he could overcome.[34] One of these means was religion. For Marx, the essence of religion was the estrangement of man from himself.[35] Religious alienation takes place in the level of "consciousness, in the inner life of man," whereas its economic version occurs in the "real life."[36]

Marx derived his theory from the understanding of Hegel and Feuerbach on religion, but turned their interpretation upside down. This is due to his understanding of man merely as a material and economic being. Because of his economic preoccupations, Marx complemented the theoretical argumentations of Hegel and Feuerbach that religion produced alienation, by claming that religion was actually a consequence of man's alienation in society. Thus, in Marx we find two understandings of religion: both a means of alienation and an aftermath of alienation. Unlike his predecessors, Marx dealt with the economic reasons for alienation. He argued that in society, labor is estranged from the laborer since the fruit of this labor goes to the bourgeoisie or the capitalist. In light of this economic alienation, religion became the aftermath of social alienation, the perpetuator of the oppressive social order, and the opium of the people.[37] Indeed, in Marx's eyes religion worked as an agent or extension of the capitalist system. It consoled the oppressed by teaching that there is meaning for their suffering. Therefore, one should combine fighting religion and the social order, because they are identical and serve the same purpose. Religion does not solve the workers' problems created by the ruling class and the capitalists, but makes their life bearable. So, it is the need of the ruling class or the capitalists to uphold religion in order to legitimize their actions.[38]

Kappen's understanding of alienation was based on Marx's writings on the subject, particularly on the "Economic and Philosophical Manuscripts." His doctoral dissertation in 1961, especially the second chapter, already dealt with the issue of alienation, including its various aspects. He categorized the term alienation into democratic alienation, material alienation, economic alienation, and religious alienation. This could also be understood as alienation from the system, alienation from the products, alienation from the productivity, and alienation from the essence of man.[39] Most of Kappen's attention, however, went to religious alienation. More particularly, he critically assessed the intellectual prejudices of Marx on religion and the inefficacy and exaggerated other-worldliness of Christianity.[40]

After his dissertation, Kappen for about eight years remained silent on alienation, but in 1969 he resumed the topic in his article on "Church and the Challenge of Social Revolution in Kerala." Here he elaborated more on democratic alienation. He criticized the democratic system in Kerala for being a relic of the feudal system. The government labeled itself as emanating from the people, by the people, and for the people. In reality, Kappen emphasized, democracy in Kerala became alienated from what it ought to be because its political outgrowth had detached itself from the ordinary life of the poor. For the poor, democracy had become nothing but a safe haven to foster the vested interests of the upper class: corruption, injustice, and inequality. Kappen especially targeted the INC. This major political group in independent India identified itself as the guardian of the democratic system, but he criticized this view and argued that it did not have support from the poor and was driven by the vested interest of the upper and wealthy class.[41]

Kappen not only elaborated on the alienation of the political system and of the INC, but also of the Church. He criticized the Church for its pro-right-wing politics and pointed up the discrepancy between Church's teachings and actions and to argue that the Church stood far away from the people. Kappen felt that the Church preferred its own "economic, denominational," and institutional interests to the values of the gospels, which were Jesus' message for the poor.[42] He attributed the concept of self-alienation to the Church to claim that the Church in Kerala alienated itself. Due to this self-alienation, he argued, the Church's role in society was taken over by the Communists, who were actually the ideological opposite of the Church. He found it indeed remarkable that in spite of the large and socially dominant Christian community, it was precisely in Kerala that the Communists gained the strongest presence in the whole of India. Kappen pointed out that the growth and development of the Communist movement in the state was due to Christian impotence. The Communist movement took up the responsibility of bridging the gap between theory and praxis. Kappen proposed three means to the Church in Kerala to regain its relevance: first, "make[ing] the message of the gospel practically relevant to the aspirations of the poor," second, preventing the "emergence of new forms of hierocracy," and third, giving greater role to the laity in "translating the social message of the Church into revolutionary action."[43]

Kappen's proposal to the alienated Church in Kerala was based on the potential co-operation between the Church and the Marxists in practical realms in spite of their ideological differences. In 1969, he noticed that the political atmosphere in Kerala of the previous years had left the Church with two options: either create a revolutionary movement which had nothing to do with the Communist movement, or critically collaborate with the revolutionary undertakings of the Communist movement. Kappen rejected both these options and suggested a new solution envisioning a de-alienation, which was practically a combination of the two options. His third way advocated the Christians form a "democratic revolutionary front" in cooperation with the people of other faiths. This new front had to critically collaborate with Communists.[44] Through this third way, Kappen had been planning out a theology of integral liberation. His proposal gained significance in the Kerala context where the Church and the Communist governments had been in conflict over many issues, such as education and land reform. He wanted to reconstruct a just social order through the Church's dialogue with committed agents of social revolution. This would essentially require from the side of the Church a constructive Church-Marxist encounter instead of the Church-capitalist alliance. Only this, Kappen stated, would be able to de-alienate both the Church and the people.

Kappen targeted the Church even more in the 1970s, particularly in his *From Faith to Revolution* (1972). He now focused on capitalistic alienation and criticized the Church's unholy relationship with the rich class and its distance from the poor. In Kappen's view, the Church became a replica of the feudal lords who enjoyed giving nominal privileges to the poor. This approach, according to him, consolidated inequality in society and weakened the Church's influence on its faithful for several reasons. First of all, most Christians became aware of the alienated nature of the Church. Secondly, many of them reevaluated their skepticism towards the Communist party because of the latter's commitment to the cause of the poor and involvement in social issues. Thirdly, they started using their franchise according to their own conscience and conviction by not giving heed to the election-time exhortations from the hierarchy of the Church through the pastoral letters of the bishops and the sermons in the parishes.[45]

After having put forward in his 1969 article the need of co-operating with the Marxists, Kappen further elaborated on this topic in 1972. He had no doubt about the need for a meaningful encounter with the Communists taking into account the significant role they had in forming the state. His argument for mutual co-operation was similar in content with that of 1969, but more explicit and intense. For instance, Kappen said that being a minority in Kerala, the Church ought to depend on other progressive institutions in order to reconstruct the social system in society. In support of this potential co-operation he referred to article 7 of the *Apostolicam Actuositatem* (1965), the Second Vatican Council decree on the apostolate of the laity, which said that "men should work together to renew and constantly perfect the temporal order." Furthermore, Kappen specified that Communism sowed the seeds of revolutionary movements in Kerala and that it had a strong relationship with the poor. This being the situation, it was impossible to construct the future of the state without Communists. However, he was totally against any uncritical co-operation with the Communists. For this, the Church had to critically analyze the means of liberation put forward by the Communists and check whether they promoted human values. He suggested a collaboration with the Communists on economic, social, and political terrains but without assimilating their philosophy. He also advocated the co-operation of the Church with other, non-Communist revolutionary movements in order to resist the Communists if the latter adopted unjust means in their journey to socialism.[46]

Kappen continued his critical approach to the concept of alienation in *Jesus and Freedom* (1977). Although he did not directly deal with Marxism in the book, he extensively used Marxist ideas and terms when analyzing the person of Jesus and the Church, as he had also done in his previous writings. *Jesus and Freedom* highlighted problems prevailing in the 1970s, such as poverty, unemployment, landless people, health issues, capitalist exploitation, low per capita income, etc. Kappen also reiterated in Marxian terms on workers' alienation from what they produced.[47] He complained that not only the product but also the means of production were expropriated from the workers. His book gave the impression that radical Christian thinkers opted to step out of the comfort zone of the hierarchical system, envisioning new vistas of integral liberation. In this mission, Kappen walked ahead of such thinkers.

In 1983, Kappen published yet another significant work, *Marxian Atheism*. Since it was a revised version of his doctoral dissertation, it contained more reflection on Marxism. In his introduction, Kappen wrote that he published this work for three reasons. Firstly, there were not many serious works in India on Marxism; secondly, the works that existed were mere reproductions of the Engelsian interpretation of Marx; and finally, Kappen wanted to present Marx as he was, i.e. without interpreting him. The book mainly dealt with Marx's theory of religious alienation, the subject of Kappen's doctoral dissertation. It was a challenge to both Marxists and adherents of religions to understand their converging and diverging points.[48]

In dealing with the concept of alienation in *Marxian Atheism*, Kappen explained its lineage from Hegel through Feuerbach and Bauer to Marx. He did so by referring to the original works of these philosophers, even though most of them were in German. The relevance of the book is that the author believed that religious alienation was still a problem in Indian society in the 1980s. Although Kappen did not explicitly express this in his book, he sympathetically highlighted the Marxian view that religion had to be abolished to affirm the true self of the human being. While analyzing Marx's thoughts, Kappen even said: "[...] the only way to get rid of religion is to change the world. The illusory happiness provided by religion can be abolished only by the promotion of man's real happiness in this world."[49] Marx also argued for the negation of

God both outside and inside of religion and nature in order to affirm the total immanence and self-sufficiency of man.[50] Kappen, however, did not promote atheism, but shared certain concerns over the godhood of Jesus (see chapter V).

In Kappen's understanding, which is in term with Marx's, religion is man's protest against the perversion of this world. In other words, he found in religion a projected world of illusion, which compensated the imperfections of human life. Eventually, the consoled man learned to reconcile himself to the social evils. In the Indian case, various prevalent religions were sponsoring their own illusory worlds. All religions became the opium of the people by taking adherents away from this immanent world to a deceptive one. Kappen extended an indirect invitation to the Indian religions to step out from their unreal worlds for the reason that they alienated them in their inner and real life. Kappen found religious and economic alienations to be complementary, particularly in the Indian context.[51] To an extent his assessment seemed accurate, because the submissive religiosity of an ordinary Indian justifies economic alienation, and this, in turn, fosters the illusory world which religion creates.

Besides *Marxian Atheism*, Kappen also regularly wrote on alienation in his articles for *Negations*. In one of them, "Alienation and the Dialectic of History" (1983),[52] he presented a rather long but condensed analysis of the concept of alienation in Marxism, which he was hitherto dealing with. Later, in 2012, Sebastian Vattamattam compiled and edited a series of six of Kappen's *Negations* articles, with the title *Marx beyond Marxism*.

The idea of religious alienation appeared in Kappen's doctoral dissertation already in 1961 and it continued to be so until the end of his life. However, over the course of the years, his criticism of religion and religious alienation intensified. Although he was already critical of religion in his dissertation, he then mostly reproduced the Marxist understanding and criticism of religion. After his dissertation, he seemingly retrieved from religious criticism until at least the late 1960s. Afterwards, however, he started publishing articles that dealt also with the idea of alienation, especially elaborating on religious alienation.

He continued this after the Vatican's disciplinary measures against him and in the 1980s even began writing more intensely about alienation.

This progressive change in his approach on religious criticism in his writings did not derive from any kind of prejudice. For instance, in spite of his increasing criticism of the alienated Church in the first half of the 1970s, Kappen also reiterated the contributions of the Church in various sectors of society including education, health care, and social work. This is also evident from the terms and phrases he used in his works. He distinguished himself from other Christian progressive thinkers of the time through his extensive use of Marxist and biblical terms and ideologies in analyzing the Church and the society. For example, he often wrote with biblical terms, such as 'kingdom,' 'prophet,' 'slaves,' 'poor,' etc. combining this with Marxist terms including 'oppression,' 'exploitation,' 'capitalism,' 'liberation,' 'revolution,' 'alienation,' etc. However, Kappen did not seem to be in total conformity with the Marxian means of de-alienation like a return from religion, the family, and the state, which is possible through revolutionary process. In sum, despite the fact that Kappen was a theologian, he showed great affinity to Marxist ideologies. But this did not mean that he was a Marxist; rather he remained a theologian who depended on Marxist ideologies. This is clear from his neutral position: Kappen was both against the Church's uncritical rejection of and unconditional co-operation with Marxism.

C.   Revolution

Revolution was a leading element in Kappen's elaboration and analysis of Marxism. He presented it as an effective means to demolish alienation and capitalism. This section will further explore this element. It will examine how Marx and Kappen interpreted the idea of revolution, its necessity, and its objectives. In this way, we will also discuss to what extent Kappen was a Marxist or whether he was just an academician making use of Marxist terms and ideologies.

For Marx, social revolution was a means in the journey of humanity towards socialism through improving the condition of the working class. In his view, wage inequality necessarily led to revolution, any revolutionary movement having its empirical and theoretical basis on private property.[53] Therefore, revolution was related to how the society tackled the working class and private property. In Marx's vision, man had to create a world for him. So, Marxism stood different from other philosophies in so far as it looked into the world.[54] This transformation was in fact an act of humanization attained through praxis. In the process of constructing a new world, man, his labor, the fruit of his labor, etc. were co-related and complementary. However, the capitalist and bourgeoisie system prevented the construction of a classless society. Marx believed that demolition of capitalism could only take place through revolution. This revolution was the outcome of certain conflicts, such as those between the "new forces of production" and the "old institutions and social organizations," between "newer rising classes" and "old ruling classes," and between "new ideas" and the "established ones."[55] The end result would be revolutionary, an epochal change.

Kappen's Understanding of Marx's Idea of Revolution

Kappen found his interest in Marx's faith in human dignity, freedom of humanity, and a retrieving of man's ability to create a new world for himself. In a way, like Marx, Kappen considered the act of transforming the world as more important than interpreting it. He wrote widely on the idea of revolution, which in substance and to an extent was a reproduction of Marxian understanding of it, although he also had different accents and interpretations. Kappen wrote about revolution in and through his entire life. After his dissertation, he started writing on the topic of social revolution along with alienation and capitalism again in 1969 with his article "Church and the Challenge of Social Revolution in Kerala."

Kappen's understanding as a Christian theologian of the Marxist concept of revolution enabled him to complement the religious criticism of Marx. His focus in the 1969 article was to explain how the Church in Kerala could be a revolutionary force, and he challenged the Church to be an agent of change. In his opinion, the Church had to first undergo an inner revolution in order to participate in the social revolutionary movement. He called this inner revolution an "ecclesial revolution." For this, the Church in Kerala had to take seriously the Second Vatican Council's catchphrase, namely "reading the sign[s] of the time," which the Latin American liberation theologians applied in progressive theologizing.[56]

The central point Kappen raised was that, being part of a secularized world, society and the Church had to come out of the primitive understanding that various deprivations of human beings were either "part of an order" or "fate."[57] Secularization, and in a way, even progressive religious leaders paved the path to social revolutions in Kerala, because they helped people to get out of the traditional religious pupas and think of the causality of various deprivations in secular terms. As a result, the urge for revolution in the human mind, whose expression was prevented due to the cultural and religious inhibitions, found a way out. Interestingly, Kappen detected the influence of the Communist movement behind the expression of this urge. He pointed out that the CPI in Kerala played a significant role in organizing the forces of revolution and defining its socio-political goals.[58] This observation was an acknowledgement of Communist contributions in the state, which is remarkable for a Christian theologian.

In the following years, Kappen published three articles which presented the concept of revolution elaborately, namely "The Christian and the Call to Revolution" (1971), "Christianity and India's Development" (1972), and "The Goals of Revolution" (1973). The main thrust of all these articles was a proper Christian participation in revolutionary movements. In the revolution that he envisaged, every Christian had the right and duty to become a revolutionary, committed to social transformation.[59] He found that traditional theology gave importance only to spiritual revolution, ignoring the social and corporeal dimension of the human being. He opted for revolution because of the presence of injustice and inequality around him, believing that justice and equality were inevitable elements of a transformed society.[60]

What should be the nature of revolution a Christian engaged in? Kappen's progressive thinking consisted of two significant conceptions of Marxism, namely revolution and freedom.[61] He advocated a revolution that was without weapons and violence. For him, revolution was the rapid and radical transformation of the existing social system, and did not necessarily require the use of violence. However, we do not find Kappen categorically repudiating violence in revolution. Besides, his approach to the concept of revolution, sometimes, conveyed the impression that non-violent means were inadequate in the process of social transformation. Even though he did not explicitly incite people to take up arms to fight social evils, he believed that power has to be encountered with power. This was clear from his argument that the goal of revolution was the destruction of something to construct something else anew.[62] From this, we may derive that destruction and power encountering power plausibly invite violence. As a matter of fact, Kappen's goal was a rapid transformation in the social system in order to reduce the disparities in society to the minimum level.[63] The social system to be changed was often the established structure with legal and moral sanction. So, revolution in practice was the restructuring of the established structure.

As a part of complementing his focus on socio-economic revolution, Kappen developed another thought, namely a revolution of attitudes and ideas. For him, socio-economic revolution without the revolution of attitudes and ideas was meaningless. Therefore, from Kappen's writings, also as a Christian theologian, we understand that both these aspects of revolution could not be fulfilled merely through collaboration with the Communists. As the Communists strived for socio-economic revolution, every Christian had to initiate a revolution of attitudes and ideas, i.e. a mental and ecclesial revolution.[64] He put forward the gospels as the inspiring agents for the latter. This conclusion from Kappen implicitly put across his discontent with institutionalized religions, which were anti-revolutionary, anti-progressive, and pro-capitalist.

Coming to the practical side, Kappen observed that a social or political revolution in India would be unfeasible mainly for two reasons. First, the left parties in India came to power through the parliamentary process, which did not give room for an "insurrectionist strategy" or "the project of smashing the bourgeois state apparatus."[65] If they still wanted to spark a revolution, they should rely on class struggle, but the parliamentary system lacked provision for it. Secondly, the presence of a "well-trained and centralized army," and the "sophisticated intelligence system" ruled out any possibility of the formation of a people's army and the subsequent political insurrection.[66] Even if Kappen believed in the need for a socio-political revolution that destructed the exploitative systems in India, he could not initiate revolution. He therefore seemed to have taken Communism for granted as the sole medium of revolution, without being able to consider other possible agents. So, the ecclesial revolution, and the revolution of the attitudes and ideas could be seen as the mitigated forms of what he essentially wanted.

Generally speaking, Kappen's idea of revolution was different from that of Marx, because the latter proposed a social and political revolution via a proletarian insurrection. For instance, in the last paragraph of *The Communist Manifesto* (1848), Marx called for a *forcible* overthrow of the existing exploitative social systems.[67] In the same year he wrote in the German newspaper *Neue Rheinische Zeitung* that revolutionary terror was the working class' means to fight the existing old systems.[68] There has been debate, ever since, about the interpretation of the term *forcible*. This question gained relevance with the appearance of the argument that Marx was in favor of peaceful revolution and only promoted violence against the existing system during the time of the composition of *The Communist Manifesto*. Yet, the reference to a peaceful revolution is also due to milder interpretations from after Marx's death.[69] Anyway, regarding the difference between Marx and Kappen over violence, we can make only a general conclusion that Marx did not explicitly avow violence and Kappen did not explicitly disavow violence.

The difference between Kappen and Marx on the means of revolution did not extend to its goals. Marxists hoped to create an egalitarian classless society. For Kappen, this classless society was nothing other than the new heaven and the new earth promised by Christianity. While Marx advocated a total destruction of the old bourgeois system, Kappen held that one should not create a new social order through the total negation of the past. He says: "revolution does not mean destroying the achievements of the past and creating a new society out of nothing."[70] In this way, the prescribed destruction of the existing social order did not mean a complete rejection of whatever positive that had been achieved in the past. We could argue that for Kappen, revolution was a continuing struggle to alleviate the miseries of the poor by opening up the prospects of an integral development, which in fact was a true process of humanizing.

Conceptualization of Revolution Continued

The very title of Kappen's first book, *From Faith to Revolution*, demanded a shift from mere faith to revolution. Kappen completed writing this book in Calicut in August 1971. The Kerala context of revolutionary movements, especially by different Communist organizations, worked as the contextual background to this work. It was primarily an attempt to analyze the response of the Church in Kerala towards the emerging revolutionary trends and organizations. Kappen did this in light of social issues and the modern Church's commitment to them. Likewise, in some of his subsequent works, he continued to write about the revolutionary undertakings of the Communist parties (mainly CPI[M] and CPI) in Kerala. But, before examining them, we will make a detailed study of his 1972 work, as it remained the most important source on Kappen's idea of revolution.

Providing a theoretical explanation about how a revolution should be, Kappen returned to his ideas about revolution, which he had previously published. First of all, revolution for him was a radical and quick transformation of an existing social system into one that was totally based on justice. The change had to be radical, not within the system but throughout the entire system. We could see this as the second stage of revolution, the first being the revolution within religious and political groups. Secondly, the change brought by revolution should not be a partial settlement of any issue that society addressed; rather, it should lead to an integral change. Most importantly, revolution was not a repair of the social system but a demolition and construction of a new one. This is a different expression of Kappen's previous observation that he preferred the transformation of society to perfection in its various aspects, i.e. economic, social, cultural, etc. Thirdly, slow and evolutionary changes cannot be considered revolutionary; rather, the change intended should be quick and planned. Slow and gradual transformation could be called sociological evolution. Revolutionary activities gained rapidity when the objective need became subjective. According to Kappen, behind every revolution there should be an elite group who converts the inarticulate objective aspirations of the exploited into articulated subjective aspirations. Therefore, he said, revolution was not a natural happening, but a deliberate process.[71]

The book also was a clear indicator of Kappen's knowledge and concern about the economic, religious, and social problems in Kerala. They included the high unemployment rate and the disequilibrium in the wage system, the poverty and economic crisis before and after the formation of the state, the relatively rational and critical understanding of society about religion and its control over the people, and the structural exploitation based on caste discrimination. Each accelerated revolutionary feeling in Kerala, and Kappen substantiated all his arguments by dealing with them in detail.[72]

Although many factors contributed to the revolutionary culture, Kappen was unsatisfied with the slow development, whether it was by the Communist government or by the Congress. In his opinion, the gap between the expectations of the poor and the possibility of it being fulfilled was huge. This disparity was mainly due to factors like growing economic inequality, price hiking, and hoarding and black marketing in the state. For this conclusion, he depended on the argument of K.

Damodaran, a prominent Marxist writer from Kerala.[73] Kappen was afraid that these drawbacks in the economy would slow down the pace of development. Moreover, the inhuman living condition of the poor was the result of the injustice of the rich minority. Not leaving the plight of the poor to a slow developing process to gradually empower them, Kappen suggested immediate and radical transformative measures. Like Marx, he also believed that revolution was not only for economic development but also for attaining justice and equality.[74]

In continuation to this, Kappen further elaborated on development, revolution, and evolution in *Jesus and Freedom* in 1977. Predominantly, he repeated what he said in 1972: transformation of society should be rapid and radical. This observation was in a sense a questioning of the conventional understanding that transformation occurred through the process of evolution. In contrast to this, and justifying his argument, Kappen stated that waiting for the slow process of evolution to take place was actually an injustice towards many generations. Rather, development should be the result of revolution. An effective revolution would take place when the society converted its protest into action. However, this action was not for overthrowing the social system but for creating a "new consciousness," with a new sense of values and a new vision of the world.[75] Kappen instructed the agents of revolution with revolutionary consciousness to stick to certain fundamental principles. He argued that revolutionary consciousness must be critical, practical, humane, communitarian, prospective, and with unconditional commitment.[76]

Kappen predominantly focused on economic revolution but shifted his interpretation of revolution towards the end of his life. In his *The Future of Socialism and Socialism of the Future* (1992), he expanded the revolutionary concept to other fields of society. He indeed advocated that struggle for socialism had to go beyond the economic or political view of society to other sectors of civil society – to multiple struggles –, such as "people against bureaucracy," "women against male domination," "students against the educational system," intellectuals "for the freedom of expression," "critical believers against religious obscurantism," and the low caste and the Dalits against discrimination and marginalization.[77] This new shift in Kappen's interpretation of revolution could be due to his more practical approach to Indian society, which required an integral liberation. An effective convergence of the struggles for the aforementioned changes had to lead to a greater social revolution. To this account, we could argue with Kappen that the religious, cultural, and civil societies had to collaborate, because an effective revolution was the summation of various minor revolutions in different sectors of society.

Therefore, the beginning of any revolution was the awareness that the existing structures and value system brought good to a minority and suffering to the majority. Kappen stated that revolution was also a conflict between the traditional structures that protected a minority and the modern social forces that represent the will of the majority. As a result, not only the destruction of the existing structure should take place but also a construction of a social structure that is in terms with human dignity and values. In Communism and Church, we find both these established structures and social forces, which require and demand respectively an inner revolution.

Kappen's Appraisal and Criticism of the Communist Movement

Kappen's appraisal and criticism of Communism were spread all through his writings. In addition to what we analyzed in the previous sections, we make a brief examination into both his approval and disapproval of Communism, especially in his writings after the second half of the 1970s. According to Kappen, the progressive policies of the Communist governments in Kerala found certain positive results in eliminating social and economic disparities. He highlighted the Communist contributions by acknowledging that they partially put an end to feudalism, liberated workers from the exploitation of the bourgeoisie landlords, contributed to improving the standard of living of the poor, and conscientized the marginalized about their rights. The CPI and the CPI[M] in Kerala deserved this appraisal for bringing about such a people-oriented atmosphere in the state.

Kappen's article "Indian Communism and the challenge of Cultural Revolution" (1985) particularly showed his passion for left ideology.[78] Interestingly, it was written immediately after the Congregation for the Doctrine of Faith had published its first document criticizing liberation theology for assimilating with Marxism.[79] Kappen recounted the revolutionary contributions of the Communist movement in some of the Indian states, especially in West Bengal, Kerala, and Andhra Pradesh. The land reform movement, initiatives towards social security and better wages for the working class, etc. according to him, were landmark achievements of Communist state governments. He also wrote that the Communist movement and parties have functioned as a political and cultural force in India.[80]

Kappen made attempts to overcome the Church's charge that Marxism subverted the notion of truth when it claimed that truth was in partisan praxis. The key concept under discussion was *praxis*.[81] Kappen explained the two-fold understanding of the term – a broader sense, i.e. man's sensuous experience and encounter with the world, and a narrower sense, i.e. a revolutionary or critical-practical activity.[82] It was the latter that transformed human beings, a transition from what they *are* to what they *ought to be*. Consequently, "the full truth of anything that exists is what it is meant to become."[83] Kappen argued that from this angle, the truth understood by Marxism and Christianity was similar. For the former, the truth of the current society was the classless society in potential and for the latter it was the Kingdom of God; and both employed *praxis* to attain their goals.[84] Therefore, any theory which helped society discover its possibilities and accelerate its striving towards a more human one, was true and valid.

Kappen's observation could not be seen as an approval of the Communists in the state by letting them escape criticism. In the 1960s, he criticized them for their deviation from original Communist ideologies. This departure, in his view, was because of the affiliation of some of the Communists to what Communism resisted – capitalism. They preached revolution in public and allied with the capitalists in private. Through such a criticism, he expressed his trust in orthodox Communism. Therefore, according to Kappen, it was unfeasible to completely entrust the future of Kerala to the Communists.[85]

Kappen became a strong critic of the Communist movement in Kerala towards the end of his life. Although he often considered Communism as an agent of revolutionary movements, he found it stood against revolution itself at a certain point of time. Communist dogmas, which in many ways were unrelated to the Indian context, prevented a proper reading of the realities and the subsequent revolution. Communism was content with electoral politics and immediate ends. To put it in Kappen's own words: "violence, intimidation, money-power, demagogy, and false electoral promises" helped it secure votes but not construct a classless society. Instead, what Indian Communism required was an original indigenous strategy for social reconstruction. It had to strengthen its democratic credibility and enter into dialogue with the Gandhian tradition. Unfortunately, the fundamental option for Indian Communism happened to be between "to change" or "to stagnate."[86] This observation reminds us of Kappen's initial criticism of Communism for its capitalist lenience in Kerala. In effect, he went back to his original critique to Communism in the state. Still, it must be noted that Kappen criticized not Communism in general, but its Kerala version, or in other words, its partisan politics. In the practical sense, Kappen had been diagnosing the problem and prescribing a means to overcome the problem.[87]

From a critical perspective, we understand that Kappen was less systematic in dealing with the idea of revolutionary Marxism. His appraisal and criticism of Marxism were scattered in his works, which in effect makes it difficult to know how Marxist he was. However, it is clear that he succeeded in using the Marxist concept of revolution in a pluralistic society by interrogating its various interpretations, including its ethical dimension. This further enabled him to argue that the Church and Communism were the two major potential revolutionary forces in the context of Kerala and India. Towards this end he constantly proposed an effective but critical cooperation between these forces. However, this cooperation would succeed only when both sides initiated internal revolution. This would invite them to redefine the system and structure in which they are established.

Having analyzed the approach of Kappen from a general framework of liberation theology, we come to the conclusion that he relied on Marxist ideologies to varying degrees in understanding and analyzing the society and the Church. Scholars had even argued that liberation theology was the result of Marxist influence on Christianity. In fact, there had been an incorporation of the Marxist social and economic analysis into the gospel message of salvation.[88] The secular interpretation of the term liberation had many things in common with Marxism. While Marx had envisioned a classless society, liberated from every form of oppression and exploitation, liberation theologians strived to bring about a classless society – a society of equity and equality – by assimilating Marxian ideologies. Classes for both Marxism and liberation theology are of the rich and the poor/the oppressor and the oppressed unlike the divisions based on caste, color, culture, and creed.[89] Generally speaking, they all criticized alienation in its different forms, as well as the institutionalization and capitalist orientation of the Church. In sum, Marxist ideologies influenced and challenged liberation theology in the Third World countries, vaguely or explicitly. This substantiated Kappen's observation that no liberation movement could function unless it was adequately supported by a social theory that not only analyzed the society but also changed the world. Kappen considered liberation theology to be the aftermath of the "fruitful confrontation between the Gospel and the philosophy of Marx."[90] The case was not different in India because, Kappen said, if there were something meaningful taking place in the field of theology in India with the task of abolishing manifold alienations, it was due to the above-mentioned confrontation. Being a progressive theologian with Marxist orientation, Kappen succeeded in maintaining a balance between the Bible and *Das Kapital*, which in fact, is an inevitable factor in the humanizing

Endnotes

[1] I depended on the "Economic and Philosophical Manuscripts" of Marx in writing this section, especially on the first manuscript which dealt with wages of labor, profit of capital, rent of land, and alienated labor. Cf. Marx, "Economic and Philosophical Manuscripts," 61-134. For more details, I also consulted Suchting, *Marx: An Introduction*; Pierson, *The Marx Reader* (1983); Bottomore, *Interpretations of Marx* (1988); Ollman, *Alienation: Marx's Conception of Man in Capitalist Society* (1976); and Carter, *Marx, a Radical Critique* (1988).

[2] Maitra, *Marxism in India*, 274.

[3] Gopalan, *Kerala, Yesterday and Today* (Malayalam), 88-91.

[4] A prominent Keralite author on Latin *American* capitalism and Communism was P. Govinda Pillai (1926-2012). Joseph, "Liberation Theology: Its Impact on Kerala Politics and Society," 257.

[5] Kappen, *Liberation Theology and Marxism*, 15.

[6] Kappen's major works in this context are "Church and the Challenge of social revolution in Kerala" (1969); *From Faith to Revolution* (Malayalam) (1972); *Jesus and Freedom* (1977); "The present cultural crisis" (1980); *Marxian Atheism*, (1983); "Towards an Indian Theology of Liberation" (1985); "In Search of a New God" (1986); *The future of socialism and the socialism of the future* (1992); and the posthumous work, namely *Tradition, Modernity, and Counter-Culture* (1994).

[7] Kappen, "Church and the Challenge of Social Revolution in Kerala," 62.

[8] Kappen, *Jesus and Freedom*, 46-7.

[9] Marx-Engels, *Selected Works*, 405.

[10] Kappen, *Jesus and Freedom*, 46-8.

[11] Kappen, *Tradition, Modernity, and Counter-culture*, 5.

[12] Pons and Service, eds., *A Dictionary of 20th-Century Communism*, 408.

[13] Kappen, *The Future of Socialism and Socialism of the Future*, 12.

[14] Kappen, *The Future of Socialism and Socialism of the Future*, 38.

[15] *GS* 22. Kappen, *From Faith to Revolution* (Malayalam), 54-5 and 62.

[16] Kappen, "Church and the Challenge of Social Revolution in Kerala," 68.

[17] Kappen, *Jesus and Freedom*, 46.

[18] Kappen, *Jesus and Freedom*, 46-7.

[19] Kappen, "The Present Cultural Crisis," 63-74.

[20] Kappen, *Liberation theology and Marxism*, 15. This work is a collection of Kappen's articles and essays.

[21] For more details, cf. Ajayan, "Mid-term Election in Kerala in 1960 and the American Government," and Issac, *The Unseen Sides of the Liberation Struggle* (Malayalam), 248-60.

[22] Kappen, "Towards an Indian Theology of Liberation," 303.

²³ Cf. Wilfred, "Religions Face to Face with Globalization," 35-42.

²⁴ Kappen, "Towards an Indian Theology of Liberation," 303.

²⁵ Kappen, "Church and the Challenge of Social Revolution in Kerala," 67.

²⁶ Kappen, "Church and the Challenge of Social Revolution in Kerala," 68.

²⁷ Kappen, *Liberation theology and Marxism*, 84.

²⁸ Bottomore, *Interpretations of Marx*, 181.

²⁹ Kappen, *Liberation theology and Marxism*, 110-1.

³⁰ Kappen, *Jesus and Freedom*, 45.

³¹ Marx, "On the Jewish Question," 39. Also cf. Ollman, *Alienation: Marx's conception of Man in Capitalist Society*, 132.

³² Marx, "Economic and Philosophical Manuscripts," 61-219.

³³ Marx and Engels, *On Religion*, 69-72.

³⁴ Chiodi, *Sartre and Marxism*, 80. For more details on Hegel's understanding of labor, cf. Bartonek, "Labour against Capitalism? Hegel's concept of Labour in between Civil Society and the State," 113-24.

³⁵ Rockmore, *Marx after Marxism*, 66.

³⁶ Marx, *Early Writings*, 156.

³⁷ Marx and Engels, *On Religion*, 69-71.

³⁸ Haralambos and Heald, *Sociology: Themes and Perspectives*, 461. A recently published article gives a simplified interpretation of the Marxist understanding of religion and alienation. Cf. Uchegbue, "A Critical evaluation of Marx's theory of Religion," 50-81.

³⁹ Kappen, "Praxis and the Emancipation of Man from Religious Alienation according to the Economic and Philosophical Manuscripts of Karl Marx," 61-87.

⁴⁰ Kappen, "Praxis and the Emancipation of Man from Religious Alienation according to the Economic and Philosophical Manuscripts of Karl Marx," 222-34.

⁴¹ Kappen, "Church and the Challenges of Social Revolution in Kerala," 65-8.

⁴² Kappen, "Church and the Challenges of Social Revolution in Kerala," 68-9. Criticism against the INC and its politically motivated mild approach to the Church is highlighted also in the writings of Marxist and non-Marxist authors. For instance, cf. Bhaskaran, *Communist Movement in Kerala* (Malayalam); A.K. Gopalan, *Kerala, Yesterday and Today* (Malayalam); and Nossiter, *Communism in Kerala*.

⁴³ Kappen, "Church and the Challenges of Social Revolution in Kerala," 73.

⁴⁴ Kappen, "Church and the Challenges of Social Revolution in Kerala," 74-5.

⁴⁵ Kappen, *From Faith to Revolution* (Malayalam), 32-3.

⁴⁶ Kappen, *From Faith to Revolution* (Malayalam), 102-4.

⁴⁷ Kappen, *Jesus and Freedom*, 32-4.

⁴⁸ Kappen, *Marxian Atheism*, 1-3.

⁴⁹ Kappen, *Marxian Atheism*, 16.

[50] Marx, "Economic and Philosophical Manuscripts," 210, cited from Kappen, *Marxian Atheism*, 10-1.

[51] Kappen, *Marxian Atheism*, 12 and 38-9.

[52] Kappen, "Alienation and the Dialectic of History," 13-9.

[53] Marx, "Economic and Philosophical Manuscripts," 77, 119, and 156.

[54] Marx-Engels, *Selected Works*, 405.

[55] Johnson, Walker, and Gray, eds., *Historical Dictionary of Marxism*, second edition, 366.

[56] Kappen, "Church and the Challenge of Social Revolution in Kerala," 75. The exhortation to read the sings of the time is from Pope John XXIII's Apostolic Constitution *Humanae Saluti*, with which he convoked the Council on 25 December 1961. For more details about the revolutionary aspects in the early life of Marx, also cf. Suchting, *Marx: An Introduction*, 30-44.

[57] Kappen, "Church and the Challenge of Social Revolution in Kerala," 63.

[58] Kappen, "Church and the Challenge of Social Revolution in Kerala," 66.

[59] Kappen, "The Christian and the Call to Revolution," 30.

[60] Kappen, "The Christian and the Call to Revolution," 38.

[61] "Economic and Philosophical Manuscripts," with which Kappen is well acquainted, treats revolution and freedom in detail.

[62] Kappen, *From Faith to Revolution* (Malayalam), 13.

[63] Kappen, "Christianity and India's Development," 129-41. Cf. Joseph, "From Development to Liberation: Perspectives in the Emergence of Liberation Theology in India," 186-8.

[64] Kappen, "The Christian and the Call to Revolution," 30-5.

[65] Kappen, "Towards a Strategy of Socialist Reconstruction," 33.

[66] Kappen, "Towards a Strategy of Socialist Reconstruction," 30-3.

[67] Marx and Engels, *The Communist Manifesto*, 120.

[68] Marx, *Neue Rheinische Zeitung*, no. 136, translated by the Marx-Engels Institute. Available at https://www.marxists.org/archive/marx/works/1848/11/06.htm [accessed on 20 October 2016]. Also cf. Marx and Engels, *The German Ideology*, 60.

[69] Singh, "Status of Violence in Marx's Theory of Revolution," 9-20.

[70] Kappen, "The Goals of Revolution," 52-3.

[71] Kappen, *From Faith to Revolution* (Malayalam), 17-9, and Kappen, "The Goals of Revolution," 52.

[72] Kappen, *From Faith to Revolution* (Malayalam), 16-21. For more details, Drèze and Sen, *India: Economic Development and Social Opportunity*, 5; Fic, *Kerala, Yenan of India*, 2-7; and Nossiter, *Communism in Kerala*, 45-65.

[73] Damodaran, *Indian Thought: A Critical Survey* (Malayalam), 480.

[74] Kappen, *From Faith to Revolution* (Malayalam), 23-4.

75 Kappen, *Jesus and Freedom*, 168-9.

76 Kappen, *Jesus and Freedom*, 170.

77 Kappen, *The Future of Socialism and Socialism of the Future*, 55.

78 *Negations*, no. 13, January-March 1985. He again published this article under the title "Whither Indian Communism?" in 1992 in his *The Future of Socialism and the Socialism of the Future*.

79 CDF, *Instruction on Certain Aspects of the Theology of Liberation*, 1984.

80 Kappen, *The Future of Socialism and the Socialism of the Future*, 40-1.

81 CDF, *Instruction on Certain Aspects of the Theology of Liberation*, VIII, nos. 2-5.

82 Kappen substantiates this by referring to Marx, "Theses on Feuerbach," 82.

83 Kappen, *Liberation theology and Marxism*, 79.

84 Kappen, *Liberation theology and Marxism*, 79-80.

85 Kappen, *From Faith to Revolution* (Malayalam), 54-5.

86 Kappen, *The Future of Socialism and Socialism of the Future*, 61-3.

87 Chandran, "Forward" to *Towards a Counter-culture* (Malayalam), 7.

88 Turner, *An Introduction to Liberation Theology*, 2. For more details, also cf. Miranda, *Marx and the Bible: A Critique of the Philosophy of Oppression* (1977), and *Communism in the Bible* (1982).

89 Fuellenbach, *Hermeneutics, Marxism and Liberation Theology*, 87-95.

90 Kappen, *Liberation Theology and Marxism*, 14.

5

Kappen on Christology

Kappen's writings clearly indicated a transition in his understanding of Jesus. This transition appears to have been a switch from his focus on Christ to a more human person. This evolution had two landmarks. Chronologically, the first began with his 1964 article "The Eucharist and the Quest of India for a New Vision of History" and concluded upon the publishing of the article "Jesus Today" in 1975. The second is from 1975 to 1993. Within the first period, Kappen made a minor shift, namely regarding the use of the term, i.e. from Christ to Jesus Christ. Beginning in 1975, i.e. in the second stage, he dropped both Christ and Jesus Christ, and consistently used the term Jesus. Furthermore, he challenged the idea of Christ, which he used in the first stage.

This chapter will further examine these key aspects of Kappen's thoughts. It is divided into three major sections. The first deals with the Christological teachings of the Catholic Church. This is in fact a prelude to the second section, which analyses in detail Kappen's Christology and explores the difference in the Christological understanding of the Catholic Church and that of Kappen. In this second section, we indeed answer certain fundamental questions. How and why did Kappen prefer the historical Jesus to the Christ of faith? How did the liberating message of the Jesus of history contribute to his progressive thinking for the pluralist Asian context? Additionally, this section researches the reasons behind the censorship of Kappen's book *Jesus and Freedom*

(1977) by the Congregation for the Doctrine of Faith in 1980. This enquiry will lead to the third section, which explores the subsequent conflict between Kappen and the Vatican, and how the Society of Jesus, especially Pedro Arrupe, then Superior General of the Society, handled the issue. This final section, which also studies the two CDF documents on liberation theology, namely *Instruction on Certain Aspects of the Theology of Liberation* (1984) and *Instruction on Christian Freedom and Liberation* (1986), inspects the Church's approach to and teaching of liberation theology. A close scrutiny of Kappen's response to these documents in 1986 will enable us to see if he changed his convictions about the Jesus of history in the post-censorship years.

A.   Catholic Christology and Asian Understanding of Jesus

The Christology of the Catholic Church is the result of an evolution of twenty centuries. In order to understand these developments, one must go back to the teaching of the ancient Church on Jesus, the challenges these teachings had to undergo in the following centuries in the form of heretical teachings, and the instruction of different Councils on such heresies. We will not make an elaborate study of the Christological development but will examine the official Church teaching on Jesus in order to see it in light of Kappen's understanding of Jesus. With this in mind, we will first briefly analyze the landmarks in the Christological development in the Church.[1]

A commonly argued thesis is that there was no need of ascertaining the godhood of Jesus in the early Church. This notion, therefore, has an implied meaning that the ancient Church considered Jesus as God. But it should not be forgotten that there were several images of Jesus in the New Testament, which could be understood and interpreted differently. Jesus as the Son of man, the Son of David, the Son of God, Messiah, the King of Israel, etc. were some of them.[2]

Therefore, the Christological development was not an unchallenged process in the history of the Church. Christological teachings evolved when there arose questions and controversies about the nature of Jesus.

The Church considered such controversies as heresies. The major currents that emerged in the first five centuries were Arianism, Apollinarianism, Nestorianism, and Monophysitism, propagated by Arius (c.256-336), Apollinarius (c.310-c.390), Nestorius (386-451), and Eutyches (378-456) respectively. Arius taught that Jesus Christ, although the Son of God, was created and was therefore subordinate to God the Father. According to him, there was a time when Jesus was not, which means Jesus had a beginning and a source or origin.[3] Apollinarius emphasized that Christ had no human spirit because it was taken over by the Logos (Word). As a result, the human nature of Jesus became incomplete. Nestorius, when he was the Patriarch of Constantinople, engaged himself in the discussion of the terms of *theotokos* (Θεοτόκος, Mother of God) and *Christotokos* (Χριστοτόκος, Mother of Christ).[4] According to Nestorius, Mary was not the mother of God, but the mother of Christ. He also believed that the two natures in Jesus, namely the human and divine, were separate and that there was no organic union between them. The Christ was a human person in the beginning and was only later joined to the divine person of God's Son. At the same time, Eutyches taught the opposite of what Nestorius believed and stated that there were not two natures in Christ, but only one – the divine nature. According to Eutyches, the human nature of Jesus no longer existed after the divine person of God's Son assumed it.

However, the Church was vigilant against such heretical teachings and adapted necessary measures. The first Council of Nicaea in 325 condemned Arianism by teaching that the Son of God is begotten, not made, and the first Council of Constantinople (381) condemned Apollinarianism.[5] In 431, the Council of Ephesus denounced Nestorius and his teachings by declaring that not man became God/Word, but that the Word/God became man. Likewise, the Council of Chalcedon condemned Eutyches' teaching in 451 by emphasizing the perfect humanity and perfect divinity of Jesus.[6] All these heresies were together addressed as the pre-Chalcedon Christological heresies, i.e. the heresies between the Councils of Nicaea and Chalcedon.[7]

Catholic Christology grew into a full swing mature discipline in theology by the 5th century and this continued to be so in the following centuries. As observed by the German Catholic theologian Walter Kasper (°1933) in his *Jesus the Christ* (1976), the modern Christological thought emerged in the second half of the 20th century, especially with the Second Vatican Council, fifteen centuries after the Council of Chalcedon.[8] Kasper gave a systematic analysis of the Christological enterprise in the Church from down the centuries. He taught that the most fundamental element in Christianity was the belief that Jesus is the Christ. Profession of faith in Jesus Christ included not only his birth from the virgin, godhood, human and divine, the second person in the Trinity, etc. but also its "universal openness and global relevance."[9]

A proper examination of the Christology of the Second Vatican Council facilitates an integral map of Catholic teaching on the person of Jesus/Christ/Jesus Christ, and its eventual development and transitions. The Second Vatican Council did not break any ground with regard to Christology, but indirectly reiterated the existing teachings of the Church. However, there were some traces of the reaffirmation of the Christological teachings of the Church in *Dei Verbum*, the Second Vatican Council document that was promulgated in November 1965. Referring to the first letter of John in the New Testament, the document asserted the eternal existence of Jesus Christ.[10] Likewise, it also recapitulated the biblical and Church teaching that the Word became man, following the will of God to reveal himself.[11] The document further taught that the full revelation of the supreme God is in Jesus Christ.[12] Instead of focusing on dogmas and doctrines, the Second Vatican Council was in fact more concerned with pastoral issues in light of the already existing dogmas and teachings of the Church. This is also clear from the pastoral orientation of *Gaudium et Spes*, another Council document, which said that Jesus restored in his people the image of God that was distorted by the sin of the first man Adam.[13]

Also, after the Second Vatican Council, Christology reaffirmed the doctrines of the Council of Chalcedon. It did not challenge either the divine or human nature of Jesus and did not question the godhood of Jesus, but rather attempted to explore the theological depths of these fundamental principles through a nuanced understanding of them. In doing so, Christologists articulated these faith principles somewhat differently in the style of expression, but remained faithful to the biblical core. For instance, the Belgian Roman Catholic theologian Edward Schillebeeckx (1914-2009) stated in 1963 – during the period of the Second Vatican Council – that "Christ is God in a human way, and man in a divine way" or that "the actions of Jesus' life as manifestations of divine love for man and human love for God."[14] Rudolf Bultmann, the renowned Lutheran theologian (1884-1976), argued for a complete separation between history and faith. At the same time, he said that the historical events in the life of Jesus should not negatively affect, but support one's faith. However, the Roman Catholic, Evangelical, and Orthodox scholars and theologians rejected Bultmann's arguments and counter-argued that a separation between faith and history was inessential.[15] Kasper again made a brilliant effort in the 1970s to synthesize "biblical, traditional, and philosophical" aspects of the life of Jesus. There one could also find a direct reference to the Christological thinking of the ancient authors, such as Athanasius, Augustine, Irenaeus, Maximus the Confessor, Tertullian, etc.[16] Thus, it is clear that the agreements and disagreements among the post-Second Vatican Council Christologists were not about the conclusions of Chalcedon regarding the human and divine natures of Jesus, but only a discussion about the way it should be comprehended.

In sum, the *Catechism of the Catholic Church* (*CCC*, 1992) provided a comprehensive understanding of the Christology that had developed in the past centuries. The *CCC* recapitulated the central teachings of the previous Councils in this regard. Number 65 of the *CCC* called Jesus "Christ, the Son of God made man." Additionally, it presented Jesus Christ as the fullness of revelation, but also denied any public revelation until his second coming. This clearly indicated that the Catholic Church did not acknowledge the revelations in other religions or in the emerging Christian sects.[17] Numbers 430 to 435 proclaimed Jesus as the only name through which humanity attained salvation. In fact, the *CCC* did not explain how Jesus was Christ, but simply presented Jesus as Christ by referring back to the biblical passages and the Church fathers.[18] So, in all this, the Christ of faith overtook the human Jesus, and this was an explicit return to the traditional Christology.

However, not everybody agreed with this. Especially among Latin American liberation theologians and Christian activists there developed a strong thought that Christology did not solely depend on traditional dogmas since it would be nothing other than scholasticism. They argued that Christological profession should also be intensely connected with the historical Jesus.[19] If it becomes so, faith becomes more than an intellectual play. While the orthodox theologians tried to stick to the Christ of faith, liberation theologians strived to explore the liberating message of the Jesus of history. From the 1960s to the close of the 1970s, they fueled activism based on the liberating message of the historical Jesus and produced a large quantity of literature on the life and message of the human Jesus. This entry of the liberation theologians and activists resulted from the perceived inadequacy of the traditional Christology in meeting the realities of their own contexts. As they were not living in a world of ancient theological and philosophical ideologies, they also did not want to subscribe to the traditional Christology, which was basically supernatural.[20] In spite of his Spanish origin, the El Salvador-based Jon Sobrino could be considered as one of the prominent figures in this area. In Sobrino's view, Christologies that excessively employed dogmatic terms "ignore or partialize the history of Jesus."[21]

Along with the Christological developments in Latin America, an Asian Christology emerged. There had been some commendable attempts from some Asian scholars to explore the Asianness of Jesus.[22] Unlike the non-Asian liberation theologians, Asian liberation theologians encountered religious pluralism and therefore did not represent Christian triumphalism. They strived to find a common ground with, for instance, Hinduism, Buddhism, and Islam. In their eyes, Lord Krishna, a leading Hindu god, had many similarities with Jesus. Both shared the incarnation: according to the Bagavat Gita, Krishna incarnated to protect the good and to set up the law of righteousness,[23] just as Jesus became flesh for the salvation of the whole world.[24] Buddhism had more differences: whereas Christians saw Jesus as God, for Buddhists, any objective understanding of the ultimate reality was an illusion.[25] Yet, as Aloysius Pieris argued, there was not necessarily a competition between Buddhists and Christians, but rather platforms of cooperation. For instance, similarities in the stories and messages of Jesus and Buddha could help Christians and Buddhists to embrace voluntary poverty and fight forced poverty.[26] Likewise, traditional Christology had nothing to do in the Islamic context.[27] According to the Islamic beliefs, Jesus was a human being and prophet of God. The Quran questioned Jesus' godhood, his sonship, and the implicit meaning of the term Christ.[28] In entering dialogue with Islam, therefore, Asian liberation theologians also had to emphasize a possible common ground – the prophethood of Jesus – along with his godhood.

For Asian liberation theologians, it was less important how Jesus, Krishna, Buddha, and Muhammad were related to God. Rather, these theologians searched for how they contributed to the salvation and welfare of humanity.[29] In this way, their interpretation of Jesus is slightly different from that of the West. Yet, their understanding was not completely new. From the beginning of Christianity, Jesus had been confessed differently according to different contexts. For instance, while Matthew wrote the gospel for the Jewish Christians and therefore used Jewish terminologies like Kingdom of Heaven and Son of David, John made use of Hellenistic terms like Logos, Light, Life, etc. Likewise, one could continue to interpret Jesus differently in different contexts. As Sugirtharajah, the Sri Lankan expert on Third World theology put it, Asian theologians' Christological formulations were inclusive, because other formulations would separate them from other religions, which would further harm the making of an equitable society.[30]

There is also a political reason for the inclusive approach of the liberation theologians. Referring to the Indian context, Stanley J.

Samartha (1920-2001), an Indian theologian who promoted interreligious dialogue, observed that exclusive theological claims had political consequences and would negatively affect harmony in society. Such claims indeed always put into question the relationship of God with the people of other faiths.[31] Therefore, an exclusivist approach suffers exclusion of each other and juxtaposes Christianity and other religions as two sides. In order to avoid this, Christology in India was very much based on religious diversity and its sensitiveness, and thus should be understood only from a pluralist perspective. Samartha's suggestion was not novel: the Federation of Asian Bishops' Conferences (FABC) had taken a similar position in 1974. As maintained by the FABC, more than proclaiming Jesus to the people of other religions in Asia, it was ideal to discover the Jesus who was present in the Asian traditions, cultures, and religions – the "Christ of the peoples of Asia."[32] As poverty and oppression were the challenges of Asia, it was not the dogmatic face of Jesus but his merciful face that should inspire the Asian people.[33] This implicitly indicated Asian Christology's striving to develop a unique path by putting aside the dogmatically overemphasized Christology of the West.[34]

Thus, from the mid-1960s Indian Christology, backed by the cultural openness of the Second Vatican Council, sharpened its search for the non-colonial Christ. This search was a challenge to the Christ of the dogma as he was thrown into a pluralist Asia from his unique status as *the* one and only Savior, *the* Son of God, *the* Christ, and *the* liberator. In such pluralist context, as put by Pieris, Buddhists were open enough to acknowledge Jesus as the aspirant for enlightenment whereas Buddha is *the* enlightened. Muslims considered Jesus as one of the prophets but Muhammad as *the* prophet. In the same fashion, it was not difficult for Hindus to look at Jesus even as one of the avatars. Unless and until the Church in Asia was given the opportunity to adapt to the pluralist context, there could not emerge an authentic Asian Christology.[35]

Although the inclusive approach was an Asian phenomenon, theologians of the West seriously and progressively approached it, particularly from the mid-1960s. For example, the Belgian Jesuit scholar Jacques Dupuis (1923-2004), who lived in India for 36 years (1948-84) and also worked as theological advisor of the CBCI, asked certain fundamental questions about the uniqueness of Jesus in a pluralist society.[36] Dupuis criticized the conventional Christology for putting forward Jesus as the only savior of humankind by arguing that it was inadequate in the present context of "religious pluralism and interreligious dialogue."[37] Schillebeeckx put forward the same view when he asked how the Church could simultaneously uphold the uniqueness of Jesus and acknowledge that there were positive values in all religions.[38] This was indeed an indirect questioning of the Church's religious imperialism and its exclusivist approach.[39] At the same time the Church believed that the Holy Spirit worked in all cultures and religions.

What Dupuis and Schillebeeckx observed should be understood in light of Leonardo Boff's opinion on Western Christology. According to Boff, imported Western Christology suffered an impoverishment in Asia since the European syncretism manipulated the "real image of the person of Jesus as well as his message."[40] There were also Asian progressive theologians who supported this view. As discussed in Chapter II, Aloysius Pieris made a clear distinction between the Euro-ecclesiastical Christ and the non-Western Christ. For him, the Dalit Christ, the Korean Christ, the Third World Christ, etc. were different but real faces of the Asian Christ.[41] This distinction exists even now in Asian Christology. To give an instance, in a paper presented at the OTC-FABC (Office of Theological Concern-FABC) colloquium on Asian Faces of Christ in Sampran, Thailand in May 2004, the Filipino progressive theologian Carlos H. Abesamis conveyed the idea that the Asian face of Jesus was a synthesis of the biblical face of Jesus, and the Asian peoples and their life-situations.[42]

B.   Kappen's Distinction between the Christ of Faith and the Jesus of History

Kappen participated in these discussions on the interpretation of Jesus. This section will examine his thoughts in this field and check whether they were in line with the official Catholic teaching on Jesus. It will also answer the question of whether Kappen was a pioneer in Asian Christology or if he followed other Christologians in this regard.

To put it straight, on the basis of the evolution in his thoughts, Kappen's understanding of Jesus is divided into two parts: pre-1975 and post-1975. As his works indicated, until 1975 Kappen was in complete conformity with the Christological doctrines of the Catholic Church. In his first English article, "The Eucharist and the Quest of India for a New Vision of History," he made use of Indian philosophical and Vedic terms and concepts, but there too remained in total agreement with the traditional theology of the Church, especially with the Eucharist and Christology.[43] Kappen understood the Eucharist as the glorified body of Christ and wrote about the incarnation of the Word of God. According to him, "[T]he Word became flesh and pitched his tent with men. He inserted himself into the flux of history, identified himself with the very stuff and texture of the universe."[44] This lenience towards orthodox theology continued in later articles, such as "Christian Participation in Social Work" (1969), "The Role of the Church in National Development" (1969), "Christianity as Liberation" (1970), and "The Christian and the Call to Revolution" (1971). His book *From Faith to Revolution* in 1972 was slightly different. In this work, he severely criticized the hierarchical Church. Yet, just as in these four articles, Kappen used either Christ (most of the time) or Jesus Christ. In 1974, glimpses of change in the usage of the terms appeared. In "The Jesus-Fellowship" (1974), Kappen only used the term Jesus and adapted a historical approach, looking at things from the point of view of the Jesus of history. He did not, however, start challenging the Christ of faith yet. Perhaps this was the last stage of his conformity to Christ.

In his view, from the point of faith, the Christ was the Word of God incarnate. However, the Christ came to the world not with a new heaven and new earth; instead, he came to teach man how to construct this new world. Also, he was not someone who came to liberate a particular group of people, but all of humanity.[45] Interestingly, as discussed in the previous chapter, he calls for revolution and elaborates on Marx in these articles. Yet, he does this with a respect for the orthodox Christology, and keeps alive the theological and spiritual invocations surrounding the Christ of faith, especially concepts like forgiveness of sin, victory over death, self-giving, love of God in crucifixion and resurrection, etc.[46]

The second stage of Kappen's Christological thinking began in 1975. His major publications with Christological references were his article "Jesus Today" (1975), and the monograph *Jesus and Freedom* (1977). In addition to this, he edited and co-authored a book under the title *Jesus Today* (1985), which included a collection of his articles dealing with Jesus. Importantly, the fundamental character of the second stage is his shift from the Christ of faith to Jesus of history. A clear distancing from Christ and an affinity to Jesus is found in "Jesus Today" (1975). He pointed out that Christian faith and practice were alienated from the historical Jesus mainly through cultic, dogmatic, and institutional lines. Consequently, a cult had developed which was centered upon Jesus, for example, the Eucharist. This took Jesus away from the common man and his ordinary experiences and reduced him to an object of worship. In fact, this view was in opposition to what he said in 1964, when he interpreted the Eucharist as the body of Jesus. As a matter of fact, it seemed that the development of cult was due to the shift from the Jesus of history to the risen Christ, and Kappen's attempt was to retrieve the former.[47] As he tried to differentiate between the two, we should assume that his shift was deliberate. Moreover, this intentional closeness towards historical Jesus is visible in the titles of many of his works after 1975, as they contained the term Jesus rather than Christ or Jesus Christ.

As discussed in the previous section, progressive Christology was initially a Western move. Soon it became popular among Latin American and Asian theologians. Jon Sobrino, in particular, is one of the pioneers in contributing to this new Christology in Latin America. His first work on Christology, *Cristología desde América Latina: esbozo a partir del seguimiento del Jesús histórico*, came out in 1976. It was in Spanish and its English translation, namely *Christology at the Crossroads: a Latin American View*, appeared in 1978, a year after Kappen's *Jesus and Freedom*. We may therefore state that Kappen was one of the pioneers of Christology in Asia. Other theologians who challenged the legacy of Catholic Christology, such as Luis Segundo and Leonardo Boff, did so after Kappen. Yet, this is not to suggest that Kappen influenced them.

Of course, Kappen was also influenced by the Western theologians. Although he did not seem to have referred to progressive theologians, such as Dupuis and Schillebeeckx, he explicitly exploited the Christological thoughts of Bultmann, Gunther Bornkamm, a student of Bultmann (1905-90), Joachim Jermias (1900-79), another German Lutheran theologian, and Norman Perrin (1920-76), an English born American biblical scholar. Accordingly, one can argue that Kappen was one of the first theologians to translate these progressive Western visions into the context of South Asia and, even more, of the non-Western world.

Kappen's full-fledged post-1975 Christology could be found in his first English book in 1977, namely *Jesus and Freedom*, after two Malayalam works in 1972 and 1973. The book was an enlarged form of his articles "Jesus Today" (1975) and "The Man Jesus: Rupture and Communion" (1976). Both in the articles and papers from 1975 and in the monograph of 1977, the central theme was the historical person of Jesus as the agent of human liberation. In addition to this, in a paper presented at the Senate Meeting of the Serampore University, West Bengal in 1976, Kappen pointed out the interconnection between the method and content of the process of the new way of theologizing by focusing on the Jesus of history.[48] Kappen, in light of the teachings of Jesus, envisioned a society that by going beyond class distinctions and exploitations cultivated an economy of giving rather than having.[49] Besides, the new society Kappen imagined consisted of people who lived for each other; the freedom of each individual would be the condition for the freedom of all in the society. The very process of theologizing was for the integral development of the humanity.

As *Jesus and Freedom* would become Kappen's masterpiece, it is essential that we analyze the contents of the book in detail. Throughout the work, Kappen discussed the historical person of Jesus and the alienated Jesus. In analyzing the historical Jesus, he elaborated concepts like human Jesus, Jesus as a prophet, his priesthood, and his miracles. Likewise, his areas of interest while discussing the alienated Jesus were cult, dogma, and institution (institutionalized Church). Contrary to what he had stated in 1964, Kappen in 1977 argued that Jesus was "less word made flesh than flesh become word"/divine.[50] It seemed that he wanted to present Jesus as one among the human beings, sharing the same flesh, blood, and feelings. Just like any other man, Jesus grew in wisdom and sought truth. Most importantly, he found Jesus as a man who was "taken hold of by God" into a divine realm. Kappen's position indicated that there was a fundamental difference between the traditional theology and his theologizing.

As a matter of fact, there were two erroneous statements from Kappen regarding the humanity of Jesus: first, the flesh becoming word, and second, Jesus being transplanted into a divine realm. These two theological approaches were in contrast to the teachings of the Catholic theology since they conveyed the idea that Jesus was in the beginning only a human person, who was later called God. In this way, Kappen preferred a Christology of ascent (from man to divine) to one of descend (from divine to man).[51] He denied an organic union between the divine and human natures in Jesus. Pointedly, this was similar to the Christological teaching of Nestorius, whom the Council of Ephesus condemned in 431, as mentioned earlier in this chapter.

Along with emphasizing the humanity of Jesus, Kappen also stressed that Jesus was a true prophet. The Christian tradition, however, had devalued the prophet in Jesus, and Kappen wanted to present Jesus as a prophet rather than as a God.[52] By referring to the liberating mission of Jesus in the gospel of Luke 4, 16-21, Kappen substantiated that Jesus as a prophet stood for the integral liberation of the marginalized. Unfortunately, this message of integral liberation had been spiritually interpreted, which further reduced the relevance of the current and material world man lived in. For Kappen, Jesus and his teachings were the role models for man's life in this world, and therefore, they could neither be monopolized by Christianity nor confined to its theological interpretations.[53]

Regarding the priesthood of Jesus, Kappen went totally against the understanding of the Church, which is that Jesus possessed eternal priesthood. Kappen, however, argued that historically Jesus could not be considered a priest. First of all, Jesus was not a priest according to the Jewish law, and secondly, neither Jesus nor the people ever claimed that he was a priest. His life was not around the altar and he never offered sacrifices. It was only because of the spiritualized interpretation of Jesus' death on the cross as a sacrifice for the world that he was called a priest.[54] For Kappen, Jesus' death was not a priestly sacrifice; it did not have a religious color, but only secular – punishment of a political criminal.

Kappen questioned the historicity of the miracles performed by Jesus asserting that reality was covered and overlaid with myths and legends. Rather than spiritually interpreting Jesus' miracles, he called for highlighting their social relevance. Through his acts, Jesus preached the primacy of love and compassion over cult. And so, for Kappen, the miracles of Jesus were the acts of a man whose spirit was taken hold by the spirit of God.[55]

Another theme that Kappen was very preoccupied with was the alienation of Jesus. It appeared in many of his publications: not only "Jesus Today," "The Man Jesus: Rupture and Communion," and *Jesus and Freedom*, but also in later texts, such as *Jesus and Culture* (1983), and "Beyond the Cult of the Dead God" (1993). According to Kappen, the alienation of Jesus is the estrangement of Jesus from his deeds, message, and life as a historical person. This alienation was a threefold phenomenon – cultic, dogmatic, and institutional. The historical Jesus who denounced every form of cult and subordinated it to justice, mercy, and love was being replaced by the glorified Christ, a creation of this very cult. Kappen reacted against the institutional and hierarchical Church of his time and observed that it was totally different from what Jesus had envisioned. *Jesus and Freedom*, as the name indicated, presented a prophet who came into the world with a message of liberation. Kappen denounced that over the centuries, Jesus was glorified, deified, and put at the right hand of God. In this way, Jesus was alienated from the historical contexts, realities, and above all from his human nature. This led Kappen to disapprove the transition of a non-cultic prophetic movement into a cultic religion that revolved around dogmatic teachings.[56]

By the cultic aspect of religion, Kappen meant the overemphasis of rituals, rubrics, devotional piety, etc. He argued that this had swallowed Christianity, which subsequently deteriorated into a mere machinery of producing rules and regulations, dogmas and doctrines. This went together with promoting pietism, but eventually fragmented Jesus, each fragment turning into the source of new devotion, for example 'The Precious Blood,' 'The Crown of Thorns,' 'The Five Wounds,' 'The Sacred Heart,' etc. Mercy, justice, and love became secondary to such devotional pietism and cultism. Jesus was alienated from what he had preached, and made an object of devotion.[57] Even more, the Church of the alienated Jesus put aside its liberating mission with preferential option for the poor. The phrase 'preferential option for the poor' appeared in Catholic social teachings only after it had been popularized by the Latin American bishops.[58]

The second line of alienation was dogmatic, which was more theoretical. Kappen argued that Greek philosophy and Roman imperialism had a vital role in Jesus' alienation. Indeed, over its history, the Church reduced Jesus to a concept, which could be interpreted differently. Yet, according to Kappen, the interpretations went to the extent of understanding Jesus as "person, nature, hypostasis, body, soul, substance, quality, quantity, essence, and existence."[59] When history threw questions at the godhood of Jesus, the Church reaffirmed his divinity. According to the Church's teaching, both the divine nature and human nature subsisted in Jesus. The Church considered Jesus as "God under the guise of man," who fully grew in wisdom and knew everything there was to know. Finally, Jesus was further taken to the world of ideas by dogmas. What prevailed in the Church at the time was a dishonest interpretation of the human conditions of Jesus, and subsequently, the Jesus of history was segregated from the company of man and made the Christ of dogma.[60] As a matter of fact, there was an indirect challenge from Kappen to the Church with regard to the divinity and godhood of Jesus. It seemed that according to Kappen, the dogmatic teachings of the Church in terms of Christology, which evolved in the past centuries, alienated the person of Jesus.

Regarding the third line of alienation, Kappen pointed out in 1972 that the power of institutions and wealth restrained the Church from its liberating mission.[61] Elaborating further, Kappen in *Jesus and Freedom* expressed his discontent with the institutional Church because it imprisoned the Jesus of history to safeguard the Christ of faith.[62] In fact, Kappen argued, theology should play the role of a critic so that the Church-given veils of Jesus could be removed and he be liberated. He used a beautiful image to explain this: we seldom meet the naked God. God, in any history or culture, appeared to people in the garb people provided him.[63] The true role of theology was to tear off the garbs history threw upon God so that man recovered the true essence of God. A true theology discovered and recovered Jesus and the original meaning of his messages, and liberated Jesus from the institutional Church. Such a theology of liberation was a potentially transformative theology that propagated changes both in religious and social realms.[64]

Although Kappen first and foremost targeted the universal Church, he did not spare the Church in India. He also observed the same failures of the Church in his native country. Institutionalism, alliance with the ruling class, cultism, dependence on stoic ethics (focusing excessively on providence and fate), overemphasis on imported theology, etc. were also explicit features of the Church in India. In many respects, Kappen stated, the Christian Church had become similar to the institutional and hierarchical religious tradition in India, especially to Hinduism with all its creed and cult. In this way, the Church has lost its relevance. Kappen therefore wanted to re-introduce the man and prophet Jesus. India did not need a God in Jesus just to increase the number of gods, but needed a prophet whose teachings would integrally liberate its marginalized and the oppressed. This required a shifting of the axis of the Church from the realm of cultism, dogmatism, and institutionalism to the realm of "personal-social life."[65]

Indeed, *Jesus and Freedom* had something concrete to do in the realm of the personal-social life. The purpose of the book seemed to be an effort to stimulate those who committed themselves to the works of human liberation. Kappen addressed the educated youth who wanted to radically commit themselves to the gospel values.[66] He wanted to provide his readers with certain visions, rather than with information. Kappen therefore did not focus on the manifold and complex interpretations of biblical scholars. The book, in fact, was a personal reflection on the human Jesus, excluding all the ubiquitous Christological definitions.

It was also evident from the book that Kappen utilized his Marxist expertise in analyzing the Church. He moderately asserted the relevance of Marxism in the Indian context and sought areas where the Church and Marxism could collaborate in creating a better society. If a new humanity was the task of both the Church and the Marxists, he said, Jesus' teachings were not an "irreconcilable opposition to the original Marxian vision of the classless society, the latter being but a secular version of the former."[67] Importantly, by equating the hopes of Jesus with those of Marx, Kappen did not want to equalize Marxism with religion. He instead expressed his hope in Marxism, and drew his socialist thoughts from the prophet Jesus.[68] At first sight, this is a confusing conclusion because according to the chronology of Kappen's thoughts, this happened the other way around. Yet, the prophetic message of the historical Jesus whom Kappen found in the gospels seems to have inspired the latter in his socialist thinking.

Apart from its content, *Jesus and Freedom* was particularly noted for Houtart's introduction to it. Houtart wrote the introduction while he was the director of the CSRR and professor of sociology at the

Université catholique de Louvain (UCL). He appreciated the originality of Kappen's approach. First of all, Kappen's focus was not a reproduction of the classical theology, but instead shedding light on the contradiction between religion and liberation, and between the institutional Church and the message of Jesus. His central point was the social experience of man, not the theological correctness. Secondly, Houtart appreciated the type of social analysis in Kappen's work. He emphasized that most of the books after Indian independence highlighted industrialist and cultural dynamism with the assistance of statistics. Social analysis accordingly became one-sidedly viewed from the top of society's ladder. Kappen was different because he looked at society from the bottom. In Houtart's view, this should be the point of departure of every progressive thinker and the hallmark of the theology of liberation.[69] Houtart purposely threw light on Kappen's criticism of the Church for its understanding of development, indirectly articulating Houtart's own anti-institutionalism, because for hm, the Church calculated development in terms of the number of educational institutions, hospitals, and charitable institutions that belonged to the Church. Thirdly, Houtart praised Kappen's explicit autonomy of thought and writing. Many liberation theologians had initially been influenced by European political theology, but some of them soon strayed from such influence by critically analyzing their own social contexts, and Kappen was one of the leading figures among them. However, Kappen did not do his social analysis by means of readymade answers to the problems of the Indian society. Rather, Houtart observed, he emphasized "re-reading the Gospels in the light of the challenge raised by today's oppressed."[70] What made Kappen recognizably different from other social thinkers of his time and context was his inclusion of social theories, especially Marxist, in analyzing social problems, and he did this job responsibly since he was in contact with true realities of the Indian society.

In a nutshell, Kappen's focus was not on the priesthood, godhood, and the miracles of Jesus; rather, he concentrated on the living contexts of humans. In spite of the fact that he published *Jesus and Freedom* with Maryknoll, his primary interest was to introduce Asians, and especially

Indians to the human Jesus. As an Asian progressive theologian, Kappen did not hold on the exclusivist approach of the Catholic Church, which unilaterally projected Jesus as the unique and universal savior, and presented itself as the custodian of truth while other religions had only ray of truth. However, this does not mean that he was an inclusivist, claiming that there could be grace and truth in other religions, and the followers might be saved. As a matter of fact, he should be labeled a pluralist – a frequent label among Asian theologians – who argued that every religion was a way to the Ultimate in its own way.[71] From a theological point of view, Kappen did not rely upon any of these means, because he did not highlight the transcendental and other-worldly aspects of religion. Conversely, he looked at religion from a sociological perspective and found liberating elements in every religion. For this reason, Kappen could be called a pluralist, but from a sociological perspective. Kappen was not completely isolated: there were also other scholars who dealt with the Asian pluralist context, both in Asia (e.g. R.S. Sugirtharajah and Stanley Samartha) and beyond (e.g. Paul F. Knit's *No Other Name?* (1985), Alan Race's *Christians and Religious Pluralism* (1982), and Gavin D'Costa's *Theology and Religious Pluralism* (1986)).

Elsewhere, Kappen wrote that Jesus "lies buried under the layers of rituals, rubrics, laws, concepts, legends, myths, superstitions, and institutions."[72] Interpretations alienated Jesus, and still they continue to take place in the Church. The Indian Christology and ecclesiology had been showing their lenience towards the Western theology of dogmas, doctrines, and symbols. Although most of the liberation theologians in India agreed upon the idea that liberation was both spiritual and material, there were certain fundamental differences among them at the same time, especially regarding how the Church and theology should be the liberating agents. In this dilemma, Kappen stood out with his understanding on the Church and Jesus. While many of the liberation theologians, such as M.M. Thomas and Samuel Rayan, projected a liberating Christ, which was more or less in conformity with the traditional theology, Kappen highlighted the liberating Jesus of history.

In fact, he blamed Indian liberation theologians for having failed to make a clear and conspicuous distinction between Jesus and Christ.

Kappen's book was immediately well received. Already in September 1977, *The Christian Century*, a Chicago based magazine, wrote that *Jesus and Freedom* facilitated a rich theology of liberation to India.[73] A second review, by Alfred T. Hennelly, who became a renowned author on liberation theology, explained Kappen's approach as Christology from below in response to the context of oppression and exploitation. Along with that, Hennelly appreciated the use of Marxist means as the hermeneutical key in Kappen's social analysis and criticism of the institutional Church.[74] In 1979, a third review of the book appeared in *The Journal of Religion*. Acknowledging the radical theological positions of Kappen, its author Robert D. Haight pointed out that the book was an appeal to the leaders of the Church in India and a call to imitate the teachings of the Jesus of the history. However, Haight criticized the lack of theological tools in interpreting the person of Jesus. He believed that this, in turn, impeded the book from going beyond local significance.[75]

Nevertheless, *Jesus and Freedom* would eventually gain international resonance and come to the attention of the CDF, which in 1980 demanded an explanation from the Society of Jesus and asked Superior General Pedro Arrupe to disavow the book. Such an incident was not exceptional. The Church monitored progressive theologians closely, especially under John Paul II. The best example was Leonardo Boff, who was silenced in 1985 for his book *Church: Charism and Power: Liberation theology and the institutional Church* (1985). Again in 1992, he received a penitential silence and soon after that he left his Order OFM and the priesthood.[76] However, Kappen was, it appears, the first Third World liberation theologian to face disciplinary action from the CDF. A few other examples include the scrutiny of the works of the Brazilian liberation theologian Hugo Assmann in 1984, the summoning of the Brazilian (Spanish Catalan-born) bishop Pedro Casaldaliga of Sao Felix do Araguaia in Rome in 1988, the excommunication of the Sri Lankan theologian Tissa Balasuriya in 1997, the posthumous notification on Anthony de Mello from India in 1998,[77] and the warning against Sobrino in 2007 for his Christological positions expressed in his works.[78] Possibly, the investigation about Dupuis' *Towards a Christian Theology of Religious Pluralism* in 1998 can also be listed here. This investigation was followed by a notification in 2001, as the CDF found the book to have "contained notable ambiguities and difficulties on important doctrinal points which could lead a reader to erroneous or harmful opinions."[79]

C.   Conflict with the Vatican

The fundamental reasons for the CDF's disciplinary action against Kappen could be broadly divided into two: his understanding of Jesus along with the criticism of the Church, and his assimilation to Marxist ideologies in his social analysis. A deeper examination of the correspondence between Kappen and the authorities from 1980 to 1982 will provide a clear picture of his response to the action taken against him. Keralite Jesuit scholar Sebastian Painadath claimed that the conservative approach of the CDF in light of the dogmas and doctrines, and its rigidity in dealing with liberation theology led to the censorship of the book.[80] However, a closer examination will demonstrate that the truth was more complex.

Following the request of the Holy See, Arrupe had to initiate certain formal procedures, including appointing a censor and asking for Kappen's explanation. In response to Arrupe's demand, Kappen wrote a ten-page explanatory letter on 15 May 1981. The letter was a reply to the critical comments of the censor. Kappen seems to have written it after mature reflection, and as a responsible member of the Society of Jesus and a theologian. He expressed his discontent on the practice of censorship based on certain criteria formulated in light of the once-and-for-all defined theological dogmas and doctrines. As long as there were such established criteria to measure the theological correctness or falseness, it was taken for granted that God had fully revealed himself at a certain point in history.[81] Kappen did not agree with this, asserting that he believed in the continuity of revelation and hence the emergence of new theologies.

Even in his response to the censorship, Kappen fiercely attacked the institutional power of the established Church, just as he had done in the book. He compared its attitude with the Crusades and Inquisition in the past, which had led to the death of thousands of people. Kappen argued that although the Church disavowed them later, it continued them in a subtler form, again 'killing' the spirit. This 'killing' was due to the Church's failure to understand God's intervention in different places and cultures. In the case of progressive theologians like Kappen, it was a killing of progressive ideologies. In other words, Kappen's response was a reminder to the Church against its predisposition in evaluating theologies from different contexts and cultures by one theology, which had been conceived and developed in the Western historical-cultural context. Kappen indeed shed light on the fundamental difference between the Western and Asian ways of thinking. If the former stressed an analytic and representational mode of thinking, the latter focused on unitive and experiential modes. Kappen was concerned that the cultural specificities of Asia were being replaced by the Western mode of thinking, which was nothing less than "cultural imperialism and colonization of the mind."[82]

Secondly, Kappen questioned the Church's traditional teaching that there is no salvation outside of the Church (*extra ecclesiam nulla salus*).[83] This axiom dated back to the 3rd century as originally found in the writings of Origen (185-254) and Saint Cyprian of Carthage (c.200-258), and later became dogma in the Church. The Lateran Council (1215) affirmed that only the subjects of the Roman Pontiff attained salvation and none outside of the Catholic Church. The dogma also came back in the *CCC* of 1992. Number 846 said: "all salvation comes through Christ the Head through the Church which is his body." It also stipulated that there was no salvation for those who refused the Catholic Church even after knowing it. For Kappen, conversely, the Kingdom of God envisioned by Jesus did not exclude non-Christians, atheists, Marxists, etc. In his eyes, it was an inclusive society here on earth, which could only be constructed in dialogue with theologians, priests, social activists, Marxists, people of other faiths, etc.[84]

Thirdly, Kappen's response to the censorship also indicated his criticism of the West's overemphasis on symbolic and conceptual theology. Such a theology often failed in taking into account the contexts outside the West, especially the Third World's social and religious contexts. Kappen did not refer to theological or scholarly sources to substantiate this. Still, for the sake of clarity, we will briefly comment on the symbolic and conceptual dimensions of theology. Fundamentally, symbolic theology is powerful and based on two hypotheses: "signs engage us with reality," and "signs that do engage can be true or false in the engaging interpretations."[85] But, the power of the classical symbolic and metaphorical language failed in effectively engaging itself in contemporary theology. In order to do so, theology has to retain its classical character, which is predominantly developed in the West, and essentially for itself. For this reason, it did not feel the need for an inclusive character. In Kappen's view, such a theology was inapplicable in Third World contexts.

It might be in light of his criticism of the representational theology that Kappen argued that the censorship against his book was out of ignorance. Although he tried to understand Jesus from a pluralist socio-religious framework, his attempt had been branded as a one-sided interpretation of the historical Jesus, his sacrificial death, his divinity, the Eucharist, etc. Interestingly, in Kappen's opinion, the same accusation could be charged against the mainstream Church for its two thousand years' organized one-sided attempts to highlight the divinity of Jesus by neglecting his humanity. So, if Kappen's one-sidedness was censorable, the Church's approach should be much more censorable. The issue of one-sidedness provoked Kappen to openly write that the censor did justice neither to his book nor to its central theme, which was "the liberating word and deed of Jesus."[86]

Kappen made clear to Arrupe in his letter that if the book was against the vested interest of the Church or its hierarchy, he was helpless and did not intend to apologize. Arrupe replied, and in a letter dated 27 May 1981, reminded Kappen of the law of the Society with regard to publication. The rule insisted the members of the Society receive permission from their superiors before they publish books, especially when the work is on doctrinal matters.[87] It was unclear if Kappen obtained permission from his superiors for his publication. Kappen's stubborn attitude made things even more complex, and this led to further correspondence between him and the CDF.

Having seen Arrupe's commitment to progressive thinking and theology of liberation, it seems that he, as a person, did not want to disown Kappen or his book. It is more logical to argue that the insistence from the CDF forced him to initiate an enquiry. Given Arrupe's positive approach to liberation theologians during the 32nd GC (December 1974-March 1975), one may assume that he somehow also subscribed to Kappen's progressive thinking. He may even have influenced Kappen. Both of them being the members of the same Society, Kappen must have heard of Arrupe's missionary life and provincialate in war-torn Japan. This does not mean that Arrupe's Marxist and progressive ideologies directly inspired Kappen. As a matter of fact, Kappen was already fascinated by Marxism in 1959, much before Arrupe became the Superior General of the Society. Yet, although Kappen completed his PhD in 1961, he started writing articles on social analysis by using Marxist tools after 1965, the concluding year of Second Vatican Council and the year of Arrupe's election as the Superior General. Both Arrupe and Kappen sought inspiration from the Second Vatican Council.[88] In addition, one may assume that Arrupe's self-proclaimed task to continue the spirit of the Council, his pro-Marxist view, and his support to progressive thinkers within his Society played a significant role in Kappen's life and writings. Kappen did not directly refer to Arrupe's works, but he must have been influenced by the atmosphere of the era.

Regardless, the whole case took a new direction when a few months later, in August 1981, Arrupe fell sick. Due to the resultant inability in administrating the Society, Pope John Paul II appointed Paolo Dezza

(1901-99) as the papal delegate to the Society in October 1981. Dezza's profile showed that he was much more loyal to the official Church. He even had assisted Pope Pius XII in formulating the dogma of the Assumption of Mary (1950) and other documents of the Church. He had also been a teacher of John Paul II at the Pontifical Gregorian University. Dezza's appointment, however, was against the will of the Society, which nominated the American liberal Jesuit Vincent O'Keefe for the interim period.[89] The Jesuits all over the world, including Arrupe, were unhappy with the Pope's decision.[90] *National Jesuit News* called the papal action as centralization of power. A group of Jesuits under the leadership of the German Karl Rahner argued that there was no constitutional legitimacy for the papal intervention.[91] Still, Dezza served the office until the Society elected Peter Hans Kolvenbach (1928-2016) as the Superior General in September1983. In 1999, John Paul II made Dezza a Cardinal, on account of his services to the Church.

While in office, Dezza followed the case of Kappen with great interest. In January 1982, he wrote a letter to Kappen asking to rectify the problems in *Jesus and Freedom* related to the dogmas of the Catholic Church. Dezza referred to the theologians who studied the book (whom he did not identify) and pointed out that Kappen was one-sided in his understanding of the teachings of Jesus. Dezza also claimed that it was the influence of liberation theology that had motivated Kappen to write against the dogmas of the Church. This reference to liberation theology presumably shows that the CDF had been pressuring Dezza on this matter, because the CDF was already disturbed with liberation theology and its so-called Marxist orientation. As a result, Dezza asked Kappen to reformulate his ideas and submit the work to Dezza.[92] Kappen, however, did not respond to this request because he had already made clear in his letter to Arrupe in May 1981 that he would not make any change at the cost of his convictions. As a result, Dezza wrote again to Kappen in May 1982 urging him to respond to the previous letter.[93]

On 12 July 1982, Kappen replied to Dezza's second letter. Despite the CDF's presumed pressure on Dezza, and Dezza's continued insistence to reformulate the book, Kappen answered that he would take at least two years for reflection and reply to the demand of the CDF. To this letter he received a reply from Dezza with more severe words of warning. The letter, written on 3 August 1982, said that without obeying the Pope and the Society of Jesus it would be difficult for Kappen to continue in the same status. This indirectly implied the possibility of an expulsion from the Society or even an excommunication from the Church.[94] Nonetheless, Kappen did not wish to yield to this threat. Instead, he replied that Dezza worked as an intermediary to execute the decisions of the Vatican bureaucracy on the Society. Additionally, he blamed Dezza for not taking his letters seriously, which he considered disrespectful towards him and the Indian Jesuits.[95] Kappen once again reiterated his convictions that he conveyed through the letter to Arrupe in May 1981.

In order to find a way out, Dezza met with Rex A. Pai, the then Provincial of India. In the meeting, the papal delegate insisted that Pai appoint someone to dialogue with Kappen. In December 1982, Dezza wrote a letter to Pai, reminding him of the duty of superiors to see that members of the Society were obedient to its constitutional norms and regulations. He advised the Provincial to discuss the matter with the Provincial of Kerala.[96] However, no further action was taken against Kappen after 1982.

Kappen had been articulating himself and reemphasizing his convictions, disregarding any potential disciplinary action against him. He refused to compromise with the criteria applied in evaluating the theological works, because he thought that such criteria were based on the Western Church and entirely mirrored its culture, tradition, and theological reflections. Kappen thought that Western theology did not necessarily fit to every particular context all around the world. In fact, in his writings, we find Kappen striving to juxtapose the West with Asia and, more particularly, India. Contrary to theology of the West, Indian theology needed an upward movement – a theology from below. This specifically was the hallmark of liberation theology. Surprisingly, it appears unusual that the CDF did not take further action against

Kappen even though he refused to concede to its demands. Sebastian Painadath shared that it was because the CDF realized the significance of *Jesus and Freedom* in a pluralist Asian society.

In sum, it is clear that Kappen had been striving to go back to the original meaning of the message of Jesus in order to gather its liberating content. This led to disciplinary action from the CDF, but Kappen was not disappointed by the censorship of his book. He found it an occasion to reflect on the institutional power of the Church.[97] He continued to criticize the Church and its theology even after the CDF ceased action against Kappen.[98] In his *Marxian Atheism* (1983), Kappen strongly repeated his 1977 criticism on transforming the prophet Jesus into a cultic Jesus and questioned the dogmatic rigidity of the Church that ignored Jesus' prophetic voice in the official Church. He sustained this criticism in the following years, especially through *Liberation Theology and Marxism* (1986). According to him, the cultic Jesus lost his uniqueness among other gods. Importantly, Kappen said this from an Indian context. Being a multi-religious land, India could more easily accommodate Jesus among its gods.[99] Kappen thus made a 'national' argument by blaming Paolo Dezza for not taking his letters seriously, which Kappen considered disrespectful towards him and the Indian Jesuits. In sum, Kappen's stubborn criticism was against the dogmatic Christology of the West, the triumphalist and imperialist Church, and the exclusivist approach of the Church. At the same time, he made use of Western theologians in order to understand Jesus. Therefore, it could be argued that Kappen is only partially original in his Christological thinking.

Endnotes

[1] In writing this section, I depend mostly on the Council documents, especially of the Councils of Nicaea I (325) and Chalcedon (451) from the early centuries, and the Second Vatican Council (1962-5) documents like *Dei Verbum* and *Gaudium et Spes* along with the *Catechism of the Catholic Church* (1992). Next to these literatures, I made use of certain secondary literature that elaborated the development of Catholic Christology over the past centuries. Some of such works consist of *Christology* (Hans Schwarz, 1998); *Jesus the Christ* (Walter Kasper, 2011); *Christ the Sacrament of the*

Encounter with God (Edward Schillebeeckx, 2014); *Christology: Origins, Developments, Debates* (Gerald O'Collins SJ, 2015); and *Toward a Christian Theology of Religious Pluralism* (Jacques Dupuis, 1997).

[2] Schwarz, *Christology*, 120.

[3] Hall, *Doctrine and Practice in the Early Church*, 122-3.

[4] Schwarz, *Christology*, 155.

[5] Council of Nicaea I, DS 130, 126.

[6] Council of Chalcedon, DS 301; *CCC* 467.

[7] Clark, Humphries, and Whitby, *The Acts of the Council of Chalcedon*, 60-75.

[8] Kasper, *Jesus the Christ*, 5.

[9] Kasper, *Jesus the Christ*, 4.

[10] *DV* 1; 1Jn 1, 2-3:

[11] *DV* 2, 17; Eph 2, 18; 2 Pet 1, 4.

[12] *DV* 7; 1Cor. 1, 20; 3, 13; 4, 6.

[13] *GS* 22.

[14] Schillebeeckx, *Christ the Sacrament of the Encounter with God*, 10-2.

[15] O'Collins, *Christology: Origins, Developments, Debates*, 4.

[16] O'Collins, *Christology: Origins, Developments, Debates*, 7.

[17] *CCC* 66-7.

[18] *CCC* 336-40.

[19] Kasper, *Jesus the Christ*, xi and 7.

[20] Among the works on Christology were Gutiérrez, *A Theology of Liberation* (1973, deals also with Christology); Boff, *Jesus Christ Liberator* (1981); Bonino, *Faces of Jesus: Latin American Christologies* (1984); and Segundo, *The Historical Jesus of the Synoptics* (1985).

[21] Sobrino, *Christology at the Crossroads: A Latin American View*, 83.

[22] To list a few contributions of Asian scholars: Samartha, *One Christ, Many Religions: Toward a Revised Christology* (1991); Sugirtharajah, ed., *Asian Faces of Jesus* (1993); Alangaram, *Christ and the Asian Peoples: Towards an Asian Contextual Christology* (1999); and Tirimanna, ed., *Asian Faces of Christ* (2005).

[23] *Bhagavad Gita*, 4. 8.

[24] Mt 9, 12; Mk 2, 17; Lk 5, 32; and Jn 3, 17.

[25] Yagi, "Christ and Buddha," 32.

[26] Pieris, "The Buddha and the Christ," 59.

[27] Malik, "Confessing Christ in the Islamic Context," 76.

[28] *Sura* 43, 59; 19, 91-3.

[29] Mohammed, "Jesus and Krishna," 23.

[30] Sugirtharajah, *Asian Faces of Jesus*, x-xi.

31 Samartha, "The Cross and the Rainbow: Christ in a Multireligious Culture," 104.

32 From the initial prayer of the First Plenary Assembly of the FABC in Taipei in April 1974. Rosales and Arevalo, eds., *For all the Peoples of Asia*, 19.

33 Alangaram, *Christ of the Asian Peoples*, 65.

34 Cone, "Asian Theology Today: Searching for Definitions," 589.

35 Pieris, *Asian Theology of Liberation*, 60-3.

36 Cf. Dupuis, *Toward a Christian Theology of Religious Pluralism*, 280-390.

37 Dupuis, *Toward a Christian Theology of Religious Pluralism*, 280.

38 Schillebeeckx, *The Human Story of God*, 165-6.

39 Schillebeeckx, *Jesus in Our Western Cultures: Mysticism, Ethics, and Politics*, 2.

40 Boff and Elizondo, "Christ in Asia: Some Aspects of the Struggles," vii-xi.

41 Pieris, "Does Christ have a Place in Asia?" 37-46.

42 Cf. Tirimanna, ed., *Asian Faces of Christ*, 21.

43 Kappen, "The Eucharist and the Quest of India for a New Vision of History," 52.

44 Kappen, "The Eucharist and the Quest of India for a New Vision of History," 56.

45 Kappen, *From Faith to Revolution* (Malayalam), 68-9.

46 Kappen, "Christianity as Liberation," 114-5, and Kappen, *From Faith to Revolution* (Malayalam), 76-8.

47 Kappen, "Jesus Today," 170.

48 Kappen, "A New Approach to Theological Education," 57-69.

49 Kappen, "The Man Jesus: Rapture and Communion," 156.

50 Kappen, *Jesus and Freedom*, 19.

51 Tilley, "Teaching Christology: History and Horizons," 266-8.

52 Kappen, *Jesus and Freedom*, 54.

53 Mk 6, 4; Lk 4, 18; 13, 22; 24, 19; 7, 16; Mt 21, 11.

54 Kappen, *Jesus and Freedom*, 130-1.

55 Kappen, *Jesus and Freedom*, 72 and 76.

56 Kappen, *Jesus and Freedom*, 17-24.

57 Kappen, "Jesus Today," 170, and Kappen, ed., *Jesus Today*, 127.

58 Cf. Curran, *Catholic Social Teaching 1981-Present: A Historical, Theological, and Ethical Analysis*, 185-6.

59 Kappen, *Jesus and Freedom*, 21.

60 Kappen, *Jesus and Freedom*, 21-2.

61 Kappen, *From Faith to Revolution* (Malayalam), 121-2.

62 Kappen, *Jesus and Freedom*, 27.

63 Kappen, "Orientations for an Asian Theology," 114.

64 Abraham, "Alternative Narratives," 158-9.

65 Kappen, *Jesus and Freedom*, 175-6 and 130.

⁶⁶ Kappen, *Jesus and Freedom*, preface, viii.

⁶⁷ Kappen, *Jesus and Freedom*, 155

⁶⁸ Interview with Sebastian Painadath SJ.

⁶⁹ Houtart, "Introduction," 14.

⁷⁰ Houtart, "Introduction," 15.

⁷¹ Knitter, *No Other Name?* 120-68.

⁷² Kappen, *Jesus and Freedom*, 60.

⁷³ *The Christian Century* 94, no. 28 (14 September 1977): 796.

⁷⁴ Hennelly, Book review, *Jesus and Freedom*, Kappen, 812-3.

⁷⁵ Haight, Book Review, *Jesus and Freedom*, Kappen, 111.

⁷⁶ Cox, *The Silencing of Leonardo Boff*, 178-88.

⁷⁷ Cf. McGovern, *Liberation Theology and Its Critics*, 286-7.

⁷⁸ *Christology at the Crossroads* (1976); *Jesus the Liberator* (1991); and *Christ the Liberator* (1999).

⁷⁹ CDF, "Notification: Father Dupuis' 'Toward a Christian Theology or Religious Pluralism,'" 605-8; Dupuis, *Christianity and the Religions: from Confrontation to Dialogue*, 87 and 90; and Dupuis, *Toward a Christian Theology of Religious Pluralism*, 388.

⁸⁰ Interview with Sebastian Painadath SJ.

⁸¹ Kappen's letter to Arrupe, 15 May 1981, KPA, 1.

⁸² Kappen's letter to Arrupe, 15 May 1981, KPA, 2-3.

⁸³ Bennett, *Understanding Christian-Muslim Relations: Past and Present*, 24-5.

⁸⁴ Kappen's letter to Arrupe, 15 May 1981, KPA, 4.

⁸⁵ Neville, *On the Scope and Truth of Theology: Theology as Symbolic Engagement*, 29.

⁸⁶ Kappen's letter Arrupe, 15 May 1981, KPA, 9.

⁸⁷ Arrupe's letter to Kappen, 27 May 1981, KPA, 1.

⁸⁸ Arrupe, "One Communist at the Service of One World," 4-20; Kappen, *From Faith to Revolution* (Malayalam), 62-3.

⁸⁹ Alessandra, (1999, Dec 22). "Cardinal Paolo Dezza, 98; Guided the Jesuits." New York Times. Retrieved from http://search.proquest.com/docview/431312673?accountid=17215 [accessed 16 February 2016].

⁹⁰ James (2012, Aug). "Of Many Things," *America, 207,* 2. Retrieved from http://search.proquest.com/docview/1037028692?accountid=17215 [accessed 16 February 2016].

⁹¹ Hitchcock, *The Pope and the Jesuits*, 177.

⁹² Dezza's letter to Kappen, 20 January 1982, KPA, 2.

⁹³ Dezza's letter to Kappen, 12 May 1982, KPA, 1.

⁹⁴ Dezza's letter to Kappen, 3 August 1982, KPA, 1.

⁹⁵ Kappen's letter to Dezza, 6 September 1982, KPA, 2.

[96] Dezza's letter to Rex A. Pai, 10 December 1982, KPA, 1.
[97] Interview with C.F. John.
[98] Interview with Sebastian Painadath SJ.
[99] Kappen, *Jesus and Cultural Revolution*, 78.

6

Kappen on Indian Religious Traditions

The Indian multi-religious and multi-cultural context inspired Sebastian Kappen. He believed that it would harness the resources of religion and culture for the purpose of social transformation. In order to achieve this, he wanted to get a deep knowledge of Buddhism, Hinduism, and related religious movements in India, especially the Bhakti movement, and to understand how they affected the social, economic, cultural, and political features of society. This chapter will examine Kappen's interpretations of these religious groups. It is divided into three major sections. The first section will focus on his search for liberating elements in Buddhism. We will examine Buddha's understanding of society and his proposals to enhance the quality of human life through the means of universal love, compassion, and the Eightfold Path. The second, third, and fourth sections are on the caste system, Bhakti movement, and Hindu fundamentalism respectively, which he used as three tools to attack Hinduism. These sections will explicate how Kappen refuted the caste-based discrimination, ritualism, and priestly hegemony in Hinduism. Caste is followed by the discussion of the Bhakti movement and its understanding of the concept of liberation. The movement started in Hinduism as a form of protest, just as Buddhism in the 5th century BCE. Also, there is a critical analysis of how Kappen interrogated the liberating and subjugating ideologies in Hinduism and how he gave meaning to the growing Hindu nationalism

(*Hindutva*). Did *Hindutva*, according to Kappen, advocate a unification of the Hindus by brushing off the caste and class differences, or did it aspire to creating a Hindu militia against a 'potential' common enemy comprised of Islam and Christianity?

Altogether, this chapter is a cross-sectional analysis of the distinctive features of Indian religious traditions, spanning from cosmic and gnostic religiosities, the caste system, cultism, priestly hegemony, and liberation, to the alarming growth of religious fundamentalism and intolerance. It will investigate, primarily from Kappen's perspective, into what degree these features found their space in Hinduism, Buddhism, and the Bhakti movement. This will further drive to Kappen's idea of ethical religiosity, which will appear at the end of the chapter. In the general framework of this research, this chapter is about Kappen's shift to the liberating elements in the Indian religious tradition. His previous encounters with Marx and Jesus also helped him in exploring the riches of Indian religious tradition from the perspective of a liberation theologian and social thinker.

Kappen lived in a pluralist society. As a Christian theologian who was constantly confronted with multiple religious ideologies, he had to take the religious groups around him into account. He was convinced that the followers of different religious groups were not inferior to Christians. This was an indirect criticism of the self-imposed supremacy of the Church. In a pluralist society, Kappen said, he could not teach that there was no salvation outside the Church. Theologians from a predominantly Christian context might not fully comprehend the real meaning of Kappen's words. However, Kappen's criticism of the Church's supremacy caught the attention of theological circles in India, especially because he phrased it in response to the censorship on his *Jesus and Freedom* in 1980.[1]

A. Buddhism as the Reservoir of Liberating Elements

Although Kappen did not dedicate volumes to Buddhism, we find references in his writings from 1983 onwards. In 1983, Kappen published

Jesus and Cultural Revolution: An Asian Perspective, in which he explored the progressive and humanizing aspects of Buddhism. Again between 1991 and 1993, he wrote three extensive articles which also dealt with Buddhism, namely "The Materialistic Conception of History and the Indian Religious Tradition" (1991), "Religious Pluralism and the Survival of Indian Democracy" (1992), and "Hindutva – Emergent Fascism?" (1993). These three articles were together published as a book in 2000 under the title *Hindutva and Indian Religious Traditions.* Additionally, Kappen had been giving lectures and presenting papers on the relevance of Buddha's teachings, even before he started writing on Buddhism. One of the first among such lectures was given at the seminar on "The Significance of Jesus for Asia" in New Delhi in 1982. The text later appeared in *Ingathering: Autobiographical Writings and Selected Essays of Fr. Sebastian Kappen* (2013), under the title "Jesus in the Indian Context."

Kappen applauded Buddha and his teachings. He appreciated him as a prophet of universal love and ethical religiosity, but also highlighted the transformative elements within Buddhism. Indeed, Kappen found a true revolutionary in Buddha because the latter questioned the existing religious and social taboos, denounced metaphysical views, and dealt with the alienated existence of human beings. The post-1982 Kappen seemed to have been deeply inspired by Buddhist ideologies, especially in shaping his thoughts. For example, Buddha's prophetic life, anthropocentric approach, Eightfold Path, moral teaching, attention to the economic roots of violence, and understanding of freedom and virtues were all inspiring elements. In what follows, we will briefly elaborate on each of them.

Kappen found Buddha prophetic in his approach to all forms of religious and social oppression, and emphasized that Buddha wanted to bring the people back from the clutches of myths to reason, from the altar to the worksite, from gods to fellow humans.[2] In fact, according to Kappen, Buddha advocated that the people realize their inner self and potentiality. Buddha was not overly concerned with metaphysical questions and magical thinking that did not directly affect human beings. This was a point of inspiration for Kappen, who became more a progressive thinker than a mere Church theologian and paid more attention to Indian society than to the renewal of the churches.[3] Metaphysical questions were about the attributes and nature of the absolute Other, which Buddha considered irrelevant in relation to the bare human life on earth. He protested against the deprivations of human beings in this world due to the craving for material things and pleasures, which generated sorrow.[4] This, as a matter of fact, was Buddha's way to tackle human alienation. In other words, Buddha taught the ways to improve the quality of life, which also was an area of Kappen's interest.

Kappen also highlighted Buddha's exhortation to affix one's own social duties to the worship one performed. Buddha's exhortation, indeed, was more an anthropocentric understanding of a religious act. He assigned social duties to the 'worship of the six quarters.' Those duties would promote the relationship between parents and children (worship of the East), teachers and students (worship of the South), husband and wife (worship of the West), between friends (worship of the North), employer and worker (worship of the Nadir), and finally, householder and ascetics (worship of the Zenith).[5] Significantly, Kappen called it an anthropocentric approach because Buddha proposed this shift from the religiosity of man-nature encounters to inter-human encounters.[6] Buddha indeed introduced the communitarian dimension of religiosity and inaugurated a new era of human ethical civilization.[7] He preferred a universal kinship to blood relations and expected that the latter would be superseded in the reign of righteousness. Also, Buddha did not preach a religion but a religiosity, which was eventually reformulated into a religion. Such an understanding of Kappen about Buddhism is different from other contemporary Christian theologians for two reasons. First, the latter were content with the general idea about Buddhism being peace loving, contemplative, and anthropocentric. Secondly, they were stuck to the theoretical and objective understanding of Buddhism. Kappen, in contrast, emphasized what society and other religious groups, especially Christians, could assimilate from it.

Buddha did not want to conceptualize everything. Rather, he looked for practical solutions. This becomes evident from the Eightfold Path he put forward. In order to have practical solutions for the various issues one comes across in everyday life, one has to apply the right means Buddha proposed. Through a proper summation of such means one ultimately achieves the goal. Again, most importantly, Kappen pointed out that Buddha did not speak of rituals, sacrifices, priests, and gods while he explained the Eightfold Path. Any of these means had much to do in attaining *nirvana* (*moksha*, liberation). Instead, Buddha suggested eight means – Eightfold Path – to *nirvana*, namely right vision, right aims, right speech, right action, right livelihood, right effort, right mindfulness, and right meditation.[8] Towards the end of his life, Buddha advised his disciples that each one should become one's own lamp. This is an invocation to trust less in the transcendental powers than the praxis-oriented Eightfold Path in attaining *nirvana*.

The central points of Buddha's morality were compassion and love. They included the whole universe: they were based on universal kinship, and not on family, clan, or caste.[9] In other words, Buddha was inclusive rather than exclusive. Even more, his concept of inclusion did consist not only of human beings but also of all other living creatures. Kappen subscribed to this, but at the same time was also intrigued by the fact that Buddha did not confine his teachings to compassion and love alone. Compassion (*karuna*) had its place as a virtue in Buddhism next to three other virtues, namely friendliness (*maitri*), joy (*mudita*), and equanimity (*upeksa*). In *Khuddaka Patha*, Buddha said that practicing charity and goodness along with restraint and self-control would help one accumulate a treasure for the future that no one could steal.[10]

Kappen also found great relevance in Buddha's discourse on the economic roots of all forms of violence. The 6th century BC, the age in which Buddha lived, witnessed a commercial growth in India, which in turn welcomed individualism, competition, profiteering, and cheating in business.[11] Buddha's social teaching clearly explicated the dignity of work and service, and demanded rightful earning of wealth.[12] Furthermore,

Buddha instructed the employer to take into account the health of the employee, to give proper food and wage, to treat the sick, and to grant leave. He aimed at morality (*dharma*) that would consider everyone equal and would replace laws without spirit. A state with such morality could surpass religious nationalism and even create a stateless society.[13]

Kappen's exploration of the liberating and humanizing elements in Buddhism shows how significant they were in contemporary India. Buddha's proposal of a casteless anthropocentric society of universal kinship and love, free of religious and priestly dominance, was still attractive.[14] Buddhism had a great impact on the Indian ethos, and the humane and tender elements in Indian religiosity owed to Buddha.[15] Yet, according to Kappen, Indian society failed to assimilate the teachings of Buddha. In a way, he agreed with what François Houtart said in 1974, that Buddhism could not deepen its roots in Indian soil because of the challenges from the Brahminic priestly hegemony and cultic religiosity.[16]

Kappen did not refer to scholars or authors on Buddhism. Although this absence made it unclear who exactly influenced Kappen in this regard, we assume that he was inspired by Houtart. The latter completed his doctoral studies in Buddhism in 1974, and he maintained contact with Kappen (e.g. writing the introduction to *Jesus and Freedom* in 1977). Kappen began writing on Buddhism a couple of years later, during and after his clash with the CDF, which may be another element in this new direction and can be considered a departure from the sensitive theme of Christology. However, the goal of Houtart's study of Buddhism was not identical to that of Kappen. While Houtart approached Buddhism from a sociological perspective, Kappen's major concern was using Buddha's teachings as an instrument to criticize the dehumanizing elements in Indian religious tradition, particularly in Hinduism. For Houtart, a religiously pluralist society was an "Eden for sociologists of religion,"[17] whereas for Kappen, it was a platform where many mutually corrective religions and cultures met at one and the same time.

The same argument could also be applied in the case of Asian liberation theologians, i.e. Kappen was not the only progressive theologian to explore the liberating elements in Buddhism. It is a common factor of Asian liberation theology that most of its proponents considered Buddhist ideologies among their sources of progressive thinking.

Some Asian liberation theologians even established centers to foster Buddhist-Christian relationships. For instance, Tissa Balasuriya, the co-founder of the Centre for Society and Religion (Sri Lanka), encouraged dialogue between the Catholic Church and Buddhism in Sri Lanka. Balasuriya considered interreligious dialogue as a source of theology and found it significant at a time of rising Buddhist nationalism in Sri Lanka especially in the second half of the 20th century. Catholic orthodox theology, in his view, was largely based on Hellenistic and Roman philosophical and theological formulations. This, however, was not the only way to understand the Divine, especially in the Asian pluralist context. He proposed an Asian theology that would take into account the pluralist context of Asia.[18] Likewise, Aloysius Pieris focused on fostering Buddhist-Christian dialogue in Sri Lanka through his Center for Encounter and Dialogue.[19] His encounter with Buddhism helped him further develop a more indigenous form of Christian prayer.[20] Most importantly, though he did not refer to anyone in particular, Pieris acknowledged the contributions of Indian liberation theologians in terms of their exploration of Buddhism. Kappen's attempt was not only to adapt the Buddhist ideologies to his progressive thinking, but also, unlike Houtart and the Asian liberation theologians, to criticize Hinduism as mentioned in the previous paragraph.

Kappen did not found any centre for Buddhist studies like his Sri Lankan counterparts, but among the Indian progressive theologians, he seems to have exploited Buddhist teachings more than others. Although some of his compatriots also dealt with Buddhism, their approach was peripheral. This was mainly due to the difference in approach between Kappen and other theologians. Whereas the contemporaries of Kappen were concerned with the renewal and building up of churches in India, Kappen's attitude was distinct. He looked towards the reconstruction of Indian society instead of confining his thoughts to certain theological and ecclesial terms.[21] For example, Samuel Rayan appreciated the spiritual heritage of Hinduism and Buddhism.[22] He said that the significance of other religions in India had to be acknowledged and creative dialogues between the Church and other faiths and ideologies should be promoted.[23] However, Rayan did so in order to rethink the mission of the Church in India and to learn how the Church could be built up in India by adapting the constructive elements in the Indian spiritual heritage. Similarly, M.M. Thomas' central focus was on the renewal of the Church in India by acknowledging other religions. Thomas remained Christocentric while dealing with other religions and found the Cross of Christ as capable of transcending the issue of religious pluralism. He even explicitly stood against Kappen's view in this regard, and refuted any form of assimilation of the ideologies of one religion by another to communicate a message.[24] Conversely, Kappen had always promoted the concept of inclusion, where the ideologies of more than one religion converged.

The new interest in understanding Buddhism was not confined to Sri Lankan and Indian progressive theologians. It was also a common phenomenon in other Asian countries like Korea. As already mentioned in Chapter II, the *minjung* theology largely made use of Buddha Siddharta (Amita Buddhism). This is a form of Buddhism that focused more on real problems, especially of the oppressed, in the present world, rather than dealing with transcendental matters.[25] Therefore, the core of the *minjung* theology was the suffering, pain, aspirations, and the struggle of the people. In terms of content, the approach of the Korean progressive theology to Buddhism seemed to be more in consensus with that of Kappen as it was more people oriented.

Kappen's knowledge of Marx and historical Jesus enabled him to absorb the liberating elements in Buddhism. By highlighting the liberating elements in Buddhism, which are interestingly similar to those of Marxism, Kappen did not try to integrate Marx to Buddhism; rather he attempted to adapt them to his progressive thinking. Moreover, Kappen's understanding of Marx and Jesus helped him explore the humanizing elements of Buddhism. For instance, Kappen found it easier to understand Buddha's teaching on casteless society, dependence on one's own potentials, human alienation, etc. from a Marxist point of view. In addition, he practiced these virtues by leading a compassionate, friendly, content, and serene life, with and among the poor, especially from the early 1970s when he started living outside of the Jesuit institutions. Likewise, his closeness to the message of the historical Jesus helped him fully comprehend Buddha's teaching on universal love and *nirvana* as loving one's enemy and the kingdom of God respectively.

B.   Hinduism

Kappen not only explored Buddhism, but also worked on Hinduism. He did so in the same years, namely in the beginning of the 1980s. One of the first works was his article "The Present Cultural Crisis: Analysis and Prognosis," which he published in his journal *Socialist Perspectives* in 1980. A second article with reference to Hinduism came out under the title "Jesus in the Indian Context." It originally was a paper he presented at the seminar on "The Significance of Jesus for Asia," held in Vidya Jyoti, New Delhi, in April 1982. His book *Jesus and Cultural Revolution: An Asian Perspective* (1983) followed these two articles. In this book, Kappen further dealt with Hindu religious ideologies. Towards the end of his life, Kappen again discussed Hinduism in two of his articles, namely "The Materialistic Conception of History and the Indian Religious Tradition" (1991) and "Religious Pluralism and the Survival of Indian Democracy" (1992). These two articles appeared in his *Hindutva and Indian Religious Traditions* (2000). Kappen's *Tradition, Modernity, and Counter-culture* (1994) also provided relevant and censuring description of the Hindu tradition, priestly hegemony, caste system, etc.

The first topics Kappen elaborated on were the concepts of transcendence and immanence in Hinduism. Although all religions gave importance to both transcendence and immanence of God, there were differences in interpretation. The concepts could be explained in two ways: either in ontic rather than in ethical terms or vice versa. Hinduism emphasized ontic terms and saw God as "one with the world of names and forms."[26] It was, in other words, a cosmic religiosity, in which God is both transcendent and immanent, i.e. God is at the same time far removed from and close at hand *in* the nature (or even *is* the nature). This inspired Kappen, and he also believed that the absolute Other (God) underwent a process of becoming, in and through nature. In his 1991 article, he presented the absolute Other in ontic terms.[27] Yet, Kappen's position was slightly different from the Christian understanding of immanence. Christian teaching about God's immanence was based on the Bible, which spoke of the presence of God among his people, the Word of God becoming flesh, and God taking the form of man.[28] Nevertheless, here the transcendental God is just dwelling among his people but not a part of this nature or nature itself. There are not many Christian theologians in India like Kappen who held the Hindu understanding of immanence. Most of his colleagues presumably wanted to avoid the risk of pantheism, which saw nature and everything in it as God.

A second inspiring aspect of the Hindu tradition was its attempt to discover the Divine within oneself. This made Hinduism different from Semitic religions, which sought the Divine outside oneself, considering it the absolute Other. Hinduism, in contrast, saw the Self (*Brahman*) within and beneath the human self (*atman*). Different spiritual activities, such as yoga and meditation (*dhyāna*), helped a person illumine the *Brahman* within.[29] By harnessing the self and the Self (*atman* and *Brahman*), a person gradually withdrew from the world of senses, actions, and passions. In effect, this was a humanizing process, which "sought to create the fully integrated man."[30] This discovering of the Divine was more a process of awareness and meditation, and therefore could be called gnostic religiosity.

Kappen's third constructive observation about Hinduism was its attitude to nature. People could see nature from two perspectives: pragmatic and religious, and Kappen emphasized that the traditional Indian mind looked at nature from a religious angle. He stressed that in Hindu culture, "nature is not something to be conquered or manipulated,"[31] but that it is the womb of everything, the source of fertility, and therefore, the mother of all creation. For this reason, there was a sense of kinship between the nature and man. Kappen referred to the *Abhijñānaśākuntalam* to elucidate this. This is a renowned Sanskrit play by Kālidāsa, a classical Sanskrit writer who lived approximately in the 5th century CE.[32] It was an expansion of a story in the *Mahābhārata*, one of the two great epics of ancient India, and described the emotional farewell of the heroine Shakuntala to the plants and animals of the hermitage where she had grown up. The piece taught the art of living and called for communion with nature. It saw nature as a self-revelation of the Divine and communicated that every creature bore the mark of the Divine. Kappen completely subscribed to these ideas and in his 1991 article called the earth the Mother Goddess.[33] In this way, he also took a position on the contemporary world of utilitarianism and exploitation of natural resources for mass production.

Of course, with these ideas, Kappen diverted from his own religion. Unlike Hindus, Christians gave priority to the ethical understanding of the transcendence and immanence of God. Transcendentally, they considered God as the absolute Other from all evils; immanently, he was in the world to lead the creation to fullness and freedom. However, Kappen was convinced that a proper dialogue between the Indian religious tradition and Christianity would help the latter complement its experience of the ethical God of the Bible with that of the Divine that was indwelling within the creation. The presence of the Divine in humans could be illuminated through mastery over the self. Therefore, Kappen proposed yogic practices in order to enable Christians to discover the self within themselves. With regard to the motherhood of nature, Kappen confronted Christianity. He asked it to consider the earth not something to dominate and subdue, as it is said in the Bible.[34] In Kappen's view, Christian tradition had to learn the art of developing a sense of kinship with nature.[35]

However, Kappen's appreciation of certain Hindu concepts did not mean that he felt entirely positive about Hinduism. On the contrary, he criticized Hindu culture for its various inherent oppressive elements. Kappen denounced Hindu culture for legitimating, sanctioning, and maintaining the system of oppression and discrimination. He primarily attacked the Hindu caste system and the hegemony of the priestly class and the scriptures. Apparently, his criticism of Hinduism outweighed his appreciation.

Kappen's criticism of Hinduism can be placed into three categories: first, to attack Hinduism he criticized the caste system, secondly, he employed the Bhakti movement into his criticism, and finally, he addressed Hindu nationalism.

Kappen's most severe criticism of Hinduism targeted the caste system and its hierarchical structure. The priestly class of Brahmins had categorized people within higher and lower castes. They had placed themselves on the top of the rank and excluded lower castes from playing a role in this process. They also created myths and legends that were favorable to the exploitation of lower castes.

In rejecting the caste system, Kappen often referred to Buddha, who indeed paid much attention to the caste system and the oppression, discrimination, and exploitation based on it. By denouncing caste, Buddha believed that nobody was Brahmin or outcast by birth. It was not birth but deeds that made one belong to a lower or an upper caste.[36] Of course, with these views, Buddha clashed with the Brahminic understanding. Yet, he went even further, and demonstrated his dislike of the caste system by choosing disciples from the low castes and outcastes. Buddha argued that no caste should be condemned nor privileged to do any particular duty. Instead, people should be categorized according to the duties they performed. People who belonged to so-called different castes could come under one group if they did the same job.[37]

Kappen emphasized that caste was a human creation and denounced the fact that it was not attributed to a child after its birth, but that a child was born into a caste. As a result, a one's social status depended not on what one did or was, but on the caste one was born in. Kappen, who as a Christian was not included in the caste system, argued that one's social status in this modern world should not be decided by caste but by wealth, power and knowledge. Therefore, the traditional ranking of status should be replaced by the criteria of merit.[38] In Kappen's opinion, progressive thinkers, including Christian and Hindu theologians, had to conscientize the marginalized and exploited sections of society to get out of the false convictions that the dominant class had instilled.[39]

According to Kappen, the caste system could be understood from a religious and a sociological point of view. As long as caste was viewed through the lens of religion and myths, it received protection from being demolished. For him, this was because Hindu sages had put forward a division between pure and impure things in human life, and extended this to various professions, classes and groups. In this way, they transformed tribes and classes into castes, assigned with certain specific duties.[40] Even more, they turned it into law by means of sacred texts, such as the *Manusmruti* (*The Laws of Manu*). Chapter X, §121 of the *Manusriti* said that a Sudra (the fourth and the last in the caste ranking) should be willing to serve Kshatriyas and Vaisyas (second and third caste groups respectively) if he/she found it difficult to earn a livelihood only by serving the Brahmin.[41]

The pure-impure division Kappen highlighted as the reason for the origin of the caste system was sanctioned by the scriptures. In the caste system purity was assessed according to the purity of the body, which depended on the family one was born to. Since there was no possibility of changing one's body, the purity or impurity remained forever, and this forbade the lower castes from transitioning from impurity to purity. *Bhagavad Gita* said that it was better to perform one's duty, even if it was lower than that of the other, than doing the duty of the other.[42] Kappen denounced such oppressive elements and even transcended this to other religions: "[...] no theologians, whether Christian of Hindu, who are responsive to human values, can unreservedly identify themselves with the religious traditions of the past."[43]

The sociological understanding of caste approached the caste system as a tool for the smooth functioning of society. It showed one's willingness to surrender to the common law. What was important here was not the status of the duty one performed, but the participation in the reciprocal nature of life in society. Eventually, the system, which had been founded for the proper functioning of the society, was instrumentalized by the powerful in order to exploit the weaker sections of society.[44] This evolved into a consolidation of the division between the people: some to serve and the rest to be served.[45]

There are numerous authors, scholars, and social reformers from religious as well as secular circles, who condemned caste before and after Kappen. We have introduced some of the Hindu social reformists from Kerala, along with Gandhi and Ambedkar, in Chapter I. However, Kappen seemed to be one of the pioneers among liberation theologians in condemning the caste system. Like him, many Christian progressive theologians criticized the caste system as oppressive and discriminating. Michael Amaladoss SJ (°1930), a contemporary of Kappen, observed that hierarchy and exclusion were the two characteristics of Indian caste system.[46] For Samuel Rayan, caste was a "powerful, divisive, and oppressive institution."[47] He found it imperative to tackle the problem of caste since it was deeply enrooted in the social, economic, religious, cultural, and political aspects of life.[48] Yet, Rayan acknowledged that this was a difficult task: even the constitution of India could only ban discrimination against the low caste, but not demolish the entire system. Some churches in India had accommodated the caste system, which Rayan considered a mockery of the gospel.[49] Although M.M. Thomas had written on Dalit theology and the caste system even before Kappen, there were Dalit liberation theologians who dismissed Thomas for the absence of any outright repudiation of the caste system in his works. Two were major accusations against him: first, he was a caste Christian (because of his Syrian Christian background; Syrian Christians are said to be upper caste converts) and second, he was a theologian with a Brahminic mindset.[50] Kappen, who also had a Syrian background, never faced such a dismissal. This was due to his explicit criticism of caste. In addition to this, as elaborated in Chapter II, many theologians from the Dalit community wrote extensively about the caste discrimination within the Church.[51]

Another aspect that Kappen discussed was the fact that Buddha repudiated every form of superstitious practices in Hindu religiosity, denounced the worship of gods, goddesses and spirits, and denied the concept of the absolute One. It is interesting to note that this denial of the absolute One was indeed against the conventional beliefs of religions. Instead, Buddha highlighted a disciplined ethical life of service that enabled one to attain salvation.[52] The communities he founded (*sangha*) had the mission of transforming this world from its sorrows to the kingdom of righteousness through ethical life. In this way, Buddha was the first to preach universal love and the rule of *dharma*.[53] The ethical society he envisaged cultivated freedom from all kinds of ignorance and subjugation. For Buddha, freedom from ignorance was the most important thing all people should attain.

In addition to caste, Kappen was also critical of the concept of priestly hegemony in Hinduism. Just as many others, he saw an interconnection between the origin of Brahminic priesthood and the settlement of the Vedic people. The latter lived according to the changing cyclical nature of the universe and consequently developed a cyclic rather than a linear consciousness. This pulled them back from thinking evolutionarily and progressively about the future. The Vedic people saw God as the cyclic rhythm of nature and they believed that he could be influenced by symbols. In order to handle these symbols, they created the priestly class. In Hinduism, the Brahminic priestly class gave importance to the way of knowledge (*jnana marga*) to reach God. A second way, devotion (*bhakti marga*), deteriorated into mere ritualism, and a third way, action (*karma marga*), was neglected. Gradually, priests put dominance on mantras and rituals, which only they could administer.[54]

In addition to his condemnation of priestly hegemony, Kappen particularly characterized Hinduism as a religion that promoted ritualistic worship to enter into a union with the Divine here in this world. Concerning rituals and sacrifices, Kappen highlighted Buddha's aversion to the Hindu tradition of animal sacrifices and the offering of gifts to gods and goddesses in exchange for their favors. Historically, Buddhism was an articulation of the popular discontent with the hegemony of the priestly class and the bloodshed in the endless animal sacrifice. Buddha totally opposed these rituals. He found no meaning in the sacrifices offered to the gods and goddesses, but also condemned the priestly intermediaries. He had a different understanding of a sage, who in his eyes ought to possess philosophical knowledge rather than the mastery over rituals.[55] As a matter of fact, Buddha's condemnatory approach both to sacrificial rituals and to the priestly class inspired Kappen to sharpen his criticism of cultic and institutional religions.

The fact that Hinduism failed to go beyond its ritualism made it an obstacle to the humanization of society. For Kappen, religion should be an agent to create a strong bond among humans and with the Divine. This bond happened mainly through individual and collective praxis, which alleviated the suffering of the people in material terms. *Jnana marga* and *bhakti marga* enabled one to know the Divine and to enter into a personal relationship with him; however, these *margas* distanced one from society. Therefore, society needed an integral approach. For this, the supremacy of the priesthood had to be challenged. The knowledge and devotion which the *jnana marga* and the *bhakti marga* generated should not be confined to the mere pleasing of the Divine; rather the same devotion that was enriched by the feeling of "contemplation, adoration, thanksgiving, surrender, and hope instinct" should urge people to create a humanized universe by means of *karma marga*.[56] This could be called a new form of religiosity that went beyond ritualism and gave equal significance to knowledge, devotion, and praxis.

In criticizing the priestly dominance, Kappen referred to the *Manusmriti*, which indeed stated that certain things like teaching, studying, and performing sacrificial rites, were reserved for the priestly class.[57] As the priestly class claimed to possess the key of the mystery of the universe, it enjoyed the freedom to control every aspect of human life. The existence of the priestly class depended very much on how effectively they tamed gods and convinced the people that ritual sacrifices were inevitable to prosperity in life. Yet, the priestly dominance was not limited to ritualism, but extended to political and economic life.[58] The kings' belief that rituals had to be performed in order to defeat enemies further granted a privileged status to the priests and even gave them decisive roles in political affairs. Since priests enjoyed a considerable share in sacrificial offerings, they also accumulated an enormous amount of wealth. Being a Catholic priest, Kappen's criticism of the priestly hegemony gained more attention as it could also be taken as a challenge to the priestly traditions of other religions, especially of his own Catholic community. Kappen's criticism pointed out his unwillingness to be part of such a hegemonic tradition.

It was at this juncture that Kappen underscored the Marxist criticism of religion – opiate of the people – and reproduced this very same phrase, but not directly referring to Marx. The "eternal passivity of the Indian masses" (Kappen talked about the lower castes, the poor, the peasants, etc.) prevented them from organizing revolts following the examples in the West. He passingly mentioned the slave revolt in the Roman Empire (BC 73), and peasant revolts in medieval Europe (mainly between 14th and 16th century AD) and the French Revolution (1789), which brought fundamental changes to European society.[59] Kappen wondered at the fact that there had never been a major revolt of the poor and the oppressed in India to shake the foundations of the Indian society. The stultifying influence of religion on the Indian mass and the blind adherence of the latter to the former was one of the reasons that led to this passivity. A radical destruction of the traditionally legitimated caste and class distinctions in the Indian society must take place. The Indian masses had to be liberated from the "psycho-structure characterized by fear, [... and] self-demeaning servility," which were the contributions of religion.[60] We presume that such a liberated mass would look through the lens of human dignity, fundamental human rights, and equality, instead of the spectacles of caste, class, and religious hegemony.

Interestingly, referring to the history of Buddhism, Kappen connected the sacrificial rituals to the social life. The middle and lower class farmers and traders of Buddha's time had been discontent with the priestly hegemony and the animal sacrifices. Animal sacrifices became both a burden on the middle and lower classes and a drain on the economy.[61] Thus, in addition to the means of Marxist and Gospel teachings that Kappen employed in his religious criticism, he also started resorting to Buddha. Yet, Kappen's affinity for the Marxist ideologies should have forced him to part with Buddha at least in this regard: for Buddha, emancipation was the freedom from the craving for material things. Conversely, for Marx, it was the dis-alienation from the product that emancipated man. Therefore, it was paradoxical to converge these two views. Still, Kappen stood for an integrated emancipation of human beings, which involved both material and spiritual aspects.[62]

C.   The Bhakti Movement

From the beginning of the 1980s, Kappen went beyond his analysis of Buddhism and Hinduism by extending his search for the liberating and humanizing factors to the Bhakti movement. This was a medieval Hindu religious movement to attain spiritual liberation, particularly focusing on individuals rather than a community. It is an umbrella for various forms of theistic devotional trends in India. Some of them were mainly centred around one god or goddess, but others had more. In both cases, the adherent of the Bhakti movement is called a *bhakta* (devotee), the one who practices *bhakti* (devotion). The Bhakti movement's origin dates back to 7th century CE in south India, and over the following centuries, particularly from the 15th century, it spread to north and east India. We cannot calculate the number of adherents since it is only a revivalist movement within Hinduism.[63] The Bhakti movement, like Buddhism, opposed the prevalent Brahminic hierarchical system, ritualistic ceremonies, and idol worship. Many *bhakti* saints condemned the discrimination within Hinduism on the basis of caste and birth. This critical approach of Hinduism seemed to have attracted Kappen. Since his use of the Bhakti movement was similar to that of Buddha's teachings, which was to criticize the practices in Hinduism, he mentioned the movement in the works in which he discussed Buddhism.

Broadly speaking, there were two ways of understanding God in the Bhakti movement, depending on the two different types of the *bhaktas – nirguna bhaktas* and *saguna bhaktas. Nirguna* and *saguna* mean 'having no quality' and 'having quality' respectively. According to the *nirguna bhaktas*, God is ineffable. He has no form or shape, no attributes, is immanent in the creation (*nirguna Brahma*), and accordingly cannot be understood in anthropomorphic terms.[64] Rama, Krishna, Allah, etc. are the names of the same God. He is present in his creation, irrespective of the species of the creation, and therefore, he should be present in all human beings – in the rich and the poor, in the low and the upper castes. *Sagunabhaktas*, in contrast, believe that God took incarnation in the forms of Rama, Krishna, Vishnu, Siva, and so on. For this reason, *sagunabhaktas* claimed that God should be worshipped in his anthropomorphic form. However, the point of agreement is that both *nirguna* and *sagunabhaktas* extolled singular devotion and personal relationship with the Divine.

The ultimate goal of personal devotion to God is *bhaktas'* liberation from bondages.[65] This is first and foremost spiritual, i.e. liberation from the five senses of a human person – taste, touch, sight, hearing, and smell – which lead to one's slavery to this material world. The *bhaktas* strive to overcome the inclinations of the material world that creep into the human person through the five senses. Their spiritual liberation takes them beyond caste inferiority. One of the hagiographical writings on Ramananda, a 14th century *bhakti* saint in north India, says that a *bhakta* is one who gives up attachment with caste. We find similar thoughts in the hagiographies of many other *bhakti* saints. They particularly focused on the themes of equality and dignity of human beings, which were salient in their lives. Modern scholars of the Bhakti movement, such as Winand Callewaert (KU Leuven), John Hawley (Columbia University, New York), Karen Pechilis (Drew University, Madison, NJ), and N.N. Battacharya (Indian author), also emphasize the importance of spiritual liberation, equality, and dignity.[66] One of the challenges the Bhakti movement faced was appropriation, a term specifically used by Winand Callewaert. Most of the *bhaktas* did not write down their poems or thoughts. They sang and taught from place to place, and their thoughts were for a long time orally transmitted before being written down by others. This interval threw doubt on the authenticity of written documents. Moreover, while being written down, most of the poems and teachings underwent a process of brahmanization. Low caste, untouchable, and Muslim *bhakti* saints, along with their poems, were appropriated by the higher castes. Such appropriation ideologically benefitted the groups that had taken over the poems.[67] Eventually, many *bhakti* sects became alienated from their original form and goal. Interestingly, Kappen noted that the domestication of the *bhakti* saints and their teachings by the Hindu orthodoxy was one of the major reasons for the weakening of the Bhakti movement.[68]

The Bhakti movement was not only relevant for religious, linguistic, and philosophical reasons.[69] The social relevance of the Bhakti movement, though subtle, cannot be totally ignored. It contained an element of protest, which scholars called an emotional religious cult against the path of knowledge (*jnana*).[70] The path of knowledge, which was considered to be the path to liberation, was only accessible to the upper castes. Conversely, the emotional relationship with a personal god, which was the trait of the Bhakti movement, made *bhakti* a path to liberation.[71] For this reason, *bhakti* became an issue between the privileged and underprivileged classes. The *bhakti* saint Bhagat Pipa even criticized the path of knowledge by saying: "if one ignores the restrictions of tradition and scripture, the one is in the company of Ram."[72] Instead of the path of knowledge, he emphasized love and devotion. In his view, liberation was not reserved to the upper castes alone but also to the low castes and the casteless. For the *bhakti* saint Raidas (c.1450-c.1520), God was compassionate, and delivered his devotees from their suffering. This implies that a *bhakta* can be an agent of God's compassion. As God showed compassion to his devotees, the *bhaktas* should be compassionate to their fellow beings, promote equality of human beings, and encourage humanitarian attitudes.[73]

Many poems also carried strong traits of social protest, especially against caste discrimination. Most of them were in vernacular languages in protest against the language of the elites – Sanskrit. Moreover, their saints-authors chose disciples from among the low castes and Dalits, which was intended to deny the sanctity of casteism and to declare all equal in society and before God. There existed no distinction between the devotees on the basis of caste or gender in the movement.[74] Again, Raidas is a good example. He was from a lower caste called *Chamar*, but he proudly acknowledged it. He wrote about the low status of his caste, birth, and trade. At the same time, he said that he was a liberated *Chamar*.[75]

It is no surprise that the Bhakti movement fascinated Kappen. In his article called "The Materialistic Conception of History and the Indian Religious Tradition," he reiterated the revolutionary and challenging factor in the Bhakti movement. This challenging factor was that a devotee's access to the Divine was unconditional. Birth, social status, sex, wealth, caste, color, etc. were not counted in the diety-devotee encounter. If God had any partiality, it was for the poor and the marginalized, not for the rich. Yet, Kappen was also critical of the movement. He noted that the scripture of the Bhakti movement – *Bhagavata Purana* – did not denounce the caste system. Unlike Buddhism, it did not struggle to eradicate the caste system. The Bhakti movement was revolutionary because it permitted a low caste to take up an occupation not assigned to his caste. Still, other than this, it did not seem to have directly challenged the existing structural evil. Instead, the movement believed that devotion (mostly emotional) would disregard and overtake the caste and class divisions via its uniting factor of love.[76]

Kappen's understanding of liberation was different from the spiritual liberation that the Bhakti movement facilitated. He intended an integral liberation, which included both social (including economic and political) and spiritual liberation. While the *bhaktas* considered devotion and the guidance of a guru as the means of liberation, Kappen believed that liberation was through revolution: of conscience, of culture, and eventually of society. Thus, rather than the spiritual aspects of the Bhakti movement, Kappen emphasized its social impact. He actually also made an appropriation, but one that was unlike that of the Brahminic priestly class. While the upper caste appropriated the *bhakti* saints and their teachings for maintaining the former's priesthood and caste domination, Kappen did it to strengthen the humanizing culture and achieve integral liberation.

D.   Kappen's Preference for an Ethical Religiosity

A close reading of Kappen's works towards the last years of his life gives us the impression that he relied on religious language to articulate his social ideas. In his posthumous publication *Jesus and Culture* (2002), Kappen wrote about the three major aspects of religiosities in India – cosmic, gnostic, and ethical. Religiosity could be interpreted as the way religious beliefs and feelings are expressed. While dealing with Hinduism, he acknowledged the positive elements in cosmic and gnostic religiosities. However, he looked forward to the evolution of these two religiosities into an ethical religiosity. Ethical religiosity, for Kappen, worked on the bond of love between man and God, and man and man. In precedent expressions of religious beliefs, man was an object, but when he reached ethical religiosity, he became the subject. Ethical religiosity challenged all understandings of traditional religiosities by means of its distinctive feature of the praxis of love for humanity.[77] While the cosmic and gnostic religiosities were individualistic, ethical religiosity was communitarian. Thus, in Kappen's ethical religiosity, we find a summation of his ideas as a social thinker and liberation theologian.

Kappen considered Buddha the first champion of ethical religiosity for the reason that the latter challenged the idiosyncrasies of the traditional religiosities, so to say, their myth, sacrifice, rituals, caste, and Brahminic domination. The ethical religiosity that Buddha envisioned replaced these features with universal love and compassion. In Kappen's view, universal love and compassion were articulated through praxis. He saw love of one's own fellow beings as the central point that should trigger any fundamental action. This love was for the integral liberation of every human person, which essentially required a denigration of everything that was oppressive and dehumanizing.[78] Kappen in this way observed the seeds of an ethical revolution in Buddhism. He believed that Buddha's repudiation of the caste system and Brahminic supremacy was potential enough in effecting both an ethical and a cultural revolution. In sum, Kappen seemed to have proposed love against hatred as the uniting factor. His proposal was relevant in a diverse society, because love promoted unity among different religious communities, whereas hatred fostered unity within each group but hostility among the groups.

On the other hand, traditional religiosities (cosmic and gnostic) did not contain ethical religiosity. Kappen reproached that they succeeded in inculcating that morality was equal to being faithful to the tradition, which was characterized by cosmic and gnostic religiosities. Moreover, traditional religiosities convinced people that conformity to this morality was a means to attain liberation (see figure 9, the crane and the pond). Kappen argued that this form of morality had to be redefined and that its dehumanizing elements had to be demolished. Therefore, Kappen's reiteration of ethical religiosity was a renewed contribution to Indian society as a transformative source to overcome the limitations of traditional religiosity. By saying renewed contribution, we mean that the ethical religiosity that Kappen proposed was a compilation of ethical religiosities he acquainted with in Buddha and the Bhakti movement.[79]

Kappen believed that ethical religiosity was the latest and highest form of religiosity ever evolved. Cosmic and gnostic religiosities were relevant only as long as men subjected themselves to nature and society.[80] Here Kappen again brought up Buddha to argue that the latter demolished magic and myth and replaced them with universal love and compassion. Buddha's instruction to his disciples was not to depend on priests and gods. Even twenty-five centuries after the Buddha, Kappen observed,

Indian religiosity continued to show proclivity to cosmic and gnostic religiosities.[81] This argument shed light on the fact that the process of evolution to an ethical religiosity had been very slow in Indian society. Kappen strongly reacted against this and strived to project ethical religiosity as it promoted communitarian aspects of liberation rather than the individual aspect.[82]

Furthermore, Kappen found ethical religiosity as an antidote to the growing religious fundamentalism in India. The struggles to reestablish the space of cosmic and gnostic religiosities against the challenges of ethical religiosity created tension in Indian society. The presence of Islam and Christianity prompted the Hindu majority to stick to its tradition and to resort to an approach of exclusion. This, according to Kappen, was *Hindutva*, which he understood in its broader sense, meaning Indian culture or civilization (versus the narrower sense of Hindu religion). Kappen saw that Indian history was being reduced to religions, and religions to Hinduism, and Hinduism to *Hindutva*. Therefore, his preference for ethical religiosity gained paramount relevance in the changing context of India.

Endnotes

[1] Kappen, "Censorship and the Future of Asian Theology," 4.

[2] Jayaseelan, *Towards a Counter-culture*, 39.

[3] Abraham, "Alternative Narratives," 133.

[4] Jayaseelan, *Towards a Counter-culture*, 39.

[5] *Sigalovada Sutta*, 27. Cf. Ling, ed., *The Buddhist Philosophy of Man: Early Indian Buddhist Sources*, 136-9.

[6] Kappen, *Jesus and Culture*, 34.

[7] For more details, cf. Kappen, "The Materialistic Conception of History and the Indian Religious Tradition," 4-6.

[8] Jayaseelan, *Towards a Counter-culture*, 39 and Kappen, *Jesus and Culture*, 32.

[9] Kappen, *Jesus and Culture*, 33.

[10] Childers, "Khuddaka Patha, a Pali Text, with a Translation and Notes," 321.

[11] Ling, *The Buddha: Buddhist Civilization in India and Ceylon*, 43-57.

[12] *Esukari Sutta*, Majjhima Nikāya 96.

[13] Yun, *Politics, Human Rights, and what Buddha said about Life*, trans. Smitheram, 60-5 and Muricken, "S. Kappen: The Man and his Contribution to the Study of Counter-Culture," 17.

[14] Cf. Pasture, "Dechristianization and the Changing Religious Landscape in Europe and North America since 1950: Comparative, Transatlantic, and Global Perspectives," 376-7.

[15] Kappen, *Jesus and Culture*, 35.

[16] Houtart, *Religion and Ideology in Sri Lanka*, 59.

[17] Houtart, *Religion and Ideology in Sri Lanka*, 1.

[18] Balasuriya, "An Asian Theology," 115-6.

[19] Pieris' major works in relation to the dialogue between the Church and Buddhism include: *Love Meets Wisdom: A Christian Experience of Buddhism* (1988); *Fire and Water: Basic Issues in Asian Buddhism and Christianity* (1996); "Liturgy and Dialogue with Buddhism: An Experiment" (1968); "Reincarnation in Buddhism: A Christian Appraisal" (1993); and "Comparative Study of Religions: Lecture Notes for Buddhist Students Studying Christianity" (2000).

[20] Pieris, "What kind of Church do we wish to be?" 428, and "Spirituality as Mindfulness," 38-51.

[21] Kuruvila, "Alternative Narratives in Contemporary Globalization: A Case Study of Visthar and Sebastian Kappen," 133.

[22] Ferm, *Profiles in Liberation: 36 Portraits of Third World Theologians*, 103.

[23] Rayan, "Inculturation and the Local Church," 15.

[24] Thomas, *Man and the Universe of Faiths*, 149-50.

[25] Rowland, ed., *The Cambridge Companion to Liberation Theology*, 48.

[26] Kappen, *Jesus and Cultural Revolution*, 67.

[27] Kappen, *Hindutva and Indian Religious Traditions* (2000).

[28] Jn 1, 14; Phil 2, 6; and Eph 4, 6.

[29] Yoga does not come within the scope of our research, but following works provide the fundamentals of this concept: Singleton, *Yoga Body: The Origins of Modern Posture Practice* (2010); Michelis, *A History of Modern Yoga: Patanjali and Western Esotericism* (2005); and Strauss, *Positioning Yoga: Balancing Acts Across Cultures* (2004).

[30] Kappen, *Jesus and Cultural Revolution*, 68.

[31] Kappen, *Jesus and Cultural Revolution*, 69.

[32] An English translation of the play is available on http://www.yorku.ca/inpar/ shakuntala_ryder.pdf. Kālidāsa, *Shakuntala*, trans. Arthur W. Ryder (1999), [accessed 23 January 2017]; Vyasa, *Mahabharata*, 11th edition, ed. and trans., Rajagopalachari (1972).

[33] *Rig Veda*, Book I, Hymn CLXIV. 33, and Kappen, "The Materialistic Conception of History and the Indian Religious Tradition," 2-3.

³⁴ Gen 1, 28: "God blessed them, and God said them, 'Be fruitful and multiply, and fill the earth and subdue it; and have dominion over the fish of the sea and over the birds of the air and over every living thing that moves upon the earth."

³⁵ Kappen, *Jesus and Cultural Revolution*, 68-9.

³⁶ Cf. *Woven Cadences of Early Buddhists (Sutta Nipata)*, trans. E. M. Hare (verses 134-6), 22.

³⁷ Pruthi, ed., *Indian Caste System*, 53 and 206.

³⁸ Kappen, *Tradition, Modernity, and Counter-culture*, 4.

³⁹ Kappen, "Orientation for an Asian Theology," 118.

⁴⁰ Cf. Kappen, "The Pure and the Impure," 118-9.

⁴¹ Bühler, *The Laws of Manu* (X. 121 and I. 91), 428 and 24.

⁴² *Bhagavad Gita*, III. 35. For details, also cf. Painadath, "Bhagavad Gita's Vision of Liberative Action," 49-65, and Maliekal, "Liberative Vision of the Vedas," 24-48.

⁴³ Kappen, "Orientations for an Asian Theology," 118.

⁴⁴ For details, cf. Mariampillai, "The Emerging Asian Theology of Liberation," 103-6.

⁴⁵ Hulton, *Caste in India: Its Nature, Functions, and Origins*, 65.

⁴⁶ Amaladoss, *A Call to Community*, xi. For more details, also cf. Lee, "The Christological Perspectives in the Theologies of Raymon Panikkar and Byungmu Ahn," 116-22.

⁴⁷ Rayan, "Theological Priorities in India," 33.

⁴⁸ Rayan, "Editorial: On Caste," 220.

⁴⁹ Rayan, "Theological Priorities in India," 34-5.

⁵⁰ Bird, "M.M. Thomas: Theological Signposts for the Emergence of Dalit Theology," 106.

⁵¹ Cf. Prabhakar, ed., *Towards a Dalit Theology* (1989).

⁵² Cf. Chenchiah, "Where Lies the Uniqueness of Christ? An Indian Christian View," 84.

⁵³ Kappen, "Towards an Indian Theology of Liberation," 35.

⁵⁴ Vattamattam, *Towards a Counter-culture* (Malayalam), 111-2.

⁵⁵ Kappen, *Jesus and Culture*, 31.

⁵⁶ Kappen, *Tradition, Modernity, and Counter-culture*, 57-9.

⁵⁷ Bühler, *The Laws of Manu* (I. 88), 24, cited in Kappen, "The Present Cultural Crisis," 4.

⁵⁸ Kappen, *Jesus and Cultural Revolution*, 35-6.

⁵⁹ Kappen, *Hindutva and Indian Religious Traditions*, 40.

⁶⁰ Kappen, *Hindutva and Indian Religious Traditions*, 43.

⁶¹ Kappen referred to the Marxist historian D. D. Kosambi (1907-66) to establish this argument. Kappen, *Jesus and Culture*, 31.

⁶² Cf. Wielenga, "Liberation Theology in Asia," 46.

[63] Ambree, ed., *Encyclopaedia of Ancient History*, 539.

[64] Callewaert and Friedlander, *The Life and Works of Raidas*, 82.

[65] *Pipa Parcai*, 1.19 and 2.1.

[66] Callewaert, *The Hagiographies of Anantdas: The Bhakti Poets of North India*, 12; Hawley, "Author and Authority in the Bhakti Poetry of North India," 272-3; Prentiss, *The embodiment of Bhakti*, 134-5; and Battacharya, ed., *Medieval Bhakti Movements in India* (1989).

[67] Callewaert, *The Millennium Kabir Vani: A Collection of Pad-s*, 2; Mohkamsing, "Machiavellian Hindutva Untamed," 105.

[68] Kappen, *Jesus and Cultural Revolution*, 45.

[69] Schoors, "Welcoming Address," 2, and Shobha, *Social Life and Concepts in Medieval Hindi Bhakti Poetry: A Socio-Cultural Study*, 1.

[70] Kappen, "The Materialistic Conception of History and the Indian Religious Tradition," 6-7, and Boyd, *An Introduction to Indian Christian Theology*, 111-2.

[71] Schomer and McLeod, eds., *The Sants: Studies in a Devotional Tradition in India*, 2.

[72] *Pipa Parcai*, 21. 4.

[73] Hawley, "Author and Authority in the Bhakti Poetry of North India," 275.

[74] Schomer and McLeod, eds., *The Sants: Studies in a Devotional Tradition in India*, 2.

[75] Hawley, "Author and Authority in the Bhakti Poetry of North India," 286, and Callewaert and Friedlander, *The Life and Works of Raidas*, 22.

[76] Kappen, "The Materialistic Conception of History and the Indian Religious Tradition," 7.

[77] Savarkar, *Hindutva: Who is a Hindu?* vii and 81.

[78] Kappen, *Hindutva and Indian Religious Traditions*, 60.

[79] Savarkar, *Hindutva: Who is a Hindu?* 113.

[80] Muralidharan et al., *Understanding Communalism* (Bangalore, 1993).

[81] Kappen, *Hindutva and Indian Religious Traditions*, 55-7.

[82] Sullivan, *Fascism*, 92, cited in Kappen, *Hindutva and Indian Religious Traditions*, 57.

[83] Gunther, *The Racial Elements of European History*, 3.

[84] Kappen, *Hindutva and Indian Religious Traditions*, 61.

[85] Houtart, "Religion and the Transition to Capitalism," 84-5.

[86] Houtart, "Religion and the Transition to Capitalism," 86.

[87] Kappen, *Hindutva and Indian Religious Traditions*, 61-4.

[88] Kappen, *Hindutva and Indian Religious Traditions*, 61.

[89] Embree, *Utopias in Conflict – Religion and Nationalism in India*, 48, cited in Kappen, *Hindutva and Indian Religious Tradition*, footnote 7, page 74. Also cf. Bender, review of *Utopias in Conflict – Religion and Nationalism in India*, 122.

[90] For a detailed analysis, cf. Jain, *The Hindu Phenomenon* (1994).

[91] *Bhagavad Gita*, II. 57.

[92] Kappen, *Hindutva and Indian Religious Traditions*, 64-5.

[93] Sen, *The Argumentative Indian: Writings on Indian Culture, History, and Identity*, 49-53.

[94] Kappen, *Hindutva and Indian Religious Traditions*, 63-4.

[95] Cosmic religiosity was based on the macrocosm and the microcosm while the gnostic religiosity concentrated on the identity of the *atman* with the *Brahman*. When the first one gave priority to magical praxis the second one focused on theoretical understanding of everything. Kappen, *Jesus and Culture*, 75.

[96] For more details, cf. Kappen, "Jesus and Transculturation," 180-1.

[97] Kappen, "Jesus and Transculturation," 181.

[98] Kappen, *Jesus and Culture*, 75-6.

[99] More on Indian religiosity is discussed in Mathew and Muricken, eds., *Religion, Ideology, and Counter-culture*, 26-7; Abraham, "Alternative Narratives in Contemporary Globalization," 145-50; and Orevillo-Montenegro, "Meeting Jesus in the Land of Spirits, Gods, Goddesses, and Tears: Christology from Asian Women's Perspective," 84-6.

[100] Kappen, "Jesus and Transculturation," 181-3.

7

___

Liberation Theology and Counter-Culture

In the 1980s, Kappen reached the apogee of his thinking, which was indeed the final stage of his intellectual transition. He published several books and articles on liberation theology and counter-culture and eventually made a permanent name as an Indian liberation theologian. This chapter will inquire into this. First, it will examine to what extent Kappen can be called a liberation theologian. In doing this, we will analyze how he employed the common and the Asian elements of liberation theology – preferential option for the poor, historical Jesus, Marxist ideologies, praxis orientation, pluralism, inculturation, and Indian religious tradition – in creating his own theology. We will also take into account how Kappen reacted to the two CDF documents about liberation theology. Then, we will contrast him to other liberation theologians and define his peculiarities. Thereafter, the chapter will unfold Kappen's counter-culture, wherein we will discuss how he defined and constructed it. This includes to what extent is he original, and how relevant and unique is his counter-culture for India. All this we do by often referring back to Kappen's ideas, criticisms, and observations that are discussed in previous chapters.

A.   Kappen as a Liberation Theologian

As previously elaborated (Chapter II), progressive thinking in theology with a preferential option for the poor emerged first in Latin American countries starting in the mid-1960s. From the beginning of the 1970s, progressive theologizing was addressed as liberation theology and the progressive Christian thinkers as liberation theologians. Although the word 'liberation' was frequent in the writings of the Latin American progressive theologians, especially after the Second Vatican Council, it was not until 1968 that Gutiérrez combined the words 'liberation' and 'theology' and popularized the concept through his *A Theology of Liberation* (1971). Kappen started using the word 'liberation' in 1970 in his article "Christianity and Liberation," in which he analyzed its spiritual and secular aspects. In his 1972 book *From Faith to Revolution*, he made an explicit mention of Camilo Torres, Óscar Romero, and Hélder Câmara, but he labeled them as revolutionaries, not as liberation theologians. In a paper presented at the Asian Theological Conference in Sri Lanka in January 1979, Kappen voiced for an Asian theology, which he did not yet call liberation theology. Actually, Kappen only started using the term 'liberation theology' extensively in the mid-1980s. His book *Liberation Theology and Marxism* and his article "Towards an Indian Theology of Liberation" – both from 1986 – are two clear examples.

In addition, Christian theologians and authors addressed Kappen as a liberation theologian before and after his death. For example, Virginia Fabella, a Filipino nun and progressive theologian, published Kappen's article "Orientations for an Asian Theology" in her 1980 *Asia's Struggle for Full Humanity*. This book was a compilation of the selected papers of renowned progressive theologians, such as Balasuriya and Pieris (Sri Lanka), Rayan (India), Carlos H. Abesamis (Philippines), and Sergio Torres (Chile), presented at the ATC in Sri Lanka in 1979. In India, progressive theologians had always referred to Kappen on account of his radical thoughts, and showed interest in publishing his articles. For example, Felix Wilfred from Tamil Nadu considered Kappen a liberation theologian and published "Towards an Indian Theology of Liberation" in the *Leave the Temple: Indian Paths to Human Liberation* (1992). In 1993, he included a book chapter on Kappen in his *Beyond Settled Foundations* from Chennai. Shortly after Kappen's death, Samuel Rayan, remembered him for his progressive theology in a two-page memoir in December 1993. Additionally, Sebastian Painadath, referred to Kappen as a liberation theologian and compiled and published Kappen's articles with progressive and revolutionary content. For instance, one such work was *Jesus and Culture: Selected Writings of Sebastian Kappen, S.J.* in 2002. Also in the secular field, Kappen is sometimes presented as a liberation theologian. O.V. Vijayan and Civic Chandran, for instance, were two important Keralite authors of Malayalam literature who found a radical and progressive theologian in Kappen. These three used to exchange ideas and thoughts, especially regarding issues of social relevance.[1]

Western authors do not seem to have often explored Kappen as a liberation theologian. Yet, Douglas J. Elwood (*Asian Christian Theology: Emerging Themes*, 1980), Christopher Rowland (*The Cambridge Companion to Liberation Theology*, 1999), etc. had introduced Kappen to the West. In addition to this, Kappen's conflict in 1980 with the CDF made him popular among the Jesuit scholars in the West.[2]

There are several reasons one may consider Kappen a liberation theologian. His progressive theology shared a number of features with Latin American liberation theology, such as the preferential option for the poor, the search for messages of the historical Jesus, the use of Marxist ideologies, the praxis oriented theology, and finally, criticism of the two CDF documents on liberation theology. All of these features were, with a possible exception to the last one for a reason of chronology, saliently present in Latin American progressive theologians and activists, such as Hélder Câmara, Óscar Romero, Gutiérrez, and even the CELAM. We will now briefly analyze these five features and discuss how Kappen also employed and encouraged them.

Kappen maintained a preferential option for the poor throughout his entire life and works, especially from the 1970s. The *locus theologicus* for Kappen was the poor and the marginalized. His life with the marginalized in the society, mainly in Cochin, Trivandrum, Chennai, and Bangalore clearly indicated his concern for the cause of the poor. It was this commitment from Kappen that prompted Houtart in 1977 to acknowledge Kappen's "option in favor of the poor and the oppressed."[3] Additionally and as already discussed, since liberation theology begins from the life experience of the poor of the lower stratum of the society, it is also called a theology from below. Therefore, Kappen's theology was also a theology from below. Theologizing from below meant, for him, interpreting the gospel in light of the cry of the poor. The rich and the cultural elite could not create a theology to liberate because they never walked in the shoes of the poor. Also, for him, the current system of theologizing and interpreting started from above and was based on rootless beliefs and concepts. Most importantly, Kappen's preferential option for the poor had an Indian character since he criticized the age-old exploitation and marginalization, that alienated the poor from their land and its resources.[4] In his criticism, Kappen referred to the Dalits, the low castes, and the landless. His book *Jesus and Freedom* and article "Towards a Strategy of Socialist Reconstruction" discussed the problems of these groups.[5] It shows that Kappen voiced for such groups even before the activism of the Dalit liberation theologians became stronger and their works started to appear in the 1980s.

The second common feature is the reference to the historical Jesus and his messages in the gospels. Kappen believed that the original message of the historical Jesus would facilitate an effective liberating mission. For this, Kappen proposed liberation of Jesus who had been hidden in the established Church for centuries.[6] This initiative, which we also find with many dogmatic theologians, such as Edward Schillebeeckz and Rudolf Bultmann, and liberation theologians, such as Juan Luis Segundo, Leonardo Boff, and Jon Sobrino, in fact challenged the legacy of Catholic Christology. Kappen turned his journals *Socialist Perspectives*, *Negations*, and *Anawim* into instruments of his liberating mission by introducing the Jesus of history and his teachings to the people. He reiterated the relevance of liberation theology in the contemporary world by pointing out that what liberation theologians said today was what the 'unknown' Jesus had proclaimed centuries back. Kappen deliberately used the term 'unknown' Jesus here, because he wanted to shed light on the real Jesus who "lies buried beneath accumulated layers of interpretations, laws, procedures, credit bills, bank accounts, and the paraphernalia of a State apparatus."[7] It was impossible to obtain access to the liberating ideologies of Jesus unless he was liberated. Kappen, like other progressive Christian thinkers, met with the unknown Jesus of history in the synoptic gospels, and he called this meeting the encounter with the Divine. Yet, the way the dominant minority had interpreted the gospel made this encounter a challenge, which Kappen called Divine challenge. No theologian could be neutral to the challenge posed by the Divine, the challenge to aspiring for the integral liberation of the human person. According to Kappen, refusing to respond to the challenge of the Divine was nothing but a denial of the Divine.[8]

The third common feature is the reliance upon Marxist ideologies. Globally, liberation theology was attracted to Communism because of the latter's protest against economic exploitation. Latin American liberation theologians, such as Gutiérrez (*A Theology of Liberation*, 1971), José Miranda (*Marx and the Bible*, 1971), and Miguez-Bonino (*Christians and Marxists: The Mutual Challenge to Revolution*, 1976), and activists like Camilo Torres, Hélder Câmara, and Óscar Romero, used Marxist ideologies as means of social analysis. In South and Southeast Asia, Kappen, Balasuriya, Pieris, M.M. Thomas, Paulose Mar Paulose, Edicio De la Torre, Carlos H. Abesamis, Ahn Byung-mu, etc. were inspired by and had made use of the liberating elements in Marxism. However, as far as the use of Marxist ideologies is concerned, Kappen stood slightly different from these Latin American and Asian liberation theologians because he employed such ideologies more often than others. We assume from Kappen's approach to Marxism that he used it primarily in his criticism of religion and only then against economic exploitation. Kappen argued that religion generated a fearful devotion to powers beyond humans, and by relying on Marx's idea of religious alienation he said that this fear alienated them. Consequently, every aspect of life was dominated by fear.[9] As a part of his religious criticism, Kappen also appreciated the Communist movement for its fight against the caste system. This is particularly evident in the Indian states with a strong Communist presence. Although the caste system was practiced in its most intense form in Kerala, the Communist movements played a vital role in weakening it. The left parties, especially the CPI and the CPI[M], considerably contributed to the uplift of the low caste and the Dalits.[10] With regard to the economic exploitation, Kappen observed that the Communist parties had been striving to organize the working class against it. They played a vital role in abolishing landlordism and distributing land to the landless.[11]

The fourth feature is the praxis orientation, which essentially differentiated liberation theology from the conventional one. While traditional theology interpreted the material deprivations of people from a spiritual point of view, even by glorifying them as means to receive God's blessings, liberation theology sought concrete solutions to such problems. Kappen criticized the theologians in Indian seminaries for taking theology as a career and forgetting the importance of praxis in theology. He believed that unless and until this praxis orientation was prioritized, theology remained not transformed into a theology of liberation. Instead, the seminaries would be havens of armchair theologians reproducing armchair theologians. Theologians instead should consider the liberation struggle of the socio-economically poor.[12] Liberation theology preferred action to theory and therefore Kappen made it clear that a true theologian should stop theologizing at a theoretical level. The new humanity he envisioned consisted of people who lived for each other.

In a paper presented at the Senate Meeting of the Serampore University, West Bengal, in 1976, Kappen pointed out the interconnection between the method and the content of the process of theologizing. At the very outset of the presentation he reiterated the relevance of a personal involvement of the teacher in what he/she taught.[13] In the following years in his life, Kappen intensified his search for orthopraxy against orthodoxy in doctrine.[14] In this way, he attempted to divert theology from theory to action. Traditional theology speaks of God as if it already knows him and then adds various attributes to him, so to say, as Kappen put it, "God is love," "God is truth," and "God is the defender of the orphan and the widow." However, Kappen criticized this way of understanding God and negated the idea that humans could know God only through the predicates they attribute to him. The predicates reduced God to certain human expressions and experiences. Instead, Kappen suggested a reformulation of the above phrases into: "love is Divine," "truth is Divine," and "caring for the orphan and the widow is Divine."[15] This was indicative of the way Kappen theologized: it started from the very act of ordinary human beings – love, truth, caring, etc.

Finally, and most importantly, Kappen's response to the two CDF documents on liberation theology – *Instructions on Certain Aspects of the Theology of Liberation* (1984) and *Instruction on Christian Freedom and Liberation* (1986) –, proved that he was a liberation theologian. Shortly after the promulgation of the second CDF document, Kappen published *Liberation Theology and Marxism* (1986) in which he criticized both documents on three counts: the Church's vague understanding of Marxism, its dualistic perception of the world, and its understanding of the poor.

Kappen's first criticism was that the *Instruction on Certain Aspects of the Theology of Liberation* was unclear about Marxism. Although the document did not explicitly reject all liberation theologies, it condemned those that uncritically borrowed from Marxism and consequently left behind orthodoxy.[16] Kappen stated that the document ruled out any possibility even of a critical assimilation and in this way implicitly insinuated that one cannot even partly adapt Marxism. He dismissed this total rejection of Marxism, pointing out that it denied the terrain of plausible dialogues.[17]

Practically, Kappen demolished almost every argument of the document against Marxism and denounced that the Church's enmity with Marxism was revealed in the former's overemphasis on the relation between Marxism and liberation theology. Ratzinger believed that liberation theologians' use of Marxist analysis would give a higher truth value to Marxist theories in society.[18] However, this cannot be a totally valid claim since many liberation theologians, including Kappen, argued that a separation between Marxist philosophy and social analysis was possible. Gutiérrez himself did not want to reduce Christianity into a revolutionary movement like Marxism and therefore stated that Marxist ideologies must be separated from Marxist analysis.[19] Arrupe shared the same view and called on liberation theologians to differentiate between Marxist social analysis and philosophy.[20] Kappen was on the same page. He denied the claim implicit in the CDF document that liberation theology resorted to the core of Marxist ideologies like atheism, this-worldly messianism, violence, dialectical materialism, and denial of human freedom and rights.[21] This seems important, though was not very original. Already before the promulgation of the CDF document, in 1982, Walter Kasper, a member of the International Theological Commission, had observed that the failure of the official Church was that it identified the ideological interpretations of Marxism with its analysis of social problems.[22]

Kappen's second criticism of the CDF was for its dualistic approach to the world. i.e. its juxtaposition of the sacred and the profane. The CDF presented the Church as a gift of God and a spiritual reality, which spoke in the name of truth. As a result, the Church gained a kind of absolute value and the power to define what was divine and profane. Kappen, however, referred to the past of the Church, an institution that misused its power to legitimize slavery, sponsor Crusades, sanction colonialism, and maintain a state apparatus including a bank (the last reference should be seen in light of the late 1970s and the early 1980s bank scandals in the Vatican). He found it paradoxical that the Church, being well engaged with such worldly affairs, accused liberation theology of making liberation a worldly program.[23] Thus it is clear that he did not agree with the CDF comment that liberation theology was a newly originated radical movement that reduced the whole essence of liberation of humanity to political and economic freedom.

Next to his criticism of the CDF for its dualistic approach to the world, Kappen objected to the Church's understanding of poverty and its attitude towards the poor. Just as many other liberation theologians, he argued that the Church spiritualized the temporal deprivations of man. Instead, they preferred to refer to the Sermon on the Mount in the gospels of Matthew (5, 1-12) and Luke (6, 20-26), where Jesus sided with the poor: "Blessed are the *poor in spirit*, for theirs is the kingdom of heaven" (Matthew 5, 3). Interestingly, Luke quoted Jesus differently: "Blessed are you who are *poor*, for yours is the kingdom of God" (Luke 6, 20). However, biblical scholars have agreed upon the conclusion that in the biblical version closer to Jesus, it is *the poor* and not *the poor in spirit*.[24] Kappen's reference to this again demonstrates his view that interpretations stayed far from the original message of Jesus and that liberation theology proposed a return to the meaning of Jesus' original message.

Regarding material deprivations, Kappen wrote that the Church had the same intentions in serving the poor as in previous centuries. Again, it was showing kindness to the slaves, giving alms to the poor, doing charity, etc. These gestures from the Church did not seek permanent solutions to the suffering of the poor, they merely treated the symptoms. At the same time, these acts were eventually spiritualized and could therefore overcome any kind of criticism on the Church's genuineness. Moreover, the Church anathematized every alternative to this strategy, including class struggle, and in this way sustained exploitation and oppression.[25] Kappen proposed a unification of the opposing agents to launch a revolution of consciousness, which ultimately would lead to the integral liberation of man. Therefore, in other words, unlike what the Church labeled, his preaching about material deprivations cannot be condemned as earthly gospel.

B.   An Asian Challenge of Traditional Theology

Kappen's concern over the second CDF document, *Instruction on Christian Freedom and Liberation*, seemed similar to that of the first, but also had some new accents. Both documents shared several similar criticisms on liberation theology. Still, in his response to the second one, his major areas of interest in particular were the Church's catholicity, triumphalism, theological imperialism, and reductionism. It sounds to be a reading of the Church from outside of the West and therefore, also taking into account the Asian background of Kappen, we consider his response a challenge to conventional and conservative theology.

First of all, Kappen doubted the catholicity of the Church in promulgating a document for the universal Church without taking into account its diverse global nature. In spite of the fact that the document addressed the faithful all over the world, it was composed in the framework of the West by referring to the Renaissance and the Enlightenment and looking at things exclusively from a Christian point of view. With regard to Latin American liberation theology, this may still have been acceptable: the predominant Christian culture there could accommodate the Christian way of analyzing things. However, Kappen questioned the functional value of such documents in the Asian context. Both the Western framework and the Christian thinking were unsuitable for the pluralist Asian societies, and the document did not take into consideration the concerns raised by Asian theologians with regard to religious and cultural pluralism.[26]

The second and third criticisms were interrelated: Christian triumphalism and theological imperialism. Both these phenomena glorified the Church as the supreme custodian of truth, morality, and justice, which in turn subordinated all religions to Christianity. Kappen, however, refuted such glorifications by referring to the failures of the Church in the past. More significantly, and from Kappen's standpoint, the CDF misused the dual meaning of the definition of the Church. The term Church can be understood in two ways: either as the hierarchical entity or as the people of God. As a result, the sinful past was attributed to the Church that was the people of God, and credit for the liberating works of the few and exceptional members of the Church went to the hierarchical Church.[27] Kappen doubted the truthfulness of the claim in the document that the Church, through its magisterium, had been trying to establish justice in the world and to witness to man's dignity in its love for the poor.[28]

Christian triumphalism and theological imperialism brought a clear shift from theo-centrism to Christo-centrism, which would finally lead to the planting of Christianity in all non-Christian cultures, as put forward in the document. It has clearly stated that "inculturation is not simply an outward adaptation; it is an intimate transformation of authentic cultural values by their integration into Christianity and the planting of Christianity in the different human cultures."[29] This type of absolute claim also reiterated that Christianity had not much to learn from non-Christian cultures and indeed, the document sponsored "ideological aggression against people of other faiths" and everything that was non-Christian. Kappen strongly condemned this and called theologians from pluralist contexts to challenge this attitude of the Church. To him, a genuine and universally applicable theology of liberation could emerge only from Asia, where Christianity confronted with other world religions.[30]

Lastly, in Kappen's point of view, the CDF's theological approach was reductionist, as it started with dogmas to arrive at ethical principles and from there went to practical guidelines. In effect, this was a downward movement. It contradicted the approach of liberation theology, and Kappen concluded that the Church had learned practically nothing from the theology of liberation. The CDF document was full of ambiguities and inconsistencies, because it did not take liberation theology in its real meaning and only tried to accommodate the thoughts of liberation theology in an age-old dogmatic-theological framework.[31] As a result, the document did not have much to do with the realities of human life in this world. It reduced structural evil to personal sin, focused on the spiritual poor, and put forth poverty as the result of original sin. This was a clear shift from the language of Medellin and Puebla.[32]

However, Kappen's criticism of the CDF documents did not mean that his theological position was totally against that of the mainstream Church. He acknowledged liberation theology as the prism to look at the world, but did not promote an uncritical acceptance of liberation theology since the latter may also have certain things that must be discarded in the future. In sum, he tried to advocate a middle position that should not be questioned by the Church nor liberation theology.[33] Therefore, we conclude that Kappen's approach was bifocal — looking back to the past and forward to the future.

According to Kappen, the Second Vatican Council and the pressing need for social justice in Asia challenged Asian progressive Christian thinkers to formulate a theology of liberation.[34] However, he observed that the liberation theology they defined did not develop as a distinctive school of thought, despite several attempts from various corners to interpret the gospel in light of the Indian cultural and religious context. Even in the beginning of the 1990s, Kappen said that liberation theology in India was only at its initial stages.[35] In his opinion, its growth remained stagnant because the Church and the traditional theologians deviated from their commitment to champion liberation. Although Kappen criticized the Church's conservative attitude, he did not fully ignore its past liberating efforts, especially the social teachings. Examples of these initiatives appeared mainly in the Church's encyclical and pastoral letters, and in Council documents like *Rerum Novarum* (1891), *Mater et Magistra* (1961), *Gaudium et Spes* (1965), *Dignitatis Humanae* (1965), *Populorum Progressio* (1967), *Octogesima Adveniens* (1971), etc. What he questioned was mainstream Church's discouraging attitude towards liberation theology in general, although liberation theology only tried to recapture the liberating aspects in the teachings of Jesus. In Kappen's opinion, it was the deviation of the mainstream Church from its prophetic responsibilities that impelled it to oppose the prophetic character of liberation theology.[36] At the same time, the signs of scientific and economic developments in the last quarter of the 20th century made Kappen think that such a boom would uproot traditional symbols and culture. Therefore, the true challenge for Christian theologians was to combine the positive values of the tradition with those of modernity. To him, in a period of transition from tradition to modernity, theologians had to strive to reconstruct society, without blindly adhering to the dominant traditional value system.[37]

Considering Kappen's understanding of liberation theology, we should distinguish between Indian and Latin American liberation theologies. By referring to Gutiérrez's definition of liberation theology ("critical reflection on Christian praxis in the light of the Word"), Kappen pointed out that Latin American liberation theology "makes little sense in India."[38] In its dealing with the Third World problems of poverty and economic exploitation, it based itself on the liberating message of Jesus in the gospels and Marxist ideologies. However, applying the same criteria in pluralist India was by and large a neutralization of the inherent potential of the Indian religious tradition. Kappen therefore strived towards a peculiar liberation theology for India. He thought that Latin America was too different and that India's religious and cultural pluralism, as well as its socio-political situation were to be taken into consideration separately.

The issue of pluralism was the major theme of the paper Kappen presented at the aforementioned ATC in 1979, in which he prioritized the existential, social, cosmic, and historical dimensions of human life in developing an Asian liberation theology.[39] In his *Liberation Theology and Marxism*, Kappen further argued that a theology evolved in such a pluralist context could not exclude the existing cultural and religious elements, and be a closed enterprise of the Church.[40] He distinguished several salient features of the Asian pluralistic context and employed them in his liberation theology, which he accordingly turned into an Asian liberation theology.

Inculturation was on the top of Kappen's agenda. Stating that every Christian in India was "first Indian and only then Christian," Kappen criticized the attitudes of the mainstream Church for instilling the conviction that Christians in India had nothing to do with the Indian religious tradition, particularly Hinduism. Instead, for him, Indian Christians were the children of the same soil and consequently, a cross-cultural and cross-religious people.[41] Kappen claimed that theologizing had to follow this context. This was the reason behind his radical invitation to Asian theologians to leave behind the traditional structure of the institutional Church and to dissociate themselves from its practices.[42] He advocated inculturation arguing that Christianity should be "enfleshed in the culture of the soil." Therefore, he also rejected any overemphasis of imported theologies. Instead, Kappen championed a theology of liberation for India by assimilating indigenous elements. Inculturation should also happen between individuals of different faiths. Kappen himself did not want to be called a Christian, but rather, disciple of Jesus, though also very much influenced by Buddha's teachings and by the concept of Divine, which could be called an impersonal god. He also thought that the Indian form of secularism, which did not deny religions and their traditions, should maintain inculturation.[43] This would further help the Church in India confront the three remarkable ways it was perceived by non-Christians, namely as an imported foreign religion, as a religion of proselytism, and as a socially and economically powerful entity through its secular institutions. Such a confrontation would help the Church provide itself with a new face.[44]

Acknowledging the Second Vatican Council's openness towards other religions and cultures, Kappen tried to assimilate non-Christian ideologies into his liberating mission. He succeeded in dealing with the plurality of India by not confining himself to the organizational structure of the Church in general nor of the Society of Jesus in particular. It was his acquaintance with the pluralist background that enabled him to comprehend and acknowledge the authenticity of different religious groups including Hinduism, which he also severely criticized.[45] Particularly and as already analyzed, the Hindu understanding of the transcendence and immanence of God, and the presence of the Divine within oneself and within nature enabled Kappen to envision an Indian liberation theology.

Kappen assimilated even more from Buddhism than from Hinduism into his liberation theology. Buddha was also concerned with the alienated people of his time and with their varying religious and cultural oppression. Kappen admired Buddha's invitation to supplant every form of discrimination and exploitation with universal love and humanism. He adapted considerably from Buddhism in order to condemn discrimination on the basis of caste and creed, and to uphold equality of all human beings. The caste divided men in terms of ritual purity, status based on birth, hierarchical order, exclusiveness in relation to other social groups, etc.[46] According to Kappen, Buddha "replaced the *varna* [caste] morality of inequality with the universal morality of compassion (*karuna*)" and promoted communitarian understanding of religiosity rather than individual salvation.[47] Going further, he emphasized Buddha's Eightfold Path, universal friendliness, and compassion as essential to true society.

According to Kappen, universal humanism demanded a combination of spiritual and secular values. He pointed out Buddha's attempts to replace religious worship with certain duties in daily life. In fact, the same attempt was explicit in Kappen's criticism of the hierarchy of institutionalized religions, which were far removed from the real life of the people. As Buddha's disciples included every kind of people, Kappen tried to reach out to all types of people in society, upholding equality and the dignity of all human beings. Since Buddhism had almost disappeared from India, mainly because of the powerfulness of Brahminism,[48] Kappen found it essential to retrieve Buddhist teachings in order to transform Indian society. Actually, transformation of society had always been a major concern of Kappen.

Finally, Kappen added the bhakti understanding of spiritual liberation to the discussion of material liberation. As already elaborated, the Bhakti movement focused more on spiritual liberation through personal devotion than on material liberation. In addition, the inclusive religiosity of the bhakti saints influenced Kappen because they valued not economic and religious status but the dignity of all human beings.[49] Moreover, the *bhaktas* were low castes, economically poor, and politically and socially not influential. Apparently, the Bhakti movement liberated the marginalized low castes and the Dalits from discrimination. This anti-cult, and anti-caste approach inspired Kappen's liberation theology for India. For him, the material aspect of human life cannot be neglected and therefore, liberation meant the material and spiritual wellbeing of all humanity. To this end, he advocated for the collaboration of various religious and secular groups and ideologies. He recognized and reiterated the significance of Jesus in the Indian context. According to Kappen, Jesus did not offer a one-sided salvation; instead, the salvation he offered was integral; it was of 'wholeness.'[50]

The above-mentioned features of Asianness greatly affected Kappen. His liberation theology incorporated an integrated sum of Asian pluralism's liberating elements into the framework of the liberating messages of Jesus. Asian liberation theologians in general were open to other religions and cultures, but not to the same degree. In India, liberation theologians, especially those of the first-generation liberation theology, do not seem to have referred to non-Christian religions with the intention Kappen had. However, in Sri Lanka, both Pieris and Balasuriya promoted dialogue with other religions, especially Buddhism, and even founded centers, namely the Tulana Research Center for Encounter and Dialogue (1974), and the Center for Society and Religion (1971) respectively, in order to strengthen inter-religious relationships. Pieris especially was very active in this field and even made indigenous Christian prayers by incorporating Buddhist elements. Surprisingly, despite the pluralist context of Philippines and South Korea, dialogue between religions, and inculturation were less discussed by liberation theologians, such as Carlos H. Abesamis and Ahn Byung-mu.[51] Instead, they resorted mainly to the gospels and Marxist ideologies. In this way, their liberation theology was closer to Latin American liberation theology than to that of India and Sri Lanka.

Kappen actually stood out from all of these liberation theologians. He did not establish a centre for religious studies and did not intend to make the Church powerful and established. Kappen not only studied religions, but also searched for their liberating elements. This was not to build the Church but to liberate the economically poor. Importantly, he adapted only the spirit of religions and cultures, and not their alienating institutional structure or hierarchy. No other contemporary liberation theologians in India seemed to have criticized religion as seriously as Kappen. According to him, established religions were obstacles to the humanization of society because of their obsolete beliefs and practices, their dogmas that curtail the freedom of thought, their distance from social ethics and justice, and the social conflict they promote in spite of the universal brotherhood they preach.[52] Kappen was looking forward to developing a secular religiosity, which respected the liberating ideologies of religion and ignored its dehumanizing character.[53]

Kappen even explicitly took distance from other contemporary liberation theologians regarding inculturation. As previously explained, there were theologians like M.M. Thomas, who discouraged inculturation of Christianity and assimilation of non-Christian ideologies already in the 1970s.[54] It is true that Balasuriya (*Jesus Christ and Human Liberation*, 1976), Pieris (*An Asian Theology of Liberation*, 1988), etc. developed their own understanding of inculturation. Indian progressive Christian theologians, in particular Rayan ("Reconceiving Theology in the Asian Context," 1985), also dealt with inculturation. However, the primary objective of these theologians was to transmit Christianity to non-Christian cultures by making use of the customs, practices, celebrations, beliefs, etc. in those cultures. Conversely, Kappen interpreted inculturation only as a study of other cultures and faiths (Buddhism, Hinduism, Dalits, Tribal people) for a better understanding, and therefore a way to assimilate the liberating elements in them. What he meant by inculturation was Indianizing Christianity for the purpose of liberation, and not Christianizing India. Endorsing Christianity's need of inculturation in the Indian soil, Kappen pointed out: "[B]eing a Christian means to have had one's being grafted on to an exotic tree which has not yet struck deep roots in the Indian soil. True Christians are as much sons and daughters of the earth as Hindus."[55] As a matter of fact, his account of inculturation was more radical than that of his contemporary progressive theologians.

Interestingly, Kappen's liberation theology was not only inspired by Asian pluralism, but also colored by Western thinkers. He indeed made some passing reference to the Austrian psychoanalyst Sigmund Freud and the German philosopher Friedrich Nietzsche. According to Kappen, there should be a transition of Indian culture from will to power to will to life, two concepts by Nietzsche and Freud respectively. Will to power is the expression of the death-instinct in human beings that tries to gain mastery over everything. Will to life is the search for freedom, self-expression, and communion with nature.[56] Thus the crux of Kappen's liberation theology could be explained as the theology transformed from will to power to will to live. Unfortunately, the ruling class, through the means of work and religion, systematically neutralizes the will to power of the oppressed and the exploited. In work, the ruling class makes use of the labor of the worker, who as a result is alienated from the product he made. In religion, the oppressed are taught to direct their urge against their own will to life. This is done mainly by glorifying asceticism, and by preaching the dignity of poverty and obedience.[57]

Kappen applauded the Gandhian criticism of Western capitalism and considered Gandhi as the most powerful spokesman of resurgent India.[58] However, he only briefly commented on Gandhi, and for instance, did not refer to Gandhi's *sarvodaya* and non-violence. This is striking since *sarvodaya* could be considered Gandhi's liberation theology. It is a Gandhian philosophy aimed at universal uplift, a concept out of the inspiration from the British writer and artist John Ruskin's book *Unto This Last* (1860). Ruskin's criticism of mainstream economic thinking influenced Gandhi because it argued against the theoretical construction of an 'economic man' who is completely detached from society and social affection. Criticizing Western materialism, Gandhi said that progress could not be limited to any particular section in the society, but for all, even of the last single person.[59] Although Gandhi's non-violence did not greatly influence Kappen, there were progressive Christian thinkers who were inspired by it. Interestingly, for instance, in a book dedicated to memory of Gandhi and Martin Luther King, Hélder Câmara wrote on Gandhi's methods of non-violent resistance.[60]

Kappen, in general, however, was critical of Gandhi and complained that Gandhism was ritualized after Gandhi. This was mainly due to three reasons, of which the first two tacitly referred to Gandhi's views and the last one explicitly criticized him. First was Gandhi's approach to the caste system. Gandhi did not intend to abolish the caste system but only strived to remove the discrimination based on caste. He merely elevated the status of the casteless untouchables by calling them Harijans, the people of God, instead of solving the fundamental problem. Secondly, Gandhi believed that religion provided moral progress to society and would therefore be an adequate tool to combat communalism in India. Kappen, in contrast, was closer to the line of Marx's criticism of religion and called religion the instrument of hegemony. Thirdly, Gandhi glorified poverty and simplicity. According to Kappen, "[T]he Gandhian tradition must shed its romanticism of poverty and its nostalgia for the simplicity of the primitive man."[61]

With these thoughts, Kappen, as a matter of fact, dovetailed with B.R. Ambedkar, the Dalit opponent of Gandhi. Ambedkar never collaborated with Gandhi and Indian National Congress, but eventually became the principal architect of the Indian Constitution and the first minister of Law. Ambedkar criticized Gandhi on the caste issue and converted to Buddhism as a protest against caste discrimination. Yet, Kappen did not make any adequate reference to Ambedkar. Likewise, he did not seem to have acknowledged the contributions of other social reformers, such as Chattampi Swamikal, Sri Narayana Guru, or Mahatma Ayyan Kali from his own native state of Kerala (whom we discussed in Chapter II). Kappen constructed his liberation theology upon the solid base paved by his forbears who fought every form of evil in the Indian society, but he only occasionally referred to or cited them.

C.   The Prophet of Counter-Culture

Kappen could rightly be called a prophet of counter-culture. Not only Kappen commented on society, but he also desperately wanted to change it. He strived to destruct the existing dehumanizing culture of alienation, oppression, and exploitation by replacing it with a counter-culture. He proposed a counter-culture that contained the liberating elements from the teachings of Marx, Jesus, and Buddha.

The English anthropologist Edward B. Taylor (1832-1917) defined culture as a "[...] complex whole which includes knowledge, belief, art, morals, law, custom, and any other capabilities and habits acquired by man as a member of a society."[62] Robert H. Lowie (1883-1957), an American anthropologist, understood culture as "the sum total of what an individual acquires from his society – those beliefs, customs, artistic norms, food-habits, and crafts which came to him not by his own creative activity but as a legacy from the past, conveyed by formal or informal education."[63] From these definitions, it is clear that culture is a multifaceted phenomenon, which is the reflection of the historically evolved and eventually refined summation of the religious and secular experiences of human beings. Kappen's definition is close to this, as he understood culture as an "organic whole of ideas, beliefs, values, and goals which condition the thinking and acting of a community or a people."[64] Even when there is an element of refinement in culture, Kappen looked at culture as a normative consciousness of people handed down from the past. Thus, the normativity of the past had to be crystallized and articulated through various means, including ethics, philosophy, art, literature, myth, cult, and economic, social, and political institutions.[65] In a diverse Indian society, however, it is relevant to ask who fashions these means. Kappen condemned the fact that it was the ruling class, who often belonged to high castes, defined these means. In his view, the caste-class character of the Indian society manipulated the culture, and this led to a cultural crisis.

The caste-class character of India was a double-edged sword, because it had both a secular and a religious dimension. As discussed in Chapter II, the low castes and the Dalits were marginalized in the economic, political, and social spheres as well as in their religious life. For this reason, according to Kappen, culture could even function as an obstacle to human emancipation. This was particularly true in India, since the low castes and the Dalits had not yet found adequate space on the cultural map. It was at this point that Kappen proposed a counter-culture, which was nothing but the demolition of the existing culture and the construction of a new one.

Counter-culture is a loosely defined yet loaded concept. It could be interpreted as a movement against the existing hegemonic system, whether it be religious, political, economic, cultural, etc. The fundamental ideology behind a counter-cultural movement is that there is no classical culture that is valid for all people and all times. The concept evolved in the 1960s in America, especially as a follow up to Beat generation. The economic boom due to large-scale industrialization and mass production improved the standard of living for a good majority of society. At the same time, there were groups of people who did not wish to share this affluence. Some young writers, artists, and wanderers rejected a society in which the majority lived lavishly, and the minority was marginalized. They called for a counter-culture that negated the ongoing culture.[66] It is interesting to note that inter alia, Jesus, Buddha, and Gandhi influenced the proponents of this counter-culture. The hippie movement that grew out of it was also inspired by Indian concepts like *sanyasa* (renunciation). Although Kappen began to use the term counter-culture in the late 1970s, its central ideas, especially as found in Allen Ginsberg (1926-97), an American poet and Herbert Marcuse (1898-1979), a German-American philosopher – two champions of counter-culture – began to appear in his works from the early period of the decade. Ginsberg and Marcuse criticized capitalism, and the former stood out with his protest against "imperialist politics, and persecution of the powerless."[67] Ginsberg himself visited India, practiced Buddhism, and sustained a good contact with

Hare Krishna movement. Despite Marcuse's criticism of Marxism in his *Soviet Marxism: A Critical Analysis* (1958), both he and Ginsberg sympathized with Marxist ideology, but advocated non-violence. Kappen shared much with the advocates of counter-culture, especially regarding the criticism of oppressive culture, capitalism, and alienation of human beings. Kappen also explored Indian religious traditions in his attempts to construct a counter-culture in and for India.

The primal elements of Kappen's counter-culture could be found in his lectures at the seminar on "Dialogue with Third World Theologians" at Maryknoll Seminary, New York, in 1979. From the 1980s, he occasionally wrote on counter-culture. The first article of this kind was "The Present Cultural Crisis," which was published in *Socialist Perspectives* in 1980. *Jesus and Cultural Revolution: An Asian Perspective* (1983), in which he dealt with Buddhism and the Bhakti movement, also provided an elaborate account of the counter-culture he proposed. It was neither a negation of tradition nor an embracing of modernity; rather, it was a stage where the humanizing elements both in tradition and in modernity converged. It then took ten years before Kappen produced a second major contribution to counter-culture. In the last year of his life, he wrote *Tradition, Modernity, and Counter-culture*, which was published in 1994, a year after his death. Yet, despite this occasional character, counter-culture was one of Kappen's central ideas.[68]

Counter-culture could also be understood as a new social structure that valued human dignity irrespective of class, caste, color, creed, economic status, etc. and that fostered universal love, ethical religiosity, and humanizing culture. In Kappen's view, counter-culture was a transformation from what was to what has to be: from cosmic to ethical religiosity, from legalistic morality to universal morality, from individual to communitarian dimension, from class to communion, from self-serving to community service, from fear to freedom, and from violence to concern. This included the religious, economic, and social dimensions of human life. Therefore, Kappen's proposal of counter-culture could be considered the climax of the evolutions in his life, in the sense that there was an essential blend of all the liberating ideologies he had come across in the teachings of Marx, Jesus, and Buddha. At the same time, just as with the previous stages of his thoughts, counter-culture could not be set apart as the last chronologically: as noted out above, Kappen had already started working on a counter-culture by the late 1970s.

The discussion of the concepts of culture and counter-culture leads to the question of the nature of the counter-culture Kappen envisioned. Kappen shared his thoughts about his country's cultural crisis during his time. Some of the symptoms of this crisis, as Kappen pointed out in 1980, were the atrocities against the Dalits, communal violence, corrupt bureaucracy and politicians, subservience of the intellectual elite to the ruling class, emerging religious fundamentalism, and the increasing capitalist culture of profiteering.[69] Interestingly, Kappen did not make any serious reference to the social, political, and communal issues of the 1970s and the 1980s, such as the state of Emergency declared by Indira Gandhi (1975), the Mandal Commission for identifying and defining the socially and economically unprivileged (1979), the Khalistan movement of the Sikh separationists (especially from the 1970 to the mid-1980s), etc. Only rarely did he mention practical issues in his country. In 1992, for instance, he wrote about the self-immolation of some high caste boys and girls in north India in protest against the Mandal Commission Report of 1990, which reserved twenty-seven per cent of the government jobs for the backward classes. Kappen was also concerned about the increase in Hindu-Muslim communal violence, and the issues related to the Ayodhya temple.[70]

Before going into the details of his counter-culture, Kappen exposed the caste-dominated culture in which the Dalits suffered discrimination. Through this, he underscored the inevitability of a counter-culture. Although India has marked tremendous advancements in the spheres of science and technology, its social theories and praxis still bear feudal and inhuman elements.[71] In Kappen's view, the upper castes had always enjoyed a high position because they are more educated and thus grabbed the top jobs. Dalits in many parts of India did not have adequate political representation. The elected upper caste representatives often promoted casteism, nepotism, and communalism.[72] He observed this in his article "Tradition and Modernity," which he published in *Negations* in 1985. An enlarged and revised version of this article appeared in his *Tradition, Modernity, and Counter-culture* in 1994. By then, several political parties by and for Dalits had emerged. For instance, the Bahujan Samaj Party (BSP), an Uttar Pradesh based political party, was formed in 1984 and became the third largest national political party in India. BSP represented the Dalits, Scheduled Castes, Scheduled Tribes, and Other Backward Castes. Interestingly, it adapted much from the ideologies of social and religious reformers, such as B.R. Ambedkar and Sri Narayana Guru. Some other less influential political parties are the Republican Party of India (1957, mainly in Uttar Pradesh, Bihar, Haryana, etc.), Viduthalai Chiruthaigal Katchi (1957, Tamil Nadu), Puthiya Tamilakam (1996, Tamil Nadu), etc. Despite these glimpses of change, in effect, the concept that all are equal in a democratic system was disregarded. What actually prevailed, as Ambedkar said, was 'graded inequality,' and as a result the development always remained uneven.[73]

Kappen's major source of inspiration was the trinity of Marx, Jesus, and Buddha (including elements from Hinduism and Bhakti movement). They can be called the three pillars of counter-culture. The search for a counter-culture and the reasons for this search are implicitly inherent in Kappen's analysis of Marxist ideologies, of the original messages of Jesus, and of the Indian religious tradition, which were discussed in the three previous chapters. Kappen did not go to a systematic analysis of the origin and growth of these sources, but inquired the liberating elements in them capable of supporting his counter-culture. He received inspiration from these pillars essentially for three goals: to assert the dignity and basic rights of human beings, to condemn any form of discrimination based on religion and caste, and to refute religious fundamentalism.

Being a Catholic priest and theologian, Kappen imbibed particularly from Jesus' criticism of hierarchical religions. Cult, law, apocalypticism, and the priestly aristocracy were the main traits of religion at the time of Jesus, which together overtook religion's prophetic character. Jesus came forward as a prophet repudiating such rigid religiosity and held high the dignity of man and his role in creating his own future. Instead of an apocalyptic expectation of the Kingdom of God at the end of the world, Jesus instructed the mass to convert this world into the Kingdom of God. Kappen introduced this prophetic Jesus to India by making him the central figure in and for the counter-culture. For Kappen, the historical Jesus was the embodiment of counter-culture, and Christianity in India could help in creating a socialist, egalitarian, and humanist society.[74] Kappen was certain about its potential since he considered early Christianity a true counter-cultural movement. In this way, Kappen called for an overthrow of cultism, Brahminic hegemony, and caste discrimination in Hinduism by inserting Jesus' prophetic protest into the Indian religious tradition. This, he believed, would strengthen the struggle for liberation already initiated by Buddhism, the Bhakti movement, Indian Christianity,[75] and Communism.

Concerning the features of the counter-culture, Kappen first of all rejected any form of fundamentalism in his reformed society. He particularly targeted the increasing religious fundamentalist trends in India. If Buddha proposed universal ethics and humanism against caste discrimination and exploitation, Kappen reiterated Buddha's ideologies in a conflict situation among different religious groups, especially of radical Hindus against Muslims and Christians. In a counter-cultural society, Kappen intended to highlight the significance of a human person's physical and material development rather than overemphasizing religious issues. People should no longer be subjugated to the domination of religions. In a society of poor, oppressed, and exploited people, beyond the liberation of the soul from the body, there should be a culture of integral liberation.[76] In other words, Kappen strived towards a culture that respected the freedom of people to fashion their own future without being influenced by religion. The central theme of his counter-culture was the dignity of human beings. According to Kappen, in the transformed society, a human person had to be nonequivalent instead of being equivalent like in the existing culture. He found it meaningless to divide humanity on the basis of ritual purity and impurity of the body.[77]

Secondly, Kappen gave a central place to inclusiveness. In his counter-culture society, secular religiosity should lead to an ethics of inclusiveness and an egalitarian culture.[78] However, there was a discord between the structure and the culture. Modern India had a Western social structure. Its economic (factories, farms, banks, markets), political (legislature, bureaucracy), and cultural (media, education) structures were basically foreign. Still, the conflicts between castes, communities, and linguistic groups increased. Kappen brought this paradox to light because the deep-rooted culture was predominantly non-egalitarian and caste based. The fundamental problem in this culture was the hierarchical distribution of rights and privileges. Thus, in the counter-culture which Kappen envisioned, the values of the dominant class should not be legitimated as universal values applicable to the low castes and the outcastes. In other words, Kappen's counter-culture should be understood neither as universalizing the values of the dominant class nor as reducing all values to that of the dominant class. Both the dominant and the subservient classes of people should surpass the caste morality and be moved to a universal morality.[79] Moreover, his counter-culture advocated a balanced vision, which promoted the autonomy of the secular disciplines like science, economy, politics, etc. along with religious ideologies.[80]

Thirdly, the counter-culture objected capitalism, which according to Kappen was a means of exploitation. In the new society that he envisioned, Kappen, like Marx, repudiated everything that promoted private property. In order to avoid economic categorization in society, he even proposed the abolition of private property. Yet, the new society should not completely legitimize Communism as the latter concentrated predominantly on economic aspects of life. A transformed society consisted not only of economic aspects, but also of social, cultural, and religious ones.

Regarding the 'how' of counter-culture, Kappen observed that in a vast society like India, a revolution of consciousness was the most effective strategy. This revolution should take place through conscientization. Although there are several means of conscientization, Kappen preferred two: literature and personal encounter with different groups of people like college students, intellectuals, etc. Kappen himself wrote more than a few books and edited journals, all aimed to a radical social change. Through his writings and personal encounters, he imparted the idea of a transformed society, which would not be provided but instead had to be constructed. Kappen himself took up the role of a prophet, criticizing the oppressive system, and conscientizing the oppressed, especially through his writings and way of life. He thought that a revolutionary had neither personal interest nor personal feelings and only aimed at the transformation of society. Therefore, he should break the conventions, customs, and morality of the established system.[81] In such initiatives, Kappen found elements of revolution of consciousness, which according to him is the basis in constructing counter-culture. Kappen put this into practice upon leaving the Jesuit institutions to live in the slum areas among the poor.

The revolution of consciousness should lead to protest, which in turn needed to be converted into action for radical restructuring of the society. Dissenting writers, poets, and activists, Kappen pointed out, should be the agents of this transformation.[82] According to him, in pluralist India, the Christians, Hindus, Muslims, Buddhists, Marxists, and such other communities and organizations had to join hands to form a wider community. Kappen called this the 'Basileic Community,' a community that strives to create an equitable society. This reflected the Kingdom of God: the Greek term βασιλεία (*Basileia*) means sovereignty, especially of God, in this world and in the hearts of people. The Latin American Basic Ecclesial Communities, which were discussed in Chapter II, influenced Kappen in imagining the Basileic Communities in India. Importantly, advocating the cooperation of different castes, cultures, and religions, Kappen emphasized that they all would enjoy the freedom to safeguard their specific identities.[83] Towards this end, he even repudiated religious conversion by claiming that it leads to conflicts and religious fundamentalism.

From Kappen's opinions it is clear that conscientization and the eventual revolution of consciousness were two deliberate processes. He strongly believed that culture was not static but constantly changing.[84] This happened in two ways: as a natural evolution or as deliberate and rapid transformation of society by one or more human agents. Kappen opted for the second way and called for a cultural revolution. This revolution should not only disown the materialist and consumerist culture but also, as he pointed out in 1980, construct a socialist society in which "people themselves will control the economic, political, and cultural process."[85] It is interesting that already in 1969, Kappen acknowledged the deliberate transformative initiatives in the Kerala society. Education, elections based on universal suffrage, and the political consciousness promoted by the leftist parties and activist groups had brought changes in the state. Kappen wanted to accelerate this.[86]

In spite of all this, however, Kappen's counter-culture was not an effortless task, especially in a context where the ruling class, the high castes, and the economically rich minority were strongly related. First of all, it had to overcome the challenge of two types of domestication – religious and secular. In the religious terrain, the high castes possessed the monopoly over the sacred scriptures, which legitimized religious hegemony. Moreover, they even appropriated the reformative movements and ideologies of the low castes, and institutionalized them in such a way that they did not pose a threat anymore. For instance, they represented social and religious reformers, such as B.R. Ambedkar, Sri Narayana Guru, and Ayyan Kali as Hindu ideologues. In this way, they brought all these underprivileged sections of society under the banner of Hinduism. Yet the fact remained that the status of the underprivileged never improved. In addition to this, domestication also happened in the secular field, particularly with the ruling class. The economic dependence of the lower castes upon the higher castes impeded the former's struggle for a counter-culture.[87] The ruling class had neutralized the revolts of the economically and socially oppressed classes by constructing political alliances with them or giving them certain nominal privileges. Nevertheless, this was only a buying of these revolting groups by the dominant class for its benefit. Even today domestication takes place in Indian society. The best example could be the alliance of the political parties that represent the Dalits and other minorities with the dominant state or national parties. In such alliances, these minor parties are not well represented, and their voice remains unheard. The catch, of course, is that staying away from such alliances keeps them off of the political map entirely.

A second challenge, next to domestication, was the ruling class's censoring of everything that is against them: screening the personnel who administer the educational institutions, text books, media, etc. Kappen gave a clear hint of this already in 1973 in his article "The Future of Christian Education and Christian Education of the Future."[88] In 1993, he indirectly repeated it in his article, namely "Hindutva: Emergent Fascism?"[89] In this way, they controlled all cultural dissemination. Censorship was not limited to the secular sectors, but also prevalent in the religious spheres. In a religion, the hierarchy represented orthodoxy, and everything that went against the hierarchy was considered to be against orthodoxy. Therefore, minority groups or individual persons could never serve as a corrective force in an established religion because they could easily be silenced. The Church's censorship of Kappen must be seen from this perspective. He thought that the true challenge of counter-culture was and is to overcome the hegemony of the ruling class and the dominant religion.

Yet another challenge of counter-culture was to transcend the past by not giving it more value than due. The beliefs that human beings were born with the evil of *karma* in the past life, or that everything in this universe is an illusion (*maya*) weakened the role of people in constructing their own future by overturning what oppressed them. If they took everything as fate, they excluded all forms of creativity.

As a result, they were seen as people incapable of free and responsible action. For Kappen, "the Indian attitude to history had always been one of indifference and not of commitment."[90] The new transformed society had to move forward from the past into a communitarian understanding of liberation. Kappen quoted A.B. Shah, the founder-president of the Indian Secularist Society (ISS): "the traditional Hindu mind is incapable of feeling a civic responsibility, wider secular loyalties, for any length of time, beyond its own kinship group."[91]

Finally, the first feature of Kappen's counter-culture – a culture without religious fundamentalism – is at the same time a challenge. By saying this he was referring to Hindu fundamentalism in India.[92] The underlying reasons for this increasing Hindu fundamentalism seemed to be the foreign character of Christianity and Islam, their aggressive proselytism, their alleged extra-territorial loyalty, and their accumulation of socio-economic power throughtheir institutions.[93] In contrast to this, Kappen's counter-culture looked forward to an ethical religiosity where the human person was the subject. India should not be a breeding ground of communalism, and for that, the ruling and the ruled had to recognize the dignity of human beings. Kappen blamed Hindu radicals for the selective approach to tradition, which in turn ignored the supreme duty (*paramo-dharma*) of non-violence, the teachings of the *Bhagavad Gita* and Buddha, friendliness (*maitri*), and compassion (*karuna*).[94] Instead of promoting such values, they highlighted the sacrificial ritualism, the priestly class that administered the sacrifices, magical religiosity, caste based discrimination, etc. as found in the scriptures like *Bhagavad Gita*, *Rig Veda*, *Yajur Veda*, and *Manusmriti* (*The Laws of Manu*). In such a context, according to Kappen, religion becomes an "instrument of domination and exploitation."[95]

Kappen's liberation theology could be seen as a gateway to his counter-culture. The central features of Kappen's liberation theology can be reduced to two: its praxis-orientation, which is shared by liberation theology in Latin America and in Asia, and its openness to and assimilation from pluralism, which is mainly of Asian liberation theology. Praxis, for Kappen, is a response to the divine challenge to create a new society by showing fidelity to the liberating message of Jesus. Yet, in his writings, he conveyed that only when Jesus is liberated first could the meaning of Jesus' message be fully comprehended. However, Kappen strived to challenge the Church in India to radicalize faith and transform this faith into praxis. By this radicalization, he did not intend the negation of the past; rather he proposed a blend of the liberating elements in the past and the present in constructing a counter-culture.

In conclusion, our analysis of Kappen's liberation theology illustrated that he was a liberation theologian in a unique way. The sources of inspiration for liberation theologians include one or more of the following: the liberating message of Jesus in the gospels, praxis-oriented interpretation of the gospels, and the liberating elements in Marxism and Indian religious tradition. However, unlike other liberation theologians, Kappen integrated all of these sources in creating an Asian theology of liberation with an Indian mark. Most importantly, his ultimate goal went beyond mere formation of a liberation theology. For him, liberation theology was not an end but a means that should support the construction of a counter-culture. Therefore, Kappen was not only a liberation theologian but also a champion of counter-culture. He argued that in a pluralist society like that of India, a cultural revolution was the most important means to finally transcending all forms of oppression and discrimination. Having been convinced of this, he used the major sources of his inspiration – Marx, Jesus, and Buddha (and other Indian religious traditions) – as pillars of his counter-culture. Even though the construction of a counter-culture against the dehumanizing and alienating elements in society is implied in the agenda of liberation theologians in general, Kappen particularly focused on it and developed it into a relevant concept. Although, Kappen referred to few Latin American liberation theologians and Western theologians while creating his liberation theology, especially in the 1970s (*From Faith to Revolution* [1972] and *Jesus and Freedom* [1977]), he did not seem to have made such reference to any works or scholars when he started his mission of counter-culture for India. It forces us to conclude that counter-culture, which was the last stage in his ideological transitions, was an original contribution from him.

Endnotes

[1] Interview with Civic Chandran, Calicut, 23 September 2014.

[2] Interviews with Georges De Schrijver SJ (13 November 2014) and Aurel Brys SJ.

[3] Houtart, "Introduction,"14-5.

[4] Kappen, "A Manifesto of Freedom," 18.

[5] Kappen, *Jesus and Freedom*, 37-9 and 164-5, and Kappen, "Towards a Strategy of Socialist Reconstruction," 34-5.

[6] Kappen, *Liberation Theology and Marxism*, 11.

[7] Kappen, *Liberation Theology and Marxism*, 11.

[8] Kappen, *Divine Challenge and Human Response*, 89.

[9] Kappen, *Jesus and Cultural Revolution*, 65.

[10] Kappen, *From Faith to Revolution* (Malayalam), 21.

[11] Kappen, "The Future of Socialism and Socialism of the Future," 40-1.

[12] Boffs, *Introducing Liberation Theology*, 80.

[13] Kappen again presented this paper in Pune in 1978 and published it in 1981. Kappen, "A New Approach to Theological Education," 57-69. In my interview with Kappen's niece Mercy Kappen in Bangalore on 19 September 2014, I learned more about the intimacy between the teacher in Kappen and what is taught.

[14] Cf. Kappen, *Liberation Theology and Marxism*, 90-1.

[15] Kappen, *Jesus and Culture*, 119.

[16] CDF, *Instruction on Certain Aspects of the Theology of Liberation*, V. 9-10.

[17] Kappen, *Liberation Theology and Marxism*, 78. Also cf. CDF, *Instruction on Certain Aspects of the Theology of Liberation*, VII. 9 and VII. 6.

[18] Illickamury, "Roman Document on the Theology of Liberation," 447-8.

[19] McGovern, *Liberation Theology and Its Critics*, 140.

[20] Kappen, *Liberation Theology and Marxism*, 79.

[21] CDF, *Instruction on Certain Aspects of the Theology of Liberation*, VII. 9.

[22] Kasper, *Der Gott Jesu Christi*, 5. For a detailed description about International Theological Commission's analysis on *Instruction on Certain Aspects of the Theology of Liberation*, cf. Gibellini, *The Liberation Theology Debate*, 44.

23 Kappen, *Liberation Theology and Marxism*, 93.

24 For more details on the interpretations of *the poor* and *the poor in spirit*, cf. Luz, "Matthew 1-7: A Commentary," 190-3; Bovon, "A Commentary on the Gospel of Luke 1:1-9:50," 224-5; and Fleddermann, *Q: A Reconstruction and Commentary*, eds. B. Doyle et al., 276-7.

25 Kappen, *Liberation Theology and Marxism*, 95-6.

26 Kappen, *Liberation Theology and Marxism*, 97-8.

27 Kappen, *Liberation Theology and Marxism*, 98.

28 CDF, *Instruction on Christian Freedom and Liberation*, nos. 20, 57, 62, and 68.

29 CDF, *Instruction on Christian Freedom and Liberation*, no. 96.

30 Kappen, *Liberation Theology and Marxism*, 101.

31 Kappen, *Liberation Theology and Marxism*, 102.

32 McGovern, *Liberation Theology and Its Critics*, 17; *Instruction on Christian Freedom and Liberation*, no. 68.

33 Kappen, *Liberation Theology and Marxism*, 77-8.

34 The statement paper presented at the ninth annual meeting of the Indian Theological Association. Kappen, "Towards an Indian Theology of Liberation," 301. It is well established by Ajith Abraham in his study on Kappen. Cf. Abraham, "Alternative Narratives in Contemporary Globalization," 129-30.

35 Kappen, "The Asian Search for a Liberative Theology," 101.

36 Kappen, *Liberation Theology and Marxism*, 12.

37 Kappen, "The Asian Search for a Liberative Theology," 108.

38 Kappen, *Liberation Theology and Marxism*, 44.

39 Kappen, "Orientations for an Asian Theology," 111-12.

40 Kappen, *Liberation Theology and Marxism*, 17.

41 Kappen, *Jesus and Culture*, 118.

42 Kappen, *Divine Challenge and Human Response*, 108.

43 Kappen, *Hindutva and Indian Religious Traditions*, 67-71.

44 Kappen, "The Asian Search for a Liberative Theology," 107.

45 Kappen, "Orientations for an Asian Theology," 23.

46 Kappen, *Tradition, Modernity, and Counter-culture*, 29.

47 Kappen, *Hindutva and Indian Religious Traditions*, 26.

48 Kappen, *Jesus and Cultural Revolution*, 38-41.

49 Kappen, *Jesus and Cultural Revolution*, 43.

[50] Kappen, *Jesus and Society*, 26-7.

[51] Ferm, *Profiles in Liberation: 36 Portraits of Third World Theologians*, 71-80.

[52] Kappen, *Tradition, Modernity, and Counter-culture*, 58.

[53] Kappen, "Towards an Indian Theology of Liberation," 307.

[54] Thomas, *Man and the Universe of Faiths*, 150.

[55] Kappen, "Historizing and Historiology as Prophecy," 245.

[56] Kappen, *Liberation Theology and Marxism*, 62-3.

[57] Kappen, *Liberation Theology and Marxism*, 62.

[58] Kappen, "The Marxian Concept of Man in the Indian Context," 125.

[59] Kantowsky, *Sarvodaya: The Other Development*, 2-3.

[60] Câmara, *Spiral of Violence*, 45-55. To know more about Gandhian non-violence, cf. Amalendu Guha, *Gandhi's Non-violence*; Zachariah, "Gandhi, Non-violence and Indian Independence," 30-5; Trivedi, "Revolutionary Non-violence: Gandhi in Postcolonial and Subaltern Discourse," 521-49; and R.E Klitgaard, "Gandhi's Non-violence as a Tactic," 143-53. For a critical understanding, cf. Vinit Haksar, "Violence in a Spirit of Love: Gandhi and the Limits of Non-violence," 303-24.

[61] Kappen, "The Marxian Concept of Man in the Indian Context," 129.

[62] Tylor, *Primitive Culture: Researches into the Development of Mythology, Philosophy, Religion, Art, and Custom*, 1.

[63] Lowie, *The History of Ethnological Theory*, 3.

[64] Kappen, "The Present Cultural Crisis: Analysis and Prognosis," 1.

[65] Kappen, "The Present Cultural Crisis: Analysis and Prognosis," 1-2.

[66] Brownell, *American Counter-culture of the 1960s*, 8-9; O'Sullivan, et al., *Key Concepts in Communication and Cultural Studies*, 66.

[67] Vendler, "Books: A Lifelong Poem including History," 81.

[68] See, for instance, Mathew and Muricken, *Religion, Ideology, and Counter-culture* (1987); Jayaseelan, *Towards a Counter-culture* (1999); and Painadath, ed., *Jesus and Culture: Selected Writings of Sebastian Kappen, S.J.* (2002).

[69] Kappen, "The Present Cultural Crisis: Analysis and Prognosis," 5.

[70] Kappen, *Hindutva and Indian Religious Traditions*, 49-51.

[71] Vikrant, "The Dharmic Mind vis-a-vis the New Society," 954.

[72] Kappen, *Tradition, Modernity, and Counter-culture*, 21.

[73] Jaffrelot, "The Politics of Caste Identities," 80, and *Dr. Ambedkar and Untouchability: Analyzing and Fighting Caste*, 35-8.

74 Kappen, *Jesus and Cultural Revolution*, 27.

75 Cf. NBCLC, *Conclusions of the Interdisciplinary Research Seminar on The Indian Church in the Struggle for a New Society*, 3.

76 Cf. Kappen, *Jesus and Freedom*, 44.

77 Kappen, *Tradition, Modernity, and Counter-culture*, 2-3.

78 Kappen, *Tradition, Modernity, and Counter-culture*, 55.

79 Kappen, *Jesus and Cultural Revolution*, 62.

80 Kappen, *Hindutva and Indian Religious Traditions*, 69.

81 Kappen, "Perspectives," 1.

82 Kappen, "Perspectives," 4-5.

83 Kappen, *Liberation Theology and Marxism*, 47 and 67.

84 Kappen, *Jesus and Cultural Revolution*, 9.

85 Kappen, "The Present Cultural Crisis: Analysis and Prognosis," 17.

86 Kappen, "Church and the Challenge of Social Revolution in Kerala," 64.

87 Kappen, *Tradition, Modernity, and Counter-culture*, 13.

88 Kappen, "Future of Christian Education and Christian Education of the Future," 59-60.

89 Kappen, "Hindutva: Emergent Fascism?" 60-3.

90 Kappen, "The Eucharist and the Quest of India for a New Vision of History," 58

91 Shah, *Tradition and Modernity in India*, 11.

92 Kappen, *Liberation Theology and Marxism*, 70.

93 Kappen, "The Asian Search for Liberation Theology," 107.

94 Kappen, *Hindutva and Indian Religious Traditions*, 53 and 61.

95 Kappen, *Jesus and Cultural Revolution*, 35-7.

Conclusion

"My preoccupation with cultural problems goes back to the early Seventies when activist groups were mushrooming up all over the country with the avowed aim of promoting human development and liberation. These groups generally shared the conviction that any meaningful action must be based on an adequate understanding of the cultural forces at work in society."[1]

These are the words of Sebastian Kappen, who sought a collective upsurge of the oppressed feeling of the poor and the marginalized. He considered this rise from the lower stratum of society a cultural revolution that negated all dehumanizing aspects of humanity. Historically, there has always been a tension between the culture of the oppressors and the culture of the oppressed, where the oppressed became dependent on the oppressor. In India "economic dependence on the upper castes [classes] impeded the lower castes [classes] and the outcastes from producing a counter-culture."[2] This dissertation has been a detailed discussion of Kappen's liberating social order, which he called counter-culture. He strived to actualize it by integrating both Eastern and Western religious and philosophical ideologies.

This dissertation's conclusion consists of three sections. The first part recapitulates Kappen's biography, focusing on the five important transitions in his life. In the second section, we make a final assessment of his oeuvre, with special attention to his sources of inspiration and major innovations. Finally, we analyze the legacy of Kappen by assessing his reception and impact on later thinkers and works.

A life of transitions

With his thoughts constantly evolving, Kappen went through a number of key transitions. As elaborated in Chapter III, at the age of twenty, Kappen joined the Society of Jesus. In 1959 he was sent to Rome for higher studies, and there he turned to Marxism: a second transition that became more pronounced in the early 1970s. This was followed by another transition, which was of theological nature – from the Christ of faith he turned to the Jesus of history. Later he focused on Asian religions, such as Hinduism and Buddhism. Finally, this led him to advocating a counter-culture.

The first transition took place when Kappen joined the Latin religious order of the Society of Jesus. This was remarkable since he was born to a Syrian Catholic family, but it was not exceptional: many Syrian Catholic youngsters who aspired to religious life joined Latin Orders (cf. page 90). This inter-ritual flow (especially in one direction: from the Syro-Malabar to the Latin Rite) provided them with the opportunity to work outside the jurisdiction of the Syro-Malabar Church. Kappen began his priestly formation at Christ Hall in Calicut, Kerala (1944-49), and went to the Sacred Heart College of Shembaganur in Kodaikanal, Tamil Nadu, for his philosophical studies (1949-52). From 1952 to 1954 he taught in St. Joseph's Interdiocesan Seminary in Mangalore, Karnataka. He did his theological studies in the De Nobili College, the Jesuit formation house at Pune, Maharashtra (1954-57), and was ordained a priest in 1957 at the end of his formation at Pune. From 1957 to 1959 Kappen underwent his Tertianship, i.e. another two years of formation specifically for the Jesuits. During this time, he also learned Indian philosophy and religion. His acquaintance with some non-conformist priests from his own family context influenced him. The Spanish Jesuit Emilio Ugarte and the French Jesuit Joseph de Finance also inspired him. Several of Ugarte's thoughts, such as the sense of social justice and the combination of Eastern and Western traditions, motivated Kappen in the beginning of his career and these returned in his later life in a more sharpened version.

The second transition in Kappen's life began with his interest in Marxism and subsequent doctoral studies in Rome. During the Jesuit formation in India, Kappen grew into a disciplined person who managed to cope with Western philosophies. When he left for Rome, he was in total conformity with the traditional religious interpretations of the scriptures both of Christianity and Hinduism. However, his exploration of the original works of Marx and the latter's religious criticism affected him. Kappen began to critically analyze religion. By pointing out Marx's intellectual prejudice on religion and Christianity's exaggerated other-worldliness, Kappen simultaneously criticized both Marx and institutionally established Church. The present research has identified the following reasons for Kappen's interest in Marx: the conformity of the Church in Kerala with Rome's approach to Communism, the impact of the People's Republic of China on Indian Communism, the upsurge of Communism in India, and the Communist-Church encounter in Kerala. Marx's thoughts, especially regarding alienation, capitalism, and revolution, influenced Kappen in his later progressive thinking and writings.

To accept some of Marx's thoughts was a difficult shift, and it took years for Kappen to come to terms with this. After his return from Rome in 1961, Kappen kept a low profile. Only in the late 1960s did he resume his scholarly activities and begin publishing on Marxism. He openly dealt with Marxism in the first half of the 1970s, and his *From Faith to Revolution* (1972) is the most telling example. Kappen was clearly influenced by the events of the 1960s, such as the Second Vatican Council (1962-65), the emergence of Latin American liberation theology (late 1960s), and the counter-cultural movements (1960s-70s). Additionally, the Belgian Catholic priest and Marxist sociologist François Houtart influenced Kappen. Their relationship can even be considered Kappen's impetus to openly flirt with Marxism.

In the mid-1970s, the third shift took place in Kappen's thoughts. After struggling with Marxism for more than a decade, he now turned to interpreting Jesus Christ. It started with his criticism of the Church.

Kappen did not conform to the over-emphasized pietism in the Church, the cult of Christ, and the capitalist orientation of the institutional Church. He challenged the Church's fixation on dogmas and doctrines, questioned the historicity of Jesus' miracles, and indirectly challenged his godhood. He opposed the view that Jesus' death on the cross was a sacrifice in order to deliver humanity from sin. He saw Jesus as a prophet rather than as the son of God and emphasized his human character and teachings. All this is clearly illustrated by means of the gradual changes in Kappen's naming of the son of God. Until the early 1970s, he did not question this and liberally used the term Christ, subscribing to the divinity and godhood of Jesus. Afterwards he preferred to use Jesus Christ, which represented the divine and human Jesus. Starting from 1975, precisely with his article "Jesus Today," we find Kappen dropping Christ, using Jesus alone, and even challenging the concept of Christ in his writings. He even claimed that both Marx and Jesus shared the same message of human liberation. This radical and unorthodox interpretation of the Son of God led to a conflict with the Vatican. Kappen was not a solitary figure here. A number of other progressive theologians, such as Leonardo Boff (Brazil), Hugo Assmann (Brazil), Pedro Casaldaliga (Spain/Brazil), Tissa Balasuriya (Sri Lanka), Anthony de Mello (India), and Jon Sobrino (Spain/El Salvador) also faced similar crisis, due either to their Christological interpretation or Marxist orientation. It should not, however, be any wonder that a Christian theologian who was attracted to Marx eventually turned to the historical person of Jesus.

By the 1980s, Kappen started exploring the liberating elements in Indian culture, and this marked the fourth stage in his intellectual transition. As an Indian progressive thinker, he was inspired by the way his country's multi-religious context could harness the resources of religion and culture for social transformation. This task demanded deep insight into both what Buddhism, Hinduism, and related religious movements, especially the Bhakti (devotion) movement taught, and *how* these affected the social, economic, cultural, and political evolutions of society. Though highly appreciative of the transformative elements in Indian religious and cultural traditions, Kappen spared no attemtps in criticizing Indian traditions. He accused them of permitting the dominant classes to establish hegemony over the rest of the society down through the centuries.

There was still a fifth and final transition in Kappen's life that was the culmination of all his previous intellectual shifts. This took place when he proposed a counter-culture. In this counter-culture, Kappen brought in the three prophets of liberation he had earlier worked with, namely Marx, Jesus, and Buddha. He criticized the oppressive and exploitative capitalist system, and condemned the cultic, institutional, and alienating character of religion in light of the teachings of these 'prophets.' Above all, however, in constructing the counter-culture, Kappen inserted Jesus as a prophet into the Indian culture. This indicated Kappen's ultimate commitment to the liberating message of the historical Jesus and his own identity as a Jesuit, even after going through several stages of ideological transitions.

In his transitions, every stage was of high importance, i.e. Kappen did not leave behind the previous stage as he moved on to a new one. Therefore, his shift from one to the next did not neglect the past; rather, he integrated them all, which included both Western and Eastern (especially Indian) theological and philosophical traditions. The point of divergence between Kappen and other progressive theologians is in terms of objectives. While his contemporaries, such as M.M. Thomas and Samuel Rayan, strived to construct, strengthen, and expand the Church, Kappen aimed at creating a reformed secular society. One of the points of his divergence was the Church position that revelation is culminated and concluded in Jesus. For Kappen, revelation was an ongoing process. The self-disclosure of the Divine is taking place even after the time of Jesus. In a similar vein, Kappen also questioned the sole authority of the Church to interpret the once-and-already-given Word of God,[3] for this arguably strangled the prospect and prospectus contextual theology – the theology from below.

Kappen's strongest weapon was his pen. His books and articles always conveyed the message of an inevitable change in society. Additionally, in the 1970s, he started publishing the journals *Anawim*, *Negations*, and *Socialist Perspectives*, which introduced readers to his liberating and revolutionary messages. Through these journals, Kappen dialogued with progressive Christian thinkers and young socially committed activists. These dialogues led to further discussions in persons and groups, primarily about how Christians should respond to the problems of poverty and injustice in India. Kappen tried to form an intelligentsia through his writings, seminars, talks, and debates in friendly circles. His writings were sharply critical and straight to the point, and he therefore could be called a man of intellectual integrity. This is clear, for instance, from his reply to the CDF's instruction in 1982 asking him to obtain permission from superiors for all future publications. In his letter to the Superior General, Kappen replied: "I have propounded nothing dangerous to the true interests of God and his reign, which is all that matters as far as I am concerned. If it poses a danger to vested interests in the church and the Society of Jesus, I cannot help it, and I intend to tender no apology."[4] Kappen's response showed his strong stance as a theologian and progressive thinker.

Innovation and Inspiration

Kappen is most commonly known as a liberation theologian. However, this dissertation has clearly substantiated that he went beyond this label. First and foremost, his theology of liberation differed from that of Latin America. By being inclusive, Kappen took a more innovative approach in defining liberation theology. Unlike Latin American liberation theologians, in addition to the synoptic gospels and Marxist ideologies, Kappen made use of Indian religious traditions to make his theology of liberation suitable precisely for the Indian pluralist context. Although Latin American and African countries underwent problems, such as economic and political oppression, and cultural domination, Asia's challenges were exceptionally multifaceted – poverty, exploitation, class, culture, caste, creed, etc. Kappen addressed these issues in the process of theologizing for Asia. Therefore, the theology of liberation that Kappen imagined was different from non-Asian ones. Interestingly, his theology of liberation was a counter-culture, which uniquely was a humanizing culture anchored on religious, political, and economic ideologies. As a result, Kappen succeeded in converting a theological concept into a secular one. In effect, Kappen objected importation not only of Western theology but also of Latin American liberation theology. He challenged the Church of India to identify and highlight its Indianness.

Being part of the Church, Kappen resorted to liberation ideologies as they exposed the theoretical bent of traditional theology that for centuries overemphasized faith at the cost of action, and flagged off an epistemological rupture with it. Third World circumstances could not endlessly import the theology of the West and disregard the former's context that required more action than theory. Admittedly, the traditional understanding of theology was different from liberation theology for its doctrinal and dogmatic character. It was a theology from above, through the *magisterium* (teaching authority) of the Church, which did not adequately consider Third World contexts and life of people.

Inculturation was one of the significant means to an Indian theology of liberation that Kappen adapted. Even in the relatively less pluralist context of Latin America, bishops emphasized that local churches must be rooted in indigenous cultures. This was an attempt to liberate Latin American identity from Neo-Scholasticism and hierarchical dominance of the traditional Church. Asian liberation theologians also encouraged inculturation, though with varying stress and objectives. Considering the pluralist Indian context, Kappen instructed local churches to promote inculturation. However, he was not entirely innovative in this field and rather drew upon Jesuit charisma. Since the start of the Jesuit mission in India in 1542, Jesuits realized that in pluralist India they had to foster a positive inter-religious relationship and adapt every positive element from Indian religious and spiritual traditions. Much like everywhere else, Jesuits in Kerala enjoyed the freedom to find their own charisma and open their own areas of mission and activism. Kappen should be considered one of the most innovative and radical figures among the progressive Jesuits of his era.

However, as previously mentioned, through inculturation Kappen did not ultimately aim to strengthen and establish the Church in India. In contrast, Kappen rejected Christian triumphalism, exclusivism, and institutionalism and considered the Church to be one of the means that could function as liberating agents in society, such as Indian religious traditions, Marxism, etc. Kappen targeted institutional and hierarchical Christianity, which he criticized, especially from the late 1960s. In the Society of Jesus as well, Kappen stood out with his radical way of life. He stepped out of the Jesuit institutions and lived among the poor in society.

Therefore, one could easily question Kappen's Christian identity. Kappen stated that he did not want to be called a Christian, but a disciple of Jesus. Still, in general terms, a disciple of Jesus is a Christian, and in this way, one could argue that Kappen was always a true Christian. However, his Christological understanding differed from that of the mainstream Catholic theology. Although he was often bracketed with other Indian progressive Christian theologians, such as M.M. Thomas and Samuel Rayan, Kappen stood out with his understanding of Jesus. While Thomas and Rayan projected a liberating Christ, Kappen highlighted a liberating Jesus. In very general terms, Christ is the glorified Son who sits at the right hand of God the Father, Jesus Christ is both human and God, and Jesus is the historical person. Kappen advocated a return from Christ to Jesus in order to explore the original message of the teachings of Jesus. This would essentially require a sloughing off of the layers of interpretations of the messages of Jesus in the history of the Church over the last twenty centuries. As a Christian theologian, he proposed the liberation of theology and Jesus from the clutches of intellectualism and cultism respectively. A Church that liberated both theology and Jesus, according to Kappen, had a role to inspire other religious groups in India. Obviously Kappen did not reject the Church, but rather projected an ideal Church. He also called Indian liberation theologians to make a clear distinction between the Jesus of history and Christ of faith. For them, just as for other Asian or Latin American progressive theologians, the distinction between these terms was not a significant decider in their theologizing and activism. Their approach seemed to be primarily pastoral, in contrast to Kappen's secular and social perspectives.

Interestingly, the historical Jesus was not Kappen's only source of inspiration. Marx, as well, influenced Kappen considerably. Kappen condemned all forms of alienation, including religious, and criticized the capitalist orientation of the Church. His advocacy for a radical change in society even went to the extent of encouraging people to revolt, though not through violence but via attitudinal, cultural, and ecclesial revolutions. This would ultimately transform into social revolution. It was a radical, innovative, and pioneering move for an Indian Jesuit. Being part of a Church that criticized Communism for promoting revolution and violence, and considered it to be the most dangerous enemy, Kappen nevertheless assimilated Marxist ideologies in his theological and non-theological thinking. With these views, he was close to other liberation theologians, both in India and beyond. However, he did not enter into debate with these others and only briefly mentioned Camilo Torres' Marxist affinity and Romero's and Câmara's call for (non-violent) revolution.

Kappen acknowledged the role of Indian Communism in radicalizing the consciousness of the intelligentsia and the poor, especially in Kerala, West Bengal, and Andhra Pradesh. He could go deeper into Marx's views since he learned German and referred to the latter's original works while Indian Marxist intellectuals and authors predominantly depended on secondary sources. However, his approach to Marxism was not as its apostle but as a social thinker who assimilated from Marxist philosophy in the process of society building. No wonder, along with his appreciation for Marxism, Kappen also criticized it on account of its ideological deviations. All in all, he was pioneering in the growing *modus vivendi*, especially in Kerala, between the Church and Marxists. Whereas their relation had been characterized by great polarization in the 1950s, this led to more pragmatic collaboration in the following decades. The Church sometimes supported local Communist candidates in elections, and the conflicts between the Church and Communists in Kerala eventually decreased.

Buddha also played a significant role in shaping Kappen's thoughts. Most significantly, Buddha's prophetic life, teachings against sacrifices and rituals, anthropocentric approach, Eightfold Path, and his understanding of freedom and virtues were all sources of inspiration to Kappen. He found a true revolutionary in Buddha because of the questions the latter raised against the existing religious and social taboos. Particularly, Buddha denounced metaphysical questions and dealt with the alienated existence of human beings. Buddhism creatively criticized the Brahminic priestly hegemony, cultism, and caste based discrimination in the Hindu system. The universal humanism which Kappen came across in Buddhist tradition inspired him to strengthen his struggle for a classless society. In the Gandhi-Ambedkar ideological conflict, Kappen seems to have been closer to Ambedkar despite Kappen's occasional reference to Gandhi. Gandhi and Ambedkar denounced hegemonic practices and caste-based discrimination in Hinduism. However, their criticisms were contradictory. Gandhi questioned discrimination based on caste, but did not consider it a social evil that must be abolished. Conversely, Ambedkar strived to eradicate caste and eventually turned his back on Hinduism and embraced Buddhism. Kappen remained in the same religious tradition throughout his life. Even in the time of his conflict with the Vatican, he tried to strike a balance between his religious and secular life.[5] He wanted to remain a Jesuit priest, but not at the cost of his intellectual integrity.[6]

Kappen's adherence to the person and message of the historical Jesus, the humanizing values of Buddha, and the revolutionary ideologies of Marx inspired him to go against institutionalism, triumphalism, and priestly hegemony in religion. Being a Christian progressive thinker, he particularly and explicitly targeted the institutional nature of the Church and the Society of Jesus. While acknowledging the contributions of the Church in India to the fields of education, health care, and social work, Kappen argued that this institutional nature alienated the Church from the people. Although he was part of the Church in Kerala and a proponent of the concept of liberation, interestingly, he never referred to the Church-led Liberation Struggle against the Communist government in Kerala in 1959. Being a strong critic of the institutional nature of the Church, Kappen must have found Liberation Struggle only as a struggle for liberating the Church institutions from government control, not liberation of the poor and the marginalized. Thus, although the Church in Kerala used the term liberation already in 1959, much before the inception of liberation theology in Latin America, it had no connection to progressive theology.

At no stages in his intellectual transition did Kappen stop evolving. In contrast, his thoughts continued to progress until he peaked with his masterpiece, namely counter-culture. In this research, we have seen that Kappen condemned the dehumanizing acts of alienation, oppression, exploitation, and injustice under the aegis of state, religion, and tradition. For him, counter-culture was a new social structure that valued human dignity and liberated human beings from all forms of dehumanizing elements in society irrespective of class, caste, color, creed, and economic status. Such a culture, he believed, would foster universal love and humanizing values. Therefore, Kappen created an essential blend of all the liberating ideologies he came across in the teachings of his trinity: Marx, Jesus, and Buddha – the three pillars of his counter-culture.

Additionally, ethical religiosity must be considered one of the most essential characteristics of his counter-culture. In Kappen's view, the prevalent Cosmic and gnostic religiosities legitimated cultism, institutionalism, and hierarchy, and were no more relevant in the counter-culture he envisaged. Cosmic and gnostic religiosities were relevant only as long as man subjected himself to nature and society. Buddha's breakthroughs, namely his denouncement of the dominance of Cosmic and gnostic religiosities and his venture into an ethical religiosity inspired

Kappen. Universal love and compassion, with which Buddha had replaced magic and myth, prompted Kappen to propose ethical religiosity as an antidote to the growing religious fundamentalism and divisive trends in India. Unfortunately, the struggle to establish the space of Cosmic and gnostic religiosities accelerated the growth of fundamentalism in India. These religiosities were basically against ethical religiosity that went beyond the borders of casteism and structured religions.

Kappen spoke out strongly against religious fundamentalism in India. Most importantly, towards the end of his life, he was anguished about the transition of Hinduism into *Hindutva* (Hinduness), the latter which he even compared with German Nazism, not only for its time of emergence but also for its *modus operandi*. This must be seen in light of increasing communal conflicts and religious polarizations in India. He intensified his criticism after the Hindu nationalist Bharatiya Janata Party (BJP) increased its foothold in Indian politics and fueled *Hindutva* in the country. His most significant contribution on this topic was his posthumous *Hindutva and Indian Religious Traditions* (2000), which was a collection of the essays he had written during the last years of his life. Kappen's strong criticism of *Hindutva* shows that he stood for religious and cultural pluralism in India.

In sum, it is clear that Kappen was not only a liberation theologian, but went far beyond and can also be labelled a progressive thinker and champion of counter-culture. Importantly, liberation theology and counter-culture are two different areas, having religious and secular nature respectively. Although Kappen's counter-culture cannot be understood as liberation theology in its typical fashion, his return to the original message of the historical Jesus resembled liberation theology, which was also a retreat to the original messages of Jesus. Since the Latin American version of liberation theology cannot be applied to the Indian pluralist context, Kappen proposed an Indian theology of liberation, which is inclusive. In Kappen's view, in a pluralist society, Jesus cannot be considered the only liberating agent. Therefore, Kappen's counter-culture inserted the liberating message of Jesus into the Indian society along and in conversation with those offered by others. This was his version of theology of liberation for India.

Legacy: Reception and Impact

To conclude, one may wonder to what extent Kappen still has relevance and influence in the contemporary world. During his life he once in a while received international attention, especially because of *Jesus and Freedom*, his conflict with Vatican, and his continued criticism of the Church even after the disciplinary action of the Vatican. In the mid-1980s, international media like *The Globe and Mail* (1985), and *The Ottawa Citizen* (1986) reported his activism.[7] Apart from this, Kappen did not garner international headlines. He died in 1993, in an age when liberation theology had started to fade globally.

Many local and national media highlighted Kappen's life, very particularly when he died. They all recounted the contributions of Kappen as a progressive thinker, author, activist, and theologian.[8] Along with that, prominent personalities from the cultural and literary world, especially in Kerala, fondly recalled the person of Kappen. The famous Keralite writer O.V. Vijayan stated that he lost a friend in his ways of philosophical thinking. Vijayan marveled at Kappen's courage to learn Marx while being within the limits of the Church, even more so at a time when the Church vehemently condemned Marxism. Civic Chandran, another famous Keralite writer, had the same view. In his opinion, Kappen sustained a balance between his religious and Marxist views. However, Kappen was also subject to criticism. Vijayan expressed his discontentment towards liberation theologians including Kappen, not mentioning Kappen's name but indirectly mentioning his experience. Vijayan recalled how he consumed a biscuit instead of the usual bread in a Holy Mass-like prayer that Kappen conducted in the former's house. In Vijayan's view, using biscuit in such an occasion was an oversimplification of one of the fundamentals of Catholicism. The central point of criticism was that many liberation theologians first used Marxism to justify Christ, then referred to Christ to justify Marx, and eventually propagated Marx, but without the help of Christ.[9]

The regional attention of Kappen further expanded to a national level in the following years. Many social thinkers, activists, and progressive theologians referenced Kappen. M.M. Thomas remembered Kappen as a "friend, philosopher and guide to a lot of young people as well as social activists" and considered himself "a friend and intellectual companion" of Kappen.[10] Bangalore based C.F. John, who was greatly inspired by Kappen, pointed to the latter's articulate communication skills. John even stated that Kappen had succeeded in inspiring the secular society more than his contemporary theologians could.[11]

Sadanand Menon, a nationally reputed arts editor, acknowledged in 2000 that Kappen was a guru and source of inspiration. Menon says: "Kappen was the obvious teacher who could lead us through the maze of Kant, Hegel, Feuerbach, Marx, Heidegger, Husserl, Wittgenstein, Cassirer, Saussure and so on, in a stimulating series of 'Study Classes.'"[12] Additionally, Kappen's criticism of organized religion, cultural imperialism, and his call for a revolution of consciousness had significant impact on Menon. Furthermore, Babu Mathew, who became the All India Catholic University Federation (AICUF) national president in 1972 and then a left-wing trade union leader, social activist, and academic, acknowledged that Kappen's ability to bring together the ideologies of Jesus and Marx had an impact on him. He even admitted that he had joined the Communist movement due to the influence of Kappen.[13]

Within the Society of Jesus, however, Kappen has received more attention, specifically for his radical way of life and ideology. According to Samuel Rayan, Kappen developed a "relentless critical quest for truth."[14] In his two-page memoir of Kappen in 1993, Rayan considered several of the latter's works still relevant for Indian Jesuits, Christian theologians, social activists, and Keralite literary writers. This appreciation from the Society of Jesus continued in the following years. The Society considers him a radical and revolutionary theologian and does not corner him because of his conflicts with the Vatican or on account of his Church criticism. Although he stepped out of Jesuit institutions in the early 1970s and lived in rented houses until his death in Bangalore, the

Society brought him back to Kerala and buried him in the cemetery of the Jesuit Kerala Province in Calicut. During my interviews with Jesuits, such as Sebastian Painadath, Georges De Schrijver, and Aurel Brys, they all conveyed the idea that Kappen succeeded in bringing great dynamism to progressive theologizing in India and still could challenge contemporary intellectuals in this regard.

Interestingly, ever since and even twenty years after Kappen's death, new publications came out in his name. Jesuits like Samuel Rayan and Sebastian Painadath, and Kappen's relatives, namely Sebastian Vattamattam and Mercy Kappen, have all valued the contributions he made to progressive theology and secular society. They collected, edited, and published many of his articles, some of which had not appeared before. Within the first ten years after his death, five major works were published: one prepared by Kappen himself before his death (1994), two compiled by Sebastian Vattamattam (1999 and 2000) and two edited by Sebastian Painadath (both in 2002). In 2012 and 2013, the latter published three more works. There exists a Wikipedia page on Kappen, which was launched by Vattamattam in 2005 and seems to have been edited more than five hundred times to date. All in all, it is clear that the legacy of Kappen is kept alive by a number of scholars, writers, Jesuits, and relatives.

Alongside, some of the studies on Kappen and the regular Kappen memorial lectures which have been organized by Visthar since 1994 (as mentioned in the Introduction as sources of this research), cherish his legacy. Even though Kappen is not explicitly discussed in many of the memorial lectures, it is still important that these events are taking place in his name and memory. They were all on themes that interested Kappen, such as development, culture, counter-culture, secularization of Indian society, democracy, and nationalism. Prominent intellectuals and activists from religious and secular sectors, such as economist and one of India's best-selling authors around the globe Ramachandra Guha, writer and critic U.R. Ananthamurthy, historian M.G.S. Narayan, theologian M.M. Thomas, and many others have been involved in this venture.

Kappen's initiatives, namely Center for Social Reconstruction and the journals – *Anawim*, *Negations*, and *Socialist Perspectives* – eventually died out. However, his commitment to Christian activism lived on. He wanted to live and mingle among the ordinary people in society. At the same time, he kept his academic profile high by engaging in dialogue with elites like university professors and other intellectuals. He collaborated also with student organizations, such as All Indian Catholic University Federation (AICUF) and the Student Christian Movement of India (SCMI).

In addition to this, his influence is explicit in the formation of the Bangalore-based non-profit secular organization called Visthar in 1989 to address the issues of poverty, gender discrimination, and social exclusion. It collaborates with civil society organizations, faith based organizations, and social movements.[15] Kappen strived to convert the proponents of Visthar, which included academics and activists from various faiths and denominations, into an influential intellectual generation, and inspire it to fight the dehumanizing capitalist culture. He hoped to construct a new social order in which the human person was the subject. According to David Selvaraj, the founder and executive director of Visthar, the organization tries to take up the prophetic role of Jesus in society. Selvaraj, remembering and acknowledging Kappen's contributions, pointed out that one cannot be a true theologian unless and until one is rooted in social science. A theologian is one who also interprets the social realities from the standpoint of Jesus the prophet.[16] Visthar can be seen as an instantiation of Kappen's plurivocal and inclusive perceptions.

Despite all these, one can claim that Kappen has been partially forgotten in history. His ideas were not irrelevant, but neither the Church nor the secular world adequately explored or further expanded on them. For the mainstream Church, he was like a radical and rebel priest and a secular thinker. His strong appeal for native theology based on a preferential option for the poor was not positively acknowledged. At the same time, secular society considered him a Christian theologian and failed to sufficiently exploit his trans-religious and counter-cultural thoughts. The Communists in Kerala also did not propagate his thoughts, possibly because he severely criticized them for deviating from the original ideologies of Marx and for degenerating to a mere political party that compromised towards capitalism.

Kappen had a very important role to play in Indian society. He not only encouraged dialogues between religions but also opened the door of cooperation and ideological exchange between religious and political groups. He did not stand for any particular faith or ideology, but championed a transformed society that does not count such differences. Again, Kappen deserves attention in the context of increasing religious fundamentalism in India (and elsewhere). He foresaw the dangers of communal polarization and interreligious tension, and thus challenged religions to be harmonizing agents that consider human beings subjects, not objects. In contemporary India, the Church lacks progressive theologians as radical and revolutionary as Kappen who can facilitate dialogue and cooperation between different ideologies. Kappen contributed to the avoidance of mutual exclusion between political ideologies and religious groups, especially between Communism and the Church, through his publications and speeches, in which he called on all sides for dialogue and collaboration. This helped religious and political factions adapt practical measures for creating a better society. At the same time, Church's relatively mild approach to the Communists in India cannot be interpreted as its approval of Communist ideologies. Kappen called on both the Church and Communists to dissociate themselves from capitalist orientation and institutionalization.

Is Kappen then still relevant as a progressive theologian? Liberation theology in India did not fully succeed in accomplishing its goal of integral liberation of human persons. With the weakening of Latin American liberation theology, many liberation theologians in India also withdrew their radical stance and preference for the poor and no longer put themselves under the banner of such a theology. In other words, theology from above regained its prominence over theology from below. However, as long as there are goals to be accomplished towards actualizing his counter-cultural society, one may argue that Kappen's radical theology still has scope in the Church and society of contemporary India. His ideologies have the potential to fight all forms of alienation, and it remains to the Church and society at large to mine out resources for a progressive course.

Endnotes

[1] Kappen, *Tradition, Modernity, and Counter-culture*, viii.

[2] Kappen, *Tradition, Modernity, and Counter-culture*, 13.

[3] Kappen, *Divine Challenge and Human Response*, 8.

[4] Kappen's letter to Arrupe, 15 May 1981, KPA, 9.

[5] Interview with C.F. John.

[6] Kappen's letter to Dezza, 6 September 1992, KPA, 3.

[7] Observer News Service Delhi, "Priests, nuns defy episcopal orders: Liberation theology splits church in India," *The Globe and Mail*, 20 April 1985. The Associated Press (AP), "Social activism among RC clergy in India causing strife in church," *The Ottawa Citizen*, 1 February 1986. *The Globe and Mail* and *The Ottawa Citizen* are two Canadian newspapers.

[8] Leading dailies and weeklies in Malayalam like *Malayala Manorama, Mathrubhoomi, Deepika*, the CPI[M]-organ *Deshabhimani*, etc. reported Kappen's death. *Times of India*, a leading English-language Indian daily on 2 September 2007, in its article, namely "The Cross and Communist," presented Kappen as one of the champions of progressive thinking in the Church in India.

[9] Vijayan, "Thoughts of an Outsider about Liberation Theology," *Malayala Manorama*, 22 May [year unclear].

[10] Thomas, "Towards and Alternative Paradigm," 13.

[11] Interview with C.F. John.

[12] Menon, "Kappen: The Advocate of Radical Consciousness," 169-71.

[13] Mathew, "Kappen the Inspirer," 174-5.

[14] Rayan, "Remembering Father Sebastian Kappen," 1.

[15] Cf. "Visthar: a Non-formal Academy of Justice and Peace," http://www.visthar. org/ [accessed 13 October 2014]. The term visthar means 'stretching out,' or 'going beyond.' Cited from *The Hindu*, 13 March 2013. http://www.thehindu.com/news/ cities/bangalore/theyre-still-stretching-boundaries/article4504113.ece [accessed 13 October 2014].

[16] Interview with Selvaraj.

Bibliography

Archival sources

Archive of the Jesuit house Sameeksha, Ernakulam, Kerala (Kappen's images).

Archive of the Gregorian University, Rome (The original copy of Kappen's doctoral dissertation: "Praxis and the Emancipation of Man from Religious Alienation according to the Economic and Philosophical Manuscripts of Karl Marx").

Archive of the Jesuit Kerala Provincial House, Calicut, Kerala (Correspondence between Kappen, his superiors, and Papal delegate, unpublished write ups, hospital documents about his death, and his images).

Archive of *Deepika*, Malayalam daily, Kottayam, Kerala (Rare issues on Kerala politics in the 1960s and 1970s).

Archive of the archdiocese of Ernakulam-Angamaly, Kerala (Rare issues of the diocesan bulletin *Ernakulam Missam* about the Kerala Church's response to Communist ideologies and government policies, and pastoral letters).

Archive of the archdiocese of Changanacherry, Kerala (Rare issues of the diocesan bulletin *Madhyasthan* about the Kerala Church's response to Communist ideologies and government policies, and pastoral letters).

Archive of *Sathyadeepam*, Catholic weekly newspaper, Ernakulam, Kerala (Rare issues about the Liberation Struggle in Kerala).

KADOC, Leuven (Catalogus Viceprovinciae Independentis Keralensis Societatis Jesu. Xavier Press, Calicut).

Oral sources (in chronological order)

Thelakkatt Paul. Interview by author. Ernakulam, 15 January 2012.

Adappur, Abraham. Interview by author. Ernakulam, 16 January 2012.

Powathil, Mar Joseph. Interview by author. Changanacherry, 20 January 2012.

Devi, Parvathi. Interview by author. Trivandrum, 22 January 2012.

Achuthan, M.P. Interview by author. Trivandrum, 23 January 2012.

Issac, Thomas. Interview by author. Trivandrum, 2 February 2012.

Eugine, Sajan. Interview by author. Trivandrum, 3 February 2012.

Houtart, François. Telephone interview by Idesbald Goddeeris. Leuven, 22 April 2014.

Painadath, Sebastian. Interview by author. Ernakulam, 15 September 2014.

Selvaraj, David. Interview by author. Bangalore, 19 September 2014.

John, C.F. Interview by author. Bangalore, 19 September 2014.

Kappen, Mercy. Interview by author. Bangalore, 19 September 2014.

Vattamattam, Sebastian. Interview by author. Kottayam, 22 September 2014.

De Schrijver, Georges. Interview by author. Leuven, 13 November 2014.

Brys, Aurel. Interview by author. Heverlee, 12 November 2016.

Publications by Sebastian Kappen (in chronological order)

"Praxis and the Emancipation of Man from Religious Alienation according to the Economic and Philosophical Manuscripts of Karl Marx." PhD diss., Rome: Pontifical University of Gregoriana, 1961.

"The Eucharist and the Quest of India for a New Vision of History." In *India and the Eucharist*, edited by Bede Griffiths, 51-60. Ernakulam: Lumen Institute, 1964.

"Christian Participation in Social Work." *Review for Religious* 28, no. 4 (1969): 586-94.

"The Role of the Church in National Development." *The Clergy Monthly* 33, no. 2 (1969): 59-75.

"Church and the Challenge of Social Revolution in Kerala." *Vaidikamitram* 3, no. 1 (1969): 25-44.

"Christianity as Liberation." *Rally* 47 (December 1970): 12-3.

"The Christian and the Call to Revolution." *Jeevadhara* 1, no. 1 (1971): 29-45.

"Christianity and India's Development." *Jeevadhara* 2, no. 7 (1972): 47-62.

From Faith to Revolution (Malayalam). Kottayam: National Book Stall, 1972.

"The Future of Christian Education and Christian Education of the Future." *Jeevadhara* 3, no. 13 (1973): 57-65.

"The Goals of Revolution." *Religion and Society* 20, no. 1 (1973): 51-61.

"The Jesus Fellowship." *Jeevadhara* 4, no. 21 (May-June 1974): 190-8.

"Jesus Today." *Jeevadhara* 13, no. 73 (1975): 169-81.

"Values in Crisis: A Socio-Philosophical Analysis of the Indian Situation." *Jeevadhara* 5, no. 25 (January-February 1975): 11-23.

"The Man Jesus: Rapture and Communion." *Religion and Society* 23, no. 3 (1976): 66-76.

Jesus and Freedom. Maryknoll, NY: Orbis Books, 1977.

"The Marxist and the Christian Dialectics of Liberation." *Journal of Dharma* 2, no. 1 (1977): 53-67.

"The Marxian Concept of Man in the Indian Context." *Indian Journal of Theology* 27, nos. 3-4 (1978): 123-36.

"Orientations for an Asian Theology." In *Asia's Struggle for Full Humanity: Towards a relevant Theology, Papers from the Asian Theological Conference, January 7-20, Wennappuwa, Srilanka 1979,* edited by Virginia Fabella, 108-22. Maryknoll, NY: Orbis Books, 1980.

"The Present Cultural Crisis: Analysis and Prognosis." *Socialist Perspectives,* no, 3 (1980): 1-21.

"A New Approach to Theological Education." In *Theologizing in India: selection of Papers presented at the Seminar held in Poona on October 26 - 30, 1978,* edited by Michael Amaladoss, T.K. John, and George Gispért-Sauch, 57-69. Bangalore: TPI, 1981.

"Perspectives." *Negations* 3 (July-September 1982): 4-5.

"Perspectives." *Negations* 7 (July-September 1983): 1-2.

"Alienation and the Dialectic of History." Negations, no. 6 (April-June 1983): 13-9.

"The Materialistic Conception of History and the Indian Religious Tradition." *Negations,* no. 8 (Oct-Dec 1983): 2-3.

Marxian Atheism. Bangalore: S. Kappen, 1983.

Jesus Today. Chennai: AICUF, 1985.

Jesus and Cultural Revolution: An Asian Perspective. Bombay: Build Publications, 1983.

Liberation Theology and Marxism. Puntamba, Maharashtra: Asha Kendra, 1986.

"Towards an Indian Theology of Liberation." In *Towards and Indian Theology of Liberation,* edited by Paul Puthenangady, 301-18. Bangalore: ITA, 1986.

"The Asian Search for a Liberative Theology." In *Bread and Breath: Essays in Honour of Samuel Rayan S.J.,* edited by T.K. John, 100-14. Anand, Gujarath: Gujarath Sahitya Prakash, 1991.

The Future of Socialism and Socialism of the Future. Bangalore: Visthar, 1992.

"Historizing Historiology as Prophecy." In *Ingathering: Autobiographical Writings and Selected Essays of Fr. Sebastian Kappen*, edited by Sebastian Vattamattam, 238-46. Kottayam: Jeevan Books, [1992] 2013.

"Jesus and Transculturation." In *Asian Faces of Jesus*, edited by R.S. Sugirtharajah, 173-88. Maryknoll, NY: Orbis Books, 1993.

Tradition, Modernity, and Counter-culture: An Asian Perspective. Bangalore: Visthar, 1994.

"Spirituality in the new Age of Recolonization." Concilium 4 (1994): 27-35.

In Search of the non-Christian Jesus (Malayalam). Kottayam: Manusham Publications, 1999.

Hindutva and Indian Religious Traditions. Compiled by Sebastian Vattamattam. Kottayam: Manusham Publications, 2000.

Divine Challenge and Human Response. Compiled by Sebastian Vattamattam. Thiruvalla: Kraistava Sahitya Samiti, 2001.

Jesus and Society: Selected Writings of Sebastian Kappen, S.J., vo. 1. Edited by Sebastian Painadath. New Delhi: ISPCK, 2002.

Jesus and Culture: Selected Writings of Sebastian Kappen S.J., vol. 2. Edited by Sebastian Painadath. New Delhi: ISPCK, 2002.

Marx Beyond Marxism: A Critical Evaluation of Marxian Philosophy. Edited by Sebastian Vattamattam. Kottayam: Voice Books, 2012.

"Ingathering." In *Ingathering: Autobiographical Writings and Selected Essays of Fr. Sebastian Kappen*, edited by Sebastian Vattamattam, 9-18. Kottayam: Jeevan Books, 2013.

"Jesus in the Indian Context." In *Ingathering: Autobiographical Writings and Selected Essays of Fr. Sebastian Kappen*, edited by Sebastian Vattamattam, 217-21. Kottayam: Jeevan Books, 2013.

"Towards a Strategy of Socialist Reconstruction." In *What the Thunder Says: A Poem and Selected Essays of Fr. Sebastian Kappen*, edited by Sebastian Vattamattam, 28-41. Kottayam: Jeevan Books, 2013.

Periodical sources

Anawim (Kappen's journal). 22 issues between 1976 and 1984 (issues 17-31, 34-37, and 3 others whose number is unclear).

Negations (Kappen's journal). 7 issues between 1982 and 1983.

Socialist Perspectives (Kappen's journal). 7 issues between 1978 and 1982.

Online sources

"A New Church: From Medellin to Puebla," http://opcentral.org/resources/wp-content/uploads/sites/11/2014/09/crisis02.pdf [accessed 8 May 2015].

"AKJM School, Kanjirappally," http://akjmschool.net/history.aspx [accessed 13 July 2015].

"D C Kizhakkemury on Fr. Sebastian Kappen," https://www.youtube.com/watch?v=KdMK0WdZeVU [accessed 08 August 2016].

"Edicio dela Torre," https://www.youtube.com/watch?v=43HMyW0n_X0 [accessed 23 March 2015].

"Fr. Mateo Crawley-Boevey, ss.cc.: Founder and Apostle of the Enthronement of the Sacred Heart," http://www.menofthesacredheartsohio.com/x_pdf/fr-mateo-final%202007.pdf [accessed 12 October 2017].

"Fr. Mateo in India," http://www.ssccpicpus.com/userfiles/file/LIBRARY/13.%20SS.CC.%20Personages/SSCC%20Brothers/20.%20Mateo%20Crawley%20(1875-1960)/Fr.Mateo%C2%B4s%20trip%20in%20India.docx [accessed 22 October 2015].

"Fr. Sebastian Kappen's Talk on Art," https://www.youtube.com/watch?v=cuuRgQzd2Lk [accessed 10 January 2016].

"Fr. Sebastian Kappen: Marxist Study Class, Part I," https://www.youtube.com/watch?v=Ng76tVHVv94 [accessed on 3 November 2016].

"Kappen Kudumba Yogam, Pala," http://www.kappenkudumbayogam.org/wp-content/uploads/2015/04/Web.pdf [accessed 17 November 2015].

"Kodikulam Grama Panchayat," http://lsgkerala.in/kodikulampanchayat/history/ [accessed 17 November 2015].

"Letter of His Holiness Pope Francis to the Bishops of India," http://w2.vatican.va/content/francesco/en/letters/2017/documents/papa-francesco_20171009_vescovi-india.html [accessed 23 October 2017].

"Medieval Source Book: John of Monte Corvino: Report from China 1305," http://legacy.fordham.edu/halsall/source/corvino1.asp [accessed 10 July 2015].

"PCLM: Poor Christian Liberation Movement," http://www.dalitchristian.com/index.php/about-pclm [accessed 06 April 2015].

"Religious Demography of India," http://www.cpsindia.org/dl/religious/summary3c.pdf [accessed 28 June 2017].

"Sebastian Kappen talks on Tradition and Modernity: Part I," https://www.youtube.com/watch?v=kP7pVKn5qoU [accessed 30 June 2017].

"Sebastian Vattamattam introducing Fr. Sebastian Kappen," https://www.youtube.com/watch?v=aOEuNeDOcEA [accessed 08 August 2016].

"St. Joseph's Boys' Higher Secondary School, Kozhikode," http://www.stjosephsboysschool.org/index.php [accessed 13 July 2015).

"St. Joseph's Interdiocesan Seminary," http://stjosephseminarymangalore.org/HISTORY.html [accessed 15 July 2015].

"The Kerala Agrarian Relations Bill, 1957," https://www.kerala.gov.in/documents/10180/622777/land%20reform1 [accessed 19 October 2016].

"The Montague-Chelmsford Reforms (1919)," http://historypak.com/montagu-chelmsford-reforms/ [Accessed 16 October 2015].

"Visthar: A Non-formal Academy of Justice and Peace," http://www.visthar.org/ [accessed 13 October 2014].

Alessandra, Stanley. (1999, Dec 22). Cardinal Paolo Dezza, 98; Guided the Jesuits. New York Times. Retrieved from http://search.proquest.com/docview/431312673?accountid=17215 [accessed 16 February 2016].

Alonso, Angela. "Hybrid Activism: Paths of Globalisation in the Brazilian Environmental Movement," Institute of Development Studies Working Paper 332 (2009): 22, http://onlinelibrary.wiley.com/doi/10.1111/j.2040-0209.2009.00332_2.x/epdf [accessed 7 June 2015].

Commission of India, Election. "Statistical Report on Election, 1954 to the Legislative Assembly of Travancore-Cochin," http://eci.nic.in/eci_main/StatisticalReports/SE_1954/StatRep_TravCochin_1954.pdf [accessed 22 July 2015].

de Mesa, Jose. "Dr. Jose De Mesa's Online Publications," http://www.dlsu.edu.ph/library/webliography/fpub/jose_demesa.asp [accessed 23 March 2015].

Goff, James G. "Puebla: Bishop's De-liberation?" NACLA Report on the Americas (July/August 1979): 43, https://nacla.org/sites/default/files/articles/A01304043_1.pdf [accessed 9 May 2015].

Goff, James G. "Puebla: Bishop's De-liberation?" NACLA Report on the Americas (July/August 1979): 43, https://nacla.org/sites/default/files/articles/A01304043_1.pdf [accessed 9 May 2015].

Hebblethwaite, Peter. "The use of Marxism," The Tablet: The International Catholic News Weekly (12 March 1983), 5. Cf. http://archive.thetablet.co.uk/article/12th-march-1983/5/the-uses-of-marxism [accessed 14 December 2015].

India, The Government of. "The Untouchability (Offences) Act, 1955," https://www.paschimmedinipur.gov.in/collectorate/podwo/acts/THE%20UNTOUCHABILITY%20_OFFENCES_%20ACT,%201955.pdf [accessed 21 July 2015].

James, SJ, Martin. "Of Many Things." *America* 207 (August 2012), http://search. proquest.com/docview/1037028692?accountid=17215 [accessed 16 February 2016].

Kālidāsa, *Shakuntala*, trans. Arthur W. Ryder. Cambridge: In Parentheses Publications, 1999, http://www.yorku.ca/inpar/shakuntala_ryder.pdf. [accessed 23 January 2017].

Kyeongil, Jung. "The Bodhi Tree and the Cross: A Buddhist-Christian Theology of Liberation," http://gradworks.umi.com/35/70/3570732.html [accessed 24 June 2015]

Marx, Karl. *Neue Rheinische Zeitung*, no. 136, trans. Marx-Engels Institute, https://www.marxists.org/archive/marx/works/1848/11/06.htm [accessed 20 October 2016].

Morley, Samuel A. Roberto Machado, and Stefano Pettinato, "Indexes of Structural Reform in Latin America," http://www.rrojasdatabank.info/eclacsa/lcl1166. pdf [accessed 24 June 2015].

Panickar, Udayabhanu L. "Narayana Guru on Conversion," http://www. hinduismtoday.com/modules/smartsection/item.php?itemid=4292 [accessed 05 November 2015].

Park, A. Sung. "Minjung Theology: A Korean Contextual Theology," http://www. biblicalstudies.org.uk/pdf/ijt/33-4_001.pdf [accessed 31 March 2015].

Patrick, Larsen. "Camilo Torres: 40 Years after the Death of a Fighter for Latin American Freedom," http://www.marxist.com/camilo-torres-catholic-marxism170206.htm [accessed 2 May 2015].

Pereira, Myron. "Locking Horns over 'the Asian Jesus,'" http://www.ucanews.com/ news/locking-horns-over-the-asian-jesus/70975 [accessed 15 April 2015].

Richards, W.J. *The Indian Christians of St. Thomas, Otherwise Called the Syrian Christians of Malabar: A Sketch of their History, and an Account of their Present Condition, as well as a Discussion of the Legend of St. Thomas.* London: Bermose and Sons Ltd., 1908, https://archive.org/stream/ indianchristian00richgoog#page/n12/mode/2up [accessed 23 April 2015].

Rosario-Cruz, Eliacin. "Remembering Padre Camilo Torres," http://eliacin. com/2009/03/remembering-padre-camilo-torres/ [accessed 8 March 2017].

S. K. Nair. "Gandhiji's Visits to Kerala-Gandhiji Remembered on 30January," http:// www.spiderkerala.net/resources/4928-GANDHIJI-S-VISITS-TO-KERALA-GANDHIJI-REMEMBERED.aspx [accessed 09 September 2015].

Sahabandhu, Jerome. "Portraying the person and works of François Houtart," http:// www.iese.ac.mz/lib/noticias/2009/houtard.pdf [accessed 11 February 2016].

Sarmiento, Nicanor. "The Awareness of the Latin American Church to the Reality of the Indigenous Cultures," http://www.sedosmission.org/web/en/mission-articles/doc_view/841-the-awareness-of-the-latin-american-church-to-the-reality-of-the-indigenous-cultures-i-part [accessed 8 May 2015].

Sikand, Yoginder. "Dalit Liberation Theology: Interview with James Massey," http://cpiarticles.blogspot.be/2005/02/dalit-liberation-theology-interview.html [accessed 06 April 2015].

Swamikal, Chattampi. *Kristhumatha Nirupanam*, http://hinduebooks.blogspot.com in 2011, [accessed 05 November 2015].

Swamikal, Chattampi. *Hindu Critique of Christianity* (Malayalam), https://archive.org/details/KristumataChedanam-ChattampiSwamikal-EnglishTranslation [accessed 10 July 2017].

The Hindu, 13 March 2013. http://www.thehindu.com/news/cities/bangalore/theyre-still-stretching-boundaries/article4504113.ece [accessed 13 October 2014].

Trueman, C.N. "India and World War One," http://www.historylearningsite.co.uk/world-war-one/india-and-world-war-one/ [accessed 24 October 2017].

Williams, Elisabeth Erin. "Liberation Theology and Its Role in Latin America," http://web.wm.edu/so/monitor/issues/07-1/6-williams.htm [accessed 24 June 2015].

Zachariah, K.C. "The Syrian Christians of Kerala: Demographic and Economic Transition in the Twentieth Century," http://opendocs.ids.ac.uk/opendocs/bitstream/handle/123456789/3027/wp322.pdf?sequence=1 [accessed 05 November 2015].

Other publications

Abesamis, Carlos H. "Some Paradigms in Re-reading the Bible in a Third-World Setting." Mission Studies 7, no. 13 (1990): 24-5.

Abey'ratna, Oscar M. *Sidelights of Christianity in Sri Lanka*. Rajagiriya: St. Stephen, 1977.

Adappur, A. *Theology Derailed* (Malayalam). Cochin: Janatha Service, 1985.

Adriance, Madeleine. *Opting for the Poor*. Kanas City: Sheed and Ward, 1986.

Aikara, Thomas and T.C. Mathew. *Deepika: The Beacon of History* (Malayalam). Media House: Calicut, 2012.

________. *The Seen Sides of the Liberation Struggle* (Malayalam). New Delhi: Media House, s.d.

Alangaram, A. *Christ of the Asian Peoples: Towards an Asian Contextual Christology.* Bangalore: Asian Trading Corporation, 1999.

Alberigo, Giuseppe. *A Brief History of Vatican II.* Maryknoll, NY: Orbis Books, 2006.

Antony, Mathew Thekkemuriyil and Idesbald Goddeeris. "Buddha, Bhakti, and Brahman: Sebastian Kappen S.J.'s Dialogue with Indian Religions." *Journal of Hindu-Christian Studies* 30 (2017) (forthcoming).

Amaladass, Anand, Sebasti L. Raj, and Jose Elampassery, eds. *Philosohpy and Human Development: Essays in Honour of Father Emilio Ugarte, S.J.* Chennai: Satya Nilayam Publications, 1986.

Amaladoss, Micheal. *Making All Things New: Dialogue, Pluralism, and Evangelization in Asia.* Maryknoll, NY: Orbis Books, 1990.

———. *A Call to Community: The Caste System and Christian Responsibility.* Anand, Gujarat: Gujarat Sahitya Prakash, 1994.

———. *Life in Freedom: Liberation Theologies from Asia.* Maryknoll, NY: Orbis Books, 1997.

———. "Liberation Theologies and Indian Experiences." *Vidyajyoti Journal of Theological Reflection* 69 (2005): 725-6.

———. Forward to *For Others with Others: Arrupe Challenges Indian Jesuits*, edited by Michael Amaladoss, ix-xii. Anand, Gujarat: Gujarat Sahitya Prakash, 2007.

Ambree, Ainslee T., ed. *Encyclopaedia of Ancient History.* London: Macmillan, 1988.

Anderson, Gerald H. "The State of Missiological Research." In *Missiological Education for the Twenty-First Century: The Book, the Circle, and the Sandals: Essays in Honour of Paul E. Pierson*, edited by J. Dudley Woodberry and Charles van Engen, 23-33. Eugene: Wipf and Stock, 1997.

Aquinas, Thomas. *Summa Theologica: Literally.* Translated by Fathers of the English Dominican Providence. New York: Benziger, 1947-1948.

Ariarajah, S. Wesley. "Liberation in World Religions." In *Dictionary of Third World Theologies*, edited by Virginia Fabella and R.S. Sugirtharajah, 124-7. Maryknoll, NY: Orbis Books, 2000.

Arndt, W., F. W. Danker, and W. Bauer. *A Greek-English Lexicon of the New Testament and other Early Christian* Literature. Chicago: University of Chicago Press, 2000.

Arrupe, Pedro. *A Planet to Heal: Reflections and Forecasts.* Rome: Ingnatian Center for Spirituality, 1975.

———. "Letter of Approval and Presentation to the Indian Assistancy." In *Jesuit Formation and Inculturation in India Today: Final Report of the Inculturation*

Commission and Conclusions of the Jesuit Conference of India, edited by Jerome Aixalá, 7-10. Anand, Gujarat: Gujarat Sahitya Prakash, 1978.

————. *Challenges to Religious Life Today: Selected Letters and Addresses I.* St. Louis, MO: Institute of Jesuit Sources, 1979.

————. *Justice with Faith Today: Selected Letters and Addresses II.* St. Louis, MO: Institute of Jesuit Sources, 1980.

————. On *Spirituality for Today's Jesuits: Five Recent Documents from Fr. General Pedro Arrupe, S.J.* St. Louis, MO: Institute of Jesuit Sources, 1980.

————. "Marxist analysis by Christians." *Origins* 10, no. 44 (16 April 1981): 690-6.

————. *Other Apostolates Today: Selected Letters and Addresses III.* St. Louis, MO: Institute of Jesuit Sources, 1981.

————. *In Him Alone is Our Hope: Texts of the Heart of Christ.* St. Louis, MO: Institute of Jesuit Sources, 1984.

————. *The Spiritual Legacy of Pedro Arrupe, S.J.* Rome: Jesuit Curia, 1985.

————. *One Jesuit's Spiritual Journey: Autobiographical Conversations with Jean-Claude Dietsch, S.J.* St. Louis, MO: Institute of Jesuit Sources, 1986.

————. *Recollections and Reflections of Pedro Arrupe, S.J.* Wilmington, DE: Michael Glazier, 1986.

————. "Marxist analysis by Christians." In *Liberation Theology: A Documentary History*, edited by Alfred T. Kennelly, 307-13. Maryknoll, NY: Orbis Books, 1990.

————. "One Communist at the Service of One World." In *Progressio: Fr. Pedro Arrupe S.J., a Man of the 'MAGIS'*, edited by Gilles Michaud, 4-20. Rome: The World Christian Life Community, 2001.

————. "Men for Others: Education for social justice and social action today." In *Pedro Arrupe: Essential Writings*, edited by Kevin F. Burke. Maryknoll, NY: Orbis Books, 2004.

Arul Raja, Maria. "A Dialogue between Dalits and Bible: Certain Indicators for Interpretation." *Journal of Dharma* 24, no. 1 (1999): 40-50.

————. "Reading the Bible from the Dalit Location." *Indian Theological Studies* 36 (1999): 87-91.

————. "Negotiating with Contemporary Social Change: Emerging Dalit Theological Sensibilities." In *Rethinking Theology in India: Christianity in the Twenty-first Century*, edited by James Massey and T.K. John, 85-104. New Delhi: Centre for Dalit/Subaltern Studies, 2013.

Arulraja, M.R. *Jesus the Dalit: Liberation Theology by Victims of Untouchability an Indian Version of Apartheid.* Hyderabad: M.R. Arulraja, 1996.

Ayrookuzhiel, A. M. Abraham. "The Ideological Nature of the Emerging Dalit Consciousness." In *Towards a Common Dalit Ideology*, edited by Arvind P. Nirmal, 81-95. Chennai: Gurukul Lutheran Theological College and Research Institute, 1991.

Bahmann, Manfred K. *A Preference for the Poor: Latin American Liberation Theology from a Protestant Perspective*. Lanham, MD: University Press of America, 2005.

Bakshi, S.R. *Gandhi and Status of Harijans*. New Delhi: Deep and Deep Publications, 1987.

Balasuriya, Tissa. *Jesus Christ and Human Liberation*. Colombo: Centre for Society and Religion, 1976.

————. "Organization for Human Rights and Development." *Human Rights Quarterly* 3, no. 3 (1981): 25-30.

————. *Planetary Theology*. Maryknoll, NY: Orbis Books, 1984.

————. "Divergences: An Asian Perspective." In *Third World Theologies: Commonalities and Divergences*, edited by K.C. Abraham, 113-9. Maryknoll, NY: Orbis Books, 1990.

Balz, H. "ochlos." In *Exegetical dictionary of the New Testament, Vol. 2*, edited by Horst Balz and Gerhard Schneider, 553-4. Grand Rapids, MI: Eerdmans, 1991.

Barba, John A. "Moral Agency in the Context of Social Sin: The Perspectives of the Latin American Bishops (CELAM) and John Paul II." PhD diss., Catholic University of America, 2011.

Bartonek, Anders. "Labour against Capitalism? Hegel's concept of Labour in between Civil Society and the State." *Culture Unbound* 6 (2014): 113-24.

Basu, Pradip. *Towards Naxalbari (1953-1967): An Account of Inner-Party Ideological Struggle*. Calcutta: Progressive Publishers, 2000.

Battacharya, N.N, ed. *Medieval Bhakti Movements in India*. New Delhi: Munishiram Manoharlal, 1989.

Bauer, Gerhard. *In Search of a Theology of Development*. Geneva: Sodepax, 1969.

Baum, Wilhem and Dietmar W. Winkler. *The Church of East: A Concise History*. London: Routledge, 2010.

Bayly, Susan. *Saints, Goddesses and Kings: Muslims and Christians in South Indian Society, 1700-1900*. Cambridge: Cambridge University Press, 1989.

Bellwinkel-Schempp, Maren. "Roots of Ambedkar Buddhism in Kanpur." In *Reconstructing the World: B.R. Ambedkar and Buddhism in India*, edited by Surendra Jondhale and Johannes Beltz, 221-44. Oxford: Oxford University Press, 2004.

Bender, Frederic L. Review of *Utopias in Conflict – Religion and Nationalism in India*. Ainslie T. Embree, *Utopian Studies* 4, no. 1 (1993): 122.

Bennett, Clinton. *Understanding Christian-Muslim Relations: Past and Present*. London: Continuum International, 2008.

Berryman, Philip. "Church and Revolution." *NACLA Report on the Americas* 30, no. 5 (March-April, 1997): 10-5.

Bethel, Leslie. *Ideas and Ideologies in Twentieth-Century Latin America*. Cambridge: Cambridge University Press, 1996.

Bhaskaran, C. *Communist Movement in Kerala* (Malayalam). Trivandrum: Chintha Publishers, 2012.

Bhatia, K.L. *Dr. B.R. Ambedkar: Social Justice and the Indian Constitution*. New Delhi: Deep and Deep Publications, 1994.

Bird, Adrian. *M.M. Thomas and Dalit Theology*. Bangalore: BTESSC/SATHRI, 2008.

————. *M.M. Thomas: Theological Signposts for the Emergence of Dalit Theology*, PhD diss., Edinburg: Edinburg University, 2008.

Bishop, George. *Pedro Arrupe, S.J: Twenty-Eighth General of the Society of Jesus*. Leominster: Gracewing, 2007.

Biswas, A.K. "Paradox of Anti-Partition Agitation and Swadeshi Movement in Bengal (1905)." *Social Scientist* 23, no. 4-6 (1995): 38-57.

Boff, Leonardo. *Jesus Christ Liberator: A Critical Christology for Our Time*. Maryknoll, NY: Orbis Books, 1981.

Boff, Leonardo and Clodovis Boff. *Introducing Liberation Theology*. Translated by Paul Burns. Maryknoll, NY: Orbis Books, 1987.

Boff, Leonardo and Virgil Elizondo. "Christ in Asia: Some Aspects of the Struggles." In *Any Room for Christ in Asia?* edited by Virgil Elizondo, et al., vii-xi. London: SCM Press, 1993.

Bonino, José M. *Faces of Jesus: Latin American Christologies*. Maryknoll, NY: Orbis Books, 1984.

Bottomore, Tom. *Interpretations of Marx*. Oxford: Basil Blackwell, 1988.

Bovon, Francois. "A Commentary on the Gospel of Luke 1:1-9:50." In *Hermeneia: A Critical and Historical Commentary on the Bible, vol. 1*, edited by Helmut Koester and translated by Christine M. Thomas, 224-5. Minneapolis: Fortress Press, 2007.

Boyd, Robin. *An Introduction to Indian Christian Theology*. Chennai: The Christian Literature Society, 1969.

Braton, Paul T. "History and Theology." In *Handbook of Latina/o Theologies*, edited by Edwin David Aponte and Miguel A. De la Torre, 236-42. Saint Louis: Chalice Press, 2006.

Brock, Sebastian P. *An Introduction to Syriac Studies*. Piscataway: Gorgias Press, 2006.

Brockman, James R. *The Word Remains: A Life of Óscar Romero*. Maryknoll, NY: Orbis Books, 1983.

————. *Romero: A Life*. Maryknoll, NY: Orbis Books, 1989.

Brown, Leslie. *The Indian Christians of St. Thomas*. New York: Cambridge University Press, 1982.

Brown, McAfee Robert. *Gustavo Gutiérrez*. Atlanta, GA: John Knox Press, 1980.

Brown, McAfee Robert. "The Roman Curia and Liberation Theology." *The Christian Century* 103, no. 19 (4-11 June 1986): 552-4.

Brownell, Richard. *American Counter-culture of the 1960s*. New York: Lucent Books, 2011.

Bruke, Kevin, ed. *Pedro Arrupe: Essential Writings*. Maryknoll, NY: Orbis Books, 2004.

Bruneau, Thomas C. "The Catholic Church and Development in Latin America: The Role of the Basic Christian Communities." *World Development* 8 (1980): 535-44.

Budde, Michael L. *The Two Churches: Catholicism and Capitalism in the World-System*. Durham: Duke University Press, 1992.

Bühler, Georg. *The Laws of Manu*. Oxford: Clarendon Press, 1886.

Burdick, John. *Looking for God in Brazil: The Progressive Catholic Church in Urban Brazil's Religious Arena*. Berkeley: University of California Press, 1993.

Callewaert, Winand M. *The Hagiographies of Anantdas: The Bhakti Poets of North India*. London and New York: Routledge Curzon, 2000.

————. *The Millennium Kabir Vani: A Collection of Pad-s*. New Delhi: Manohar, 2000.

Callewaert, Winand M. and Peter G. Friedlander. *The Life and Works of Raidas*. New Delhi: Monohar, 1992.

Câmara, Helder. *Church and Colonialism*. Translated by William McSweeney. London: Sheed and Ward, 1969.

————. *Spiral of Violence*. Translated by Della Couling. London: Sheed and Ward, 1971.

Carter, Alan B. *Marx, a Radical Critique*. Brighton: Wheatsheaf Books Limited, 1988.

CBCI. "Declaration of CBCI on Evangelization." *Indian Ecclesiastical Studies* 13 (1974): 1-20.

CDF. *Instruction on Certain Aspects of the Theology of Liberation.* Washington, DC: United States Catholic Conference, 1984.

————. *Instruction on Christian Freedom and Liberation.* Washington, DC: United States Catholic Conference, 1986.

————. "Notification: Father Dupuis' 'Toward a Christian Theology or Religious Pluralism.'" *Origins* 30, no. 38 (2001): 605-8.

CELAM. *New Evangelization, Human Development, Christian Culture.* Translated by Philip Berryman. Santo Domingo: Bishops' Committee for the Church in Latin America, 1993.

Centrum Ignatianum Spiritualitatis. *Follow-up on General Congregation XXXII: Unedited Papers, Articles, Experiences and Bibliography on the General Congregation.* Rome: Centrum Ignatianum Spiritualitatis, 1975.

Century, Christian. "Backing for the Poor." *Christian Century* 103 (1986): 408-9.

Chandran, Civic. Forward to *Towards a Counter-Culture* (Malayalam), by Sebastian Vattamattam, vii-xiii. Kottayam: Manusham Publications, 2008.

Chenchiah, P. "Where Lies the Uniqueness of Christ? An Indian Christian View." In *Readings in Indian Christian Theology*, vol. 1, edited by R.S. Sugirtharaja and Cecil Hargreaves, 83-92. London: SPCK, 1993.

Chentharassery, T.H.P. *Ayyan Kali* (Malayalam). Trivandrum: s.n., 1979.

Chethimattam, John B. "Towards a Theology of Liberation." *Jeevadhara* 2, no. 7 (1972): 25-34.

Childers, R.C. "Khuddaka Patha, a Pali Text, with a Translation and Notes." *Journal of the Royal Asiatic Society of Great Britain and Ireland*, New Series 4, no. 2 (1870): 309-39.

Chiodi, Pietro. *Sartre and Marxism.* Sussex: The Harvester Press, 1976.

Clark, Gillian. Mark Humphries, and Mary Whitby, *The Acts of the Council of Chalcedon.* Translated by Richard Price and Michael Gaddis, Translated Texts for Historians, Vol. 45. Liverpool: Liverpool University Press, 2005.

Cleary, Edward L. *Crisis and Change: The Church in Latin America Today.* Maryknoll, NY: Orbis Books, 1985.

Colonnese, Louis Michael, ed. *The Church in the Present-Day Transformation of Latin America in the Light of the Council: Second General Conference of Latin American Bishops, Bogotá, 24 August, Medellin, 26 August - 6 September, Colombia, 1968.* Bogotá: CELAM, 1970.

Cone, James. H. *Liberation: A Black Theology of Liberation*. Philadelphia and New York: J.B. Lippincott Company, 1970.

————. "Asian Theology Today: Searching for Definitions." *The Christian Century* 96, no. 19 (1979): 589-91.

Cousineau, Madeline R. "Preferential Option for the Poor." In *Encyclopedia of Religion and Society*, edited by William H. Swatos, Jr., 374-5. Walnut Creek, CA: Altamira Press, 1998.

Cox, Harvey. *The Silencing of Leonardo Boff: The Vatican and the Future of World Christianity*. Bloomington: Meyer-Stone Books, 1988.

Curran, Charles. *Catholic Social Teaching 1981-Present: A Historical, Theological, and Ethical Analysis.*Washington, DC: Georgetown University Press, 2002.

D'Souza, Hermon. *In the Steps of St. Thomas*. Chennai: The Diocesan Press, 1983.

Damodaran, K. *Indian Thought: A Critical Survey*. s.l.: Karen Haydock, 1967.

de Souza, Teotónio R. "Why Cuncolim Martyrs? An Historical Re-Assessment." In *Jesuits in India: In Historical Perspective*, edited by Teotónio R. de Souza and Charles J. Borges, 35-47. Macao: Instituto Cultural de Macao, 1992.

Dhanuraj, D. "Story of 1957 Education Bill in Kerala." Working paper. Ernakulam: Centre for Public Policy Research, 2006.

Drèze, Jean and Amartya Sen. *India: Economic Development and Social Opportunity*. Oxford: Oxford University Press, 1995.

Drogus, Carol Ann. "The Rise and Decline of Liberation Theology: Church, Faith, and Political Change in Latin America." *Comparative Politics* 27, no. 4 (1995): 465-8.

du Toit, Brian M. "The Mahatma Gandhi and South Africa." *The Journal of Modern African Studies* 34, no. 4 (1996): 643-60.

Dupuis, Jacques. *Toward a Christian Theology of Religious Pluralism*. Maryknoll, NY: Orbis Books, 1997.

————. *Christianity and the Religions: from Confrontation to Dialogue*. London: Darton, Longman, and Todd, 2002.

Embree, Ainslie T. *Utopias in Conflict – Religion and Nationalism in India*. Delhi: Oxford University Press, 1990.

Enrique, Dussel. *A History of the Church in Latin America: Colonialism to Liberation, 1492-1979*. Grand Rapids: Eerdmans, 1981.

Fabella, Virginia. "Liberation." In *Dictionary of Third World Theologies*, edited by Virginia Fabella and R. Sugirtharajah, 122-4. Maryknoll, NY: Orbis Books, 2000.

Fatehi, Kamal. "Capital Flight from Latin America as a Barometer of Political Instability." *Journal of Business Research* 30, no. 2 (1994): 187-95.

Ferm, Diane W. *Third World Liberation Theologies: An Introductory Survey.* Maryknoll, NY: Orbis Books, 1986.

————. *Profiles in Liberation: 36 Portraits of Third World Theologians.* Mystic: Tewnty-Third Publications, 1988.

Ferrao, Filipe Neri. "Keynote Address of Archbishop Filipe Neri Ferraro at the Inaugural Session of the International Conference 'In Honour of St. Francis Xavier: Jesuit History, Culture and Identity.'" In *Jesuits in India: History and Culture,* edited by Delio de Mendonca, 12-7. Anand, Gujarat: Gujarat Sahitya Prakash, 2007.

Ferroli, Domenico. *The Jesuits in Malabar,* vol. 1. Bangalore: Bangalore Press, 1939.

————. *The Jesuits in Malabar,* vol. 2. Bangalore: The National Press, 1951.

Fic, Victor M. "Peaceful Transition to Communism in India, 1954-1957: A Comparative Case Study of Kerala." PhD diss., The Indian School of International Studies, 1962.

————. *Kerala, Yenan of India: Rise of Communist Power 1937-1969.* Mumbai: Nachiketa Publications, 1970.

Fleddermann, H.T. *Q: A Reconstruction and Commentary,* edited by B. Doyle et al. Leuven: Peeters, 2005.

Forrester, Duncan B. *Forrester on Christian Ethics and Practical Theology: Collected writings on Christianity, India, and the Social Order.* Farnharm, Surrey, and Burlington, VT: Ashgate Publishing Company, 2010.

Fortescue, Adrian. *The Lesser Eastern Churches.* London: Catholic Truth Society, 1913.

Foster, Douglas A. "The Historiography of Christianity in Ecumenical Perspective." In *Telling the Churches' Stories: Ecumenical Perspectives on Writing Christian History,* edited by Timothy J. Wengert and Charles W. Brockwell, Jr., 121-32. Grant Rapids: Eerdmans, 1995.

Frykenberg, Robert Eric. *Christianity in India: From Beginning to the Present.* Oxford: Oxford University Press, 2008.

Fuellenbach, John. *Hermeneutics, Marxism and Liberation Theology.* Manila: Divine World Publications, 1989.

Gama, Vasco da. *The First Voyage of Vasco da Gama 1497-1499.* Translated by E.G. Ravenstein. London: Hakluyt Society, 1898.

Gandhi, D.N. "Ambedkar and Separate Electorates Issue." *Economic and Political Weekly* 26, no. 21 (25 May 1991): 1328-30.

Gandhi, M.K. *Satyagraha in South Africa: The Selected Works of Mahatma Gandhi*, vol. 2. Edited by Shriman Narayan and Translated by Valji Govindji Desai. Ahmedabad: Navajivan Publications, 1968.

Gibellini, Rosino. *The Liberation Theology Debate*. Translated by John Bowden. London: SCM, 1987.

Gilson, Etienne. *Thomism: The Philosophy of Thomas Aquinas*. Toronto: Pontifical Institute of Medieval Studies, 2002.

Girardi, Giulio. *Faith and Revolution in Nicaragua: Convergence and Contradictions*. Maryknoll, NY: Orbis Books, 1989.

Gispert-Sauch, G. "The Concept of Person and Indian Thought - An Attempt at a Cross-cultural Dialogue." In *Philosophy and Human Development: Essays in Honour of Father Emilio Ugarte, S.J.*, edited by Anand Amaladass, Sebasti L. Raj, and Jose Elampassery. Chennai: Satya Nilayam Publications, 1986.   27.

Gokhale-Turner, Jayashree B. "Bhakti or Vidroha: Continuity and Change in Dalit Sahitya." *Journal of Asian and African Studies* 15 (1980): 29-42.

Gopalan, A.K. *Kerala, Yesterday and Today* (Malayalam). Fourth edition. Trivandrum: Chintha Publishers, 2010.

Gough, Kathleen. "Kerala Politics and the 1965 Elections." *International Journal of Comparative Sociology* 8, no. 1. (1967): 55-88.

Gunther, Hans F. K. *The Racial Elements of European History*. Translated by G. C. Wheeler. London: Methuen & Co. LTD, 1927.

Guru, Nataraja. *The Word of the Guru: Life and Teachings of Narayana Guru*. Ernakulam: Paico Publishing House, 1968.

Gutiérrez, Gustavo. *A Theology of Liberation: History, Politics, and Salvation*. Maryknoll, NY: Orbis Books, 1973.

————. *We Drink from Our Own Wells: The Spiritual Journey of a People*. 1984.

————. *On Job: God-talk and the Suffering of the Poor*. Maryknoll, NY: Orbis Books, 1987.

————. "The Meaning and Scope of Medellin." Translated by Margaret Wilde. In *The Destiny of the Present: Selected Writings*, 59-101. Maryknoll, NY: Orbis Books, 1999.

Haight, Robert D. Review of *Jesus and Freedom* by S. Kappen. *The Journal of Religion* 59, no. 1 (January 1979): 111.

Haksar, Vinit. "Violence in a Spirit of Love: Gandhi and the Limits of Non-violence." *Critical Review of International Social and Political Philosophy* 15, no. 3 (2012): 303-24.

Hall, Stuart G. *Doctrine and Practice in the Early Church*. Grand Rapids, Michigan: William B. Eerdmans Publishing Company, 1991.

Haralambos, Michael and Robin Heald. *Sociology: Themes and Perspectives*. Slough: University of Tutorial Press, 1980.

Hardgrave, Jr., Robert L. "The Mappilla Rebellion, 1921: Peasant Revolt in Malabar." *Modern Asian Studies* 11, no. 1 (1977): 57-99.

Harris, Louie. "The Theology of Struggle: Recognizing Its Place in Recent Philippine History." *Kasarinlan: Philippine Journal of Third World Studies* 12, no. 2 (2006): 83-107.

Harrison, Selig S. *India: The Most Dangerous Decades*. Princeton, NJ: Princeton University Press, 1961.

Hatada, Takashi. *A History of Korea*. Santa Barbara, CA: ABC Clio Press, 1969.

Hawley, John Stratton. "Author and Authority in the Bhakti Poetry of North India." *The Journal of Asian Studies* 47, no. 2 (May 1988): 269-90.

Hennecke, Edgar. *New Testament Apocrypha*. Edited by Wilhem Schneemelcher and translated by R. McL. Wilson. London: Lutterworth, 1965-1973.

Hennelly, Alfred T. Review of *Jesus and Freedom* by S. Kappen. *Theological Studies* 38, no. 4 (1 December 1977): 812-3.

———. ed. *Liberation Theology: A Documentary History*. New York: Orbis Books, 1990.

Hitchcock, James. *The Pope and the Jesuits: John Paul II and the New Order in the Society of Jesus*. New York: National Committee of Catholic Laymen, 1984.

Horn, Gerd-Rainer. "Left Catholicism in Western Europe in the 1940s." In *Left Catholicism 1943-1955: Catholics and Society in Western Europe at the Point of Liberation*, edited by Gerd-Rainer Horn and Emmanuel Gerard, 13-44. Leuven: Leuven University Press, 2001.

Houtart, François. *The Challenge to Change*. Editedy by Mary Anne Chouteau. New York: Sheed and Ward, 1964.

———. *Religion and Ideology in Sri Lanka*. Bangalore: TPI, 1974.

———. Introduction to *Jesus and Freedom*, by S. Kappen, 3-16. Maryknoll, NY: Orbis Books, 1977.

Houtart, François and Emile Pin. *The Church and the Latin American Revolution*. New York: Sheed and Ward, 1965.

Houtart, François and André Rousseau. *The Church and Revolution: from the French Revolution of 1789 to the Paris Riots of 1968; from Cuba to Southern Africa; from Vietnam to Latin America*. Maryknoll, NY: Orbis Books, 1971.

————. *Church and Development in Kerala*. Bangalore: TPI, 1979.

————. *Genesis and Institutionalization of the Indian Catholicism*. Louvain-la-Neuve, UCL: Centre de recherches socio-religieuses, 1981.

————. *Size and Structures of the Catholic Church in India: The Indigenization of an Exogenous Religious Institution in a Society of Transition*. Louvain-la-Neuve, UCL: Centre de recherches socio-religieuses, 1982.

————. *The Great Asiatic Religions and their Social Functions*. Louvain-la-Neuve, UC: Centre de recherches socio-religieuses, 1982.

————. "Social Functions of Religion in Pre-Capitalist Societies: The Case of Kerala." *Social Scientist* 23, no. 1-3 (1995): 91-108.

Hulton, J.H. *Caste in India: Its Nature, Functions, and Origins*. Mumbai: Oxford University Press, 1973.

Illickamury, Cyprian. "Roman Document on the Theology of Liberation: A Theological Appraisal." *Jeevadhara* 15, no. 90 (1985): 439-53.

Indian Theological Association, Statement of the, "Towards an Indian Theology of Liberation." In *Towards and Indian Theology of Liberation: The Statement Papers and the Proceedings of the Ninth Annual Meeting of the Indian Theological Association*, edited by Paul Puthanangady, 8-23. Bangalore: ITA, 1986.

Irvine, Andrew B. "Liberation Theology in Late Modernity: An Argument for a Symbolic Approach." *Journal of the American Academy of Religion* 78, no. 4 (2010): 921-60.

Issac, Thomas. *The Unseen Sides of the Liberation Struggle* (Malayalam). Trivandrum: Chintha Publishers, 1999.

Jaffrelot, Christophe. "The Politics of Caste Identities." In *The Cambridge Companion to Modern Indian Culture*, edited by Vasudha Dalmia and Rashmi Sadana, 80-98. Cambridge: Cambridge University Press, 2012.

————. *Dr. Ambedkar and Untouchability: Analyzing and Fighting Caste*. London: Hurst and Company, 2000.

Jagatheesan, A. "St. Francis Xavier." In *The St. Thomas Christian Encyclopedia of India*, vol. 1, edited by G. Menachery, 16-21. Trichur: The St. Thomas Christian Encyclopedia of India, 1982.

Jain, Girilal. *The Hindu Phenomenon*. New Delhi: UBS Publishers Distributers, 1994.

Jayakumar, S. *Dalit Consciousness and Christian Conversion: Historical Resources for a Contemporary Debate*. New Delhi: ISPCK, 1996.

Jayasankar, A. *Communist Rule and Liberation Struggle* (Malayalam). Calicut: Mathrubhumi Books, 2012.

Jayaseelan, L. *Towards a Counter-Culture Sebastian: Kappen's Contribution*. Delhi: ISPCK, 1999.

Jeffrey, Robin. "Matriliny, Marxism, and the Birth of Communist Party in Kerala, 1930-1940." *Journal of Asian Studies* 38, no. 1 (1978): 77-98.

————. "Temple-Entry Movement in Travancore, 1860-1940." *Social Scientist* 4, no. 8 (1976): 3-27.

Jesus, Society of. *Catalogus Viceprovinciae Madurensis*. Madurai: Typis De Nobili, 1949, 1950, and 1951.

————. *Documents of the Thirty-Second General Congregation of the Society of Jesus*. Washington, DC: The Jesuit Conference, 1975.

————. *Documents of the Thirty-First General Congregation*. Washington, DC: Conference of Major Superiors of Jesuits, s.d.

John, T.K, ed. *Bread and Breath: Essays in Honour Samuel Rayan S.J.* Anand: Gujarat Sahitya Prakash, 1991.

Johnson, Elliot, David Walker, and Daniel Gray, eds. *Historical Dictionary of Marxism*, second edition. New York: Rowman and Littlefield, 2014.

Johnson, Matthew V. "Black Theology." In *Encyclopedia of Religion*, second edition, vol. 2, edited by Lindsay Jones, 963-967. New York: Thomson Gale, 2005.

Jones, Kenneth W. *The New Cambridge History of India: Socio-religious Reform Movements in British India*. Cambridge: Cambridge University Press, 1989.

Joseph, George Ghevarghese. *George Joseph, the Life and Times of a Kerala Christian Nationalist*. s.l.: Orient Blackswan, 2003.

Joseph, K.M. "Liberation Theology: Its Impact on Kerala Politics and Society." PhD diss., Mahatma Gandhi University, 1997.

Joseph, Muricken K. "From Development to Liberation: Perspectives in the Emergence of Liberation Theology in India." PhD diss., Duquesne University, Pittsburg, 1985.

Kallumkalpurayidom, Antony. "The involvement of the Kerala Church in Politics." *Jeevadhara* 1, no. 1 (1971): 61-71.

Kananaikal, Jose. *Christians of Scheduled Caste Origin*. New Delhi: Indian Social Institute, 1986.

Kantowsky, Detlef. *Sarvodaya: The Other Development*. New Delhi: Vikas Publishing House, 1980.

Kariyil, Antony. *Church and Society in Kerala: A Sociological Study*. New Delhi: Intercultural Publications, 1995.

Kasper, Walter. *Der Gott Jesu Christi*. Mainz: Matthias-Grünewald, 1982.

________. *Jesus the Christ*. London: Clark, 2011.

Kaye, Cecil. *Communism in India*. Kolkata: Editions India, 1971.

KCBC. "Pastoral Letter." *Vedaprachara Madhyasthan* 32, no. 5 (1959): 137-44.

Keer, Dhananjay, ed. *Dr. Ambedkar: A Memorial Album*. Mumbai: Popular Prakashan, 1982.

Keogh, Dermot. *Church and Politics in Latin America*. New York: St. Martin's Press, 1990.

Klitgaard, R.E. "Gandhi's Non-violence as a Tactic." *Journal of Peace Research* 8, no. 2 (1971): 143-53.

Knitter, Paul F. *No Other Name?* Maryknoll, NY: Orbis Books, 1985.

Kochuparampil, Xavier. "The St. Thomas Christians of India: Ecumenical and Missiological Challenges." *Exchange* 25, no. 3 (1996): 243-60.

Koilparampil, George. *Caste in the Catholic Community in Kerala*. Cochin: Department of Sociology, St. Theresa's College, 1982.

Koodapuzha, Xavier. *Indian Church History*. Kottayam: OIRS, 1980.

________. *Faith and Communion of the Indian Church of the St. Thomas Christians*. Kottayam: OIRS, 1982.

Krishna, P.S. "Synthesising the Gandhi-Ambedkar-Narayanaguru-Marx Visions for Dalit Liberation." *Social Change* 41, no. 1 (2011): 1-41.

Kumbalakuzhy, Kuriakose. ed. *Image* (Malayalam). Kottayam: Prathichaya Publishing Trust, 2010.

________. *Liberation Struggle* (Malayalam). New Delhi: Media House, 2010.

Kunnath, George. "Smouldering Dalit fires in Bihar, India." *Dialect Anthropology* 33, nos. 3-4 (2009): 309-25.

________. "Anthropology's Ethical Dilemmas: Reflections from the Maoist Fields of India." *Current Anthropology* 54, no. 6 (2013): 740-52.

Kunnukal, Thomas V. "Jesuit Education in India Today and Tomorrow." In *Jesuits in India: In Historical Perspective*, edited by Teotónio R. de Souza and Charles J. Borges, 99-111. Macao: Instituto Cultural de Macao, 1992.

Kuriakose, M.K. *History of Christianity in India: Source Materials*. New Delhi: ISPCK, 1999.

Kuriedath, Jose. *Authority in the Catholic Community in Kerala*. Bangalore: Dharmaram Publications, 1989.

Kurup, K.K.N. *Peasantry Nationalism and Social Change in India*. Allahabad: Chugh Publications, 1991.

Kurup, K.K.N. and K.J. John. *Legacy of Basel Mission and Herman Gundert in Malabar*. Calicut: Gundert Death Centenary Committee, 1993.

Kuruvila, Ajith Abraham. "Alternative Narratives in Contemporary Globalization: A Case Study of Visthar and Sebastian Kappen." PhD diss., Pacific School of Religion, Berkeley, 2011.

Kuruvila, Kadakkal P. "The Incarnation and the Cross: The Inseparable Paradigms for an Indian Christian Theology of Incarnation and Liberation." PhD diss., Faculty of the Lutheran School, Chicago, 1999.

Küster, Volker. "Jesus and the Minjung Revisited: The Legacy of Ahn Byung-Mu." *Biblical Interpretation* 19, no. 1 (2011): 1-18.

Kwang-Sun, David Suh. "A Biographical Sketch of an Asian Theological Consultation." In *Minjung Theology: People as Subjects of History*, edited by Kim Yong Bock, 15-37. Maryknoll, NY: Orbis Books, 1981.

Lee, Chanseok. "The Christological Perspectives in the Theologies of Raymon Panikkar and Byungmu Ahn: Toward and Asian Christology." PhD diss., Drew University, Madison, 2005.

Lee, Jung Young. "Minjung Theology: A Critical Introduction." In *An Emerging Theology in World Perspective: Commentary on Korean Minjung Theology*, edited by Jung Young Lee, 3-29. Mystic, CT: Twenty-Third Publications, 1988.

Lernoux, Penny. *Cry of the Poor: The Struggle for Human Rights in Latin America, the Catholic Church in Conflict with the U.S. Policy*. Harmondsworth: Penguin Books, 1980.

————. *People of God: The Struggle for World Catholicism*. New York: Viking, 1989.

Levine, Daniel H. *Popular voices in Latin American Catholicism*. Princeton, NJ: Princeton University Press, 1992.

Lieten, Georges Kristoffel. "Education, Ideology and Politics in Kerala 1957-59." *Social Scientist* 6, no. 2 (1977): 3-21.

Ling, Trevor. *The Buddha: Buddhist Civilization in India and Ceylon*. London: Pelican Books, 1976.

————. ed. *The Buddhist Philosophy of Man: Early Indian Buddhist Sources*. London: Everyman's Library, 1981.

Louis, Prakash. "Discriminated Masses of India: Dalits and Minorities." *The New Leader* (March 16-31, 2004): 10-2.

Lowie, Robert H. *The History of Ethnological Theory*. New York: Rinehart and Co., 1937.

Luz, Ulrich. "Matthew 1-7: A Commentary." In *Hermeneia: A Critical and Historical Commentary on the Bible*, vol. 1, edited by Helmut Koester and translated by James E. Crouch, 190-3. Minneapolis: Fortress Press, 2007.

Maitra, Kiran. *Marxism in India: From Decline to Debacle*. New Delhi: Roli Books, 2012.

Maliekal, Louis. "Liberative Vision of the Vedas." In *Towards an Indian Theology of Liberation*, edited by Paul Puthanangady, 24-48. Bangalore: ITA, 1986.

Malik, Alexander J. "Confessing Christ in the Islamic Context." In *Asian Faces of Jesus*, edited by R.S. Sugirtharajah, 75-84. London: SCM Press, 1993.

Manalel, J.C. "Should the Church be Poor?" *Jeevadhara* 3, no. 16 (1973): 330-8.

Manickam, Sundararaj. *Studies in Missionary History: Reflections on a Culture-contact*. Chennai: Christian Literature Society, 1988.

Mariampillai, D. Bosco. "The Emerging Asian Theology of Liberation in the Documents of the Federation of Asian Bishops' Conferences 1974-1986." PhD diss., St. Paul University, Ottawa, 1993.

Martin, Christopher F.J, ed. *The Philosophy of Thomas Aquinas: Introductory Readings*. London: Routledge, 1989.

Martinez, Gaspar. *Confronting the Mystery of God*. New York and London: Continuum International Publishing, 2001.

Marx, Karl. "On the Jewish Question." In *Karl Marx: Early Writings*, edited and translated by T.B. Bottomore, 1-40. New York: McGrow-Hill Book Company, 1964.

————. "Economic and Philosophical Manuscripts." In *Karl Marx: Early Writings*, edited and translated by T.B. Bottomore, 61-134. New York: McGraw-Hill Book Company, 1964.

————. "Theses on Feuerbach." In *Karl Marx: Selected Writings in Sociology and Social Philosophy*, edited by T.B. Bottomore and Rubel. London: Penguin, 1975.

Marx, Karl and Frederic Engels. *On Religion*. Moscow: Foreign Language Publishing House, 1957.

Marx, Karl and Frederic Engels. *The Communist Manifesto*. Harmondsworth: Penguin Books, 1967.

————. *The German Ideology*. Moscow: Progress Publishers, 1976.

Marx-Engels, *Selected Works*, vol. 2. Moscow: s.n., s.d.

Mason, Philip. *Christianity and Race: The Burroughs Memorial Lectures, 1956*. London: Lutterworth Press, 1956.

Massey, James. "Dalit Movements." In *A Dictionary of Asian Christianity*, edited by Scott W. Sunquist, 220-1. Cambridge: William B. Eerdmans, 2001.

Mathew, Babu. "Kappen the Inspirer." In *Counter-culture Perspectives: Selected Kappen Memorial Lectures*, edited by Koshy Mathew and Mercy Kappen, 174-5. Bangalore: Visthar, 2013.

Mathew, Philip and Ajit Muricken, eds. *Religion, Ideology, and Counter-culture: Essays in honor of S. Kappen.* Bangalore: Horizon Books, 1987.

Mathothu, Kurian and Sebastian Nadackal, eds. *The Church of St. Thomas Christians Down the Centuries.* Pala: Kurian Mathothu, s.d.

Mattes, Claudio. "Liberation Theology." In *The Brill Dictionary of Religion*, vol. 2, edited by Kocku von Stuckrad, 1095. Leiden and Boston: Brill, 2006.

McGovern, Arthur F. *Liberation Theology and Its Critics: Toward an Assessment.* Maryknoll, NY: Orbis Books, 1989.

Menacherry, George. *The St. Thomas Christian Encyclopedia of India*, vol. 2. Trichur: s.n., 1973.

Menon, A. Sreedhara. *Kerala History and its Makers.* Chennai: S. Viswanathan Printers and Publishers, 1987.

————. *Social and Cultural History of Kerala.* New Delhi: s.n., 1989.

————. *A Survey of Kerala History.* Kottayam: D C Books, 2007.

Menon, P.K.K. *The History of Freedom Movement in Kerala: 1600-1885.* Government of Kerala, 1970.

Menon, Sadanand. "Kappen: The Advocate of Radical Consciousness." In *Counter-culture Perspectives: Selected Kappen Memorial Lectures*, edited by Koshy Mathew and Mercy Kappen, 169-73. Bangalore: Visthar, 2013.

Miranda, José P. *Marx and the Bible: A Critique of the Philosophy of Oppression.* London: SCM Press, 1977.

————. *Communism in the Bible.* London: SCM, 1982.

Miras, Joseph A. "Doing Theology in the Philippines: A Study on the Theological Methods of Selected Filippino Contemporary Theologians." PhD diss., Catholic University of Leuven, 1991.

Moffett, Samuel Hugh. *A History of Christianity in Asia: Beginnings to 1500.* San Francesco: Harper Collins, 1992.

Moffet, Samuel Hugh. *A History of Christianity in Asia: 1500-1900.* Maryknoll, NY: Orbis Books, 2005.

Mohammed, Ovey N. "Jesus and Krishna." In *Asian Faces of Jesus.* Edited by R.S. Sugirtharajah, 9-24. London: SCM Press, 1993.

Mohkamsing, Narinder. "Machiavellian Hindutva Untamed." *Totalitarian Movements and Political Religions* 11, no. 1 (March 2010): 103-6.

Moltmann, Jurgen. *The Trinity and the Kingdom of God*. London: SCM Press, 1981.

Monte, Gustavo Pena. "Pope Paul's Visit to Bogotá Focuses on Poverty Problems." *The Voice* 10, no. 24 (1968): 1-28.

Muralidharan M, P.K. Michael Tharakan, and S. Kappen, eds. *Understanding Communalism*. Bangalore: Visthar, 1993.

Muricken, Ajit. "S. Kappen: The Man and his Contribution to the Study of Counter-Culture." In *Religion, Ideology, and Counter-Culture*, edited by Philip Mathew and Ajit Muricken, 9-31. Bangalore: Horizon Books, 1987.

Nair, A. Balakrishnan. "The Dynamics of Kerala Politics." *The Indian Journal of Political Science* 55, no. 3 (July-September 1994): 251-60.

Namboothiripad, E.M.S. *Communist Party in Kerala* (Malayalam). Trivandrum: Chintha Publishers, 1986.

————. *E.M.S. on Education* (Malayalam). Trivandrum: Chintha Publishers, 2009.

————. *Religious Faith and the Communists* (Malayalam). Trivandrum: Chintha Publishers, 2012.

Nandi, Proshanta. "Communism through the Ballot Box: Over a Quarter Century of Uninterrupted Rule in West Bengal." *Sociological Bulletin* 54, no. 2 (2005): 171-194.

NBCLC, *Conclusions of the Interdisciplinary Research Seminar on The Indian Church in the Struggle for a New Society*. Bangalore: NBCLC, 1981.

Neill, Stephen. *The Story of the Christian Church in India and Pakistan*. Grand Rapids: William B. Eerdmans, 1970.

————. *A History of Christianity in India: The Beginning to AD 1707*. Cambridge: Cambridge University Press, 1984.

Nemade, Bachandra. "The Revolt of the Underprivileged." *Journal of Asian and African Studies* 15 (1980): 113-23.

Neville, Cummings Robert. *On the Scope and Truth of Theology: Theology as Symbolic Engagement*. New York and London: T&T Clark, 2006.

Nirmal, Arvind P., ed. *Towards a Common Dalit Ideology*. Chennai: Gurukul Lutheran Theological College and Research Institute, 1991.

Nossiter, T.J. *Communism in Kerala: A Study in Political Adaptation*. London: The Royal Institute of International Affairs, 1982.

————. *Marxist State Governments in India: Politics, Economics and Society*. London and New York: Pinter Publishers, 1988.

O'Collins, Gerald. *Christology: Origins, Developments, Debates.* Waco, TX: Baylor University Press, 2015.

O'Sullivan, Tim, et al. *Key Concepts in Communication and Cultural Studies*, second edition. London: Routledge, 1994.

Öktem, Kerem Gabriel. "A Comparative Analysis of the Performance of the Parliamentary Left in the Indian States of Kerala, West Bengal and Tripura." *South Asia: Journal of South Asian Studies* 35, no. 2 (2012): 306-28.

Ollman, Bertell. *Alienation: Marx's Conception of Man in Capitalist Society*, second edition. Cambridge: Cambridge University Press, 1976.

Omvedt, Gail. *Dalits and the Democratic Evolution: Dr. Ambedkar and the Dalit Movement in Colonial India.* New Delhi: Sage, 1994.

Oommen, George. "The Emerging Dalit Theology: A Historical Appraisal." *Indian Church History Review* 34, no. 1 (June 2000): 19-37.

Pablo, Richard. *Death of Christendoms, Birth of the Church.* Maryknoll, NY: Orbis Books, 1987.

Paikada, Mathew. *Indian Liberation Theology as an Authentic Christian Theology: Hermeneutical and Theological Perspectives on Dialogue, Inculturation, and Dialogue.* New Delhi: Intercultural Publications, 2000.

Painadath, Sebastian. "Bhagavad Gita's Vision of Liberative Action." In *Towards an Indian Theology of Liberation*, edited by Paul Puthanangady, 49-65. Bangalore: ITA, 1986.

__________. "Preface." In *Jesus and Culture: Selected Writings of Sebastian Kappen, S.J.*, edited by Sebastian Painadath, vii-xiv. New Delhi: ISPCK, 2002.

Pallath, Paul. "The Syro-Malankara Catholic Church." In *Important Roman Documents Concerning the Catholic Church in India*, edited by Paul Pallath, 261-2. Kottayam: OIRSI, 2004.

__________. *Important Roman Documents Concerning the Catholic Church in India.* Kottayam, OIRSI, 2004.

Parappally, Jacob. *Emerging Trends in Indian Christology.* Bangalore: IIS Publications, 1995.

Pastor, Manuel. "Capital Flight from Latin America." *World Development* 18, no. 1 (1990): 1-18.

Pasture, Patrick. "Multi-faceted Relations between Christian Trade Unions and Left Catholicism in Europe." In *Left Catholicism 1943-1955: Catholics and Society in Western Europe at the Point of Liberation*, edited by Gerd-Rainer Horn and Emmanuel Gerard, 228-46. Leuven: Leuven University Press, 2001.

————. "Religious Globalization in Post-war Europe: Spiritual Connections and Interactions." *Archiv für Sozialgeschichte* 51 (2011): 63-108.

————. "Dechristianization and the Changing Religious Landscape in Europe and North America since 1950: Comparative, Transatlantic, and Global Perspectives." In *Dechristianization in North America and Western Europe, 1954-2000*, edited by Nancy Christie and Michael Gauvreau, 367-402. Toronto and London: University of Toronto Press, 2013.

Pathil, Kuncheria. "What happened at Poonamallee?: A Brief Report." In *Towards an Indian Theology of Liberation*, edited by Paul Puthanangady, 1-7. Bangalore: ITA, 1986.

Paulose, Paulose Mar. "Be a Dissenting Minority." In *Out of Control: Official Report of the Asia Youth Assembly, Delhi: September 25 - October 10, 1984*, edited by Chris Tremewan, viii. Toa Payo: CCA, 1985.

————. "Liberation Theology and Marxism." In *Religion, Ideology, and Counter-Culture*, edited by Philip Mathew and Ajit Muricken, 195-205. Bangalore: Horizon Books, 1987.

————. *Spirituality for Struggle: A Selection of Lectures and Sermons*. Thiruvalla: CSS, 1999.

Pelton, Robert S., ed. *Monsignor Romero: A Bishop for the Third Millennium*. Notre Dame: Notre Dame University Press, 2004.

Peña, Milagros. "Theology in Peru: An Analysis of the Role of Intellectuals in Social Movements." *Journal for the Scientific Study of Religion* 33, no. 1 (1994): 34-5.

Perumalil, H.C. and E.R. Hambye, eds. *Christianity in India: A History in Ecumenical Perspective*. Alleppey: Prakasam Publications, 1972.

Pfeil, Margaret R. "Toward an Understanding of the Language of Social Sin in Magisterial Teaching." PhD diss., Notre Dame: Notre Dame University, IN, 2000.

Phan, Peter C. "Jesus Christ with an Asian Face." *Theological Studies* 57 (1996): 399-411.

————. "Reception of and Trajectories for Vatican II in Asia." *Theological Studies* 74 (2013): 302-20.

Philip, T.M. *The Encounter between Theology and Ideology*. Chennai: Christian Literature Society, 1986.

Pieris, Aloysius. "Liturgy and Dialogue with Buddhism: An Experiment." *Dialogue* 15 (1968): 1-12.

________. "Towards an Asian Theology of Liberation: Some Religio-Cultural Guidelines." In *Asia's Struggle for Full Humanity*, edited by Virginia Fabella, 75-95. Maryknoll, NY: Orbis Books, 1980.

________. *An Asian Theology of Liberation*. Maryknoll, NY: Orbis Books, 1988.

________. *Love Meets Wisdom: A Christian Experience of Buddhism*. Maryknoll, NY: Orbis Books, 1988.

________. "Does Christ have a Place in Asia?" In *Any Room for Christ in Asia?* edited by Virgil Elizondo, et al. London: SCM Press, 1993.

________. "Reincarnation in Buddhism: A Christian Appraisal." *Concilium* 5 (1993): 16-22.

________. "The Buddha and the Christ." In *Asian Faces of Jesus*, edited by R.S. Sugirtharajah, 46-56. London: SCM Press, 1993.

________. *Fire and Water: Basic Issues in Asian Buddhism and Christianity*. Maryknoll, NY: Orbis Books, 1996.

________. "Christ Beyond Dogma: Doing Christology in the Context of the Religions of the Poor." *Louvain Studies* 25 (2000): 187-231.

________. "Comparative Study of Religions: Lecture Notes for Buddhist Students Studying Christianity." *Dialogue* 27 (2000): 134-53.

________. "Buddhism as a Challenge for Christians." In *Christian Approaches to Other Faiths: A Reader*, edited by Alan Race and Paul M. Hedges, 177-82. London: SCM Press, 2009.

________. "Spirituality as Mindfulness: Biblical and Buddhist Approaches." *Spiritus: A Journal of Christian Spirituality* 10, no. 1 (2010): 38-51.

________. "What kind of Church do we wish to be?" *The Month* 33, no. 11 (2000): 428-35.

________. *The Genesis of an Asian Theology of Liberation: An Autobiographical Excursus on the Art of Theologizing in Asia*. Kelaniya, Colombo: Tulana Research Centre, 2013.

Pierson, Christopher. *The Marx Reader*. Cambridge: Polity Press, 1997.

Pillai, K. Bhaskara. *Chattampi Swamikal*. Trivandrum: s.n., 1978.

Pillai, P. Gopinadhan. *Left Movement and Agrarian Relations 1920-1995*. New Delhi: South Asian Publishers, 2003.

Pillai, G.K. *A History of Congress in Kerala*. Trivandrum: Prabhat Books, 1986.

Pinto, Ambrose. "The achievements of the Jesuit educational mission in India and the contemporary challenges it faces." *International Studies in Catholic Education* 6, no. 1 (2014): 14-32.

Planas, Ricardo. *Liberation Theology: The Political Expression of Religion.* Kansas City, MO: Sheed and Ward, 1986.

Podipara, Placid. *Thomas Christians.* Mumbai: St. Paul's, 1970.

———. *The Rise and Decline of the Indian Church of the Thomas Christians.* Kottayam: OIRSI, 1979.

Polak, Millie Graham. *Mr. Gandhi: The Man.* London: Allen, 1931.

Pons, Silvio and Robert Service, eds. *A Dictionary of 20th-Century Communism.* Princeton, NJ and Oxford: Princeton University Press, 2010.

Pope John XXIII. *Pacem in Terris.* Papal Encyclical, 1963.

Pope John Paul II. *Catechism of the Catholic Church.* 1992.

Pope Paul VI. *Gaudium et Spes.* Pastoral Constitution, 1965.

———. *Apostolicam Actuositatem.* Decree on the Apostolate of the Laity, 1965.

———. *Populorum Progressio.* Papal Encyclical, 1967.

———. *Octogesima Adveniens.* Apostolic Letter, 1971.

Pope Pius XI. "*Christo Pastorum Principi*, Apostolic Constitution concerning the Erection of a new Ecclesiastical Province of Antiochean Rite for the Syro-Malankara Faithful in the Malabar region of the East Indies." In *Important Roman Documents Concerning the Catholic Church in India*, edited by Paul Pallath, 264-73. Kottayam: OIRSI, 2004.

Pope Clement VIII. "*In supremomilitantis*: The Imposition of Portuguese Patronage over the Church of Angamaly." In *Important Roman Documents Concerning the Catholic Church in India*, edited by Paul Pallath, 68-73. Kottayam: OIRSI, 2004.

Pope Pius XI. *Quadregesimo Anno.* Papal Encyclical, 1931.

———. *Divini Redemptoris.* Papal Encyclical, 1937.

Pope Pius XII. *Ad Apostolorum Principis.* Papal Encyclical, 1958.

Prabhakar, M.E., ed. *Towards a Dalit Theology.* New Delhi: ISPCK, 1989.

———. "Developing a Common Ideology for Dalits of Christian and Other Faiths." In *Towards a Common Dalit Ideology*, edited by Arvind P. Nirmal, 53-79. Chennai: Gurukul Lutheran Theological College and Research Institute, 1991.

Prabhu, George Soares. "Jesus the Prophet." *Jeevadhara* 4, no. 21 (1974): 206-17.

Prashad, Vijay. *Untouchable Freedom: A Social History of a Dalit Community.* Oxford: Oxford University Press, 2000.

Prentiss, K. Pechilis. *The embodiment of Bhakti.* New York: Oxford University Press, 1999.

Pruthi, R.K., ed. *Indian Caste System*. New Delhi: Discovery Publishing House, 2004.

Pui-lan, Kwok. *Discovering Bible in Non-Biblical World*. Maryknoll, NY: Orbis Books, 1995.

Puthanangady, Paul, ed. *Towards an Indian Theology of Liberation: The Statement Papers and the Proceedings of the Ninth Annual Meeting of the Indian Theological Association*. Bangalore: ITA, 1986.

Puthumana, George. "A Christian Evaluation of Kerala Politics." *Jeevadhara* 1, no. 1 (1971): 72-87.

Raj, Ruble. "Politics of Educational Management." PhD diss., Mahatma Gandhi University, Kottayam, 2003.

Rajayyan, K. "Sri Narayana Guru and Social Reform." *Journal of Kerala Studies* 3 (1976): 43-4.

Rajkumar, Peniel. *Dalit Theology and Dalit Liberation: Problems, Paradigms and Possibilities*. London and New York: Routledge, 2010.

Rayan, Samuel. "Human Well-being on Earth and the Gospel of Jesus." *Jeevadhara* 2, no. 7 (1972): 35-46.

————. "Wealth and Power and the Catholic Church in India." *Jeevadhara* 3, no. 16 (1973): 337-58.

————. "Editorial: On Caste." *Jeevadhara* 11 (1981): 203-31.

————. "Inculturation and the Local Church." *Mission Studies* 3, no. 1 (1986): 14-27.

————. "Instruction on Christian Freedom and Liberation: Some reflections of the Document." *Jeevadhara* 16, no. 93 (1986): 225-54.

————. "Early Christianity as Counter-Culture." In *Religion, Ideology, and Counter-Culture*, edited by Philip Mathew and Ajit Muricken, 113-43. Bangalore: Horizon Books, 1987.

————. "Theological Priorities in India." In *Irruption of the Third World: Challenge to Theology*, edited by Virginia Fabella and S. Torres, 30-41. Maryknoll, NY: Orbis Books, 1988.

————. "Commonalities, Divergence, and Cross-Fertilizations among Third World Theologies." In *Third World Theologies: Commonalities and Divergences*, edited by K.C. Abraham, 195-214. Eugene: Wipf and Stock Publishers, 1990.

————. "Remembering Father Sebastian Kappen." Archival source, KPA, Calicut, Kerala.

Reddy, E.S. and Gopalakrishna Gandhi, eds. *Gandhi and South Africa: 1914-1948*. Ahmedabad: Navajivan Publications, 1993.

Rending, Andrew, ed. *Christianity and Revolution: Thomas Borge's Theology of Life*. Maryknoll, NY: Orbis Books, 1987.

Robinson, Rowena. *Christians of India*. Thousands Oak: Sage Publications, 2003.

Rocha, Zilso. *Helder, the Gift: A Life that Marked the Course of the Church in Brazil*. Petrópolis: Editora Vozes, 2000.

Rockmore, Tom. *Marx after Marxism*. Oxford: Blackwell Publishing, 2002.

Rosales, Gaudencio B. and Catalino G. Arevalo, eds. *For all the Peoples of Asia*. Maryknoll, NY: Orbis Books, 1992.

Rowland, Christopher, ed. *The Cambridge Companion to Liberation Theology*. Cambridge: Cambridge University Press, 1999.

Rush, Valerie. "CELAM III: Policy is Science, Growth." *Executive Intelligence Review* 6, no. 9 (6 March 1979): 55-7.

Sadasivan, S.N. *A Social History of India*. New Delhi: APH Publishing Corporation, 2000.

Samartha, Stanley J. *One Christ, Many Religions: Toward a Revised Christology*. Maryknoll, NY: Orbis Books, 1991.

————. "The Cross and the Rainbow: Christ in a Multireligious Culture." In *Asian Faces of Jesus*, edited by R.S. Sugirtharajah, 104-23. London: SCM Press, 1993.

Samuel, George. "The Prospects and Challenges of Ecclesiology in the Contemporary Indian Context with Special Reference to the Theology of M.M. Thomas." PhD diss., Faculty of the Lutheran School of Theology, Chicago, 2002.

Sato, Hiroshi. "Social Security and Well-being in a Low-income Economy." *The Developing Economies* 42, no. 2 (2004): 288-304.

Savarkar, Vinayak Damodar. *Hindutva: Who is a Hindu?* second edition. Mumbai: Veer Savarkar Prakashan, 1969.

Sawyer, Frank. *The Poor are Many: Political Ethics in the Social Encyclicals, Christian Democracy, and Liberation Theology in Latin America*. Kampen: Kok, 1992.

Schillebeeckx, Edward. *Jesus in Our Western Cultures: Mysticism, Ethics, and Politics*. London: SCM Press, 1987.

————. *The Human Story of God*. London: SCM Press, 1990.

————. *Christ the Sacrament of the Encounter with God, The Collected Works of Edward Schillebeeckx*, vol. 1. London: Bloomsbury, 2014.

Schmink, Marianne and Charles H. Wood. *Contested Frontiers in Amazonia*. New York: Columbia University Press, 1992.

Schoenfeld, Benjamin N. "Kerala in Crisis." *Pacific Affairs* 32, no. 3 (1959): 235-48.

Schomer, Karine and W.H. McLeod, eds. *The Sants: Studies in a Devotional Tradition in India*. New Delhi: Motilal Banarsidass, 1987.

Schoors, A. "Welcoming Address." In *Early Hindi Devotional Literature in Current Research: Proceedings of the International Middle Hindi Bhakti Conference (April 1979) Organized by the Katholieke Universiteit Leuven*, edited by Winand M. Callewaert, 1-3. Leuven: Department of Oriental Studies, 1980.

Schubeck, Thomas L. "Liberation Theology." In *Encyclopedia Christianity*, edited by Geoffrey W. Bromiley and David B. Barret, 259. Grand Rapids, Michigan: Brill, 1993.

Schwarz, Hans. *Christology*. Grand Rapids, MI: Eerdmans, 1998.

Segundo, Juan L. *The Historical Jesus of the Synoptics*. Maryknoll, NY: Orbis Books, 1985.

Selvaraj, A. *Christianity and Social Transformation: The Kerala Story*. Trivandrum: ICRO, 2002.

Sen, Amartya. *The Argumentative Indian: Writings on Indian Culture, History, and Identity*. London: Penguin Books, 2005.

Shah, A.B. and C.R.M. Rao, eds. *Tradition and Modernity in India*. Mumbai: Manaktalas Books, 1965.

Shastry, B.S. "Marques de Pombal and the Jesuits of Goa." In *Jesuits in India: In Historical Perspective*, edited by Teotónio R. de Souza and Charles J. Borges, 49-59. Macao: Instituto Cultural de Macao, 1992.

Shobha, Savitri Chandra. *Social Life and Concepts in Medieval Hindi Bhakti Poetry: A Socio-Cultural Study*. Meerut: Chandrayn Publications, 1983.

Sin, Cardinal Jaime. "The Future of Catholicism in Asia." *Indian Missiological Review* 1, no. 1 (1979): 15.

Singh, Jitendra. *Communist Rule in Kerala*. New Delhi: Diwan Chand Indian Information Centre, 1959.

Singh, Prerna. "Wellness and Welfare: A Longitudinal Analysis of Social Development in Kerala, India." *World Development* 39, no. 2 (2010): 282-93.

Singh, Rustam. "Status of Violence in Marx's Theory of Revolution." *Economic and Political Weekly* 24, no. 4 (1989): 9-20.

Singleton, Mark. *Yoga Body: The Origins of Modern Posture Practice*. Oxford: Oxford University Press, 2010.

Smith, Christian. *The Emergence of Liberation Theology: Radical Religion and Social Movement Theory*. Chicago: University of Chicago Press, 1991.

Soares, Aloysius. *Catholic Church in India: A Historical Sketch*. Nagpur: Government Press and Book Depot, 1964.

Sobrino, Jon. *Christology at the Crossroads: A Latin American View*. Maryknoll, NY: Orbis Books, 1978.

———. *Archbishop Romero: Memories and Reflections*. Translated by Robert R. Barr. Maryknoll, NY: Orbis Books, 1990.

———. "The Winds in Santo Domingo and the Evangelization of Culture." In *Santo Domingo and Beyond*, edited by Alfred T. Hennelly, 165-235. Maryknoll, NY: Orbis Books, 1993.

———. *The Principle of Mercy: Taking the Crucified People from the Cross*. Maryknoll, NY: Orbis Books, 1994.

Suchting, W.A. *Marx: An Introduction*. Brighton: Wheatsheaf Books Limited, 1983.

Sugirtharaj, Felix N. "Developing a Common Dalit Ideology: Is it a Myth of Reality?" In *Towards a Common Dalit Ideology*, edited by Arvind P. Nirmal, 121-6. Chennai: Gurukul Lutheran Theological College and Research Institute, 1991.

Sugirtharajah, R.S., ed. *Asian Faces of Jesus*. London: SCM Press, 1993.

———. "Liberation Theologies." In *Dictionary of Third World* Theologies, edited by Virginia Fabella and R. Sugirtharajah, 129. Maryknoll, NY: Orbis Books, 2000.

Sullivan, Noel. *Fascism*. London and Melbourne: Dent and Sons, 1983.

Suna, Nimai C. "A Theology of Suffering: A Biblical and Theological Engagement with key Themes of Christian Dalit Theology." PhD diss., Trinity International University, Deerfield, 2007.

Sunder, B. Shyam. *They Burn: The 160000000 Untouchables of India*. Bangalore: Dalit Sahitya Academy, 1987.

Sung-Hae, Kim. "Liberation and Inculturation: Two Streams of Doing Theology with Asian Resources." *Inter-Religio* 12 (1987): 67-83.

Sweetland, Dennis. "Liberation Theologies." In *The Modern Catholic Encyclopedia*, edited by Michael Glazier and Monika K. Hellwig, 483-7. Collegeville, MN: Liturgical Press, 2004.

Swiderski, Richard M. *The Blood Weddings: The Knanaya Christians of Kerala*. Chennai: New Era Publications, 1988.

T, Ajayan. "Mid-term Election in Kerala in 1960 and the American Government." *History and Sociology of South Asia* 2, no. 2 (2017): 212-20,

Tamez, Elsa. "Liberation Theology." In *Encyclopedia of Religion*, vol. 8, edited by Lindsay Jones, 5438. New York: Johnson Gale, 2005.

Thannikot, Antony. "The Liberating Church." *Jeevadhara* 4, no. 22 (1974): 319-32.

Tharsiuse, Culas Nicholas. "Christian Faith, a Liberative Praxis in India: An Analysis and Assessment of the Theology of Samuel Rayan." PhD diss., KU Leuven, 2001.

Thekkedath, Joseph. *History of Christianity in India, Vol. 2: From the Middle of the Sixteenth Century to the End of the Seventeenth Century (1542-1700)*. Bangalore: Theological Publications in India, 1982.

Thomas, M.M. *Salvation and Humanization*. Chennai: Christian Literature Society, 1971.

————. *Man and the Universe of Faiths*. Chennai: Christian Literature Society, 1975.

————. "Towards an Alternative Paradigm." In *Counter-Culture Perspectives: Selected Kappen Memorial Lectures*, edited by Koshy Mathew and Mercy Kappen, 13-9. Bangalore: Visthar, 2013.

Thundiyil, Cyriac. *The Hidden Agenda*. Mannanam: Sanjos Publication, 2006.

Tilley, Terrence W. "Teaching Christology: History and Horizons." In *Christology: Memory, Inquiry, and Practice*, edited by Anne M. Clifford and Anthony J. Godzieba, 265-76. Maryknoll, NY: Orbis Books, 2003.

Tirimanna, Vimal, ed. *Asian Faces of Christ*. Bangalore: Asian Trading Corporation, 2005.

Tisserant, Eugene. *Eastern Christianity in India: A History of the Syro-Malabar Church from the Earliest Time to the Present Day*. London: Longmans, 1957.

Toolan, David S. "Heresy or Hokum in Sri Lanka?" *America* 176, no. 4 (1997): 4-5.

Torres, Sergio and John Eagleson, eds. *The Challenge of Basic Christian Communities: Papers from the International Ecumenical Congress of Theology, February 20-2 March 1980, Sao Paulo, Brazil*. Maryknoll, NY: Orbis Books, 1981.

Treto, Raul Gomez. *The Church and Socialism in Cuba*. Maryknoll, NY: Orbis Books, 1988.

Trivedi, H. "Revolutionary Non-violence: Gandhi in Postcolonial and Subaltern Discourse." *Interventions-International Journal of Postcolonial Studies* 13, no. 4 (2011): 521-49.

Turner, J. David. *An Introduction to Liberation Theology*. Lanham: University Press of America, 1993.

Tylor, Edward B. *Primitive Culture: Researches into the Development of Mythology, Philosophy, Religion, Art, and Custom*, vol.1. London: John Murray, 1871.

Uchegbue, Christian O. "A Critical evaluation of Marx's theory of Religion." *American Journal of Social Issues & Humanities* 1, no. 2 (November 2011): 50-81.

Ugarte, Emilio. *Ideal Personality*. AICUF: Chennai, 1961.

————. *Lay Sanctity the Need of the Hour*. Trichy: Catholic Truth Society of India, 1962.

————. *Vacation and Psychology*. Shembaganur: SHC, 1963.

————. *Philosophical Psychology*. Shembaganur: SHC, 1964.

————. *Experimental Psychology*. Shembaganur: SHC, 1972.

Vaidyar, C.R. Kesavan. *Thoughts of Sri Narayana* (Malayalam). Kottayam: s.n., 1972.

Varghese, Sam. "New Insights of Ecclesiology in Sebastian Kappen's Understanding." *Master's College Theological Journal* 1, no. 1 (March 2011): 60-82.

Varier, M.R. Raghava. *Village Communities in Pre-colonial Kerala*. Mysore: Place Names Society of India, 1994.

Vattamattam, Sebastian. *Towards a Counter-culture* (Malayalam). Kottayam: Manusham Publications, 2008.

————. "Sebastian Kappen (1924-1993)." In *Marx Beyond Marxism*, S. Kappen, edited by Sebastian Vattamattam. Kottayam: Voice Books, 2012.

Vendler, Helen. "Books: A Lifelong Poem including History." *The New Yorker* (13 January 1986): 81.

Verstraeten, A. "Jesuit Colleges in India in the Restored Society." In *Jesuit Education in India*, edited by G. Naik, 52-64. Gujarat: Gujarat Sahitya Prakash, 1987.

Vikrant, Swami. "The Dharmic Mind vis-a-vis the New Society." In *The Indian Church in the Struggle for a New Society*, edited by Amalorpavadass, 954-7. Bangalore: NBCLC, 1981.

von Lazar, Arpad. *Latin American Politics: A Primer*. Boston: Allyn and Bacon, 1971.

Vos, Rob, et al., eds. *Who Gains from Free Trade? Export Led-led Growth, Inequality, and Poverty in Latin America*. London and New York: Routledge, 2006.

WCC. *The Uppasala Report 1968*. Geneva: World Council of Churches, 1969.

Webster, John C. B. *The Dalit Christians: A History*. New Delhi: ISPCK, 1994.

Wielenga, Bastiaan. "Liberation Theology in Asia." In *The Cambridge Companion to Liberation Theology*, edited by Christopher Rowland, 39-62. Cambridge: Cambridge University Press, 1999.

Wilfred, Felix. *Leave the Temple: Indian Paths to Human Liberation*. Maryknoll, NY: Orbis Books, 1992.

————. *Beyond Settled Foundations: The Journey of Indian Theology*. Madras: University of Madras, 1993.

————. "Religions Face to Face with Globalization." *Concilium* 5 (2001): 35-42.

__________. *On the Banks of the Ganges: Doing Contextual Theology*. New Delhi: ISPCK, 2005.

Windmiller, Marshall. "Constitutional Communism in India." *Pacific Affairs* 31, no. 1 (1958): 22-35.

Wright, Erik Olin. *Class Structure and Income Determination*. New York: Academic Press, 1979.

Yagi, Seiichi. "Christ and Buddha." In *Asian Faces of Jesus*, edited by R.S. Sugirtharajah, 25-45. London: SCM Press, 1993.

Yun, Hsing. *Politics, Human Rights, and what Buddha said about Life*. Translated by Robert H. Smitheram. Hacienda Heights: Buddha's Light Publishing, 2011.

Zachariah, Benjamin. "Gandhi, Non-violence and Indian Independence." *History Review* 69 (March 2011): 30-35.

Zeyen, Thomas E. *Jesuit Generals: A Glimpse into a Forgotten Corner*. Scranton, PA: The University of Scranton Press, 2004.

Zogaria, Donald S. "The Social Bases of Communism in Kerala and West Bengal." *Problems of Communism* 22, no. 1 (1973): 16-24.

www.ingramcontent.com/pod-product-compliance
Lightning Source LLC
Chambersburg PA
CBHW020239160726
47987CB00019B/63